FARM EQUIPMENT OF THE
ROMAN WORLD

FARM EQUIPMENT
OF THE
ROMAN WORLD

K. D. WHITE

CAMBRIDGE UNIVERSITY PRESS

CAMBRIDGE

LONDON · NEW YORK · MELBOURNE

Published by the Syndics of the Cambridge University Press
The Pitt Building, Trumpington Street, Cambridge CB2 1RP
Bentley House, 200 Euston Road, London NW1 2DB
32 East 57th Street, New York, NY 10022, USA
296 Beaconsfield Parade, Middle Park, Melbourne 3206, Australia

Library of Congress catalogue card number: 70–82450

SBN: 0 521 20333 3

First published 1975

Printed in Great Britain
at the
University Printing House, Cambridge
(Euan Phillips, University Printer)

CONTENTS

v

CONTENTS

PART THREE: Utensils made of Earthenware, Stone, Metal, Wood and Leather
page 105

PART FOUR: Miscellaneous
205

PLATES

(*between pp. 222 and 223*)

1*a* Pony drinking from a trough fed from a well by means of a swipe (*tolleno*). *Photo*: Bardo Museum, Tunis.

  b Raising irrigation water from the Nile with the Archimedean screw (*cochlea*). *Photo*: Peter Clayton.

  c Oak cylinder-block of a double-action force-pump. *Photo*: Landesmuseum, Trier.

2*a* Fine and coarse flour-sieves (*cribra*), mortars and other milling equipment. *Photo*: Vatican Museum.

  b Donkey-mill (*molae asinariae*).

  c Stone *mortarium* for grinding grain. *Photo*: National Museum of Antiquities, Scotland.

  d Bronze wine-strainer (*trulla*). *Photo*: British Museum.

3*a* Vine-trellis (*pergula*) with grape-clusters and a bird eating the fruit. *Photo*: Archaeologisch Instituut der Rijksuniversiteit Utrecht.

  b Worker carrying grapes in a fruit-picking basket (*qualus*). *Photo*: Archaeologisch Instituut der Rijksuniversiteit Utrecht.

  c Life on an African farm. To l., seasonal offerings to the mistress of the estate. In foreground, r., a fence (*vacerra*) enclosing an orchard. *Photo*: Bardo Museum, Tunis.

4*a* and *b* Hard (*sporta*) and soft (*fiscus*) types of basket from Roman Egypt. *Photos*: University College London.

  c Wine-making equipment from Agedincum in central France, including grape-baskets, mortars (*mortaria*), a fork and piles of *marc de raisin*. *Photo*: Studio Allix, Sens.

5*a* Winnowing grain with the *vannus*; carrying away the sifted grain in a basket (*corbis*). *Photo*: Mittelrheinisches Landesmuseum, Mainz.

  b Two labourers carrying manure to the fields on a hurdle (*crates stercorariae*). *Photo*: National Museum of Antiquities of France.

  c Two slaves carrying merchandise in netted baskets (*cophini*). *Photo*: Deutsches Archäologisches Institut, Rome.

6*a* Oxen for sacrifice wearing muzzles (*capistra*). *Photo*: Deutsches Archäologisches Institut, Rome.

  b Road transport in Asia Minor. Four-wheeled goods wagon drawn by mules, followed by a two-wheeler drawn by oxen. *Photo*: British Museum.

7 Vintage scenes. To l., two-wheeled cart with solid wheels and wicker body, carrying grapes to the press; above, picking grapes; to r., treading vat (*forus, labrum*). *Photo*: Deutsches Archäologisches Institut, Rome.

8 *a* Braying donkey equipped with basketry panniers (*clitellae*). *Photo*: British Museum.
  b Wicker-work farm cart of traditional pattern. *Photo*: Author.

9 *a* Dock-worker carrying a wine-*amphora* from a merchantman to a lighter. *Photo*: The Mansell Collection.
  b Replica of a river barge loaded with wine-casks (*cupae*), and stacked *amphorae* encased in basketry for sea transit. *Photo*: Landesmuseum, Trier.

10 *a* Oil-storage jars (*dolia olearia*) deeply buried in the ground. *Photo*: The Mansell Collection.
  b Sampling and sale of wine direct from the *cella vinaria*. In centre, ladling out wine into an *amphora*; top r., tally-clerk with notebook; bottom r., a buyer enjoys a tasting. *Photo*: B. Ashmole, *The Ince Blundell Catalogue* (The Clarendon Press, Oxford).

11 *a* Nubian slaves serving wine from flagons (*lagoenae*) to guests at a fashionable party. *Photo*: Bardo Museum, Tunis.
  b Goatherd milking a goat into a shallow bowl (*mulctrum*). *Photo*: J. Powell.

12 *a* Man superintending the boiling of a cauldron (*cortina*) on a fire. *Photo*: British Museum.
  b Two men carrying an *amphora* full of wine on a pole.
  c Roofed market stall with stacked *amphorae*. *Photo*: Deutsches Archäologisches Institut, Rome.

13 *a* Storage jars (*seriae*), Naples. *Photo*: National Museum, Naples.
  b Toilet basin (*labrum*) in the changing room (*apodyterium*) of the Forum Baths.
  c Cook-shop (*thermopolium*) in Herculaneum. The six storage jars (*dolia*) in the counter base contain remains of cereals and vegetables.

14 *a* Pastoral scene on a Roman sarcophagus. In centre, shepherd with his crook (*pedum*); to l., shepherd feeding his dogs.
  b Ploughman directing his team with a long goad (*stimulus*).
  c An African farm-worker tapping down olives with long canes. *Photo*: Bardo Museum, Tunis.

15 *a* Basket-making. A labourer brings a bundle of osiers (*salix*); in front of a building, a second man weaves a basket over a frame of crate-rods.
  b Pressing the grapes with the simple lever-press.
  c Pitching wine-jars. One worker smears the inside of a storage-jar with pitch; a second man stirs the liquid pitch on the fire.

16　To l., a labourer brings a full sack of grain to be measured; c., a *modius* measure; beside it an official with a document in his r. hand; with his l. he runs through the sample. *Photo*: Editions Arthaud.

FOR ISOBEL

PREFACE

This book, like its older companion (*Agricultural Implements of the Roman World*, Cambridge, 1967), began life as an assortment of notes, jotted down from time to time in the process of working through the relevant literary evidence on Roman farming, and laying the foundations for a full-scale study of its principles and practice, which finally appeared in 1970 (*Roman Farming*, London, 1970). As the pile accumulated it became evident that, whereas 'amphora' and 'vannus' were household words, other containers, with much less familiar, and sometimes outlandish, names, kept cropping up, and presented, as in the case of farm implements, a growing number of identification problems. Consideration of these items, and the problems they posed, led on to more general thinking about the uses of the various containers and receivers employed in the harvesting and processing of crops, and about the methods of transport used in getting the various farm products in and out of store and to the market. Attempts to solve some of the problems connected with these different operations proved abortive, since the available technical manuals were either defective or mutually contradictory, or simply muddled. Confusion of nomenclature, form and function on the part of editors and translators provided further encouragement to the notion of compiling a comprehensive catalogue of this material, using both literary and archaeological data, and following the method adopted in the planning of the volume on farm implements, which had proved useful to general readers as well as to specialists. Examination of the equipment used in vine and olive cultivation, and in the processing of their respective products, indicated a need to extend the scope of the study so as to embrace the entire range of farm equipment, apart from the implements and machines used in cultivation. Behind the problem of identifying the artefacts themselves lay that of identifying the raw materials from which they were made, and the sources of those materials, the rushes, reeds and willows for the many types of baskets and frails, together with the flax, hemp, esparto grass and leather which furnished the necessary rope and cordage. In the last-named area of enquiry, as well as in that of food processing, the *Natural History* of Pliny yielded an immense amount of miscellaneous information, some of it of great value, and which provided a pointed contrast to the feeble contributions made to these topics by the usual reference works available to English readers. An excellent starting-off point was provided by Cato's inventory of equipment (*De Agri Cultura* 10 and 11), but valuable information was to be found over a wide spectrum of literary sources, including those sections of Justinian's *Digest* which deal with inheritance, and furnish important lists of items making up the *instrumentum fundi*, and which distinguish carefully between those items which are essential to the running of an establishment, and those deemed inessential.

The archaeological material abounds in pitfalls for the unwary. Thus in looking over the range of earthenware containers in everyday use, the researcher who tries to match up a literary name such as 'lagoena' or 'cophinus' with particular shapes or sizes of vessel must needs begin his museum investigations virtually from scratch; the museologists have long since abandoned the confident labelling of containers with specific names (usually Greek), and now content themselves with the use of safe, non-committal terms such as 'pot' or 'jug'. This is surely all to the good; we can now take our classified literary references along to the collections of artefacts with an open mind, uninfluenced by the former conventional epithets. It is fashionable to question the value of this type of enquiry; indeed, there are those who would dimiss it as mere pedantry; of course there is some truth in the criticism, at least so far as non-technical references are concerned, though here and there the reader may concede that a more precise definition, aided by appropriate parallels, has served to clarify the argument, or give point to the narrative. With the technical references the critic is on weaker ground; failure to establish the precise meaning may lead, for example, to great inaccuracy in the reconstruction or restoration of a complex artefact or a piece of machinery such as an oil mill or a screw press. Glaring examples of such inaccuracies abound in the most widely-used translations of Vitruvius and Pliny. The need for accuracy is most obvious in those inventories and catalogues of equipment which are of great importance to the economic historian of classical times, whether they occur in the agronomists (Cato, Palladius), in individual inscriptions, in the legal Codes, or in the Price Edict of Diocletian. In a significant number of cases, it is the juxtaposition of the various classes of evidence, literary, lexical and archaeological, that has helped both to identify the term, and to indicate the range of use of the item to which it refers. (For a full discussion of these aspects of the topic the reader is referred to the Introduction to Part III, pp. 107 ff.)

Aim of the present work

This book attempts to do two things: first, to sort out the names of all recorded items of farm equipment: secondly, to identify, where possible, the shapes, sizes and functions of each particular item, using both literary and archaeological evidence in the search: lastly, to indicate the relevance of the study of particular items (e.g. bulk containers) to the socio-economic context by drawing attention to such matters as the sources of supply of the raw materials used in their manufacture, to questions of supply and demand, to cost factors and so on. I have endeavoured to serve the interests of different users of the book in a number of ways. Thus, in addition to the discussions of individual items, which may help the reader of Latin literature to identify a particular object mentioned by the author he happens to be reading, some of the more complex operations, involving several different processes, such as those involved in the making of wine, the extraction of olive oil or the preparation of meal and flour from grain, have been described at length, the various items of equipment used being inserted, with their English equivalents, at the appropriate places in a continuous narrative (see for example the account of wine-making 'From vintage to storeroom' at pp. 112 ff.).

The organization and arrangement of the material

Agricultural Implements of the Roman World was concerned with the implements and machines used in the raising of crops up to the point of removal for storage and/or processing. The present volume, while complementary to its predecessor, deals with an even greater quantity of items, exhibiting great differences in material, design and function. Classification by function, as in the earlier volume, seemed at one stage to be the most appropriate method, but the extended practice of using the same container for several different purposes, coupled with the fact that containers represented by far the largest single category, led to the abandonment of this plan in favour of an untidy but useful combination of two systems of classification: by function, and by the material used. The four parts into which the contents are divided are classified as follows:

Part One is classified by function, and contains the following sections:

1. Rolling, stamping and grinding equipment

2. Vine-props

3. Fencing

4. Ropes, cordage and netting

5. Measuring instruments

6. Water-raising devices.

Part Two is classified by material, and consists of items made from basketry (chiefly containers).

Part Three is also classified by material, and deals with containers and receivers made of earthenware, stone, metal, wood and leather.

Part Four comprises a miscellaneous group.

The Illustrations

The text-figures, prepared by Miss Susan Bird, have been inserted in the margins so as to coincide with the relevant discussions, and references are given at the conclusion of each discussion to easily accessible representations of the particular item, and to the location of extant specimens. In view of the variety of types and their wide dispersal a catalogue raisonné has not been attempted.

Acknowledgements

The extent of my obligations to experts in many diverse disciplines, as well as to classical colleagues in many parts of the world, will be evident to even the most casual reader of this book. I remember with special gratitude the warm welcome given to me by the many museums and libraries in which I worked on various portions of it – the generous provision of reading space where this was obviously at a premium, and the unprompted provision of bibliographical and other references which have saved me many hours of tedious searching in unfamiliar fields. In this regard my particular thanks are due to the Director and Librarian of the German Archaeological Institute in Rome, to John Ward Perkins, Director of the British School at Rome, and to John Hayes of the Royal Ontario Museum, Toronto. I should also like to take the opportunity of acknowledging two continuing debts: first, to Sir Roger Mynors, who for more than a decade has administered a salutary blend of castigation and encouragement to my work, secondly, to my friend and colleague Nan Ure, of Reading, who has generously acted as a one-woman steering committee, directing my enquiries into the appropriate channels with cheerful tolerance. This book is appropriately dedicated to my wife, who through the length of days has borne with my irritability, kept all supporting services going in full swing, and contrived at the same time to meet the increasing demands of her own professional commitments.

Reading   K.D.W.
March 1973

ABBREVIATIONS

AIRW	K. D. White, *Agricultural Implements of the Roman World*, Cambridge, 1967
Amelung, *SVM*	H. Amelung, *Die Skulpturen des Vatik nischen Museums*, 2 vols., Berlin, 1903–8
André, *Lexique*	Jacques André, *Lexique des termes botaniques en latin*, Paris, 1956
Ath. Mitt.	*Mitteilungen des Deutsches Archäologisches Instituts, Athenische Abteilung*
Billiard, *L'Agriculture*	Raymond Billiard, *L'Agriculture dans l'antiquité d'après les Géorgiques de Virgile*, Paris, 1928
Billiard, *La Vigne*	Raymond Billiard, *La Vigne dans l'antiquité*, Lyons, 1913
Blümlein, *Bilder*	Carl Blümlein, *Bilder aus dem römisch-germanischen Kulturleben*, 2nd ed., Munich/Berlin, 1926
Blümner, *Privataltertümer*	Hugo Blümner, *Die römischen Privataltertümer*, Handbuch der Altertumswissenschaft 4. Bd., 2. Abt., 2. Teil, Munich, 1911
Blümner, *Technologie*	Hugo Blümner, *Technologie und Terminologie der Gerwerbe und Künste bei Griechen und Römern*, 4 Bde., Leipzig, 1875–87
Brehaut	*Cato the Censor on Farming*, trans. by Ernest Brehaut, New York, 1933
BSA	*Annual of the British School at Athens*
Cabrol-Leclercq	F. Cabrol and H. M. Leclercq, *Monumenta ecclesiae liturgica*, Paris, 1900–
Callender	M. H. Callender, *Roman Amphorae*, Oxford, 1965
Calza–Becatti, *Ostia*	G. Calza and G. Becatti, *Ostia*, 4th ed., trans. by C. H. Pennock and R. Meiggs, Rome (Istit. dello Stato), 1961
Calza–Becatti, *Scavi*	G. Calza and G. Becatti, *Scavi di Ostia*, vols. I–VI, Rome, 1953–69
Cichorius, *Traianssäule*	C. Cichorius, *Die Reliefs der Traianssäule*, Berlin, 1896–1900
CIL	*Corpus Inscriptionum Latinarum*
Corp. Gloss.	*Corpus Glossariorum Latinorum*, ed. G. Goetz, Leipzig, 1888–1923
Crova, *Edilizia*	B. Crova, *Edilizia e tecnica rurale di Roma antica*, Milan, 1942
Dict. Ant.	*A Dictionary of Classical Antiquities*, ed. by W. Smith, W. Wayte and G. E. Marindin, 2 vols., London, 1891

Dilke, *RLS*	O. A. W. Dilke, *The Roman Land Surveyors: an introduction to the Agrimensores*, Newton Abbot, 1971
D–S	Ch. Daremberg and E. Saglio, *Dictionnaire des antiquités grecques et romaines*, 5 vols., Paris, 1877–1991
Drachmann, *AOMP*	H. Drachmann, *Ancient Oil Mills and Presses*, Copenhagen, 1932
E–M	A. Ernout and A. Meillet, *Dictionnaire étymologique de la langue latine*, 4th ed., Paris, 1959
Espérandieu, *Gaule*	E. Espérandieu, *Recueil général des bas-reliefs, statues et bustes de la Gaule romaine*, Paris, 1907–66
Farnell, *CGS*	G. S. Farnell, *The Cults of the Greek States*, 5 vols., Oxford, 1896–1909
Feldhaus, *Technik*	F. M. Feldhaus, *Die Technik der Vorzeit, der Geschichtlichen Zeit und der Naturvölker: ein Handbuch*, 2nd ed., Munich, 1965
Forbes, *SAT*	R. J. Forbes, *Studies in Ancient Technology*, Leiden, 1955–
Forc.	E. Forcellini, *Totius Latinitatis Lexicon*, 4 vols., Patavii, 1771
Hellas and Rome	W. Zschietzschmann, *Hellas and Rome: the Classical World in Pictures*, 3rd ed., London, 1959
HGT	*Histoire générale du travail*, 1. *Préhistoire et antiquité*, L.-R. Nougier, Paris, 1959
Hilgers	W. Hilgers, *Lateinische Gefäßnamen* (*Bonner Jahrbücher*, Beih. 31), Düsseldorf, 1969
Hooper–Ash	*Cato and Varro*, trans. by W. D. Hooper and H. B. Ash, Loeb Classical Library, London/New York, repr. 1960
Hopfen, *FIATR*	H. J. Hopfen, *Farm Implements for Arid and Tropical Regions*, Rome, 1960 [FAO Agricultural Development Paper, no. 67]
Hörle, *Hausbücher*	J. Hörle, *Catos Hausbücher, Studien zur Gesch. u. Kultur des Altertums*, Paderborn, 1929
Jasny (1944)	N. Jasny, *The Wheats of Classical Antiquity*, Baltimore, 1944
JHS	*Journal of Hellenic Studies*
LS	C. T. Lewis and C. Short, *A Latin Dictionary*, Oxford, 1880
LSJ	H. G. Liddell and R. Scott, *A Greek–English Lexicon*, 9th ed., ed. by H. Stuart Jones, Oxford, 1940
MAAR	*Memoirs of the American Academy in Rome*
Mau–Kelsey	A. Mau, *Pompeii*, trans. by F. W. Kelsey, New York/London, 1899
MEFR	*École française de Rome, mélanges d'archéologie et d'histoire*
Meiggs, *Ostia*	R. Meiggs, *Roman Ostia*, Oxford, 1960
M-L	W. Meyer-Lübke, *Romanisches etymologisches Wörterbuch*, 3rd ed., Heidelberg, 1930–2
Moritz, *Grain-mills*	L. A. Moritz, *Grain-mills and Flour in Classical Antiquity*, Oxford, 1958

NS	*Notizie degli scavi di antichità*
OED	*Oxford English Dictionary*
OHT	C. Singer, E. J. Holmyard and A. R. Hall, *A History of Technology*, 5 vols., Oxford, 1954–8
OLD	*Oxford Latin Dictionary*
Paoli, *Vita romana*	U. E. Paoli, *La vita romana*, 9th ed. trans. by H. Macnaughten, Rome, 1968
PBSR	*Papers of the British School at Rome*
Pernice	Erich Pernice, *Die hellenistische Kunst in Pompeji*, 6 vols., Pompeji/Berlin, 1925–38
R-E	A. Pauly, C. Wissowa and W. Kroll, *Realencyclopädie der classischen Altertumswissenschaft*, Stuttgart, 1894–
Rich, *Dict. Ant.*	A. Rich, *A Dictionary of Roman and Greek Antiquities*, 4th ed., London, 1874
Rostovtzeff, *SEHRE²*	M. Rostovtzeff, *The Social and Economic History of the Roman Empire*, 2nd ed., ed. by P. M. Fraser, Oxford, 1958
Scheuermeier, *Bauernwerk*	P. Scheuermeier, *Bauernwerk in Italien, der italienischen und rätoromanischen Südschweiz*, Erlenbach/Zürich, 1943
Sydenham, *CRR*	E. A. Sydenham, *The Coinage of the Roman Republic*, London, 1952
Taylor, *RVA*	L. R. Taylor, *Roman Voting Assemblies*, Michigan, 1966
TLL	*Thesaurus Linguae Latinae*
Vigneron, *Le Cheval*	P. Vigneron, *Le Cheval dans l'antiquité gréco-romaine*, 2 vols., Nancy, 1968
Walters, *HAP*	H. B. Walters, *A History of Ancient Pottery*, London, 1905
W–H	A. Walde, *Lateinisches etymologisches Wörterbuch*, 3rd ed., revised by J. B. Hofmann, Heidelberg, 1938
White, *RF*	K. D. White, *Roman Farming*, London, 1970

PART ONE

1

ROLLING, STAMPING AND GRINDING EQUIPMENT

This chapter deals with a number of implements concerned with the operations of stamping, pressing and grinding of surfaces and materials. The first three (*cylindrus*, *festuca* and *pavicula*) were used for rolling, ramming or consolidating earth, the remainder (*pilum*, *pila*, *mortarium*, *fistula* and *mola*) for stamping, bruising or grinding the seeds of cereal grains and other plants so as to produce meal or flour.

1. Cylindrus (-i, m.) (fr. Gr. κύλινδρος), (i) geom. a solid circular figure whose ends consist of equal circles; (ii) a *roller* for levelling and consolidating soil

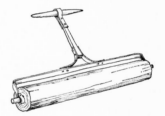

Fig. 1. Cylindrus

No entry in *R-E.*
Not in Varro, *LL.*

(a) Isid. *Etym.* 20. 14. 9 (*De instrumento rustico*). 'The *roller* is a round stone shaped like a column, which has obtained its name from its capacity to roll. On this Vergil writes (*Georg.* 1.178): "the threshing floor especially must be levelled with a huge roller"': cylindrus lapis est teretis in modum columnae, qui a volubilitate nomen accepit. de quo Vergilius (*Georg.* 1.178): area cum primis ingenti aequanda cylindro.

(b) *Corp. Gloss.* s.v. 'cylindrus'. cylindrus κύλινδρος III 200.16; 262.59. lapis volvilis IV 34.59 (volubilis *cd.*). cylindrus. est fustis quo aratores glebas castrorum quassant V 617.49. cylindrum lapis volubilis IV 95.20 (*Serv. in Georg.* 1.178). semicolumnium V 35.7; 495.21, etc. cylindri margaritae rotundae V 653.37 (Iuvenal. II.61).

(c) Cato 129 (on making a threshing-floor). 'To make a floor for threshing corn: break the soil up fine, sprinkle generously with oil-lees and let it absorb as much as possible. Pulverize the ground and level off with a *roller* or tamper': aream, ubi frumentum teratur, sic facito. confodiatur minute terra, amurca bene conspargatur et conbibat quam plurimum. comminuito terram et *cylindro* aut pavicula coaequato.

(d) Colum. 10.318–21 (on the sowing of basil); cf. *ibid.* 12. 3. 34. 'At this time too on fallow ground well trenched and watered (sow and) press down the seeds of basil, and compress the soil with heavy *rollers*, lest the heat of earth

3

turned to dust burn up the seedlings, or the tooth of the tiny ground-flea creeping in assail it, or the greedy ant ravage the seeds':

> tum quoque proscisso riguoque insparsa novali
> ocima comprimite, et gravibus densate *cylindris*,
> exurat sata ne resoluti pulveris aestus,
> parvulus aut pulex inrepens dente lacessat,
> neu formica rapax populari semina possit.

(*e*) Pliny, *HN* 17. 73 (on sowing cypress-seed). 'The seed is sown in April, after the earth has been levelled with *rollers* or tampers; it is sown thickly and a layer of earth a thumb deep is sieved over it': seritur Aprili mense, area aequata *cylindris* aut paviculis,[1] densum, terraque cribris superincernitur pollicis crassitudine.

(*f*) Virg. *Georg.* 1. 178 (cited by Isid. at *a* above).

(*g*) Colum. 11. 3. 34 (on sowing the herb basil). 'Basil too is usually sown at this season; the seed after being covered with soil is carefully pressed down with a tamper or *roller*. If you leave the soil loose, the seed usually rots': fere etiam his diebus ocima seruntur, quorum cum semen obrutum est, diligenter inculcatur pavicula vel *cylindro*. nam si terram suspensam relinquas, plerumque corrumpitur.

DISCUSSION

Material and design

The only surviving references to the material of which this implement was made are late (passages *a* and *b*), and they indicate that it was of hewn stone, shaped into cylindrical form. There are no indications of size in our sources, but it is evident that rollers of two different sizes would be required to serve the different purposes mentioned, that is, (1) the levelling and consolidation of the surface of the threshing-floor (*area*) (passage *c*), and (2) the compression of the finely-graded soil in a seed-bed (passages *d* and *g*). Rich (*Dict. Ant.* s.v. 'cylindrus') is very misleading; aware that revolving cylinders were known to Roman farmers and nurserymen, he nevertheless illustrates his text with an implement still in use in Anatolia, consisting of a solid tree-trunk drawn over the ground by an animal. This would serve as a primitive form of leveller; but it does not illustrate our implement, which was clearly intended to be used for consolidating, as well as levelling, a surface.

The threshing-floor roller

The authorities give no indications of size, but rollers of this type are still made of moulded concrete, and are commonly from 1·25 m to 1·5 m in length, with a diameter of between 30 and 37 cm. The two processes could be carried out separately, a heavy drag being used for levelling, and

[1] Urlichs: volviculis *Mayhoff*: vulvoalis *aut* vulgo alis *aut* vulgivalis *codd.*

a rammer (*pavicula*) for consolidating the surface (passages *c, g*). The *cylindrus* could combine both operations. Palladius' chapter on the preparation of the threshing-floor (7. 1) refers only to a round stone (*rotundus lapis*), with a 'piece of broken column' (*columnae . . . fragmentum*) as a substitute. Saturating the layer to be consolidated with oil-lees (*amurca*) was thought to be effective against ants, as well as protecting the surface against mud-formation after rain, the oily constituent of the lees acting as a water-repellant. Cylinders of this primitive type are still to be found on farms in parts of Italy and Spain. They are also used for consolidating the surfaces of gravel tennis-courts as a cheap substitute for the conventional iron roller.

The seed-bed roller

For a tree-nursery (passage *e*), or a garden seed-bed (passages *d, f*), a much smaller roller is needed, though still heavy in relation to its size (see Columella's 'gravibus densate cylindris' – passage *d*). A discarded kitchen rolling-pin makes a good tool for this purpose, and is sometimes used by gardeners for consolidating the seed-bed when propagating from very small seeds, or seeds with a long germination period. Columella's recommendation (passage *g*) is correct: the seeds of basil are very small, and must be sown with only a thin covering of soil if germination is to be effective. Consolidation with a roller is a good protection against surface pests (passage *d*). The pressure also helps to preserve moisture. Pliny (passage *e*) makes no mention of consolidation after sowing the seed of the cypress; as frequently elsewhere he seems to misunderstand his source; if too much soil scattered over it will cause the seed to 'twist back under the ground', how will it respond to the second method of 'merely treading it into the ground' (*HN* 17. 74)?

2. Festuca (-ae, f.), (i) = *calamus, stipula, stalk*; (ii) *rod, cane*; (iii) *rammer* (cf. *pilum*); (iv) *pile-driver* (Caes. *BG*)

Not in Isidore.

(*a*) *R-E* VI 2. 2224 [Mau].

(*b*) Varro, *LL* 5. 136, s.v. 'rastellum' (= *stipula*). 'In the meadows during the haymaking men rake together the *stalks* with it (viz. the wooden rake)': homo in pratis per fenisicia eo (rastello) *festucas* corradit.

(*c*) Fest. p. 76 L; p. 86 M. 'Hay, from which also the *stalk* gets its name': fenum, unde etiam et *ferula* vocata est.

(*d*) *TLL* s.v. 'festuca'. 1 festuca, -ae, f. [orig. incert. nisi cf. est c. fenum vel c. ferula Th.] Paul. Fest. p. 86 ... *TLL* notes the form *fistuca* as the vulgar form, very common in later, especially ecclesiastical, writers.

Fig. 2. Festuca

(e) *Corp. Gloss.* s.v. 'festuca'. festuca κάρφος, ῥάβδος II 71. 45. κάρφος II 339. 23, etc. fistuca κάρφος II 407. 16. festucum κάρφος II 428. 41 (Arch. I. 578).

(f) *Pers. Sat.* 5. 174–5 (on *ambitio*). 'The goal of our search is here, right here; not in the *rod* wielded by the stupid lictor':

> hic hic quod quaerimus hic est,
> non in *festuca*, lictor quam iactat ineptus.

(g) Cato 28. 2 (on transplanting trees); quoted by Pliny, *HN* 17. 87. 'When you set them in the trench, bed them in top soil, then spread earth over them to the ends of their roots, tread it down thoroughly, and then pack it as tightly as you can with *rammers* and bars. This is the most important thing': in scrobe quom pones, summam terram subdito; postea operito terra radicibus fini, deinde calcato pedibus bene, deinde *festucis* vectibusque calcato quam optime poteris; id erit ei rei primum.

(h) Pliny, *HN* 36. 185 (on paved flooring). 'The original paved floors were, I believe, the ones we call "foreign" and "indoor" floors. In Italy these were beaten down with *rammers*. This at least is what may be inferred from the name': pavimenta credo primum facta quae nunc vocamus barbarica atque subtegulanea, in Italia *festucis* pavita. hoc certe ex nomine ipso intellegi potest.

(j) Caes. *BG* 4. 17. 4 (building of the bridge over the Rhine). 'Having lowered the beams and set them in position in the river-bed with the aid of cranes, he drove them in with *pile-drivers*': tigna cum machinationibus inmissa in flumen defixerat *festucisque*[1] adegerat.

DISCUSSION

There is much confusion in the ordinary works of reference about the spelling, the etymology and the range of meaning of this word. (1) *Spelling*: LS give the separate forms *festuca*, 'stalk, straw', and *fistuca*, 'ram, beetle, pile-driver'. *OLD* gives *fistuca* as alternative form, noting that *f.* in the sense of 'pile-driver' may be a separate word. One may suspect confusion with the common word *fistula*, 'pipe'. (2) *Etymology*: Uncertain, according to *OLD* (see passage *d*). (3) *Range of meaning*: Examination of the passages cited shows that there is no need to suggest two separate words. The first meaning of *festuca* may well be 'stalk' (passage *b*; cf. *ferula* in passage *c*). Columella (8. 5. 7) couples it with *surculus*, 'twig'. Assuming a single root, we should expect *festuca* as instrument to resemble a stalk or cane, but made of wood. The few Glossary references point in the same direction, equating *f.* with κάρφος, 'dry twig', and ῥάβδος, 'stick'. I believe the *festuca* to be distinct from the *pavicula* (*q.v.*, where I have identified the latter as a 'tamper' or 'punner', that is, an instrument for consolidating a surface). A 'rammer', on the other hand, is designed for

---

[1] fistucia *a*, festuculisque *b*.

use in an earlier phase in the process of paving, that of forcing down the stones in a heavy concrete mix such as *opus Signinum*. The two stages are in fact clearly distinguished by Columella (1. 6. 15) in his account of the construction of a granary, where the earth floor, after being dug over and soaked with *amurca*, is then 'consolidated with rammers' (*pilis condensatur*), and then overlaid with a special mixture of broken tile, *amurca*, lime and sand. After this process, the surface 'is beaten down and smoothed off with tampers (*paviculis*)'. *Festuca* should therefore be identified with *pilum*, a pestle, the tapered design of which is very well suited to the task of ramming. Rammers are necessary for setting up fencing poles, and many other jobs around the farm. In pre-mechanized days they were used for road-making, and will certainly have been used by Roman road-construction gangs, though no account survives. Caesar's pile-drivers (passage *j*), will have been similar in shape, but of massive size.

3. Pavicula (-ae, f.) (fr. *pavire* to 'stamp', 'pave'), *tamper*, '*punner*', for consolidating a surface

Not in Varro, *LL*; not in Isidore.

(a) See *R-E* s.v. 'pavimentum', XVIII. 2307–24 [van Buren]: comprehensive discussion.

(b) Corp. Gloss. s.v. 'pavicula'. paviculae ὁμαλιστῆρες II 140. 28; = 43. 36 (*add. e*).

Fig. 3. Pavicula

(c) Cato 91 (on making a threshing-floor). 'To make a threshing-floor: dig over thoroughly the ground where you intend to make it. Then give it a good sprinkling of oil-lees, letting it soak in. Next break up the clods thoroughly, level the ground, and pack it with *tampers*; then spread a fresh layer of oil-lees and let it dry': aream sic facito. locum ubi facies confodito. postea amurca conspargito bene, sinitoque conbibat. postea comminuito glebas bene. deinde coaequato et *paviculis* verberato. postea denuo amurca conspargito sinitoque arescat.

(d) Colum. 1. 6. 13 (on making a granary). 'The best storage place for grain ... is a granary with a vaulted roof, the earth floor of which, before paving, has been dug over and soaked with fresh unsalted oil-lees, and consolidated with rammers like *opus Signinum*. Then, after it has dried off thoroughly, the surface is overlaid in the same way with a pavement of broken tile, which, instead of absorbing water, has been combined with oil-lees mixed with lime and sand; this is then beaten down with greater force by *tampers* and smoothed off': sedem frumentis optimam ... horreum camera contectum, cuius solum terrenum, priusquam consternatur, perfossum et amurca recenti non salsa madefactum velut Signinum opus pilis condensatur. tum deinde cum exaruit, simili modo pavimenta testacea, quae pro aqua receperint amurcam mixtam calci et harenae, supersternuntur et *paviculis* inculcantur atque expoliuntur.

7

(e) Colum. II. 3. 34 (on raising the herb basil). 'The seed after being covered with soil is carefully pressed down with a *tamper* or roller': quorum cum semen obrutum est, diligenter inculcatur *pavicula* vel cylindro.

DISCUSSION

The derivation of the term (from *pavire* 'to pave, lay down paving') indicates the general class of ramming or tamping instrument required. The main references (passages *c* and *d*) are concerned with two processes, the mixing of the ingredients making up the finished surface, and the preparation and finishing of the surface itself. Cato's threshing-floor is very economical, being made of earth combined with *amurca*; in this case the breaking up and mixing would be done by means of a multi-tined hoe (*rastrum*), which was the usual implement for breaking up clods left after ploughing. Columella's granary pavement (passage *d*) is formed by breaking up and incorporating tile with lime, sand and oil-lees; this part of the job requires a different instrument, the heavy pestle or pounder (*pilum*). See further s.v. 'pilum', p. 9. In both cases the surfaces must be consolidated after levelling; this job needs an implement with a flat surface. In the absence of identifiable representations of the *pavicula* we must assume that it resembled the tampers which are still used by road repair gangs for consolidating small tar surfaces, or by public service employees for restoring road surfaces after the installation of gas or water supplies. They are known in the trade as 'punners'. The instrument consists of a flat plate of heavy-gauge iron mounted on a solid handle usually about five feet in length, the operator lifting it to the full stretch of his arms and driving it into the ground as he releases it 'magna vi', as Columella puts it.

Extant representations

I know of no certain representations of any of the above implements. Rich (*Dict. Ant.* s.v. 'festuca') illustrates his article with a drawing taken from a fort-construction scene on Trajan's Column (Cichorius, *Traianssäule*, Taf. XIV, Bild 39), in which a soldier is alleged to be engaged in tamping down the end of a course of bricks with a club-shaped instrument; but the instrument is much too long for this purpose; Cichorius correctly identified it as a straight-edge used to check the level before commencing the next course of bricks.

Extant specimens

I have not come across any identifiable specimens.

4. Pilum (-i, n.), (i) *pestle* (large), *pounder*; (ii) mil. t.t. *pilum*; dimin.
pistillum (-i, n.), *pestle* (small), *grinder*

Fig. 4. Pilum and
mortarium (*a*)

5. Pila (-ae, f.), mortar (= *mortarium*)

W–H s.v. 'pilum'. *pilum* from *pist-lum*, cf. dimin. *pistillum* and *pistor*
'miller' from *pinsere* 'to pound'.

(*a*) *R-E* xx 2. 1333–69, s.v. 'pilum' [A. Schulten] contains virtually nothing on
the implement, being almost wholly devoted to *pilum* (ii).

(*b*) Varro, *LL* 5. 138. 'The pilum "*pestle*" is so named because with it they
"*pisunt*" "pound" the emmer; from this the place where this is done is
called a "*pistrinum*" "mill"': *pilum, quod eo far pisunt, a quo ubi id fit
dictum pistrinum . . .*

(*c*) Isid. *Etym.* 4. 2. 5 (*De instrumentis medicorum*). 'The *mortar* "pila" is a hollow
vessel suited to the needs of doctors . . . Varro however tells us of a certain
Pilumn[i]us who lived in Italy, who looked after the "pounding" (pulverizing?) of the fields, whence come the terms pestle-men (?) "pilumni"
and millers "pistores". This man then was the inventor of the pounder and
mortar with which the emmer is pounded': *est enim pila vas concavum et
medicorum aptum usui . . . Varro autem refert Pilumn[i]um quendam in
Italia fuisse, qui pinsendis praefuit arvis, unde et pilumni et pistores. ab hoc
igitur pilum et pilam inventam, quibus far pinsitur, et ex eius nomine ita
appellata. Cf. *ibid.* 4. 2. 4; 11. 1. 28 (*pilum* derived from *pila*).*

(*d*) *Corp. Gloss.* s.v. 'pilum'. *pilum pistillum* II 589. 45. *pistillum vel vas concave
(pilo et pistillo)* V 576. 1; 510. 28. *unde contunditur quicquid in pila
tunditur* IV 143. 27 (cf. Isid. IV. II. 5. XI. I. 28); 553. 34.

(*e*) Cato 10. 5 (oliveyard inventory). 'One wooden *mortar*, one fuller's *mortar*
. . . two *mortars*, four *pestles* – one for beans, one for emmer, one for seeds
and one for cracking kernels': *pilam ligneam I, fullonicam I . . . pilas II,
pilum fabarium I, farrearium I, seminarium I, qui nucleos succernat I.*

(*f*) *Ibid.* 14. 2 (homestead fittings and equipment). 'One small *mortar* for crushing wheat, one fuller's mortar': *paullulam pilam ubi triticum pinsat I,
fullonicam I.*

(*g*) Pliny, *HN* 18. 112 (how to prepare groats (*alica*) from emmer). 'Its grain is
pounded in a wooden *mortar*, to prevent it from being ground to flour by
the hard stone': *tunditur granum eius in pila lignea ne lapidis duritia
conterat.*

6. Mortarium (-i, n.), (i) small *grinding-mortar*; (ii) large *stone mortar* for the
oil-mill (*trapetum*); (iii) *mixing-bowl* (cul.)

(*h*) W–H s.v. fr. *mer in gr. μαραίνω; cf. *moretum*, a 'dish of pounded herbs'.

(*j*) *R-E* s.v. 'mortarium' XVI I. 319–21 [A Hug.].

(*k*) Isid. *Etym.* 4. 11. 6 (*De instrumentis medicorum*). '"*Mortar*" because it is here
that seeds are reduced to powder and seasoned when they are "dead"

Fig. 5. Mortarium (*b*)

9

("mortua")': *mortarium, quod ibi iam semina in pulverem redacta et mortua condiantur.*

(*l*) Non. p. 543. 22. 'The *mortar*, in which they grind things which have to be broken down': *mortarium, in quo teruntur quae solvenda sunt.*

(*m*) Cato 74 (recipe for bread-making). 'Recipe for kneaded bread. Wash your hands and a *mixing-bowl* thoroughly. Put meal in the bowl, add water gradually and knead thoroughly': *panem depsticium sic facito. manus mortariumque bene lavato. farinam in mortarium indito, aquae paulatim addito subigitoque pulchre.*

(*n*) Cato 22 (how to adjust the oil-pulping mill (*trapetum*) – in the Table of Contents the title 'how to construct the oil-mill' is incorrect). 'The mill-stone should be separated from the bottom of the *mortar* by the breadth of the little finger. You must take care not to let the stones rub against the sides of the mortar': *digitum minimum orbem abesse oportet ab solo mortari. orbes cavere oportet nequid mortarium terant.*

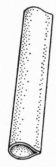

Fig. 6. Fistula

7. Fistula (-ae, f.) (fr. *findere, fissum*), (i) *pipe, esp. water-pipe*; [(ii) *reed-pipe* (mus.)]; (iii) *mortar* for stamping hard grains

Not in Varro, *LL*, except with meaning (i) 'water-pipe'.

(*o*) *R-E* s.v. 'fistula' refers to s.v. 'Wasserleitungen', but no reference is given to Pliny's *fistula serrata* (passage *s*).

(*p*) Isid. *Etym.* 19. 10. 29 (*De constructione*). '*Water-pipes* are so called because they pour out water and let it (flow). στολα is the Greek word for "make to flow"': *fistulae aquarum sunt dictae quod aquas fundant et mittant. nam* στολα *Graece mittere est.*

(*q*) Pliny, *HN* 19. 66 (on growing cucumbers). 'Also if the flower is passed down into a *pipe* they grow to a remarkable length': *iidem in fistulam flore demisso mira longitudine crescunt.*

(*r*) Cato 10. 3 (oliveyard inventory; list of iron implements). 'One *mortar* for emmer': *fistula farraria I.*

(*s*) Pliny, *HN* 18. 97 (on methods of pounding and milling cereals). 'In Etruria they pound the ears of emmer, after roasting them, with a pestle shod with iron at the top, in a *mortar* that is serrated, and fitted inside with grooves radiating from the centre, so that, if they pound it forcibly, the grains are merely splintered and the iron gets broken. Over most of Italy they use a bare *pestle*, also wheels turned by water flowing past, and a millstone': *Etruria spicam farris tosti pisente pilo praeferrato, fistula serrata et stella intus denticulata, ut, si intenti pisant, concidantur grana, ferrumque frangatur. maior pars Italiae nudo utitur pilo, rotis etiam quas aqua verset obiter et mola.*

DISCUSSION

To the reader for whom home-baked bread is at best a distant memory of childhood, and stone-ground meal an eccentricity associated with health-food addicts, the various pounding and grinding processes mentioned above will require a good deal of explanation. A further difficulty arises from the fact that basic terms such as *mortarium* and *pila*, *pilum* and *pistillum*, were used of widely differing operations. To avoid unnecessary duplication, *mortarium* and *fistula*, the only terms in the series not derived from a common root, are included in the general heading 'pilum', and the commentary is arranged to cover all of them.

Types and sizes

Three related kinds of operation are mentioned in the passages cited above: first, that of grinding substances to a fine powder (*terere*, *conterere*, *in pulverem redigere*), as in the making of pills in the dispensary (passage *k*), a process now confined to the laboratory; this grinding was effected in a hemispherical stone bowl or mortar (*pila*, *mortarium* (i)), using a small, heavy instrument with a rounded end of highly polished stone (*pilum*, more commonly *pistillum*) as mentioned by Isidore (passage *c*); secondly, that of pulping the olives after the initial pressing; for this operation a heavy stone mortar was used, with a pair of millstones (*orbes*) set to revolve inside the bowl (passage *n*); see Appendix A, pp. 225 ff., for details; thirdly, the operation of crushing the grains of wheat, barley or emmer to make groats (*alica*) or other kinds of farinaceous porridge (*puls*). For this they used a long, heavy, double-ended pounder (*pilum ligneum*), working in a narrow mortar (*pila lignea*, *fistula*), made from a hollowed-out piece of tree-trunk. These wooden mortars were either plain (passages *e*, *g*) or grooved on the inside, as described by Pliny (passage *s*). The appearance of Cato's mortar for pounding emmer in a list of ironware (passage *r*) implies the use of some form of iron cladding. A different version of the small mortar, closely resembling in shape the corn-measure (*modius*), appears on a relief from Sens (see Pl. 4*c*). The term *mortarium* was also applied to a mixing-bowl, usually of earthenware, used for blending, mixing and kneading flour, meal and other mixtures for making bread and cakes (passage *m*). The wide, rather flat bowl (*mortarium* (iii)) is mentioned frequently by Apicius in his cookery-book (e.g. 43. 2; 131. 4, etc.), and is well known from surviving examples (see Hilgers, nos. 52–5, p. 69; Pl. 2*c*).

Uses

All the above varieties of mortar occur in Cato's lists (passages *e* and *f*). His oliveyard inventory (passage *e*) mentions four different types of pounder for making meal from beans, emmer and ordinary wheat, and one for cracking the kernels of nuts. These would vary in weight according to the type of seed to be crushed. His launderer's 'mortar' is also well known from paintings depicting work in the fuller's establishment (see below). The process of making meal from emmer (see Pliny's recipe for *alica* at *HN* 18. 112 ff.) was both tedious and laborious; a first pounding was needed to remove the tenacious 'wrappings' from the grain (Pliny appropriately calls these 'tunicae'), followed by a second pounding to break the kernel (*medulla*), 'the motive power for the pestle, as is well known, being supplied by chained convicts as a penal task'. The importance of pearl barley (*polenta*), groats (*tragum, alica*) and other pulses in the Roman diet is frequently stressed by Pliny, e.g.: 'It is clear ... that for a long time the Romans lived on porridge, not on bread, since even today foodstuffs are also called "pulmentaria"' (18. 83). In grinding the hulled grains, care had to be taken to produce meal, not powder (see passage *g*).

The frequency of references to these various pounding operations in the Roman writers suggests that these pulses were not completely displaced by baker's bread. The point seems to have escaped the notice of modern commentators; thus Forbes, in a lengthy treatment of the subject of food in classical antiquity (*SAT*, III, 84 ff.), devotes much space to the evolution of milling techniques, but confines the topic of grinding and crushing by manual apparatus to a brief mention in the preceding chapter (at p. 57), while Pliny's description of the process of making groats is misplaced in yet another section, that on the diet of ancient Greece (*ibid.* p. 96). Finally, in a chapter entitled 'Crushing', with subdivisions on pressing, grinding and pounding, the author provides important information on querns and animal mills which is essential to his earlier discussions on food. The persistence of older methods is given prominence by Pliny when he observes that the 'improved' Etruscan method of grinding emmer was no improvement at all, since most of Italy continued the tedious task of milling it with the smooth pestle (passage *s*). These large pounding pestles are still used widely in under-developed countries. I have myself used a double-ended locally made *pilum* and *fistula* of identical design to those illustrated by Forbes (see below, 'Extant specimens'), for the purpose of crushing whole maize when the machine-ground product was in restricted supply owing to a severe drought.

Fig. 7. Mola manualis

8. Mola (-ae, f.) (cf. Gr. μύλη, 'mill'), a *millstone*; pl. **molae** (-*arum*, f.) (cf. Gr. μύλαι), (i) '*grinders*', *molars*; (ii) a *mill*, turned by manual, animal- or water-power; **molae aquariae,** a water-mill; **molae oleariae,** an oil-mill (see Appendix A)

(a) *R-E* s.v. Μύλη, XVI 1. 1064–72 [Aug. Hug]. Comprehensive treatment, providing a complete list to date (1933) of all archaeological finds and monumental evidence on the various kinds of mills.

(*b*) Cato 10. 4 (oliveyard inventory). '1 *donkey-mill*, 1 pushing-mill, 1 Spanish mill': *molas* asinarias unas, trusatiles unas, Hispaniensis unas.

(*c*) *Ibid.* 11. 4 (vineyard inventory). '3 *donkey-mills*, 1 pushing-mill': *molas* asinarias tres, trusatiles unas.

(*d*) Pliny, *HN* 36. 155 (on curious stones). 'Varro also records that *turning millstones* (?) have been found (?) at Bolsena': idem (i.e. Varro) tradit *molas versatiles* Volsiniis inventas.

(*e*) Pallad. 1. 42 (inventory of farm equipment). 'If you have a plentiful supply of water, the mill should receive the effluent of the baths, so that you may construct a *water-mill* in that place, and have your corn ground without the labour of animals or men': si aquae copia est, fusoria balnearum debent pistrina suscipere, ut ibi formatis *aquariis molis* sine animalium vel hominum labore frumenta frangantur.

(*f*) Ovid, *Fast.* 6. 317–18 (the primacy of Vesta, goddess of the hearth). 'Hence the miller keeps the hearth and the Mistress of the hearth, and the *millstones* of pumice turned by the she-ass':

> inde focum servat pistor dominamque focorum
> et quae pumiceas versat asella *molas*.

(*g*) Gellius, *NA* 3. 3. 14 (early life of the dramatist Plautus). 'Varro and several other writers have recorded that the *Saturio*, the *Addictus* and a third play . . . were written by Plautus in a mill-bakery, at a time when . . . in order to earn a living, he had hired out his labour to a miller for turning the *mills* called "*pushing-mills*"': sed enim Saturionem et Addictum et tertiam quandam . . . in pistrino eum scripsisse Varro et plerique alii memoriae tradiderunt, cum . . . ob quaerendum victum ad circumagendas *molas*, quae *trusatiles* appellantur, operam pistori locasset.

(*h*) Juvenal, *Sat.* 8. 67–9 (noble lineage has no value nowadays). 'The grand-children (of a racing champion) are told to change owners at rock-bottom prices . . . slow-footed and fit only for *turning the mill*': dominos pretio mutare iubentur/exiguo . . ./segnipedes dignique *molas versare* nepotes.

(*j*) Varro, *RR* 1. 55. 5 (on the making of olive oil). 'So that the piles (of olives) may pass in the order of picking through the jars and oil vessels to the "trapeta", which is an *oil-mill* consisting of hard roughened stones': ac [ut] primus quisque acervos demittatur per serias ac vasa olearia ad trapetas, quae res *molae oleariae* ex duro et aspero lapide.

(*k*) Colum. 12. 52. 6 (on making olive oil). 'For making oil, however, the *olive-mill* is better than the revolving mill': oleo autem conficiendo *molae* utiliores sunt quam trapetum.

(*l*) Paul, *Sent.* 3. 6. 36 (on the *instrumentum fundi*). 'Included in the basic equipment are items furnished for the gathering of crops, such as baskets, trays, sickles and scythes, also *olive mills*': fructuum cogendorum causa comparata instrumento cedunt, velut corbes, alvei, falces messoriae et fenariae, item *molae olivariae*.

13

DISCUSSION

(1) *Hand-operated mills*

The singular noun 'mola' has the meaning 'millstone', the plural being used, normally with a defining adjective, as in passages *b–d*, etc., of a milling device, consisting of two stones. In an earlier section (above, pp.) we have discussed the various stamping and pounding instruments used for preparing meal and flour from cereal grains. Crushing and pounding were essential processes in the preparation of barley, emmer and other husked grains, but the expansion in the use of the more convenient naked wheats, such as common bread-wheat (*triticum vulgare*) and hard or 'macaroni' wheat (*triticum durum*) led to the growth and improvement of milling as distinct from crushing devices, in which the meal or flour is produced by rubbing the grain between two roughened stones instead of pounding with pestle and mortar. The oldest form of grain-mill is the saddle-quern, which consists of a stationary lower stone over which the upper stone is moved to and fro, first away from, then towards the operator, who is usually represented in a kneeling position. The hand-quern is familiar from Egyptian statuettes, and surviving specimens have been found on numerous prehistoric sites all over Europe. This primitive pushing-mill underwent a number of improvements in classical times: these included the invention of a lever to ease the burden of the task, and of a hopper and slot to allow the grain to flow continuously on to the grinding surface. This 'hopper-rubber' is pushed to and fro over the lower stone, both upper and lower surfaces being grooved for more effective pulverizing of the grain. The type is mentioned by Virgil (*lapis incusus* at *Georg.* 1. 275), and this is also the mill used in the anonymous poem called the 'Mixed Salad' (*Moretum*), which contains the only surviving description of a very familiar daily process. This simple 'pushing-mill' (*molae trusatiles* [passages *b, c, g*]) continued to be used for grinding salt and for other culinary purposes long after the introduction of more efficient devices. Little is known for certain about the introduction of rotary motion into the process (full discussion in Moritz, *Grain-mills*, pp. 103 ff.); Cato's 'Spanish' mill (passage *b*) may well have been of this type (see Fig. 7). Diffused throughout the Roman world, the rotary hand-mill survived alongside the much more efficient animal-powered mills made possible by the introduction of rotary motion.

(2) *Animal-operated mills (molae asinariae)*

While the making of flour by means of the traditional hand-quern or a modification of it was never completely displaced by mills using more efficient sources of power (legionary soldiers, for example, continued to grind their own meal in the old way in imperial times), the bakers whose products fed the growing populations of Rome and other urban centres drew their flour from donkey-driven mills of the type familiar to every visitor to Pompeii or Ostia. This type of mill consisted of a conical or bell-shaped lower stone (the *meta*), which remained stationary while the hollowed and 'waisted' upper stone (the *catillus*), was made to revolve about it. The grain, dispensed from a hopper (*modiolus* – q.v.), was ground as it passed between the upper and lower stones, while the flour collected round the circular base (see Fig. 8 and Pl. 2 *b*). For an up-to-date, well documented account of these mills see Moritz, pp. 74–96. While donkeys provided the most common motive power (Suetonius (*Gaius* 39) reports that the emperor Caligula created a serious bread-crisis by commandeering the mill-animals for one of his more spectacular public performances), worn-out horses were also employed (Juv. *Sat.* 8. 67 – other literary references in Moritz, p. 100), 'their somewhat higher upkeep costs being offset by their higher output and by the small initial outlay' (Moritz, p. 100). The erroneous view that slaves were also employed in place of animals to drive these mills dies hard (see Forbes, *SAT*, III, 145).

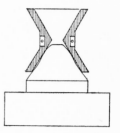

Fig. 8. Mola asinaria

(3) *Water-powered grain-mills (molae aquariae)*

The undershot 'Vitruvian' water-wheel (*rota aquaria*), which seems to have made its first appearance in Italy in the course of the first century B.C. (see below, 'Water-raising Devices', pp. 44 ff.), was subsequently provided with a reduction gearing to give a vastly increased power output for milling grain. At least two centuries elapsed before it began to be widely used. Pliny's reference to it (above, passage *s*) seems to imply that it cannot have been common in his day, while the manner of its appearance in Palladius' list of farm equipment more than three centuries later 'shows both that it was well enough known not to need detailed description . . . and still uncommon enough not to be installed as a matter of course' (Moritz, p. 138). These brief, casual references to a new and potentially revolutionary source of power are typical of Roman writers, as well as exasperating! The Vitruvian mill (see his account of the water-wheel in *De Arch.* 10. 4) could grind about forty times as much grain per day as the donkey-mill, that is, about 3·6 tons of grain per day. Yet there was no dramatic 'take-over' by the new device; the emperor Diocletian's Price

Edict of A.D. 301 contains a list of four types of mill – the horse-mill, priced at 1,500 *den.*, the donkey-mill, at 1,250 *den.*, the water-mill at 2,000 *den.*, and the hand-mill at 250 *den.* In fact, all three devices survived the fall of the Roman Empire in the West. For a summary treatment of the factors limiting the extension of technical innovations and improvements see my *Roman Farming*, pp. 446 ff., and for a full discussion of the problems relating to the spread of the water-mill see Marc Bloch's essay in *Ann. d'hist. écon. et sociale* VII, 538 ff. (now available in English in *Land and Work in Mediaeval Europe*, selected papers by M.B., trans. by J. E. Anderson, London, 1966, 136 ff.).

Economics of the various milling devices

Numerous estimates have been made of the relative efficiency of the milling devices discussed here. Yet in spite of the large quantity of surviving material in the form of querns, millstones and complete donkey-mills, the only detailed experiments so far carried out are those done with a Romano-British quern at Lewes in Sussex, and described by Moritz. Two donkey-mills were reconstructed and are now in the National Museum at Naples, but the reconstructions are unsatisfactory, and any results obtained from them would be valueless. Forbes (*SAT*, III, 94) states that a donkey-mill (dimensions not given) could grind $3\frac{1}{2}$ bushels per day, equivalent to 200 lb., but his figure of 12 tons per day for the water-mill (see above), is not forty times this quantity! It has been shown by Jasny (1944) that the high price of wheat, together with the very low power-output per bushel required for grinding the coarse meal (no more than $\frac{1}{2}$ h.p. per bushel compared with $1\frac{1}{2}$–2 h.p. in a modern mill) meant that grinding costs could have amounted to no more than 10 per cent of the total. This would provide at least part of the explanation of the fact that the more efficient devices did not drive out other methods. The girls that ground at the mill did not all 'stay their busy hands', as the poet optimistically predicted (Antipater of Thessalonica (?) in *Anth. Pal.* IX 418; translated in *OGV* no. 592); and donkeys and worn-out hacks continued to plod around the bakeries for many centuries to come.

Extant representations

(1) *of pestles and mortars.* I know of no representations of the large *pilum/mortarium* on Roman monuments, but there is a good representation of the pounding technique on a red-figured Attic *amphora*, now in the Hermitage, Leningrad, which shows two women standing at either side of a large mortar, each holding a double-ended pestle, which is tapered in the centre to form a hand-grip. They are working as a pair, and

alternately lifting and lowering their pestles, which are raised high to get maximum drive. The vase is little known; reproduced by F. Bourriot in *HGT*, vol. IV, pl. 31.1 Paris, 1959. Forbes (*SAT*, III, fig. 36, p. 149) has a drawing of a 'primitive mortar and pestle', of exactly the same design and proportions as the one mentioned earlier (p. 11) (see Fig. 4); the small diameter of the mortar in relation to its length explains Pliny's choice of the word 'fistula' in passage *s*, p. 10.

(2) *of hand-querns*. Moritz provides three illustrations: pl. I (*a*) a wooden model of a woman grinding with a movable upper stone on a sloping slab, from Asyut in Egypt, dated *c.* 2000 B.C., now in the British Museum; (*b*) a working model in terracotta from Rhodes, also in the British Museum, and dated to the middle of the fifth century B.C.; (*c*) a terracotta figurine of a man working a saddle-quern from Thebes, dated to the late sixth century B.C., now in the Louvre.

(3) *of animal-driven mills*. The best-known example is a bas-relief of a horse-driven mill, part of a sarcophagus now in the Vatican (Rome, Museo Chiaramonti, Inv. 497, Taf. 68), and often reproduced (e.g. *RF* pl. 79). Moritz (*Grain-mills*, pl. 5(*b*)) displays it to best advantage, since the photograph covers the whole fragment, including part of an adjoining mill, and the hindquarters of a second horse. The artist has idealized his subject, and provided a first-class animal; in fact, as we have seen (above, p. 15) only broken-down hacks were used. Maiuri (*Guide to Pompeii*, 8th ed., p. 57), notes the oil lamp on a ledge at the rear, indicating that the operation was carried on through the night. The more familiar donkey is presented on a well-preserved sarcophagus, that of P. Nonius Zethus, also in the Museo Chiaramonti collection (Inv. 683, Taf. 84; Moritz, pl. 7(*a*); see Pl. 2*a*). Full accounts of all important representations in Moritz pp. 74 ff.

Extant specimens

(1) *Hand-querns*. All the types mentioned above, from primitive saddle-querns to rotary hand-mills, are represented from a great variety of sites (see e.g. E. C. Curwen in *Antiquity* XI (1937), 133–51; XV (1941), 15–32.

(2) *Molae asinariae*. 'The examples found at Pompeii alone run into three figures' (Moritz, p. 74). Two different sizes are represented, and the Naples Museum contains a reconstruction of each; as noted in the previous discussion, however, these reconstructions are uncertain, the smaller model (Moritz, pl. 4(*a*)) being described incorrectly as a *mola trusatilis*, and furnished with crossbars for working by slaves, and the upper fittings provided for the larger model (*ibid.* pl. 4(*b*)) do not tally with the evidence of either of the two Chiaramonti representations (*ibid.* pl. 5(*b*) and pl. 7).

There are good photographs of mills *in situ* in Moritz, pl. 5(*a*) (two sizes of mill): 6(*a*) (two *metae* which have lost their *catilli*); 9(*a*) and (*b*) (details of *meta* and *catillus*); 10(*a*) and (*b*) (mills *in situ* at Pompeii and Ostia).

(3) *Molae aquariae*. No complete specimen of the water-mill has survived; nor can the Saalburg remains, which include an iron spindle fitted at one end with a pinion, and at the other with a pair of dovetails for slotting into the lower millstone, be demonstrably connected with a water-mill (for details see Moritz, 125 ff.). The main lines of its design are, however, determined by Vitruvius' description (*De Arch.* 10. 4–5), see Fig. 12, p. 44. The earliest water-mill known from substantial remains was located at Venafrum. The wheel, the timber of which had completely disintegrated, had nevertheless left a clear enough impression to allow of identification and reconstruction (in the Naples Museum) as a wheel of Vitruvian type with compartments (*pinnae*), as shown in Moritz, pl. 4(*a*). For scanty traces of mills on the Janiculum at Rome see A. W. van Buren and G. P. Stevens in *MAAR* 1915–16, 59 ff. and 1933, 69 ff. The most complete water-mill complex so far known was found in Athens, just south of the Stoa of Attalus (now the Agora Museum), in 1933. The remains are fully described and illustrated by A. W. Parsons (*Hesperia* v (1936), 70 ff.) who notes that the wheel was of the overshot type, and must have been fitted with buckets. The entire system provides a remarkably clear illustration of the text of Vitruvius: 'the mill was planned and built nearly 500 years after Vitruvius wrote. It might as well have been five years or fifty as far as the actual installation is concerned, for once the principle was discovered, this simple application of it must have been rapidly developed' (Parsons, *art. cit.*).

Survival

On the history of the water-mill see M. Bloch, *Land and Work in Mediaeval Europe*, selected papers, trans. by J. L. Anderson, London, 1967, 136–68.

2

VINE-PROPS

This chapter deals with the numerous types of prop used by vine-dressers for supporting and training vines. Made usually of wood or cane, they range from simple forked sticks for raising the young vine-shoots clear of the ground so as to prevent them trailing to the more or less elaborate systems of framing designed to control and direct the growth of the mature vine. The somewhat formidable list of terms may be conveniently subdivided into (a) single props, (b) various kinds of timber frames used for the same purpose, whether by way of temporary or permanent support to the tree or plant; to the former group belong *adminiculum, palus, patibulum, pedamen, pedamentum, pertica, ridica, statumen,* and *sudes*; to the latter *cantherius, compluvium, iugum* and *pergula*. Many of the terms are used in both a general and a specific sense: thus at 17. 174 Pliny uses *pedamentum* of a prop generally, while elsewhere (e.g. at 17. 187) it means the vertical member of a frame to which cross-bars (*iuga*) are added at intervals. Other terms are confined to a specific meaning: thus of single props *palus* usually has the generic meaning 'stay', *pertica* means a round pole, while *ridica* means a stake formed by splitting a tree into two or four sections (see Colum. 4. 33. 4).

The *loci classici* for the various methods of propping vines are Varro, *RR* 1. 8 and Columella 4. 12 (initial propping); 16–17, 19 (framing); 26 (selecting props). Pliny (17. 164–6) gives a short summary of the various methods employed.

(a) Varro, *RR* 1. 8. 'The profitability of growing vines depends on the kind of vineyard, for there are several: some are low-growing, and need no *stakes*, as in Spain; others are trained up, the so-called "yoked vines", to which class Italian vines mostly belong. In connection with this latter class, two terms are in use, *props* ("pedamenta") and *espaliers* ("iuga"). The supports on which the vine runs vertically are called "pedamenta", and those on which it runs crosswise are called "iuga"; from this comes the name "yoked vines". Of these yokes four kinds are usually employed, *poles*, reeds, cords and withies: poles are used in the Falernum district, reeds around Arpi, cords around Brindisi, and withies around Milan. . . . Similarly, there are as a rule four kinds of *props*; the first is a stout post, made of oak or juniper, called the "ridica" – the best prop for use in the vineyard; the second best is a *stake* made from a *branch* ("pertica"), a hard wood

being preferred as being more durable ... the third, used only as a substitute when the first two are unobtainable, is obtained from the reed
plantation ... the fourth is the natural prop made of the vines, where the
vineyard consists of vines running from tree to tree; some people call these
traverses "rumpi"': aliae enim humiles ac sine *ridicis*, ut in Hispanis, aliae
sublimes, quae appellantur iugatae, ut pleraeque in Italia. cuius generis
nomina duo, *pedamenta* et *iuga*. quibus stat rectis vinea, dicuntur pedamenta;
quae transversa iunguntur, iuga; ab eo quoque vineae iugatae. iugorum
genera fere quattuor, *pertica*, harundo, restes, vites: pertica, ut in Falerno,
harundo, ut in Arpano, restes, ut in Brundisino, vites, ut in Mediolanensi.
... *pedamentum* item fere quattuor generum: unum robustum, quod
optimum solet afferri in vineam e querco ac iunipiro et vocatur *ridica*;
alterum *palus* e *pertica*, meliore dura, quo diuturnior. ... tertium, quod
horum inopiae subsidio misit harundinetum. ... quartum est pedamentum
nativum eius generis, ubi ex arboribus in arbores traductis vitibus vinea fit,
quos traduces quidam rumpos vocant.

(*b*) Colum. 4. 12. 'Attention to the propping of the vine follows the pruning.
But the first year does not yet require a strong *prop* ("palus") or *stake*
("ridica"); I have noticed that generally a young vine settles down better
with a *support* ("adminiculum") of moderate size than with a stout *prop*
("palus"). And so we shall attach each young vine either to two old reeds,
in case any new ones strike root;[1] or if local conditions permit, to *brier
canes* ("de vepribus hastilia"), to which single *cross-bars* may be tied along
one side of the row – the sort of *frame* ("iugum") which farmers call a
"cantherius" or "gelding"': putationem sequitur iam pedandae vineae
cura. verum hic annus nondum vehementem *palum* aut *ridicam* desiderat;
notatum est enim a me plerumque teneram vineam melius *adminiculo*
modico quam vehementi palo adquiescere. itaque aut veteres, ne novae
radicem agant, harundines binas singulis vitibus applicabimus, aut si regionis
conditio permittit, *de vepribus hastilia*, quibus adnectantur singulae transversae *perticae* in unam partem ordinis quod genus iugi *cantherium* vocant
rustici.

(*c*) Pliny, *HN* 17. 164–6. 'There are five kinds of vineyard – with the branches
spreading about on the ground, or with the vine standing up of its own
accord, or else with a *prop* ("adminiculum") but no *cross-bar* ("iugum"),
or propped with a single cross-bar, or trellised with four *bars* in a rectangle ... A vineyard with the single cross-bar is arranged in a straight row
which is called a "*gelding*" ... The cross-bar is made from a pole or a reed,
or else from a rope of hair or hemp, as in Spain and at Brindisi. More wine
is produced from a square-framed vine ("compluviata vinea"); this is
divided into compartments of four by the same number of cross-bars':
quinque generum hae (vineae): sparsis per terram palmitibus aut per se vite
subrecta, vel cum *adminiculo* sine *iugo*, aut pedatae simplici iugo, aut
compluviatae quadriplici. ... simplici iugo constat porrecto ordine quem
canterium appellant ... iugum fit *pertica* aut *harundine*, aut crine funiculove
ut in Hispania Brundisique. compluviata copiosior vino est, dividitur in
quaternas partes totidem iugis.

[1] The point is that a new reed could easily strike root, and deprive the young vine-shoot
of vital nourishment.

20

(d) Colum. 4. 26. 1 (on work to follow the annual pruning of the vines).
'For making a firm prop the *live prop* is better than the *stake*, and not just
any prop; the best kind of all is the olive split with wedges, the oak and the
cork, and any other wood of similar strength. The *round pole* holds third
place': cui (i.e. vineae) stabiliendae melior est *ridica palo*, neque ea quaelibet;
nam est praecipua cuneis fissa olea, quercus et suber, ac si qua sunt similia
robora. tertium obtinet locum *pedamen teres*.

(e) Colum. 11. 2. 12. 'One workman can cut down, strip and sharpen a
hundred *stakes* a day; he can also split, smooth on both sides and sharpen
sixty oak or olive-wood *props*': palos una opera caedere et exputatos acuere
centum numero potest; *ridicas* autem quernas, sive oleagineas findere, et
dedolatas utraque parte exacuere numero sexaginta.

(f) Colum. 4. 16. 3. 'If this stake is placed midway between the rows (of vines),
it must be either pushed well down or driven to a greater depth by first
making a hole in the ground with a *small stake* so that it may more easily
support both the trellis and the fruit': sive medio interordinio pangetur (is
palus), vel deponendus est vel, prius *paxillo* perforato solo, altius adigendus,
quo facilius et iugum et fructum sustineat.

DISCUSSION

The variety of terms employed emphasizes the meticulous care devoted
to the various systems used in cultivating the vine. Hard woods were
naturally preferred for props, and split timber (*ridica*) was found to be more
durable than poles (*pedamen teres*). I find no evidence of the use of 'treated'
poles, that is, of coating the portion to be embedded in the ground with
pitch or other preservative. Hardening the ends by firing (*praeurere*),
though unnoticed by the agronomists, is frequently mentioned in military
contexts (e.g. Caes. *BG* 7. 73. 6, Tac. *Ann.* 4. 51), and may well have been
standard practice on the farm.

There are some individual preferences in the use of terms: thus Varro
(passage *a*) uses *pedamentum* and *iugum* for the single-prop and frame-
systems respectively, while Columella and Pliny oppose *adminiculum* to
iugum (Colum. 4. 12; Pliny 17. 164). At 4. 26. 1 Columella uses the verbs
adminiculare and *iugare* for this purpose.

Of the various terms corresponding to our words 'stake', 'pole',
'standard' and the like, some are used with a wider, others with a more
restricted, range of meaning. Thus *palus* is the ordinary term for a straight
stake sharpened to a point, as in the tally-check recorded on the wall of a
farm building near Boscoreale: 'palos acutos DC, non acutos DCC,
summa MCCC' (*CIL* IV 6886; cf. Colum. 11. 2. 12: 'palos una opera
caedere et exputatos acuere centum numero potest'). These were commonly used in fencing, the stakes, as Varro tells us, being 'planted close

and intertwined with brushwood' (*RR* 1. 14. 1). In viticulture *palus* is commonly distinguished from *ridica*, a prop made from a living tree, usually of oak, juniper, olive or cypress (Varro, *RR* 1. 8. 4; Colum. 4. 26. 1, etc.), and from *pertica* (ii), properly a support made from the branch of a tree (Varro, *RR* 1. 8. 4: 'palus e pertica'). At 4. 26. 1 Columella gives his order of preference in the choice of single vine-props: a *ridica* is better than a *palus*, and a round pole (*pedamen teres*) is inferior to both.

Patibulum. Like the term *furca* and its diminutive *furcilla* the word *patibulum* (lit. a 'spreader', from *pateo*), was used by Cato and Pliny of a fork-shaped prop; in both passages it seems that we have to do with a temporary support: Cato (26 and 68) includes *patibula* among the various pieces of equipment that have to be stored away after the vintage and pressing, to be brought out next year; and Pliny's single use of the term (*HN* 17. 212) refers to the strange practice of a wine-farmer of Novara, who trained the bearing shoots of his vines on props to increase the yield, a practice which Pliny rightly deplores!

Statumen, like *pedamentum*, means either a single prop (Colum. 4. 2. 1, 16. 2, etc.), or a timber standard used in the construction of a frame (*iugum*) (Colum. 4. 16. 4). It is also used of the reed props used to support the spiralling system known as *vitis characata* (Colum. 5. 4. 1).

Iugum had two common meanings, (i) the 'single-yoke' frame (Pliny's 'simplex iugum' at 17. 164f.), which consisted of a single standard, fitted at the top with a cross-bar, as described in detail by Columella (4. 12), and popularly known as the 'horse' or 'gelding' (*cantherius*); (ii) the multiple system of four of these frames joined together to form a quadrangular frame (*compluvium*), so called from its obvious resemblance to the opening in the roof of the *atrium* of a Roman house (Pliny, *HN* 17. 164, 166). The commentators are far from satisfactory on the design of the *simplex iugum*. Thus Rich (*Dict. Ant.* s.v. 'iugum') describes it as consisting of *two* uprights and a cross-piece, connecting it, not with the yoke of a chariot or cart, but with the cross-bar of a loom (a much rarer meaning, and quite unsuitable in the context of vine-propping). It seems more natural to connect the *simplex iugum* with the yoke and pole of a plough or wagon than with the military symbol of ignominious surrender, a pair of upright spears with a third laid across the top. But the use of the term *cantherius* = 'gelding' as synonym does not clinch the meaning either way. For different explanations of the *compluvium* see L. Storr-Best, *M. T. Varro on Farming*, London, 1912, 31, n. 1; White, *RF*, 232, and fig. 2 (i); W. F. Jashemski in *American Journal of Archaeology*, 77. 1 (1973), 34, and ill. 3.

Pergula. The common term for an ornamental arbour (It. 'pergola') forming an avenue, *pergula*, was also used of a vine of prolific growth, from which more than eight shoots were permitted to develop: 'a vine of this size', writes Columella, 'has more of the appearance of a pergola than of a vine' (4. 21. 1). The term is also used in this sense by Pliny (*HN* 14. 11) and by Palladius (3. 12. 5, 3. 12. 3). The shade provided by the *pergula* system made it particularly suitable for dessert grapes (Pl. 3*a*). For illustrations of the various systems of vine-training see *RF*, pp. 234 ff. (with accompanying diagrams).

Paxillus (-i, m.) (Gk. πάσσαλος), small *stake*, *peg*, Varro *ap.* Non. p. 153 (see below, *Corp. Gloss.*)

Not in Varro, *LL*.

(*a*) Isid. *Etym.* 11. 15. 45. '"Maxillae", "jaws", are a diminutive form of "malae", "cheeks", just as "paxillus", "peg", is the diminutive formed from "palus", "stake"': maxillae per diminutionem a malis; sicut *paxillus* a palo.

(*b*) *Corp. Gloss.* s.v. 'paxillus'. paxillum palum IV 374. 44; V 170. 10; 318. 37. palum qui in pariete figitur V 472. 39. mensura est modica vel palus qui in pariete figitur V 509.37 (v. pauxillus). paxillis palis V 642. 42 (Non. 153. 5).

(*c*) Colum. 4. 16. 3 (on staking vines). 'By first making a hole in the ground with a *small stake*': prius *paxillo* perforato solo.

(*d*) *Ibid.* 8. 8. 3 (on making nesting-boxes for pigeons). 'Boards should be placed on *pegs* driven into the walls': *paxillis* adactis tabulae superponantur.

(*e*) Pliny, *HN* 17. 154 (on propagating figs). 'Nine-inch slips are planted in holes made in the ground with *small stakes*': dodrantales (surculi) *paxillis* solo patefacto seruntur.

DISCUSSION

As the above passages show, the diminutive form of *palus* was used to cover any kind of small pointed stake, from the planter's dibble (passages *c*, *e*) to a strong wooden peg, driven into a wall to support a light shelf (*b*), or, as in passage *d*, a nesting-box. For the two-pronged implement used for planting see *AIRW*, pp. 109 ff.

Survival

The dibble is still an essential item among the gardener's tools; the commercial type is now of metal, usually fitted with a cross-bar.

3

FENCING

Barriers to mark off cultivated areas, and to fence in or keep out animals, have been a familiar feature of farm-sites from prehistoric times. They range from rough layers of stones removed from fields to earth banks, planted hedges and solid walls. They serve a variety of purposes, such as keeping livestock or protected game within bounds, protecting low-lying fields from inundation and exposed slopes from erosion, or simply for the purpose of discouraging marauders or trespassers. In an early chapter of his *De Re Rustica* Varro makes Scrofa conclude his discussion of housing and stabling with a short account of the different methods used in making enclosures (1. 14). This is the only complete account of the subject that has come down to us, apart from a short statement by Vitruvius (2. 8). At the same point in his account of the homestead Columella merely refers in passing to the need of high walls to protect the unstalled animals kept on the farm, and of fenced enclosures to protect the garden and the orchard (1. 6. 4). He also gives detailed instructions for building a post-and-rail fence for a game-park (9. 1. 3). The relevant terms are *saepes* (a hedge – general term), *saepimentum* (an enclosure – general term), *clatri* (*clatra*), a barrier in the form of a grille, *vacerra* (post) and *ramex* (rail or cross-bar), the two last-named terms being used specifically for this type of wooden fence.

1. saepes (-is, f.), *hedge, fence*

2. saepimentum (-i, n.), *enclosure*

Not in Varro, *LL*.

(a) Isid. *Etym.* 15. 9. 6. (*De munitionibus*). 'Hedges are *enclosures* for crops; hence their name': *sepes* munimenta satorum sunt; unde et appellatae.

(b) Varro, *RR* 1. 14. 1 (on enclosures). 'The first type is the natural *enclosure*, generally planted with brush or thorn. Having roots, and being alive, it has nothing to fear from the blazing torch of the mischievous passer-by. The second type is the rustic *fence*, made of wood, but dead: it is made either of stakes set up close and intertwined with brush, or of thick posts with holes bored in them and with *rails* drawn through them, usually two or three to each standard': primum naturale *saepimentum*, quod opseri solet virgultis aut spinis, quod habet radices ac vivit, praetereuntis lascivi non metuet facem ardentem. secunda *saeps* est agrestis e ligno, sed non vivit: fit aut palis statutis crebris et virgultis implicatis aut latis perforatis et per ea foramina traiectis longuris fere binis aut ternis.

(c) Pliny, *HN* 17. 101 (on the origin of grafting). 'A careful farmer, making a protective *fence* around his house, put an ivy-wood base beneath the posts to prevent them rotting; but the posts . . . created life of their own from the vitality of another plant': agricola sedulus casam *saepis* munimento cingens, quo minus putrescerent sudes limen subdidit ex hedera; at illae . . . suam ex aliena fecere vitam.

(d) Virgil, *Georg.* 1. 270 (on work allowed on feast-days). 'Extending a *fence* in front of the grainfield': segeti praetendere *saepem*.

(e) *Ibid.* 2. 371 (on vine-cultivation). 'Fences must be woven and all stock kept out': texendae *saepes* etiam et pecus omne tenendum.

(f) *Moretum* 61–2 (a simple garden fence). 'Adjoining the cottage was a garden, protected by re-used[1] reeds with light stems, and widely-spaced osiers':

> hortus erat iunctus casulae, quem vimina pauca
> et calamo rediviva[1] levi munibat arundo.

DISCUSSION

Saepes

As a generic term, *saepes* may be used of a living (passage *b*), or a dead fence (passages *c, e*). Pliny's account (passage *c*) of the origin of grafting describes a phenomenon familiar enough to any gardener working under sub-tropical conditions, where freshly-cut stakes will easily strike root when firmly bedded-in as fencing-poles, and is reminiscent of Lucretius' famous description (5. 1361 ff.).

Varro's reference (passage *b*) to the risk of fire from a 'mischievous passer-by' underlines the disadvantages of having your farm close to a main highway, as pointed out by Columella (1. 5. 7).

Different types of fencing compared

Varro (passage *b*) says nothing about the comparative costs or durability of the different types of enclosure. Pliny's story (*c*) underlines the obvious fact that, in the absence of any references to creosote or pitch to arrest decay (see above, p. 21), the dead fence would only be preferred where it was required to be movable (enclosures for stock), or where a solid barrier

---

[1] redimita *VBGΓ Cat. Trag.* d. rediviva *MPEFSh.* (*Ellis*). E. J. Kenney (*OCT*) retains *rediviva* without comment and notes *recidiva* 5 prob. Heinsius. *Redivivus* is commonly used of restored buildings or re-used materials. See below, p. 26.

was needed, and a wall would be out of the question on grounds of expense, as in a game-preserve (*vivarium*); see below, s.v. 'ramex', 'vacerra'.

The live fence was usually made of vigorous shrubs such as butcher's broom (*ruscus aculeatus*) or from the numerous types of thorn-bush (*spina*), such as Christ-thorn (*paliurus australis*), wild rose (*rosa sempervirens*), and brambles (*rubi*), mentioned by Columella (11. 3. 4 ff.) and Palladius (1. 35. 4). By contrast, and in keeping with the humble background of the story, the hedge described in the *Moretum* (passage *f*) consists of a thin curtain of osiers intertwined with re-used reeds (clearly the strong *arundo donax*, used also in olive-picking – see Appendix A, p. 226), making a fence that is partly 'live' and partly 'dead'.

The dead fence was constructed in two ways; either by setting up posts at regular intervals, and filling up the intervening spaces with woven material in the form of withies or broom, so as to form a continuous screen of hurdles (passage *b*), or by the post-and-rail method (see below).

In his lengthy account of the establishing of a kitchen-garden Columella makes some useful observations on the economics of fencing. A strongly constructed enclosure here was absolutely essential against both human and animal marauders, especially the latter: a single donkey can wreck a succession of vegetable plantings overnight! He begins by quoting Democritus, who condemned brick walls as subject to damage by rain, and stone as much too expensive (11. 3. 2), and then goes on to describe a method 'whereby, without much trouble, we can make a garden secure from the depredations of men and animals'. 'A quick-set hedge (*vivam saepem*)', he tells us, 'was preferred by the oldest authorities on two grounds: (1) as less expensive, (2) as more durable.' His thorn-bush hedge is made by laying in two parallel trenches lengths of old ships' cables (*nautici funes*), smeared with an adhesive mixture containing the seed. The plants are then trained up a row of sticks placed between the trenches, and the result is an impenetrable screen produced at little cost. See below, s.v. 'restis', p. 35.

3. Clatri (-orum, m.) (fr. Gr. κλῆθρον, 'a bar, bolt'), *grille*, us. of vertical bars; also **clath-**; also **clatra** (-orum, n.); **clatratus**, -a, -um, adj. (fr. *clatrare*), *fitted with bars*

Not in Varro, *LL*; not in Isidore.

(*g*) *Corp. Gloss.* s.v. 'clatri'. clatri κανόνες οἱ ἐν θυρίσι ὀβελίσκοι II 101. 78. ligna volubilia in caveis IV 35. 32 (clitri); V 179. 25. clatris id est lignis volubilibus quae sunt in caveis V 653. 49. Cf. clatrum *pearroc* (*AS*) V 352. 38.

(*h*) Cato 4 (on stabling for oxen). 'Have *barred* feed-racks; the *bars* should be a foot apart': faliscas *clatratas, clatros* interesse oportet pede.

(*j*) Plaut. *Mil.* 377–9. 'SCEL. Extraordinary though! how could she have got over there from here? there's no through passage, no garden, not a window that isn't *barred*': SCEL. nimis mirumst facinus quomodo haec hinc huc transire potuit./nam certo neque solarium est apud nos neque hortus ullus/neque fenestra nisi *clatrata*.

4. Ramex (-icis, m.) (fr. *ramus*, 'branch'), *cross-bar, rail*

5. Vacerra (-ae, f.), *post-and-rail fence*

No entries in *R-E*.

Not in Varro, *LL*; not in Isidore.

(*k*) *Corp. Gloss.* s.v. 'vecerra'. vecerra est stipes ubi religantur v 625. 4.

(*l*) Colum. 9. 1. 3–4 (on enclosing a game-park (*vivarium*)). '(Where neither stone nor brick serves the purpose of the owner) reason demands that they (the animals) should be enclosed within a *post-and-rail fence*; this is the name given to a sort of *lattice-work* ("clatri") made of oak or cork, since olive-wood is hard to come by ... the timber ... has several holes bored in its sides, and is set up firmly in the ground at regular intervals around the perimeter; *bars* are then passed through the holes to bar the passage of the wild animals': ratio postulat *vacerris* includi: sic enim appellatur genus *clatrorum*; idque fabricatur ex robore querneo, vel subereo. nam oleae rara est occasio. ... stipes compluribus locis per latus efforatur, et in circuitu vivarii certis intervenientibus spatiis defixus erigitur: deinde per transversa laterum cava transmittuntur *ramices*, qui exitus ferarum obserent.

DISCUSSION

Barriers or grilles made of vertical bars

The post-and-rail fence of passage (*l*) is described as a 'sort of *clatri*', that is, a type of barrier consisting of bars. The dictionaries (e.g. LS s.v., *OLD* s.v.) emphasize the idea of lattice-work, but Cato's feed-racks (passage *h*) will surely have conformed to the traditional pattern of close-set vertical bars, and Columella's fish-barriers, mentioned in his account of an ancient 'fish-farm' in coastal waters (8. 17. 10) are clearly of the same type, being carefully distinguished from the 'brass gratings with small holes' (*aenei foraminibus exiguis cancelli*) fixed in front of the outflow channels (8. 17. 6). The barred window of passage *j* will also have been a vertical *grille* rather than a *trellis*.

27

The post-and-rail fence

Where each upright had to be bored with an auger (*terebra*), a fence enclosing a circuit of 10 *iugera*, with poles at 8-foot intervals and 3 rails to a post, would require a total of 2,700 poles, and more than 8,000 holes. No wonder Columella regards this system as suitable for some of the vast tracts of land in Gaul and certain other provinces, where there is 'an abundant supply of timber and everything else that is needed' (9. 1. 4). Varro has a brief reference to this type of fencing (see above, s.v. 'saepes', passage *b*). Continuous fences need to be provided with gates; but I have not come across any references to their design or construction. Where both staff and animals are continually passing in and out, gates must be both strong and well-hung; one might therefore have expected some discussion of the topic, but I can recall none. Nor do monumental sources feature them. Walled gardens and farm boundary walls are frequently represented, but in these examples the gates are represented as solid structures.

Extant representations

Representations of any type of fencing, except the popular wooden trellising, seem to be rare. I have noted only the following:

(1) *Carthage:* the Dominus Iulius mosaic (T. Prêcheur-Canonge, *La vie rurale en Afrique romaine d'après les mosaïques* (Paris, 1962), *Inventaire*, no. 8, pl. IV). In this mosaic pavement, now in the Bardo Museum, Tunis, there is an orchard in the r. foreground, protected by a post-and-rail fence (see above, pp. 26f.), the spaces between the two horizontals being filled by criss-cross timber (see Pl. 3*c*).

(2) *Zliten, Tripolitania:* the farm mosaic contains, in addition to a large central panel depicting threshing with horses and cattle, two smaller panels, one of which shows a garden bounded by a wall of solid masonry, with an ornamental gate leading into the fields where women are plying their hoes. Now in the Tripoli museum (Aurigemma, *Africa Italiana* 2 (1926), 91, fig. 57; Rostovtzeff, *SEHRE*[2], pl. LIX 3).

4

ROPE, CORDAGE AND NETTING

There is scarcely a department of economic activity, whether in factory or farm, in the transport of goods by land, river or sea, on the building site or in the workshop, where extended lengths of rope, cable or belting are not in regular use, as they have been from very early times. Although the range of raw materials has vastly increased in modern times with the addition to the list of natural fibres of cotton, jute and sisal, and of drawn steel wire, linked steel cable, and artificial fibres such as nylon, the traditional materials have not been entirely supplanted, and the methods of manufacture, apart from mechanization, have undergone no basic changes from antiquity until the present day. If an Egyptian rope-maker of the third millennium B.C. were set down in a modern rope-making establishment, he would soon become familiar with the processes.

Raw materials

Fibrous material for making rope and cordage was obtained from a variety of plants, the most important of which were hemp (*cannabis sativa* L.) and flax (*linum usitatissimum* L.), both plants being widely cultivated in classical times (see Pliny, *HN* 19. 2–25 – a comprehensive account of flax and the range of its uses, *ibid.* 173–4 – where hemp is dismissed as 'exceedingly useful for ropes'). Other sources of fibre included the bark (*cortex*) of certain trees (Pliny, *HN* 16. 34 ff. – a full account), and a wide variety of rushes (*iuncus*) (for the varieties see André, *Lexique*, s.v. 'iuncus'). The Greek equivalent of *iuncus*, namely σχοῖνος, is also the generic term for rope or cord; on the strength of this, it has been suggested that rushes were probably the earliest fibre-producing plants known to the Greeks. The term 'esparto grass' is used of the products of two distinct species of plant: (1) *Stipa tenacissima* L., a perennial grass which grows wild in North Africa and in the Mediterranean steppe areas of southern Spain. (2) *Lygeum spartum* Loefl., the true 'sparto', which is a cultivated plant, still extensively grown in Almeria, Murcia and other parts of southern Spain, and used for making matting, rope, cord and shoes. Both plants yield a similar fibre, with similar commercial uses. Not unnaturally, the two plants have been confused by Pliny's editors, as well as by the author himself! On the introduction of esparto into Spain see Pliny, *HN* 19. 26 ff., where reference is also made to the fact (?) that the vast quantities required for many different purposes were produced in a district on the coast round Cartagena less than 100 miles long and 30 miles wide. Pliny also commits himself to the statement that 'the cost of carriage prevents it being transported any considerable distance' (*ibid.* 30). Cato however (ch. 135) informs his readers that they can get all kinds of 'cordage' (*spartum omne*) at Capua; unless Cato is using the term loosely, regardless of the material, it would seem that in his day Italian rope-manufacturers had no difficulty in securing supplies of the raw material.

Manufacturing problems

The extraction of the fibre from flax, hemp and esparto grass involves a number of tedious and time-consuming processes. In the case of flax these include binding and drying, 'rippling' to remove the bolls, followed by 'retting', that is, lengthy immersion in water. After drying the stalks are beaten with sticks to detach the woody portions of the plant from the fibres. The crude fibre is then removed by a scraping process known as 'skutching', and refined by roughing and hackling, to be finally spun into yarn, if linen is to be made. The elaborate series of processes is clearly described by Forbes (*SAT* IV, 28 ff.), who notes that present-day procedures are virtually identical with those used in antiquity. The processing of flax and esparto grass was the most troublesome of all, since the fibres had to be pulled by hand, and the pullers had to wear gaiters and have their hands protected by gauntlets (Pliny, *HN* 19. 27). This task is now carried out by special pulling-machines. There are several reasons for the pulling process: 'the flax tends to deteriorate at the point of the cut, and weeds are gathered up with the stems when they are cut. Moreover, with cutting, about 6 inches of straw is left in the field . . . and there is a consequent loss of fibre' (R. H. Kirby, *Vegetable Fibres, Botany, Cultivation and Utilization* (London/New York, 1963), p. 20).

Esparto grass. The plant does not seem to have been exploited in the western Mediterranean area before the Carthaginian conquest of southern Spain in the third century B.C. (Pliny, *HN* 19. 26); as a competitor with the older fibres obtained from flax and hemp it had the special advantage of greater durability under wet conditions: 'Though on dry land, ropes made of hemp are preferred, esparto is actually nourished by being plunged into water . . . it is used in all countries for ship's rigging, for mechanical appliances in the building trade, and for other essential requirements of daily life' (Pliny, *HN* 19. 29–30).

Palm-leaves, which were available in quantity in Egypt, North Africa and parts of southern Spain, also yield a suitable fibre: 'the leaves have a knife-like edge ... and are divided into two flanges ... these are split open to make ropes and plaited wickerwork and sunshades' (Pliny, *HN* 13. 30).

Leather for ropes. In addition to these natural fibres leather was used for a wide variety of purposes. Strips of rawhide (Ger. 'Lederriemen') were employed to make ropes for operations requiring a capacity to withstand great tension, as well as durability, as in the case of the press-ropes (*funes torculi*) for the wine- or olive-press. Cato 135. 6 gives an interesting account of how a press-rope is made from twisted rawhide strips, and of the type of splicing needed to give a working length under tension of 51 feet. Similar strips were also used to make the longer 'traces' for plough teams or carriage mules.

Technique of rope-making

The twisting of the strands could be done by hand, but the reverse twisting required for the manufacture of multiple-stranded cordage with a high breaking-strain demands a powerful holding device at one end, and a spinner at the other. The two-man technique is very ancient. It makes its first appearance on a wall-relief in the Mastaba of Prahhetep and Akethetep at Sakkara (date *c.* 2600 B.C.; Fifth Dynasty), where a man and a boy are shown 'twisting ropes of boat-building', as the inscription says. In another scene a boy replies to the man's request for rope by passing over two coils of light cordage, saying, 'My father, here is your rope.' An Eighteenth Dynasty wall-painting from Thebes (*c.* 1500 B.C.) shows a much more sophisticated method. The instruments used, which include a metal cartridge enclosing the rope-end, and a heavy ball, and the details of the method, have been clearly described and interpreted by Feldhaus (*Technik*, s.v. 'Seile'). Blümner's earlier interpretation (*Technologie*, I, 302 f.) is incorrect. Forbes's lengthy account of textiles and related topics (*SAT*, IV) ignores the subject of rope-making completely, and there is very little information in the usual dictionaries of antiquities. Mechanical spinning may have come into use by the late fifth century B.C., if we accept one of the explanations offered by a scholiast on a well-known passage in Aristophanes' comedy the *Peace*, which refers to the voracious eating habits of the dung-beetle (*Peace* 33 ff.); see further Blümner, *Technologie*, I, 305, n. 1.

The stranding of cordage. The first stage in the conversion of suitably prepared fibres into cordage is the spinning of the yarn, which is essentially a plaiting process (see above, p. 31). The yarns are then stretched to get an even tension. After that the yarns are formed into strands, and the strands into rope. In order to ensure stability of the rope, the direction of twisting must be reversed at each stage: 'when two or more strands are combined by twisting them together, they must each at the same time be twisted in the opposite sense, so that they do not untwist when they are released' (K. R. Gilbert in *OHT* I, 454).

Terminology

The term 'rope' is used of all types of cordage of a diameter of 1 in. or more. Twisted cords of less diameter are known as cords, twines and lines (in descending order). Rope is made up of a number of *strands*, which in turn are made up of a number of *yarns*, which are twisted from the basic fibre. No account of rope-making survives from classical antiquity, but we get some light on the terminology from Pollux, s.v. ἄρκυς, 5. 27 (on nets), where Xenophon (*Cyn.* 2. 4) is cited on the various stranding standards for different kinds of hunting-nets. The yarns (τόνοι) could be made up into nine-stranded cordage, with three threads (λίνοι) to each of three yarns for the fine ἄρκυς (purse-nets), running up to 12- and 16-stranded types for the heavier ἐνόδια (road-nets), and δίκτυα (heavy hunting-nets). For rope-making, yarns of 15 threads were employed, making ropes of 45 threads.

The Egyptian rope-maker in the wall-painting is using four yarns (perhaps a core and the usual three yarns for plaiting. Hug (passage *a*) is surely incorrect in identifying Cato's 'torus' at 135. 4 with τόνος = 'yarn'. Cato is using the word in its common sense of 'knot', as required for the splicing of the lengths of rawhide strips for his press-rope (see below, s.v. 'lorum', p. 35). Among the other terms, both *funis* and *restis* are regarded by the lexicographers as general terms (the etymologies are uncertain). Varro's list of fibres which can be produced on the farm (see s.v. 'restis', passage *e*) implies a difference of meaning; and the definition of *funis* as 'restis longa et crassa' (Nonius, followed by *TLL*), taken together with its regular use for 'pulley-belts' and 'press-ropes', suggests that in contexts where a specific meaning is required *funis* refers to the heavier, and *restis* to the lighter, kinds of rope. This impression is strengthened by Festus (s.v. 'restis' – passage *d*), where *restes* are presumably the corded units from which *funes* are made. Other passages (e.g. Colum. 11. 3. 5 – see s.v. 'restis', passage *f* – and Isidore – passage *b*) show clearly that both words could be used in the most general sense. *Linea* and *tomix* are similarly differentiated in usage, the former being used of heavier, the latter of lighter, types of cord. Columella's reference (see s.v. 'tomix', passage *c*), with its adjectives 'palmea' and 'iuncea', suggests an untwined fibre corresponding to our 'raffia', which is also a palm-leaf fibre, while *linea*, with its wide range of meanings, including sewing-thread, fishing-line and plumb-line, must have been made of twisted fibre. The four common terms may be very roughly equated with our 'rope', 'cord', 'twine' and 'string'.

Note: The principal technical problems relating to the manufacture of cordage in antiquity have been adequately dealt with above. Since the passages that follow appear to offer few special difficulties of interpretation, notes on particular points take the place of the usual discussion section.

1. Funis (-is, m.) (Gr. σχοῖνος), *rope* (general term); dimin. **funiculus** (-i, m.), thin rope, *cord*

No entry in *R-E.*

Not in Varro, *LL.*

(a) Isid. *Etym.* 20. 4. (*De funibus*). 'Ropes are called "funes" because in former times they were covered in wax and used for lighting. Hence the word "funalia" (torches)': *funes dicti quod antea in usum luminis fuerint circumdati cera; unde et funalia.*

(b) Isid. *Etym.* 20. 10. 5: only of tapers of waxed cord in a candelabra (see *a* above).

(c) Fest. 165 M. 'The junior pontiff is to weave ropes from straw, that is, to make cords with which the pigs can be attached': *pontifex minor ex stramentis napuras nectito, id est funiculos facito, quibus sues adnectantur.*

(d) *Corp. Gloss.* s.v. 'funes'. Funis σχοῖνος II 450. 20. σχοινίον II 450. 16. funis σχοῖνος II 511. 9. σχοινίον II 515. 21. κᾶλος ἢ σχοῖνος II 337. 47, etc.

(e) Cato 135 (where to buy farm equipment). '*Pulley-belts* . . . should be bought at Capua . . . L. Tunnius of Casinum, and C. Mennius, son of L. Mennius of Venafrum, make the best *press-ropes*': *funes subductarios* . . . Capuae (emito) . . . *funem torculum* siquis faciet, Casini L. Tunnius, Venafri C. Mennius L.F.

(f) *Ibid.* '*Cords* (i.e. traces) for the wagon (to be) 15 feet long, for the plough . . . 8 feet': in plostrum . . . *funiculum* P. XV, in aratrum . . . *funiculum* P. IIX.

(g) Colum. 12. 52. 8 (preparations for the olive-picking); cf. *ibid.* 12. 18. 3 (vintage). '(There must be) *ropes* of hemp and esparto-grass': *funes cannabini spartei.*

(h) Vitruv. 1. 1. 8 (the architect must know the mathematics of weaponry). 'He must be able to carry out correctly the tuning of ballistae . . . for . . . there are holes of equal tension, through which *ropes* made from twisted sinews are stretched by means of capstans and levers': *praeterea balistarum . . . temperaturas possit recte facere . . . sunt foramina homotona,[1] per quae tenduntur suculis et vectibus e nervo torti funes.*

---

[1] hemitoniorum *codd.*: homotona *Philander.*

(j) Pliny, *HN* 17. 174 (materials used in training the vine). 'When the shorter shoots are intertwined with brushwood to form a kind of *rope*, the festoons made from them are called "rope-trellises"': cum breviores palmites sarmento iunguntur inter se *funium* modo, ex hoc arcus ⟨facti⟩[1] *funeta* dicuntur.

(k) Ed. Diocl. 11. 3 (on goat or camel hair). 'Hair twisted into rope den. 10': pilorum ad *funem* confectorum p̄ unum ✕ decem.   1 lb.

2. Linea (-ae, f.) (fr. *linum*, 'flax'), (i) *twine, cord, string*; (ii) *plumb-line*; (iii) *line* (geom.)

Not in Varro, *LL*.

Isid. *Etym.* 3. 12. 6 (*De figuris geometriae*) only in sense (iii).

(a) *R-E* VI 2, s.v. 'Flachs', 2461 ff. [Olck].

(b) *Corp. Gloss.* s.v. 'linea'. linea γραμμή, σειρά, ὁρμιά, κτλ. funis γραμμή, σειρά ... σπάρτος. II 435. 25 (linia) ἀκολουθία III 454. 64; 485. 1.

(c) Varro, *RR* 1. 23. 6 (on making plantations for cutting). 'Have a place where you can sow hemp, flax, rush, esparto-grass, so that you can weave shoes for the oxen, *twine*, cord and rope': (alio loco) sic ubi cannabim, linum, iuncum, spartum (seras), unde nectas bubus soleas, *lineas*, restis, funes.

(d) Cic. *Q.F.* 3. 1. 1 (a builder's error). 'Diphilus had set up the columns out of the perpendicular, and out of alignment with one another. These he will naturally take down; some day he may learn how to use the plumb-bob and *line*': columnas neque rectas, neque e regione Diphilus conlocarat; eas scilicet demolietur: aliquando perpendiculo et *linea* discet uti.

(e) Sen. *De Clem.* 12. 'In this way you can keep wild animals shut up by means of *cords* and feathers': sic feras *lineis* et pinna clausos contineas.

(f) *Pallad.* 3. 9. 10 (on planting vine-shoots). 'We shall use the following arrangement for planting. Keeping the intervals which we have decided to maintain (between the plants) we shall mark a *cord* with white markers or any other distinguishing tag; then, having stretched our cord over the bed, we shall fix twigs or reeds where each vine is to appear': sed ad ponendum utemur hoc ordine. *lineam* servatis his spatiis, quae placuerit custodire, candidis signis vel quibuscumque notabimus: tunc tensa per tabulam linea in eis locis surculos vel calamos figemus, ubi vitis unaquaeque ventura est.

3. Lorum (-i, n.) (Gr. ἱμάς), *thong, strap* (of leather); pl. *reins*; adj. **loreus,** -a, -um, *made of thongs*, cf. p. 38.

Not in Varro, *LL*.

Isid. *Etym.* 20. 16. 3 (*De instrumentis equorum*) has only 'reins', lora.

(a) *R-E* XIII 2. 1449-50 [Hug]. Superficial treatment: no information on how the long leather ropes ('Lederriemen') of passage *c* were made. *Ibid.* s.v.

    1 arcus ⟨facti⟩? *Rackham*: ⟨fiunt⟩ qui *vel* ⟨f.⟩ quae *Warmington*.

'pellis' XIX 1. 369 [K. Schneider]. Almost entirely devoted to leather for clothing or military uses. Nothing on thongs, straps, etc.

(b) *Corp. Gloss.* s.v. 'lorum'. lorum ἱμάς II 124. 28, etc. (w. variations between *lorum* and *lorus*). ἡνία II 325. 20; III 273. 19. funis II 586. 43. lora ἱμάντες III 174. 5; 194. 25. retinacula IV 450. 31 (gl. Verg.).

(c) Cato 135 (where to buy farm equipment). '(The rope) should have nine leather *thongs*, two fingers in width, at each splice': (*lora*) habeat in toros singulos VIIII lata digitos II. '*Leather reins* for the cart 36 feet, and for the plough 26 feet; *traces* 27½ feet; yoke straps for the cart 19 feet ... for the plough, *yoke straps* 12 feet': lora retinacula in plostrum P. XXXVI, ad aratrum P. XXVI, lora praeductoria P. XXVII S, subiugia in plostrum *lora* P. XIX ... in aratrum subiugia *lora* P. XII.

4. Restis (-is, f.), *rope* (gen.), *cord* (?); cf. *funis*

Not in Varro, *LL* (exc. 8. 66: pl. *restis* and *restes*).

(a) *R-E* s.v. 'restio' 1 A. 1. 676 [Hug].

(b) Isid.*Etym.* 20.4. 1 (*De funibus*). 'They are called "restes", *ropes*, either because they hold "rates", rafts, together, or because they are used for stretching "retia", nets': *restes*, sive quod rates contineant, seu quod his retes tendantur.

(c) *Corp. Gloss.* s.v. 'restis'. restis σχοινίον μικρόν II 174. 1. σχοινίον II 450. 16, etc. σπαρτίον II 435. 23. spartin II 524. 22.

(d) Paul. Fest. s.v. 'funis', p. 357. '*Cords* (?) from which ropes are made': *restes*, ex quibus funes fiunt.

(e) Varro, *RR* 1. 22. 1 (on self-sufficiency). 'Do not buy anything outside which can be grown on the farm or produced by the workers, in general, articles ... made of hemp, flax, rushes, palm fibre, and bulrush, such as ropes, *cordage* and matting': quae nasci in fundo ac fieri a domesticis poterunt, eorum nequid ematur, ut fere sunt quae ... fiunt de cannabi, lino, iunco, palma, scirpo, ut funes, *restes*, tegetes.

(f) Colum. 11. 3. 5 (how to make a brier hedge). '(Mix the seeds of the brier with meal made from bitter vetch), sprinkle this mixture with water, and smear it on old ships' *cordage* or any other kind of *rope* ... lay it in furrows half-filled with the loose soil (dug out from the trench) and piled up in the autumn': quae farina cum est aqua conspersa, inlinitur vel nauticis veteribus *funibus* vel quibuslibet aliis *restibus* ... resolutaque humus, quae erat autumno regesta, usque ad mediam sulcorum altitudinem reponitur.

(g) Juv. *Sat.* 3. 226ff. (country pleasures are simple and cheap). 'Here (you can have) a little garden-plot, and a shallow well that needs no *rope*, sprinkling with an easy lift your tender seedlings':

> hortulus hic puteusque brevis nec *reste* movendus
> in tenuis plantas facili diffunditur haustu.

5. Tomix (-icis, f.) (fr. Gr. θῶμιξ), *cord, string*; perh. conn. w. *funis*

Not in Varro, *LL*; not in Isidore.

(a) *Corp. Gloss.* s.v. 'tomix'. vestis (restis?) leviter torta IV 293. 5; V 517. 2. Cf. Festus Pauli p. 357. 1.

(b) Fest. 356 M 488 L. 'The Greek name *thomices* is given to lightly twisted cords made from unworked hemp and esparto grass, from which ropes are made. Lucilius (1324): "We have seen him bound with hempen cords." Oppilius Aurelius said that the soft cushion, which he had on his neck to prevent the rope chafing, is called a *tomix*.' ⟨. . . thomices Graeco⟩ nomine appellantur ⟨ex cannabi inpolita⟩ et sparto leviter tortae ⟨restes ex quibus funes⟩ fiunt. Lucilius (1324): 'vidimus vinctum thomice ⟨cann⟩abina'. Op[p]illius Aure⟨lius . . . mol⟩lem pulvillum, quem in ⟨collo habent, ne restis⟩ laedat tomicem vo⟨cari⟩.

(c) Colum. 12. 32 (to make horehound wine). 'Then make little bundles (of horehound), tie them with *string* made from palm or rush, and let them down into a (small) wine-jar': deinde fasciculos facito et *tomice* palmae aut iuncea ligato et in seriam mittito.

(d) Vitruv. *De Arch.* 7. 3. 2 (making a base for stuccoing vaulted ceilings). 'When the ribs have been fixed in place, Greek reeds are to be bruised and bound to them with *cords* of Spanish broom, as the curvature requires': asseribus dispositis tum *tomice* ex sparto hispanico harundines graecae tunsae ad eos, uti forma postulat, religentur. Cf. Pallad. 1. 13 (*De cameris canniciis*).

6. Rete (-is, n.), us. pl. **retia** *net, netting*; also **retis** (-is, f. and m.); dimin. **reticulum** (-i, n.), *small net*

Not in Varro, *LL*.

(a) *R-E* I A. 688–91 [Hug]. Etym. dub. perh. conn. w. root of *rarus*, 'widely-spaced' or 'spaced at intervals' (see *AIRW*, p. 161 on the meaning of *dentes rari*, and cf. *rarum solum*, 'open' soil, as opp. to *spissum*, 'dense').

(b) Isid. *Etym.* 19. 5 (*De retibus*). 'They are called "retes", nets, either because they "hold back" (*retinere*) the fish, or from the "restes", *cords*, with which they are stretched': *retes* vocatae sive a retinendis piscibus, sive a restibus quibus tenduntur.

(c) *Corp. Gloss.* s.v. 'rete'. rete δίκτυον III 462. 38; 477. 38. retis σαγήνη II 174. 36. . . . λίνον κυνηγετικόν II 361. 18. retia δίκτυον, etc. (as above). . . . δίκτυα θήρατρα, ἄρκυες καὶ στάλικες, πλέγματα III 259. 50 (unde?) . . . retia proprie piscatorum III 256. 42 (unde?). retibus, cassibus, saginis, quibus pisces capiuntur V 479. 59.

(d) *Corp. Gloss.* s.v. 'reticulus'. γύργαθος καὶ κροκόφαντος II 174. 14. reticulum γύργαθος II 174. 15; III 132. 46. κεκρύφαλον II 347. 26 (cf. Iuvenal. ed. Friedländer, praef. p. 108); III 369. 64. ὄγκινος II 378. 53 (retinaculum H). cassiculum IV 386. 57.

(e) Varro, *RR* 3. 5. 11 (Varro's aviary at Casinum); cf. *ibid.* 14. 'In the entrance, on the right and left sides there are colonnades, arranged with stone columns in the outside rows. .... while from the top of the wall to the architrave, and from the architrave down to the base the colonnade is covered with a *net made of hemp*': in limine, in lateribus dextra et sinistra porticus sunt primoribus columnis lapideis ... ordinatae, cum a summa macerie ad epistylum tecta porticus sit *rete cannabina* et ab epistylo ad stylobaten.

(f) Varro, *RR* 3. 11. 3 (on keeping ducks). 'The entire enclosure is covered with a wide-meshed *net*, to prevent an eagle flying in or a duck flying out': idque saeptum totum *rete* grandibus maculis integitur, ne eo involare aquila possit neve evolare anas.

(g) Colum. 12. 53. 1 (recipe for making 'gleucine' oil). 'Then spices, which have not been sifted, and not even pounded into small pieces, but lightly broken, should be placed in a small *net* made of rush or linen, and let down into the above mentioned quantity of oil and must': tum aromata non cribrata, sed ne minute quidem contusa, verum leviter confracta in *reticulum* iunceum aut linteum adici, et ita in olei atque[1] musti prae⟨dictum modum⟩ demitti.

(h) Paul. *Dig.* 33. 7. 22 (on the *instrumentum fundi*). '*Nets* for wild boars (are included in the "instrumentum fundi"), if the profit from the estate arises for the most part from hunting': *retia* apraria ... si quaestus fundi ex maxima parte in venationibus consistat.

NOTES AND REFERENCES

The following references will be found useful in varying degrees:

R-E, s.v. 'Binsen', III 476–80 [Wagler]. On rushes and articles made from them.

Ibid. s.v. 'Flachs', VI 2461–84 [Olck]. On flax and linen: a comprehensive study.

Ibid. s.v. 'Hanf', VII 2313–16 [Orth]. On hemp and its products.

Ibid. s.v. 'pellis', XIX. 1. 369–371 [K. Schneider]. Almost entirely devoted to leather for clothing and military uses. Nothing on reins, straps, etc.

Ibid. s.v. 'restio', I A. 1. 674–6 [Hug]. On rope and its manufacture.

Notes on ropes and cordage

Apart from Pliny's valuable account of some of the raw materials from which ropes and cordage were made (see above, pp. 29 ff.), and scattered references in Vitruvius and other technical writers, Cato is our main source of information. There are references to rope in four chapters of the

---

[1] atque *S*: aut quae *AR* – praedictum modum demitti *scripsi*; predemitti (pondo de- *h*²) *SAR*: *Hedberg*.

De Agri Cultura, viz. 3. 5. (*bis*); 12; 63; 135. Three types of rope are mentioned in connection with the lever-press, and six in connection with wagon-harness. Unfortunately the text of the conclusion of chapter 3, which contains an important list of ropes required for the press, is very confused, and commentators have resorted to much emendation of the text. Since some of the identifications are uncertain, it seemed best to give a list, with some interpretative notes.

Ropes for the lever-press. As may be seen from the diagram of the simple lever-press (Appendix A, Fig. 43), two sets of ropes were required for lowering and raising the press-beam. Each was connected to a pulley-block (*troclia*), and the lowering-rope (*funis loreus*) was attached to a capstan (*suculus*) with sockets for the insertion of handspikes (*vectes*). In Cato's inventory (ch. 12), there are two other sets of ropes, the *funes subductarii*, which are the lifting-ropes, and the *funes meliponti*. This very rare word (only in Cato 3. 5 and 12) was interpreted by Billiard (*La Vigne*, p. 451) as a heavy rawhide rope coiled round the press baskets when set in position with their load of grape- or olive-pulp to enable them to withstand the great lateral pressure as the beam came down. This interpretation receives support from monumental representations, some of which show such coils (e.g. *OHT* II, 113, fig. 81). But the ropes depicted here are ordinary twisted fibre-ropes; rawhide ropes would be quite unsuitable for this purpose, since they could not form a coil; they would also be too expensive. I assume also that the lifting ropes were of fibre, not leather, for they would not be subjected to the great strain of the press-ropes. In fact Cato's phrasing supports the distinction between the press-ropes and the others. In chapter 63 the press-rope is referred to as *funis torculus*, but here the press-ropes appear without the descriptive adjective; if the others were of leather *funes lorei* would lose its distinctive meaning; they are in fact the only ropes in the inventory which are made of leather.

Harness-ropes. Reference is made to these items in ch. 63 and again in ch. 135. 5. The 'rope of rawhide for a wagon' (*funis loreus in plostrum*) has to be 60 feet long. Brehaut (comm. on 63) correctly interprets this item: a rope of such great length and of high breaking strain could only have been necessary for hitching a number of oxen to pull an exceedingly heavy load, 'as possibly in hauling home an olive-pulping mill' (ch. 22 – Brehaut, *loc. cit.*, n. 1). All the other items mentioned, which include reins and traces, are apparently of rawhide.

5

MEASURING INSTRUMENTS

The list of instruments discussed here is strictly limited, comprising (1) the *ciconia*, a testing device mentioned by Columella in connection with trench-digging: (2) the *groma* or surveyor's cross-staff: (3) the *decempeda* or *pertica* (iii), the standard measuring-rule used by surveyors. For a description of the *chorobates*, the *dioptra* and other surveying instruments the reader is referred to O. A. W. Dilke's *Roman Land Surveyors*, Newton Abbot, 1971.

1. Ciconia (-ae, f.), lit. a *stork*; (i) an *instrument* for testing the correct shape and depth of a trench (Colum.[1]); (ii) a *swape* or *shaduf* for raising water for irrigation at a higher level (= *tolleno*), for which see below, chapter 6, 'Water-raising Devices'

(i) = a device for testing trenches; not mentioned in this sense by lexicographers or by the Glossaries; elsewhere only by Columella (the instrument is partly the author's own invention).

No entry in *R-E*.

> Colum. 3. 13. 11 (on trenching ground for vines). 'But our ancestors, inventing a sort of instrument for measuring this work, have constructed a vertical bar ("regula"), in the side of which a small rod ("virgula"), projecting outwards at a height corresponding to the depth of trench required, makes contact with the topside of the trench. The country folk call this type of measuring instrument a "stork". .... (in order to avoid fraud) we (i.e. Columella himself) have added certain parts to this instrument in order to do away with quarrels and disputes between rival parties. We have fastened two pieces crosswise fashion in the form of the Greek letter X, of a spread equal to the width the trencher intends his furrow to attain; and to the centre point, where the pieces are joined, we have attached that old-fashioned "*stork*", so that it will stand at right-angles to it as if on a sub-base. Then, on the traverse rod, which is at the side, we have attached a workman's plumb-line': sed huic operi exigendo quasi quandam machinam commenti maiores nostri regulam fabricaverunt, in cuius latere virgula prominens ad eam altitudinem, qua deprimi sulcum oportet, contingit summae ripae partem. id genus mensurae *ciconiam* vocant rustici ... nam duas regulas eius latitudinis, qua pastinator sulcum facturus est, in speciem Graecae litterae X decussavimus, atque ita mediae parti, qua regula

[1] Only used by Columella in this sense.

committitur, antiquam illam *ciconiam* infiximus, ut tamquam suppositae basi ad perpendiculum normata insisteret; deinde transversae, quae est in latere, virgulae fabrilem libellam superposuimus.

The *ciconia* (lit. 'stork') was an instrument designed to test the accuracy in width and depth of trenches, and thus prevent dishonest or slovenly work. In its simpler form it consisted of an upright piece of wood (*regula*), with a cross-bar attached to it at right angles, the upright defining the depth, and the cross-bar the width, required to be dug. It was placed in the trench at intervals. The instrument could however be set up slantwise so as to conceal irregularities in width or depth, and so deceive the overseer. Columella's improved version, as his description makes plain, could only be set square to the trench, and the addition of a plumb-line would prevent disputes between overseer and contractor by showing at once whether the bottom of the trench had been correctly excavated and properly aligned. Accuracy of levels was of prime importance in farm irrigation and drainage schemes.

Monuments. No illustration of the instrument is known. Rich (*Dict. Ant.* s.v. 'ciconia') reproduces a conjectural diagram taken from J. G. Schneider's edition of *Scriptores Rei Rusticae*, vol. II, Leipzig, 1794. Our suggested reconstruction (Fig. 9) corresponds more closely with the requirements of the text.

Survivals. Sets of simple 'T' squares are still used by foreman drain-layers for testing the level of trenches for drainpipes, but they are set in the upright position.

Fig. 9. Ciconia

2. Groma (-ae, f.), also **gruma** (-ae, f.), **stella** (-ae, f.), *surveyor's cross-staff*

Not in Varro; not in Isidore.

(*a*) *R-E* VII 2. 1881–6 (Schulten).

(*b*) *Corp. Gloss.* s.v. 'gruma'. γνώμων II 36. 18; 264. 7. διόπτρα ἡ τῶν μέτρων (γεωμετρῶν *Vulc.*) II 278. 25. βασιλικὴ γνώμη II 36. 23. gauma (gruma *adg*) ὁραια (διοπτρα? ὄπτρα *Scal.* ὁριαία *Buech. scil.* μηχανή. ὁρμιά *Volkmann*) τεκτονικὴ II 32. 26. gruira fust⟨ic⟩ellus horologii II 581. 36.

(*c*) *Fest. Gloss.²* IV. p. 217ᵃ (p. 490 L; p. 96 M). groma appellatur genus machi-nulae cuiusdam, quo regiones agri cuiusque cognosci possunt, quod genus Graeci γνώμονα dicunt. Non. p. 63 M est groma mensura (?) quaedam, qua fixa viae ad lineam deriguntur. NIPS. grom. p. 285, 17 percuties gromam. *ibid.* manente groma (*opp.* ex alia parte ferramenti). Hyg. *mun. castr.* 12 ferramento groma superponatur.

Fig. 10. Groma

DISCUSSION

The *groma*, or surveyor's cross-staff, was relatively simple in design, and was used for setting out the boundaries of all types of land-allocation based on a gridded system, the most familiar of which is that known as centuria-tion, commonly based on a rectangle of 20 × 20 *actus*, or *c*. 700 × 700 metres. The *groma*, as we now know from a specimen actually found in the house of a surveyor in Pompeii in 1912, consisted of a vertical rod, partly encased in bronze, from the top of which projected a hinged arm, fitted at its outer end with a socket. Into the socket was fitted a pair of cross-bars meeting at right angles, and from the ends of each of these hung a plumb-line. The staff was fixed in the ground beside the inscribed stone pillar which marked the base of the rectangular grid. A line was then 'sighted' by means of ranging-rods (*metae, signa, perticae*), the four 'com-pass points' were next adjusted to this sight-line, and the squares were then marked out with the *groma*. By this relatively simple method of surveying very large blocks of settlement were laid out, mainly to accommodate veteran soldiers, in Lombardy, the Istrian peninsula around Aquileia, parts of Dalmatia, and over the greater part of what is now Tunisia (see John Bradford, *Ancient Landscapes*, London, 1957, pp. 145–216, with numerous air photographs of the above centuriated systems; for a brief summary, with a list of Italian colonial sites, E. T. Salmon, *Roman Colonization under the Republic*, London, 1969, pp. 21–4).

Extant representations

A representation of the *groma*, as viewed from above, appears on a funerary relief from Ivrea (*Eporedia*) in North Italy, in the heart of a centuriated area, dedicated to a professional surveyor, one Lucius Aebutius Faustus. The relief is now in the Museo Civico, Ivrea: D–S s.v. 'stella', vol. IV 2, p. 1506, fig. 6627; M. Della Corte, *Monumenti Antichi*, 28 (1922), p. 18, fig. 1. The tripod-base suggested by Espérandieu (D–S, *art. cit.*) is disproved by the fragments found at Pompeii, which include the 12 in. gouge-faced spike. The museum at Pompeii contains a reconstruction of this *groma*. See now Dilke, *RLS*, p. 50.

Extant specimens

The Pompeian *groma*, which was discovered, appropriately enough, in the house of a Pompeian land surveyor, but in a fragmentary state, has been fully described and reconstructed in a masterly study by M. Della Corte, *art. cit.*, pp. 1ff. His fig. 2 (p. 29) shows the fragments of bronze and iron as found; fig. 4 shows the pointed end of the *calcio*, which was of bronze and iron, with a wooden core. The point is ingeniously faced with gouged surfaces meeting in sharp edges to help the instrument to bed down in a vertical position. The *groma* is shown as reconstructed at fig. 13. A copy of Della Corte's reconstruction is in the Science Museum, London. Original finds are in the Museo Nazionale, Naples.

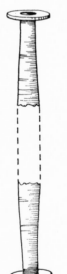

Fig. 11. Pertica

3. Pertica (-ae, f.), (iii) = **decempeda**, *surveyor's ranging-rod*

(*a*) *R-E* XIX 1. 1059–60 [A. Schulten].

(*b*) Isid. *Etym.* 15. 15. 2 (on land measurement). 'The *ranging-rod* is two paces, that is ten feet, in length. The ranging-rod derives its name from carrying, as if it were derived from "portica"': pertica passus duos (habet) id est pedes decem. pertica autem a portando dicta, quasi portica.

(*c*) *Corp. Gloss.* s.v. 'pertica'. pertica κανών, κάμαξ II 148. 39. κανών, κοντός II 493. 52, etc.

(*d*) Anon. *De Mensuris* (in *Die Schriften der römischen Feldmesser* I (ed. Blume *et al.*, Berlin, 1848) 371. 20ff. (on units of linear measurement). 'We see that the *measuring rods* are adjusted to the terrain, that is, to the fertility of the soil. Some are fixed at ten feet, some have two feet added, while others are fifteen or seventeen feet long, with the proviso however that shorter units of measurement are assigned to more fertile, longer to less fertile soils': perticas autem iuxta loca vel crassitudinem terrarum, ... videmus esse dispositas, quasdam decimpedas, quibusdam duos additos pedes, aliquas vero XV vel X et VII pedum diffinitas, ita dum taxat ut crassioribus terris minores mensuras, sterilioribus maiores tribuissent.

(*e*) Prop. *Eleg.* 4. 1. 130. 'The dismal *measuring-rod* has filched away the wealth amassed by cultivation': abstulit excultas pertica tristis opes.

(*f*) Serv. ad Virg. *Ecl.* 9. 7 (on land confiscation by the Triumvirs). 'Octavius Musa, the land-surveyor appointed by Augustus, had stretched out his *measuring-rod* right up to that place, that is, for a distance of fifteen miles into the *ager Mantuanus*, there being insufficient land (for distribution) in the *ager Cremonensis*. Augustus had been insulted by the people of Mantua, because, so he alleged, they had rounded up his flocks when grazing on the Public Land': usque ad eum locum *perticam* militarem Octavius Musa porrexerat, limitator ab Augusto datus, id est per quindecim milia passuum agri Mantuani, cum Cremonensis non sufficeret, offensus a Mantuanis, quod pecora eius in agro publico aliquando clausissent.

DISCUSSION

The *pertica* in the special sense was normally a rod ten feet in length (hence the common abbreviation 'decempeda'). Since the plots assigned to veteran soldiers in military colonies were measured with it, it is also referred to as *pertica militaris*, especially in contexts dealing with the dispossession and eviction of existing property-holders to make way for new colonists (see passage *f* above).

Extant representations

The *pertica* is often displayed on coins and engraved gems alongside the settler and his plough, which is the usual symbol of colonial veteran settlements.

Extant specimens

Three end-pieces of measuring-rods were found at Enns in upper Austria. The first two (a pair) are 8·5 cm long, with a slight taper, and flat circular ends, enabling exact alignment of two rods. 'Thus, if an actus, 120 ft., needed to be measured, two 10 ft. rods each used six times would suffice' (Dilke, *RLS*, p. 71, who gives other interesting details). For a full account of other surveying devices the reader may now refer to Dilke, *RLS*, pp. 66–81, with numerous text-figures.

Survival

(1) *Of the term.* Fr. 'perche'; Eng. 'perch' (obs.), a unit of linear measurement equivalent to a 'rod' or 'pole', and measuring $5\frac{1}{2}$ yards; four perches made a 'chain' and ten chains a 'furlong'.

(2) *Of the instrument.* The contemporary surveyor's ranging-rod is banded at 1 ft. intervals in red, white and black. We do not know whether the divisions of the *pertica* were similarly marked. The variations in length noted by Anon. *De Mensuris* (passage *c*) as related to the terrain surveyed still apply; the 'standard' length today is six feet, but five-foot and twelve-foot rods are used for similar reasons.

6

WATER-RAISING DEVICES

The importance of irrigation to the ancient Italian farmer is clearly emphasized by Cato's order of profitability for different types of land-use, where the vineyard tops the list, with an irrigated garden (*hortus inriguus*) in second place. The subject of water-supply for agricultural purposes has been fully treated elsewhere (see my *Roman Farming* (1970), pp. 146–72). Here we shall confine our attention to the water-raising devices in use on the farm. But here our difficulties begin. The fact that the topic is ignored by all but one of the agricultural writers might be regarded as ground for supposing that little or no use was made of mechanical methods, but casual literary references and monumental evidence present a different picture.

The evidence

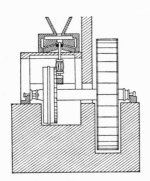

Fig. 12. Tympanum

Vitruvius (*De Arch.* 10. 4. 1–7) gives instructions for making the following machines: (1) the *tympanum* or compartment water-wheel, turned by men on a treadmill; 'does not raise the water to a great height, but draws a large amount in a short time'; gives an abundant supply of water 'for irrigating gardens or diluting salt in salt-pits' (4. 1–2); (2) the bucket-wheel (no distinctive name given); no compartments, hence larger wheel giving greater height can be used as a treadmill (4. 3); (3) the bucket-hoist; using the same wheel and treadmill, the axle is made to turn an endless chain of bronze buckets (*situli*), giving a still greater lift. No information is given on the lift available with any of these wheels; (4) the undershot water-driven wheel (*a*) for lifting water, as in (2); (*b*) with horizontal gearing for grinding corn; (5) the *cochlea* or water-screw, turned by men using a treadmill; the machine is efficient, in that it hoists a continuous flow of water, but it does not have as high a lift as the wheel; (6) the *Ctesibica machina* or piston-pump, a twin-cylinder, hand-operated water-lifting pump, worked by suction; the use of this machine in classical times has been denied (see below, s.v. 'organum pneumaticum'). Pliny (*HN* 19. 60) mentions three methods used for drawing water for irrigation from a well: (1) *rota scil. aquaria*, the well-rope passing over a spindle fixed at the well-head; (2) *organa pneumatica*,

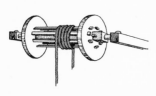

Fig. 13. Rota aquaria

the suction-pump (= Vitruv. 6); and (3) *tolleno*, the 'shaduf', known also as *ciconia*, the swing-beam, with which the water is collected from a lower level, and swung on a horizontal beam with a counterweight (for a full description see *RF*, pp. 156f.).

Archaeological evidence. Three of these devices are confirmed for agricultural use from monumental evidence, viz. the *cochlea*, the *rota aquaria*, and the *tolleno*, and one (the *organum pneumaticum*) from surviving specimens. The use of the *tympanum* cannot be proved from independent evidence, but Vitruvius was writing for users, not for students, and his statement is unequivocal (above, p. 44).

(a) *RE* s.v. 'Wasserleitungen', VI A. I (1955), 470–80 [A. W. van Buren]. Part of a comprehensive treatment of the whole topic of water-supply. *RE* s.v. 'Archimedes', II 538–9 [Hultsch]. *RE* s.v. 'cochlea', IV I. 155 [Hultsch]; *RE* s.v. 'Heron 5', VIII 2. 992–1080 [Tittel]; *RE* s.v. 'Ktesibios', 'Ctesibica machina', XI 2076 [Orinsky]. The entry s.v. 'tolleno' VI A. 1677–9, by F. Lammert, deals with military engines only.

(b) Isid. *Etym.* 20. 15. 1–3 (*De instrumentis hortorum*). 'The *wheel* ("rota") takes its name from the fact that it 'runs' ("ruat"): it is a contrivance for drawing water from a river. Lucretius (5. 516): "as we see the streams turning the *wheels* and the scoops". The *scoop*, that is the wheel, takes its name from "drinking up" ("aurire"), the water. The *roller* ("girgillus") takes its name from turning in a circle ("girus"); it is a movable piece of wood on a crossbeam from which the rope with bucket or skin is let down into the well to draw up water. Gardeners give the name *swape* ("telo") to the long wooden instrument they use to draw water. It is called a "telo" because of its length; among the Greeks anything long is called τηλόν . . . The Spaniards call this instrument a "*stork*" ("ciconia"), because it imitates the bird of the same name, as they lift (it) up full of (?) water, and drop the beak, while it clangs': *rota dicta quod quasi ruat: est enim machina de qua e flumine aqua extrahitur*. Lucretius (5. 517):

> ut fluvios versare rotas atque austra videmus.

austra autem, id est rota, ab auriendo aquam[1] dicta. *girgillus*, quod in giro vertatur: est enim lignum in transversa pertica mobile ex quo funis cum situla vel utre in puteum demittitur auriendae aquae causa. *telonem* hortulani vocant lignum longum quo auriunt aquas. et dictum telonem a longitudine: τηλόν enim dicitur iuxta Graecos quidquid longum est . . . hoc instrumentum Hispani *ciconiam* dicunt propter quod imitetur eiusdem nominis avem, levantes aqua[2] ac deponentes rostrum, dum clangit.

(c) *Corp. Gloss.* s.v. 'ciconia'. ciconia πελαργὸς μηχανή II 100. 34. κηλώνειον φρέατος ciconia, telleno (v. tolleno) II 349. 1. Cf. Isid. 20. 15. 3.

(d) *Corp. Gloss.* s.v. 'girgillus'. rota hauritoria Scal. V 601. 4 (= Osb. p. 264). est mergus V 620. 3.

[1] aqua *KT: corr. Lindsay.* [2] aqua *U* aquae (ue) *BVT om. C.*

45

(e) *Corp. Gloss.* s.v. 'haustra'. rota hauritoria (-ium gloss. Scal.) qui (!) et girgillus v 601. 33 (cf. Osb. p. 277). Cf. Isid. 20. 15. 2. haustra id est rota ab hauriendo aqua⟨m⟩ dicta v 170. 7. rotarum modii (radii Madvig; modioli?; cf. P. Salmas. Pl. ex. 589 B) v 649. 4 (Non. 13. 3).

(f) Non. 13. 3 f. 'The pots on the wheels are correctly called *scoops* ("austra") because they "scoop up" ("auriendo") the water': *austra proprie dicuntur rotarum cadi ab auriendo.*

(g) Paul. Fest. s.v. 'tolenno', p. 490 L; p. 356 M. tolenno est genus machinae, quo trahitur aqua, alteram partem praegravante pondere, dictus a tollendo.

(h) *Corp. Gloss.* s.v. 'cochlea' *vel* 'coclea'. κοχλιός II 517. 50; 540. 25, etc. cochlia, coclea κοχλίας II 354. 36. coclia miaci (h.e. μύακιν) II 563. 33. coclea ascensus qui circuit v 351. 43 (cf. Vulg. 3 Reg. 6. 8, etc.). . . . cocleas bicani (βυκάνη?) III 554. 22, etc. Cf. Isid. 12. 6. 48.

(j) Pliny, *HN* 19. 60 (on laying out a kitchen-garden (*hortus*)). 'We ought certainly to have kitchen-gardens adjoining the farm-house, and they should be thoroughly irrigated, if possible by a river running past them; if not, with irrigation water supplied from a well by means of a *pulley* or *suction-pumps* or by scooping with a *swing-beam*': hortos villae iungendos non est dubium riguosque maxime habendos, si contingat, praefluo amne, si minus, e puteo *rota organisve pneumaticis* vel *tollenonum* haustu rigatos.

(k) Hor. *Odes* 3. 10. 9–10 (the poet pleads with his mistress). 'Away with the pride that Venus disapproves, lest as the *wheel* spins the rope slip back (into the water)':

> ingratam Veneri pone superbiam
> ne currente retro funis eat *rota*.

DISCUSSION

Problems of interpretation are few but difficult. Mistranslations abound (notable is Rackham's interpretation of *organa pneumatica* as 'windmills'!), and the different senses of *rota* have not been clearly differentiated, nor has any scholar attempted, so far as I know, to discuss the meaning of *organa pneumatica*. These problems will now be discussed in turn.

1. *Rota in its various meanings.* Cato's vineyard list includes a *rota aquaria* and a *situla aquaria*. This is surely the simple rope and bucket with the improvement of a roller (*rota, girgillus*) (see fig. 13), the term being used in exactly the same sense at 3. 6, where it is an alternative to pulley-blocks for lifting up the press-beam (see Brehaut *ad loc.*). The proportion of either of his model estates devoted to irrigated lands would not have justified the use of a water-wheel, and the Loeb editor's windmill is many centuries too soon! On the other hand, Vitruvius' water-wheels are intended for the large-scale operator, such as Pliny also has in mind. 'The kitchen-gardens', he says, 'are to be fully irrigated (*maxime riguos haben-*

dos)', and the alternative devices he mentions are in a different class from the humble well-rope and bucket affair, even when improved by the addition of a roller. The referenceto the bucket-chain in Lucretius (passage *b*) is all the more significant in that its operations are introduced to explain an unfamiliar feature of the movement of the heavenly bodies, by which they are driven up the celestial sphere in reverse, as a bucket-chain and its scoops (*austra*) are turned in reverse motion by the water flowing past, whe nthe power is not applied. Vitruvius (10. 5. 10) calls these scoops *modioli* (see below, s.v. 'modiolus', pp. 167 ff.).

2. *Organa pneumatica.* The commentators are strangely silent on the identification of Pliny's *organa pneumatica* (passage *j*). I am convinced that he is referring to the piston-pump known as the *Ctesibica machina*, described several times by Hero of Alexandria (*Pneumatika* 1 28, etc.), and by Vitruvius (*De Arch.* 10. 7). Most of Hero's pumps are quite small affairs, used for compressing air or pumping water, but his reference at *Pneum.* 1 28 to a 'siphon', used for fire-fighting, is to a double-action water-pump, with two cylinders and a swivelling nozzle. At least four devices answering to Hero's description have been found, one of them (from Silchester, near Reading), actually sitting at the bottom of a well (Pl. 7*c*). See further Feldhaus, *Die Technik,* s.v. 'Pompe:12, Kolbenpompe', giving details. In view of this evidence I find it impossible to accept Forbes's categorical pronouncement that 'antiquity did not know the suction-pump' (*SAT* II, 30).

3, 4. *The cochlea and the tolleno.* The *cochlea* or Archimedean screw is still very much in use in Egypt and other parts of the Middle East (see Pl. 1 *b*), as is the *tolleno* or shaduf (see Pl. 1 *a*). Both are known from monuments, the *cochlea* from a Pompeian painting, showing a slave turning a small *cochlea* with his feet (Rostovtzeff, *SEHRE*[2] pl. LIII, 5), the *tolleno* from a north African mosaic pavement with many agricultural scenes from Oudna, now in the Bardo Museum, Tunis (*RF*, pl. 4, p. 56).

5. *The girgillus.* This word, not noticed by LS, is

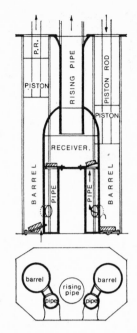

Fig. 14. Organum pneumaticum

Fig. 15. Cochlea

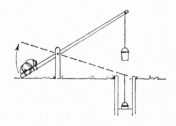

Fig. 16. Tolleno

Fig. 17. Girgillus

defined by E–M (s.v.) as 'cylindre tourné par une manivelle pour tirer de l'eau d'un puits moulinet, dévidoir'. They further suggest that the word, whose etymology is unknown, may reflect the sound of the operation (cf. Eng. 'gurgle'). It is clearly the late Latin word for the wooden roller set over the well-head on which the bucket-rope was wound, as Isidore neatly explains (passage *b*). Representations of wells so equipped show a serrated surface on the cylinder to prevent the rope from slipping (see e.g. Fig. 14 = D–S s.v. 'puteus', vol. IV, fig. 5894, p. 780).

6. *The (h)austrum*. Marked * by the lexica, the word appears only twice (Lucr. 5. 116 (passage *b*), and Non. 13. 3 (passage *f*), the latter presumably a gloss on the former. It seems evident that Nonius is referring, not to the compartment-wheel (*tympanum*) with its wedge-shaped boxes (*modioli*, q.v.), first described by Vitruvius, but to the primitive 'wheel of pots' (*cadi*), turned by animal-power, and still in use in the Middle East. Nonius goes on to refer to the Lucretius passage, but confuses the discussion by making *austra* the equivalent of the *modioli* of the Vitruvian water-wheel.

PART TWO
EQUIPMENT MADE OF BASKETRY

INTRODUCTION

TECHNICAL AND ECONOMIC ASPECTS
OF TRANSPORT ON THE FARM

Heavy loads were moved by ox-wagon, lighter weights by donkey- or mule-drawn carts, or by pack-saddle (see below, pp. 79 ff.). Cato's vineyard inventory (*RR* 11) includes two carts drawn by donkeys; these are presumably light two-wheeled types fitted with solid wheels like the one carrying a load of grapes on the great pergula mosaic from Cherchel (J. Lassus in *Libyca* 7. 2 (1959), 257–69). The much larger olive farm calls for three 'larger wagons' (*plostra maiora*), which were presumably four-wheelers of light construction, but larger capacity (see below, s.v. 'plaustrum', p. 81); cf. the Pompeian wall painting depicting a four-wheeler for bulk wine transport (below, s.v. 'culleus', p. 139). Associated with bulk transport in the northern provinces, where wine was matured and conveyed in wooden casks, are a number of Gallo-Roman reliefs depicting heavy four-wheelers drawn by pairs of mules, as on the Langres relief (Espérandieu, *Gaule*, IV no. 3232), which shows a heavy wagon loaded with a single cask (on these containers see below, s.v. 'cupa', p. 143). In Italy, on the contrary, wheeled transport was restricted by the mountainous nature of much of the terrain, and cultivation was regularly carried out on hillsides too steep for cartage except by men or pack-animals. The point is neatly illustrated in Cato's inventories; in addition to its three larger wagons, Cato's olive farm requires four asses, one for the animal-drawn grain-mill, and three for carrying manure by pannier ('asinos ornatos clitellarios qui stercus vectent III' – 10. 1). This form of transport is still the rule in the more mountainous regions of the Mediterranean area, such as South Italy, Sicily and many parts of Spain (see below, s.v. 'clitellae', p. 97).

But the varied activities of the typical mixed farm necessitated a great deal of handling, most of it by means of baskets or sacks, with or without the aid of load-distributing or load-easing devices. These included hurdles fitted with poles (see below, s.v. 'crates'), shared two-man shoulder-loading with the load suspended from a pole (see below, s.v. 'amphora'), and the one-man 'bucket-yoke', a device which was extremely common, though almost unrecorded (see below, s.v. 'scirpea', 'sirpiculus'). One of the most important of these devices, the wheelbarrow, was unknown to the West before mediaeval times.

Limitations to the use of land transport

The conventional view, based partly on lack of an efficient harness for horses, partly on the high price quoted for wagon-transport in the Price Edict of Diocletian (XVII. 1 ff.), that the movement of bulky goods by land was severely restricted, has received fresh support from P. A. Brunt (review of my *Roman Farming*, *JRS* 62 (1972), 156), who relates the deficiency to the aim of self-sufficiency on large estates. But animal-drawn wagons did not provide the cheapest form of road transport in classical times; the evidence for the use of pack-animals is somewhat scanty, but the same applies to many other departments of ancient life; and Varro's casual reference (*RR* 2. 6. 5) to the use of trains of pack-asses (*aselli dossuarii*) by traders in the major agricultural products of corn, wine and oil merits close attention. Large quantities of bulky produce can be easily conveyed by this method; the Edict gives standard loads for wagons (1,200 lb.) and for camels (600 lb.) but gives none for pack-asses, 'because', as Blümner drily observes, 'they loaded the asses with as much as they could possibly carry, much as they still do in the East' (*Maximaltarif*, 145). The question is a difficult one, and needs further study (see Conclusion, pp. 218 ff).

MATERIAL FOR MAKING CONTAINERS:
SOURCES OF SUPPLY AND ORGANIZATION

Basketry

The economic importance of a regular source of supply of broom, willow and reed for weaving into basketry is well attested: in Cato's list of investment preferences (1. 7), the willow-plantation (*salictum*) holds third place in profitability, being bettered only by the vineyard and the irrigated market-garden (on the economic importance of the willow-plantation see further Pliny, *HN* 16. 174–7). The large numbers of woven containers, of solid or flexible type, required on the farm could be supplied by the farm hands, without recourse to outside purchase, by turning to account the inevitable 'dead' periods occasioned by winter or bad weather. In an interesting section of his Calendar (*RR* 11. 2. 90f.) in which the work for November is under discussion, Columella draws attention to the short periods of daylight available for outside work, and goes on to give a list of jobs that can be done by artificial light (*in lucubratione*). These include the cutting and sharpening of vine-props, the making of bee-hives out of fennel or bark, of frails and baskets from palm or broom, and of hampers from osiers (see p. 215).

On the sources of supply for basketry see Appendix B, pp. 233–9.

Earthenware

Apart from the northern provinces, where coopered casks predominated, earthenware containers were standard for bulk storage and transport of most dry and liquid farm products, as well as for the retailing and domestic handling of wine and oil. Only on large estates, however, was there sufficient demand to warrant the cost of setting up a pottery for producing them. In Cato's list (135) of the best sources of supply for items not produced on the farm, only two special types of woven container are mentioned, but large pottery containers (*dolia, labra*) are to be purchased at Venafrum (the nearest town).

Other materials

Stone was often used for large, vat-type containers, the common tufa being very easily worked. It should be noted that the shallow stone kitchen sink persisted in England until the late nineteenth century, when it was displaced by cheaply produced porcelain. *Bronze* was employed for the making of utensils needed for the boiling of liquids (water, must, etc.). Cato's inventory for the olive plantation includes a bronze cauldron (*aenum*, q.v.) to hold thirty *amphorae* (*c.* 183 gallons). Lead was also used (see Forc. s.v. 'plumbeus'). The list includes dug-out containers of *wood*, and complete skins of animals were also used. Where the same type of vessel was made from different materials, these are usually distinguished in the sources by the use of appropriate adjectives, viz. *aeneus, plumbeus*, etc.

CLASSIFICATION OF CONTAINERS MADE OF BASKETRY

Having no metal cheaper than bronze for making containers, the Roman farmer was heavily dependent on earthenware, basketry and, to a much lesser extent, on wood for containers. Earthenware and metal items are dealt with in Part Three, while Part Two is concerned with those made from basketry and wood. Basketry included what are called 'crate-rods' as well as the 'withies' made from osiers or other pliant materials. Cato refers curtly to both in a list of instructions on how to prepare various articles made of timber: 'withies that are ripe, and willow-rods should be gathered at the right time, so that there may be material for making new baskets and mending old ones' (31).

The broadest distinction, as shown in the distribution of items in the following list, is that between true baskets, which are woven by horizontal plaiting over a vertical framework of rods, and containers of the sack type which have no framework. Even this broad distinction cannot be rigidly applied; thus *corbis* and *qualus* are sometimes used of flexible containers. Nor, again, can precise distinctions either of form or function be established, e.g. as between *corbis* and *calathus* (the latter a loan-word from Greek). Similarly, *fiscella*, *qualus* and *saccus* are lumped together by D–S as synonymous with *colum*, a sieve or filter. Sometimes, however, the shape can be to some extent determined from the known function: thus the *fiscus* or rush-basket, mentioned frequently by Columella as being used for pressing olives, must evidently have been both large and of some depth (see below, s.v. 'fiscus', pp.   ff.). It would, however, be pointless to draw too rigid boundaries between artefacts which served many different purposes.

ON THE MAKING OF BASKETS

No account of the processes of making hard or soft basketry has come down to us. This is not particularly surprising. The plaiting techniques involved are simple and traditional, and have remained basically unchanged over the centuries. A few surviving representations show basketmaking in progress. The best-known example is provided by one of the winter panels from the great Seasons Mosaic from Vienne, now in the Museum of National Antiquities at St-Germain-en-Laye, near Paris (see Pl. 15 a). This panel, which is very well preserved, shows a basketmaker seated at his work. He has already made the holes in the solid base of the basket; now, having inserted the crate-rods, he is engaged in plaiting the withies, pushing each successive layer into position as he goes. To his right another workman arrives with a load of freshly-cut crate-rods. Basket-making is listed by Columella, along with the preparation of poles and vine-props, as work that can be carried out under artificial light (11. 2. 90). The thrifty farmer is encouraged to obtain some compensation through these activities for the time lost owing to the short length of the winter working day. One or two technical terms may be noticed: *corbium costae* (Pliny, *HN* 16. 75) refers to what are called in England 'crate-rods', that is, the ribs which provide the rigid framework for the basket. It does not appear that any surviving account has provided us with the name of the bands used to strengthen the basket at its mouth (and sometimes lower down). Blümner (*Technologie* 1, 304, n. 6) wrongly identified the word *fibula* as 'fastener', hence 'brooch' in this connection. These are in fact wooden pegs or pins, which were used for many different purposes (see

Brehaut's note on Cato, *RR* 12. 1). *Circulus* would seem to be appropriate, but Pliny uses the term only to denote barrel-hoops (16. 75, cf. 14. 132).

ORDER OF TREATMENT

Although even the technical writers are often imprecise, and different terms are used to designate the same type of container, we shall try to establish from the evidence the basic design and function of each, giving attention also to important specialized uses. Following the distinction drawn earlier between rigid, framed types of basketry and the flexible 'sack' variety, we discuss them in that order, beginning with containers.

7

HARD BASKETRY

Fig. 18. Corbis

1. Corbis (-is, comm.), a *basket*; dimin. **corbula, corbicula**

No separate entry in *R-E*.

(*a*) Varro, *LL* 5. 139. 'Those means by which field produce and other necessary items are transported. . . . (of these) *baskets* (were so named) from the fact that into them they piled up corn-ears or other things': quibus comportantur fructus ac necessariae res . . . *corbes* ab eo (dictae) quod eo spicas aliudve quid corruebant.

(*b*) Isid. *Etym.* 20. 9. 10. '*Baskets* are so called because they are woven together from curved rods': *corves* dicti, quia curvatis virgis contexuntur.

(*c*) Isid. *Etym.* 20. 14. 13. 'Baskets, *frails* and sieves for the wine-press, through which the must flows': qualos *corbes* colaque prelorum, per quos[1] mustum fluit.

(*d*) *Corp. Gloss.* s.v. 'corbis'. corbis εἶδος κοφίνου II 116. 51. κόφινος (corbes et corbis) II 354. 32. corbes κόφινος II 518. 21. covel (*AS*) v 354. 54. corbem fiscina⟨m⟩ cophinum graece v 278. 56. fiscinam, cophinum v 627. 45. corbula κόφινος II 354. 32; 492. 65.

(*e*) Cato 136 (contract for harvesting grain on shares). 'In the country around Casinum and Venafrum on good soil [the owner] should give the share worker the eighth part of the *basket*; on fairly good soil, the seventh': in agro Casinate et Venafro in loco bono parti octava *corbi* dividat, satis bono septima.

(*f*) Varro, *RR* 1. 50 (on harvesting methods for grain). 'To throw the ears into the *basket*': spicas in *corbem* conicere.

(*g*) Cic. *Pro Sest.* 38. 'He covered himself with a *reaper's basket*': messoria se *corbe* contexit.

(*h*) Colum. 6. 3. 5 (on fodder). 'If we do not feed them on grain, it is enough to supply them with a *fodder-basket* each, containing twenty modii of dried leaves or thirty pounds of hay': si grano abstinemus, frondis aridae *corbis pabulatorius* modiorum viginti sufficit, vel faeni pondo triginta (cf. *ibid.* 11. 2. 99).

(*j*) Varro, *RR* 1. 15 (on methods of training the vine). '(The elm) often supports and gathers many *baskets* of grapes': (ulmus) quod et sustinet saepe ac cogit aliquot *corbulas* uvarum (cf. Colum. 12. 52. 8).

[1] quae? *Mynors, fortasse recte.*

(k) Pallad. 3. 10. 6 (new method of transplanting vine-cuttings). 'There is another economical way of transplanting a vine from the live plantation ("arbustum"); you make a *small basket* of osiers': est et aliud de transferenda ex arbusto vite compendium; fit ex vimine *parva corbicula.*

(l) Cato 11. 5 (vineyard inventory). '20 Amerian *baskets*': corbulas Amerinas XX.

(m) *Ibid.* 31. 1 (equipment for harvesting olives). 'Ripe osiers and willow-shoots should be gathered at the right time as material for making *baskets* and mending old ones': vimina matura, salix per tempus legatur, uti sit unde *corbulae* fiant et veteres sarciantur.

(n) Ulp. *Dig.* 18. 6. 1. 4 (on purchasing wine 'in cask'). 'If the storage jars have not been emptied, the seller must do what the old authorities recommended, viz. measure the contents *by the basketful*, and pour them out': quod si non sint evacuata (*scil.* dolia) faciendum, quod veteres putaverunt, *per corbem* venditorem mensuram facere et effundere.

DISCUSSION

Shape

Rich (*Dict. Ant.* s.v.) describes *corbis* as 'a basket of wickerwork, made in a pyramidal or conical shape'; but there is no literary evidence to support this restricted notion of shape, and the illustration he provides (taken from a fresco) might well serve as a flower basket, but would hardly pass as a receptacle for grain or fodder (passages *e, f, g*). Isidore's derivation from *curvus* (passage *b*), though technically incorrect, and rejected by many commentators, is however accepted by Walde–Hofmann (s.v. 'corbis'), quoting the Middle Irish word 'corb', a wagon, which links it firmly with the basketry container used widely for transporting bulky loads (see further s.v. 'plaustrum', pp. 102 ff.). As for Isidore's other reference, a basket made of rods and withies would not have served as a sieve (passage *c*). Mynors' simple correction of 'quos' to 'quae' removes the absurdity and restricts the application of the relative clause to the last item on the list, the 'cola prelorum' (see the critical note to passage *c*). Pliny's discussion at 16. 35, where *corbes* are grouped with 'certain rather capacious containers' (*patentiora quaedam*), used for carrying corn at harvest and grapes at vintage (*messibus convehendis vindemiisque*), adds to the impression of a curved receptacle as distinct from the straight-sided baskets used in many other operations.

Size

The English 'bushel-basket', as used by market porters, holds the equivalent of 4 *modii*, so that Columella's fodder-basket (passage *h*) will have been five times that size, and a 'reaper's basket' (passage *g*) was big enough for a man to hide in. None of the above references suggests that the *corbis* was of a standard size. The one undisputed fact is that it could be very large, while the diminutive form *corbula* seems to have been reserved for the smaller fruit-picking basket (passage *j*). Palladius' 'very small basket' (passage *k*) will probably have been only a few inches in diameter.

Corbulae Amerinae. Cato's vineyard inventory includes two kinds of container for picking and transporting the grapes to the vats: (1) forty 'planting baskets' (*quala sataria*) or forty wooden trays (*alvei*); (2) twenty 'Amerian baskets'. The quantities of each of the two items required makes it clear that the *quala sataria* or *alvei* were to be used for picking, the *corbulae* for transporting, the grapes. See further Part III, Introduction (p. 112), on this part of the vintage. It is typical of Cato's thrifty attitude that he advises using equipment originally designed for a different purpose. *Quala sataria* is slightly ambiguous: I think it means baskets used to carry seedlings from nursery beds to where they were to be planted out. As for the diminutive in *corbulae Amerinae*, it has no force. The 'local' adjective (*Amerinus*) is fairly common as descriptive of a particular shape developed in a district (here a famous wine-growing area, home of the well-known Amerian grape). The difference of function is shown much more clearly in a passage from the *Digest* (below, s.v. 'qualus', p. 60, passage *h*).

The phrase 'per corbem'. We have at least two pieces of evidence (*e* and *n* above) to show that measurement of crops 'by the basket' was common. This natural and easy way of calculating the amount harvested was used both for corn harvest and for the vintage; in both cases the work was commonly done by hired gangs on a contract basis (see e.g. Cato 136, and *RF*, pp. 347ff.), the contractor taking his agreed share in kind.

Monuments

Representations of the *corbis messoria* are often found, like the *modius* or *calathus* (q.v.), as an attribute of the corn-goddess Ceres (Overbeck, *Kunstmythologie*, Atlas, Demeter, pl. XVII, 6). They are also common on reliefs depicting farm operations:

(1) D–S s.v. 'corbis', I, 2, p. 1504, fig. 1942 illustrates part of a relief now in the Louvre. On the l., a wagon loaded with deep conical baskets full of grapes; to r., behind the oxen drawing the wagon, a grape-picker with a full basket fastened to his back by cords.

(2) Espérandieu, *Gaule*, IV, nos. 2852, 2853. Two fragments from a Gallo-Roman funeral monument now in the Museum of Sens, showing, among other equipment used in wine-making, four empty fruit baskets

(two stacked inside each other), and two similar baskets full of grapes (Pl. 4*c*).

Fruit-picking scenes also occur frequently on wall-paintings and mosaics. In the Seasons mosaic from St-Romain-en-Gal the baskets used in picking table grapes (*RF*, pl. 55) and apples (*RF*, pl. 64) are identical in design, being round, shallow, and without handles, with apparently rather less than half the capacity of a bushel basket. The apple-picker, who is half-way up the ladder for another picking, has handed a full basket to the second man, who is carrying it across his shoulders, supporting it with his right hand. The pergula mosaic from Cherchel (Pl. 3 *b*) shows a man with a much wider basket carrying table grapes on his shoulders. From a mural painting of the early fourth century in the house of Trebius Iustus on the Via Latina, Rome, comes a representation of a labourer carrying grapes (?) in a much larger square basket fitted with leather (?) loops for carrying.

Survival

(*a*) *Of the name.* It. corba, corbella, corbellino; Fr. corbeille.

(*b*) *Of the container.* Most of the traditional types still to be found in Italy can be matched with Roman originals. See Scheuermeier, *Bauernwerk*, I, *passim*. A very striking example is on p. 347, pl. 135, a basket without a handle carried on the neck, and resembling very closely the fruit-picking basket depicted on the St-Romain panel (above).

2. Qualus (-i, m.), also **qualum** (-i, n.), *basket, frail*; dimin. **quasillus** (-i, m.), a woman's *work-basket* (for wool, etc.), see also s.v. 'calathus'

No entry in *R-E*.

Not in Varro, *LL*.

(*a*) Isid. *Etym.* 20. 14. 13. '*Baskets*, frails and sieves for the wine-press, through which the must flows': *qualos corbes, colaque prelorum, per quae mustum fluit.*

(*b*) *Corp. Gloss.* s.v. 'qualus'. qualus σώρακος, κόφινος II 166. 15 (cf. margo), κόφινος II 354. 32; III 32. 13; 461. 68; 484. 9; κάλαθος II 337. 12 (qualis *codd. corr. a e*). ἠθμός (ἤθρος *cod.*), διυλιστήρ II 166. 14 (qualos *cod. corr. c*). cofinus, corbis II 591. 1. mand (*AS*) v 385. 44. qualum cofinum 383. 13. quali per quos vinum defluit v 556. 38. qualos corbes quibus uvae portantur v 237. 46. corbes colaque prelorum; per quos mustus fluit a colando v 238. 1 (Virg. *Georg.* II 242: cf. Serv.). coffinos v 326. 37. V. cophinus (squalum).

(*c*) *Corp. Gloss.* s.v. 'quasillus'. quasillus κάλαθος II 166. 45. quasillum κάλαθος III 198. 12. castillum κάλαθος III 21. 3. quaxillus dirivativum a qualo II 591. 2.

(*d*) Cato 11. 5 (vineyard inventory). 'Forty *planting-baskets* or forty picking-trays': *quala sataria vel alveos* XL.

Fig. 19. Qualus

PART TWO

(e)   Cato 23 (requirements for the grape-harvest). 'Let *baskets* be got ready': *quala* parentur.

(f)   Colum. 10. 81–3 (on garden work in the spring). 'Then let the kitchen-gardener glut the hungry earth with rich loam or asses' solid dung or that of cattle, carrying *baskets* bursting with the weight':

> rudere tum pingui, solido vel stercore aselli,
> armentive fimo saturet ieiunia terrae,
> ipse ferens olitor diruptos pondere *qualos*.

(g)   Virgil, *Georg.* 2. 242–3 (on preparations for the vintage). 'Take down from the grimy walls close-woven baskets and strainers for the wine-press':

> tu spissos vimine *qualos*
> colaque prelorum fumosis eripe tectis.

(h)   Paul, *Dig.* 33. 7. 8 (in the list of equipment – *instrumentum fundi*). 'Vintagers' baskets and hampers in which the grapes are collected': quali vindemiatorii exceptoriique in quibus uvae comportantur.

(j)   Pallad. 4. 10. 16 (on grafting the persimmon-tree). 'The grafted shoots must be completely protected above the graft by a *frail* or a small clay vessel': insiti surculi *qualo* desuper omnino muniendi sunt vel fictili vasculo.

(k)   Colum. 8. 3. 4 (an inferior type of nest for hens). 'What some people do when they forcibly drive pegs into the walls and hang *wicker baskets* on them': quod quidam faciunt, ut, palis in parietes vehementer actis, *vimineos qualos* superimponant.

(l)   Colum. 9. 15. 12 (how to strain honey from the comb). 'A *wickerwork basket*, or a bag rather loosely woven of fine withies shaped like an inverted cone of the type used for straining wine, is hung up in a dark place': *saligneus qualus*, vel tenui vimine rarius contextus saccus, inversae metae similis, qualis est quo vinum liquatur, obscuro loco suspenditur.

(m)   Cato 133 (how to layer fruit and other trees). 'To make them root while still attached to the tree, take a pot perforated at the bottom, or a *small basket*, pass a small branch through it, then fill the basket with earth, pack it in and leave it on the tree. When it is two years old, cut off the young branch below (the basket) and plant it, basket and all. By this method you will be able to get rooted plants of any variety of tree that you want': in arboribus radices uti capiant, calicem pertusum sumito tibi aut *quasillum*: per eum ramulum transerito; eum quasillum terra impleto calcatoque, in arbore relinquito. ubi bimum erit, ramum tenerum infra praecidito, cum quasillo serito. eo modo quod vis genus arborum facere poteris ut radices bene habeant.

The above recipe is repeated much less succinctly by Palladius (3. 10. 6), where the term used is *corbicula*.

(n)   Propertius 4. 7. 41 f. 'And if some gossiping slave has praised my beauty, she punishes her with heavier stints of wool in unfair *baskets*':

> et graviora rependit iniquis pensa *quasillis*
> garrula de facie si qua locuta mea est.

Note: qualus is often loosely used for *quasillus*, e.g. Hor. *Od.* 3. 12. 4f.: 'tibi *qualum* Cythereae puer . . . aufert'.

Design

As the passages cited show, *qualus*, like *corbis*, is a generic word for a container of rigid basketry, which, like the *corbis*, could be employed for various purposes. On the inevitably inconclusive evidence of the surviving references, it would appear that in the vineyard and orchard *qualus* was more common in the sense of a shallow picking-basket (Cato's reference (passage *d*) to the use of sowing-baskets for this purpose is valuable), and *corbis* in the sense of the larger basket for collection and transport to treading-vat or fruit-store. The *Digest* inventory, however (passage *h*), uses *qualus* for both sizes of basket employed in the vineyard, defining them functionally by means of the adjectives *vindemiatorius* and *exceptorius*, the latter term being otherwise unrecorded. Rich (s.v. 'qualus') is unsatisfactory; misinterpreting Columella at 9. 15. 12 (passage *l*), he insists that the *qualus* had a conical shape. As the *Digest* reference makes clear (passage *h*), *quali* were used, not for straining wine (the term for strainer is *colum*, q.v.), but as receptacles; a conical shape would be impossible. All that Columella is saying in passage *l* is that you may use *either* a basket of wickerwork *or* a *saccus* of the type used for straining wine. The baskets most frequently depicted on monuments with agricultural themes are fruit baskets. The common shape is that of a bucket, and the rim is usually strengthened by a thick band of plaited material (see above, s.v. 'corbis', p. 57). There is usually no handle. The tapered shape and the absence of handles make it easy to stack them in large quantities when not in use, as shown very clearly on a sculptured frieze from Sens (C. France) (see Pl. 4*c*; Espérandieu, *Gaul*, IV, 2852; Rostovtzeff, *SEHRE*[2], pl. XXIV 3). The shape, which is traditional, and still found in all fruit-growing countries (see e.g. D. Wright, *Baskets and Basketry*, London, 1959, p. 67, fig. 115, from St Ives, Hunts, England), will have served well enough for the honeycomb operation (passage *l*).

Materials

All the usual materials were used for plaiting.

Special types of qualus

The diminutive *quasillus* was chiefly used to denote the household basket of similar design for holding the wool and other materials used in spinning and weaving. Rich (*Dict. Ant.* s.v. 'quasillariae') stresses the importance of this department of an ancient household, and notes the frequency of representations of beaker-shaped baskets in this context (cf. also below, s.v. 'calathus', pp. 70 ff.).

Fig. 20. Canistrum

3. Canistrum (-i, n.; pl. **canistri** Pallad.), *open basket*, esp. for bread or fruit

(a) *R-E* III. 1482 [Mau].

(b) Varro, *LL* 5. 120. '"Trublia", "bowls", and "canistra", "*bread baskets*", though people think they are Latin, are in fact Greek words': tryblia et *canistra*, quod putant esse Latina, sunt Graeca.

(c) Isid. *Etym.* 20. 9. 8 (*De vasis repositoria*). 'The *bread-basket* is woven from split reeds, whence its name; others derive it from the Greek': *canistrum* fissis cannis contexitur; unde et nuncupatum: alii Graecum adserunt.

(d) *Corp. Gloss.* s.v. 'canistrum'. canistrum κανοῦν III 321. 45, etc. κανίσκιον III 321. 46. sporta V 174. 25. virgis palmarum texitur V 354. 21. fissis cannis contexitur, unde et nuncupatum. alii graecum asserunt V 174. 26. canistris canistellis V 636. 38. ferculis V 174. 24.

(e) Pallad. 12. 17. 1 (the Greek method of oil making). 'The *frails* (?) should be made of willow-reeds, since this type is said to improve the oil': salignis *canistros* fieri debere virgultis, quia genus hoc oleum dicitur adiuvare.

(f) Virg. *Aen.* 8. 180–1 (Evander feasts the Trojans). 'And they pile in *baskets* the gifts of Ceres prepared for eating, and serve the wine':

onerantque canistris

dona laboratae Cereris Bacchumque ministrant.

(g) Cic. *Att.* 6. 1. 13 (various commissions for Atticus). 'I've ordered the Rhosian ware. But look here! What are you going to get up to? You usually feed us on vegetarian fare served on fern-pattern dishes and in sumptuous *baskets*. What shall I expect you to serve up on earthenware?': Rhosica vasa mandavi. sed heus tu! quid cogitas? in filicatis lancibus et splendidissimis *canistris* holusculis nos soles pascere; quid te in vasis fictilibus appositurum putem?

(h) Ovid, *Met.* 8. 674–5 (Philemon and Baucis entertain the gods). 'Here are nuts, figs mixed with wrinkled dates, and plums, and sweet-smelling apples in open *baskets*':

hic nux, hic mixta est rugosis carica palmis

prunaque et in patulis redolentia mala *canistris*.

DISCUSSION

Canistrum provides an instructive example of one sort of difficulty in classifying containers. By far the most common meaning is 'open basket', used for handing round bread (passage *f*) or fruit (passage *h*), or even vegetarian fare (passage *g*), at table, that is, if Atticus' 'magnificent baskets' were really made of basketry. More probably they were made of silver shaped to resemble an ordinary bread-basket. Translators and commentators on the passage offer no help. The *canistrum* of passage *e*, which seems to be the sole instance of the term in the agronomists, cannot possibly have been of this type, since the context requires a flexible bag-type container which could be put under the press. It must surely be Palladius' term for the classical *fiscus* and its compounds (see below, s.v. 'fiscus' p. 88), that is, the rush bag in which the olives were squeezed. As we have already seen, *corbis* and *qualus* sometimes refer to the same type of flexible bag (see above, p. 54). Rich (*Dict. Ant.* s.v. 'canistrum') describes it as a large flat open basket, whence the adjectives *patulum* (passage *h*) and *latum* (Ovid, *Fasti* 2. 650). But these references only prove that *some canistra* were broad. He also uses the derivation from Gr. κανοῦν, a basket, to identify *canistrum* with the flat shallow baskets carried on their heads by Athenian girls (*kanephoroi*), in well-known acts of worship (Rich, *Dict. Ant.* s.v. 'canephora'). But the word may well have been derived directly from κάναστρον, so that the identification proposed, though attractive, remains unproved.

Extant representations

The shallow bread-basket can be readily identified, for it appears frequently in cult-scenes connected with the worship of Demeter/Ceres, as in Rich's illustration (*Dict. Ant.* s.v.), from a Pompeian wall-painting now in the National Museum at Naples; C. L. Ragghianti, *Pittori di Pompei*, Milano, 1963, Tavole fuori Testo, no. 30.

Survival

(*a*) *Of the word.* It. 'canestro' (m.), flower-basket, also 'canestra' and cpds. with the more general meaning of basket (e.g. 'canestraio' (m.), a basket-maker, and 'canestrata' (f.), a basketful; Eng. 'canister', us. of a cylindrical metal container, corrupted to 'can' (prop. U.S. colloq.).

(*b*) *Of the 'bread-basket'.* Scheuermeier, *Bauernwerk*, II, 320, Pl. 52, top r. (among a collection of kitchen equipment from Grottamare, Marche, Italy).

4. Cista (-ae, f.) (fr. Gr. κίστη), *basket*; dimin. **cistella** (-ae, f.), **cistula** (-ae, f.)

Not in Varro, *LL.*

(*a*)   *R-E* III 2. 2591–606 [Mau].

(*b*)   Isid. *Etym.* 20. 9. 8. 'The *small basket* ("cistella") takes its name from the ribs of reed or wood of which it is woven': *cistella a costis ex canna vel ligno quibus contexitur nominata.*

Fig. 21. Cista

(c) *Corp. Gloss.* s.v. 'cista'. cista κύτις II 357. 18. κίστη II 349. 58, etc. λάργαξ, κίστη, κοιτίς (κοιτης *cod.* κοίτη *e* κύτις). κόφινος II 101. 17. cest (*AS*). arcula II 573. 4. corbis IV 35. 2; 495. 23. cistas corbes grandes IV 318. 42; V 277. 1 (cista *cod.*); 351. 55 (*item*). *ubi lectum sit* V 639. 57 (= Non. 91. 22).

(d) *Corp. Gloss.* s.v. 'cistella'. cistella capsella V 565. 30. a costis ex canna, etc. V 565. 36 (cf. Isid. xx 9. 8). cistellam γλωσσόκομον II 101. 18. Cf. Fulgent. p. 50 (*Comm. Ien. 6. 2*).

(e) *Corp. Gloss.* s.v. 'cistula'. cistula sporta V 349. 20.

(f) Colum. 12. 56. 2 (recipe for pickling turnips). 'After that arrange the turnips in a *square wickerwork basket*, which should be of open yet firm weave, and made of thick withies. Then place on top of them a board so fitted that it can, if need be, be pressed down inside the basket right to the bottom': et postea in *quadratam cistam vimineam*, quae neque spisse, solide tamen et crassis viminibus contexta sit, rapa componito: deinde sic aptatam tabulam superponito, ut usque ad fundum, si res exigat, intra cistam deprimi possit.

(g) Pliny, *HN* 15. 60 (on preserving apples). 'M. Varro says that all other fruit of the apple sort should also be wrapped up individually in fig-leaves ... and stored in *wicker baskets* or else smeared over with potters' earth': (M. Varro iubet) cetera mala et foliis ficulnis ... singula convolvi *cistisque vitilibus* condi vel creta figulinarum inlini.

(h) *Tabula Hebana* 18 (on voting procedure). 'He (viz. the returning-officer) is to order fifteen large withy *baskets* to be set in front of his dais as receptacles for the voting tablets': *cistas* XV vimineas grandes poni iubeat ante tribunal suum in quas tabel[lae suffra]giorum demittantur.

DISCUSSION

The fact that this word is derived directly from Gr. κίστη has led to some misunderstanding. Mau (passage *a*) points out that whereas κίστη can mean 'a box' (Ger. 'Kasten', Eng. 'chest', 'kist'), the meaning in Latin is always that of a basket. Mau has little else to say that is relevant to our subject, the remainder of a lengthy discussion being taken up with funerary *cistae* and the *cista mystica*. The wide range of meanings attached to this term includes the official voting-baskets (passage *h*) into which the voters at elections cast their voting-tablets, and the *cista mystica*, the special container in which the sacred utensils connected with the cults of Bacchus and Ceres were carried in procession. The word is often rendered into English by its derivative 'chest', which suggests an object made out of wood. In fact, all containers bearing this name were made of woven basketry (passages *f*, *g*, *h*). Columella's use of the adjective *quadratus* (*f*) indicates that a square shape was unusual. Several of the containers to which the term was applied were in fact cylindrical (e.g. *cista* = voting-basket, and *cista* = *capsa*, a case for holding books – see Juv. *Sat.* 3. 206, etc.), and all were almost certainly closely related in design. The diminutives *cistella* and *cistula* are of frequent occurrence in colloquial Latin, generally with true diminutive force.

Extant representations

Rich's illustration (s.v. 'cista 1') is described as 'copied from a Roman bas-relief', but no provenance is given. Its nearest modern relative is the cylindrical laundry basket. *Cista* = *cistella*, the voting-basket, is best known from a silver denarius issued by L. Cassius Longinus (52–50 B.C.), perhaps to commemorate the passing of the *Lex Cassia Tabellaria* by L. Cassius Ravilla in 137 B.C. This law introduced the secret ballot at elections (Sydenham, *CRR* no. 935, pl. 26). The *cista mystica* is also well known from coins and bas-reliefs (e.g. as shown on the 'cistophoric tetradrachm'); for a fine example issued to commemorate the marriage of Antony and Octavia, and dated 39 B.C., see Sydenham, *CRR* no. 1197, pl. 29.

Extant specimens

For more elaborate versions in bronze see the *cistae* found at Praeneste and Labicum (Rich, *Dict. Ant.* s.v. 'cista 5').

Survival

(a) *Of the name.* Sc. 'kist', Eng. 'chest', etc., It. 'cista'.

(b) *Of the container.* Scheuermeier, *Bauernwerk*, II, 411, pl. 335, large square-sided basket, woven from chestnut bark, with the name 'cista da lessia'.

5. Cumera (-ae, f.), also **cumerum** (-i, n.) (Varro, *LL*), (i) *large basket*; (ii) *smaller container*; (iii) *box, chest*

(a) *R-E* IV 2. 754 [Olck].

(b) Varro, *LL* 7. 34. 'So at a wedding he is called a "camillus" who carries the box': itaque dicitur nuptiis camillus qui *cumerum* fert.

(c) Paul. Fest. s.v. 'cumerum', p. 43 L; p. 50 M. cumerum vas nuptiale a similitudine cumerarum quae fiunt palmeae vel sparteae ad usum popularem, sic appellatum. Cf. *ibid.* p. 63 (also known as 'camillum').

(d) Porph. ad Hor. *Epist.* 1. 7. 30. cumera vasi frumentarii genus factum ex vimine admodum obductum.

(e) *Corp. Gloss.* s.v. 'cumera'. cumera vas frumentarium v 283. 20. cumeras (cumerus? cf. Festus Pauli p. 50. 7) vas f⟨r⟩umentarium v 627. 49.

(*f*) Hor. *Sat.* 1. 1. 53 (the folly of avarice). 'Why do you praise your granaries more than our *corn-bins*?': cur tua plus laudes *cumeris* granaria nostris? Note Schol. *ad loc.* cumeram dicimus vas ingens vimineum in quo frumenta conduntur ... sive cumerae dicuntur vasa fictilia similia doliis, ubi frumentum suum reponebant agricolae.

(*g*) Hor. *Epist.* 1. 7. 29 f. (fable of the vixen in the corn-bin). 'Once upon a time a thin little vixen had squeezed through a narrow crack into a *corn-bin* (?) and after a feed she tried to get out again with her body distended, but all in vain':

> forte per angustam tenuis vulpecula rimam
> repserat in *cumeram* frumenti, pastaque rursus
> ire foras pleno tendebat corpore frustra.

DISCUSSION

Olck (*R-E* s.v. 'cumera') distinguishes four different items to which this term is applied: (1) A large wicker container for the storage of grain for domestic use, woven, according to Festus (passage *c*) from strips of palm or esparto grass. These ordinary domestic storage bins were evidently also made of earthenware (see the scholiast's comment on passage *f*), and this latter must have been the type envisaged in the fable of the vixen (passage *g*). Even with her body distended the animal would surely have been able to gnaw her way out of a basket! (2) A small container (Olck gives no references for this type). (3) A box or chest (a generic term, like *cista*). (4) A small box containing the ritual salted meal (*mola salsa*) used in connection with the ancient marriage ceremony known as *confarreatio*, and carried by the *camillus* (passage *b*) (Olck says 'by priests'). It was so called, says Festus (*c*) from its resemblance to the corn-bin.

Extant representations

D–S s.v. 'camilli', 1. 2, 859, fig. 1053 show a *camillus* holding an oblong box for incense. Although a careful distinction is drawn between this incense-holder and the box for the salted meal (no. 4) no representation of the type is given either s.v. 'confarreatio' or s.v. 'matrimonium'.

Fig. 22. Scirpea

6. Scirpea (-ae, f.), *hamper*; dim. **scirpiculus** (-i, m.), *small basket*, esp. *flower-basket*

These are the better forms, from *scirpus*, a reed. Also found are the forms **sirpea, sirpicula.**

No entry in *R-E*. Not in Isidore.

(*a*) Varro, *LL* 5. 139. 'The *wicker-hamper* which "sirpatur" ("is plaited") of osiers, that is, woven by binding them together, in which manure or something else is conveyed': *sirpea, quae virgis sirpatur, id est colligando implicatur, in qua stercus aliudve quid vehitur.*

(b) *Corp. Gloss.* s.v. 'scirpea'. *Eorisc* (AS) v 392. 38, lebrae (*vel* Ierb *AS*) de qua mata (!). Conficitur v 389. 42. *Scirpa* qui(a) antiqui stori⟨i⟩s utebantur, *quae de scirpo fiunt* v 579. 30.

(c) Cato 10. 3. '3 manure *hampers*': *sirpeas* stercerarias III. *Ibid.* 11. 4. '1 manure *hamper*': *sirpiam* stercerariam I.

(d) Varro, *RR* 1. 23. 5. 'In yet another place thickets should be planted so that you may have osiers for making woven articles such as *wicker wagon-bodies*, winnowing-baskets and hurdles': *et alio loco virgulta serenda, ut habeas vimina, unde viendo quid facias, ut sirpeas, vallus, crates.*

(e) Ovid, *Fast.* 6. 680. 'On the wagon there was a broad *hamper*': *in plaustro scirpea lata fuit.*

(f) Varro, *RR* 2. 2. 9 (on the public cattle-trails). 'I had flocks that wintered in Apulia, and spent the summer in the Reatine mountains, these two widely separated ranges being lined by public cattle-trails, like a pair of "*buckets*" by their cross-piece': *mihi greges in Apulia hibernabant, qui in Reatinis montibus aestivabant, cum inter haec bina loca, ut iugum continet sirpiculos, sic calles publicae distantes pastiones.*

(g) Colum. 10. 304–5 (gathering flowers in the garden). 'With dark-red hyacinths pile high your *basket* woven from gray willow-twigs':

> cano iam vimine textum
> *sirpiculum* ferrugineis cumulate hyacinthis.

(h) Plautus, *Capt.* 815 'With fish-*baskets*': *sirpiculis piscariis.*

DISCUSSION

Scirpea. The literary references indicate that this was a large hamper made of plaited bulrushes (*scirpus*). Most of the passages refer to a large container for manure (passages *a* and *c*), which was mounted on the platform of a wagon (passage *e*). The *plaustrum* (see below s.v., pp. 79 ff.) was only a strong wooden platform mounted on a pair of solid wheels, on which a variety of containers, e.g. barrels (*cupae*) or large skins for wine (*cullei*), as well as *scirpeae*, could be mounted. Similar removable units are nowadays provided for the small farmer, enabling him to make maximum use of one or two trucks, and reducing his capital outlay.

Sirpiculus. The diminutive form denoted a small container made of soft plaited work, and used for a variety of purposes, as the three passages (*f, g, h*) indicate. Neck-loading by means of a 'yoke' (*iugum*), resembling that worn on the farm by milkers up to very recent times, will have been very common, since Varro's expression (passage *f*) is proverbial, and aptly suits the topography. The 'buckets' were small panniers, similar to the soft-woven types still used in many parts of southern Europe for the

PART TWO

transport of goods by pack-mule. Columella's *sirpiculus* (passage *g*) is one of three different terms used by him for flower-basket in his book on gardening; the others are *canistrum* (*v.* 277), and *calathus* (*v.* 300); obviously the name cannot be identified with any specific type (see Rich, *Dict. Ant.* s.v. 'sirpicula').

Extant representations

(*a*) *Of the* scirpea. I have not been able to locate any.

(*b*) *Of the* sirpiculus. The 'neck-yoke pannier' is well illustrated on a fifth-century Boeotian *cantharos*, depicting a man with a yoke across his shoulders, from which hang two open-weave containers filled with pottery (*CVA* III 5, Belgique, 114) now in the Cinquantennaire, Brussels; see A. D. Ure in *JHS* 61 (1951), 194.

Survival

(*a*) *Of the term.* None. The Eng. 'skip' is from old Norse 'skeppe'.

(*b*) *Of the object.* Several examples of the *scirpea* have been noted from Italy (Scheuermeier, *Bauernwerk* II, 368). The manure hamper mounted on an ox-drawn cart from Borno, Lombardy, bears a striking resemblance to the bas-relief reproduced by Rich (see Fig. 22).

7. Sporta (-ae, f.), *basket, cage, sieve*; dimin. **sportella** (-ae, f.), **sportula** (-ae, f.)

Not in Varro, *LL*.

(*a*) *R-E* s.v. σπυρίς III A. 2. 1891–2 [Hug].

(*b*) Isid. 20. 9. 10 (*De vasis repositoriis*). 'The *broom-basket*, so-called either because it is usually made from broom, or because it is used for carrying things out': *sporta vel quod ab sparto fieri solet, vel quod exportet aliquid*.

(*c*) *Corp. Gloss.* s.v. 'sporta'. sporta σπυρίς II 187. 33; 436. 16, etc. aut ab spartu quasi spartea[s] aut ⟨ab⟩ a⟨s⟩portando v 647. 68.

(*d*) Cato 11. '3 strainers for wine-lees': *sportae faecariae III*.

(*e*) Colum. 8. 7. 1 (on fattening hens). 'For this purpose you need a place which is very warm and has very little light, where the birds may be suspended, each shut up in a separate narrow coop or a *plaited cage*, but confined in so tight a space that they have no room to turn round': *locus ad hanc rem desideratur maxime calidus, et minimi luminis, in quo singulae caveis angustioribus vel sportis inclusae pendeant aves, sed ita coarctatae, ne versari possint*.

(*f*) Colum. 12. 6. 1 (on making hard brine). 'Then place in the water a *basket made of rushes or broom*, which must be filled with white salt': *tum indito sportam iunceam vel sparteam, quae replenda est sale candido*.

68

(g) Pliny, *HN* 18. 77 (on making starch). 'When it is quite soft but before it turns sour, it is strained through a linen cloth or a *sieve* made of broom': emollitum, prius quam acescat, linteo aut *sportis* saccatum.

(h) Martial 10. 37. 17–18 (in praise of life in Spain). 'While I speak, look, your angler comes home with empty *creel*, but the hunter is at hand, exulting in the badger he has trapped':

> dum loquor, ecce redit *sporta* piscator inani,
> venator capta maele superbus adest.

(j) Ulp. *Dig.* 33. 9. 3. 11 (on equipment regarded as essential). 'Stores of grain or pulse, kept perhaps in small chests, *baskets* or any other similar items which are kept for the purpose of plenishing the provision store or larder will not be included, but only those things are included without which the larder cannot be properly kept': nec frumenti nec leguminum thecae (arculae forte vel *sportae*) vel si qua alia sunt, quae horrei penuarii vel cellae penuariae instruendae gratia habentur, non continebuntur, sed ea sola continentur, sine quibus penus haberi non recte potest.

DISCUSSION

Material

The term is evidently derived from *spartum* (1) = our 'Spanish broom' (see above, Part I, pp. 29f.). The type of basket denoted by the term *sporta* was usually made either from broom or rush (passage *f*); cf. Gr. σπυρίς, 'woven basket'.

Design

The references suggest that the term *sporta* was applied to two distinct types of object: (1) A plaited *basket* of broom or rushes used for various purposes, and especially as a fishing-creel (passage *h*), the shape of which is well known from the monuments. (2) A strainer made from broom or rushes (passages *d, g*). Columella's use of the adjectives *iuncea* and *spartea* shows that *sportae*, like many other basketry items, were made from a variety of plaiting material, according to the purpose required, or for economic reasons (see above, p. 52). The selection of materials for strainers will presumably have depended on the required percolating capacity (see further s.v. 'fiscus', 'colum'). Rich (*Dict. Ant.* s.v. 'sporta') recognizes only the first of the two meanings. The entry in D–S (IV 2, 1443–5) is inadequate, and offers no illustrations.

The *Digest* reference (passage *j*), where *sporta* is coupled with *arcula* as an example of the sort of container to be found in the provision-store (*penus*) does not appear to fit either of the categories already discussed. Dry stores such as meal, beans or lentils were normally kept in bins (*lacus, lacusculi*), as Columella tells us in his account of farm buildings (1. 6. 9f.).

Arcula (a small chest or box, a casket) presumably means a small bin (of wood?) in which the daily supplies of dry produce were kept. *Sporta* must here imply a 'mealsack' made of finely woven material, providing another example of a shift of meaning taking place with the passage of time (see e.g. Palladius' use of *canistrum* for a flexible container, above, pp. 62 f.).

Extant representations

Rich (*Dict. Ant.* s.v.) shows a fishing-creel from a well-known statue of a young fisherman in the National Museum, Naples. Columella's hen-coop (passage *e*) will have been more spherical than this, and with a narrower opening.

Extant specimens

Hard baskets of the type have survived from Roman Egypt (Pl. 4 *a*). See Sir F. Petrie, *Objects of Daily Use*, London, 1927, pl. XLII, nos. 172–4.

Survival of the term

It. 'sporta' a shopping basket.

The diminutives

Sportella and *sportula*, diminutives of *sporta*, are not used by any of the agricultural writers. *Sportella* is quite common meaning a small basket in which cakes, fruit, etc. were passed round at the table, while *sportula*, used occasionally as = *sporta* (i), e.g. by Plautus (*Stichus* 289), where it means a fishing creel, normally refers to the basket of provisions handed out by opulent Romans to their retainers, and later to either a money-dole or to any kind of gift.

Fig. 23. Calathus

8. Calathus (-i, m.) (fr. Gr. κάλαθος), also **calathum** (-i, n.), *hand-basket*

No entry in *R-E*.

Not in Varro, *LL*.

(*a*) Isid. *Etym.* 19. 29. 3. 'A *hand-basket* is a light container made of flax, canes or rushes, for carrying a daily ration or for picking flowers. The Greek term for wood is κᾶλα, from which is derived the word "calathus". The Latin word for "calathus" is "quasillum"': *calathum leve gestamen ex lino vel cana aut ex iunco factum, in qua vel pensa ponuntur vel leguntur flores.* κᾶλα *enim Graece lignum est, a quo derivatum est* calathum. *nam Latine quasillum dicitur.*

(*b*) *Corp. Gloss.* s.v. 'calathus'. κάλαθος III 263. 25. . . . τάλαρος II 451. 20; 263. 24. cophinus vel canistrus (!) v 444. 22. canistrum vel qua[s]illum v 493. 36

70

(cf. Festus Pauli, p. 47. 6; Serv. in *Ecl.* II 45; Isid. XIX 29. 3). poculi genus V 173. 42. calatum canistrum est id est cartallum IV 31. 7, etc. caladi similitudo liliorum V 275. 30. calati cyathi; scyphi V 173. 40. calthis canistris IV 213. 28.

(c) Fest. s.v. 'calathus'. *calathos* Graeci, nos dicimus quasillos.

(d) Pliny, *HN* 21. 23 (of the lily). 'Narrow at the base, it swells out gradually like a *hand-basket*': ab angustiis in latitudinem sese laxantis effigie *calathi*.

(e) Vitruv. *De Arch.* 4. 1. 9 (on the invention of the Corinthian capital). 'The nurse collected the goblets, arranged them in a *hand-basket*, carried it to the monument, and set it on the top . . . the *hand-basket*, as it happened, was set on the root of an acanthus': nutrix pocula collecta et composita in *calatho* pertulit ad monumentum et in summo conlocavit . . . is *calathus* fortuito super acanthi radicem fuerat conlocatus.

(f) Virg. *Aen.* 7. 805–7 (the warrior-maid Camilla). 'The warrior-maid, no woman with hands accustomed to the distaff and *work-baskets* of Minerva, but a girl hardened to bear the brunt of battle, her speed outstripping the winds':

> bellatrix, non illa colo *calathisque* Minervae
> femineas adsueta manus, sed proelia virgo
> dura pati, cursuque pedum praevertere ventos.

(g) Juv. *Sat.* 2. 54–5 (on effeminate men). 'You men teaze out the wool, and bring back your finished work in full *baskets*':

> vos lanam trahitis *calathisque* peracta refertis
> vellera.

(h) Colum. 7. 8. 3 (on cheese-making), cf. 10. 397. '(After the milk has thickened under heat) it should be transferred immediately to bags or *baskets* or moulds; for it is of the utmost importance that the whey should drain away as quickly as possible and become separated from the solids': et confestim cum concrevit liquor in fiscellas aut in *calathos* vel formas transferendus est. nam maxime refert primo quoque tempore serum percolari et a concreta materia separari.

(j) Virg. *Georg.* 3. 400–4 (on making goat's milk cheese). 'What they have milked at daybreak and in the daytime they press at night; what they milk in the dark and as the sun goes down the goatherd carries off in *baskets* at daybreak, and goes to town; or they soak it in a little brine and put it by for winter':

> quod surgente die mulsere horisque diurnis,
> nocte premunt; quod iam tenebris et sole cadente,
> sub lucem exportans *calathis* adit oppida pastor;
> aut parco sale contingunt hiemique reponunt.

DISCUSSION

The word is of frequent occurrence in all periods, and the multiple identifications with *canistrum*, *cophinus* etc. presented by the Glossaries might suggest that the main problem here, as with *cophinus* (q.v.), is to decide what it was not. But Pliny's inverted comparison of nature's work with that of the potter (passage *d*), coupled with Vitruvius' story of the origin of the Corinthian capital, in which the inverted 'bell' represents the discarded basket (passage *e*), makes identification certain. Correspondence with numerous representations in art of vessels of this shape used as work-baskets for wool clinches the meaning. The shape also fits the requirements of a cheese-making basket (passages *h* and *j*). The uses noted by Isidore (passage *a*) require the addition of a handle. He also mentions *calathus* in a list of drinking-cups (20. 5. 5).

Calathus and *quasillus*

The identification given by Festus (passage *c*) is amply supported by other evidence. *Calathus* is one of several instances where the native Latin word and the Greek loan-word are both in common use. In addition, each is metrically acceptable in hexameter verse.

The calathus as symbol. Both in art and literature, the *calathus* symbolizes the ancient ideal of the home-loving housewife, occupied with her distaff. Virgil (passage *f*) calls it 'Minerva's basket', as he paints the contrasted portrait of the warrior-maid Camilla, the very antithesis of the woman who minds her loom.

Extant representations

(1) *As work-basket.* Rich (*Dict. Ant.* s.v.) shows an illustration of the work-basket, with wool and other materials, from a Pompeian wall-painting representing the work-basket of Leda. Penelope is of course constantly represented with the *calathus* (cf. Blümner, *Technologie*, I, p. 118) and figs. 37–41; D–S I 2, 812ff. (with numerous references).

(2) *As drinking-cup.* Rich (*ibid.*) refers to one of the miniatures in the Vatican Virgil (*Vat. lat.* 3225), illustrating *Ecl.* 5. 71: 'vina novum fundam calathis Ariusia nectar', in which a vessel of the inverted bell type appears in the hands of a cupbearer.

(3) *In the vineyard.* E. Saglio (D–S, *art. cit.*) says, without citing evidence, that the word was also used of a metal container of identical design, e.g. as carried by a vintager walking alongside a wine-press in a Pompeian painting (fig. 1001).

(4) *As attribute or emblem.* The calathus appears frequently on the heads of certain divinities, notably Demeter/Ceres; see e.g. Farnell, *CGS*, III, pl. 3, a votive terra-cotta from Eleusis showing her wearing the high *calathus* which closely resembles that worn by a Greek Orthodox priest; *ibid.* pl. 18, a *pelike* from Kertch in the Crimea, now in the Hermitage, Leningrad, showing the more usual shallow type. Yet another symbolic

type is illustrated by D–S (*art. cit.*, fig. 1002), a sestertius of Trajan, showing a huge *calathus* filled with fruit and mounted on a four-horse chariot (G. Zoëga, *Numi Aegyptii*, Roma, 1787, XIV, no. 84: Z. suggests a possible connection with an Isiac festival).

9. Cophinus (-i, m.) (fr. Gr. κόφινος), (i) *basket*, for carrying earth, manure, etc. (ii) *hamper*, '*skip*'

Not in Varro, *LL*.

Fig. 24. Cophinus

(*a*)   *R-E* s.v. 'cophinus' IV 1. 1211–13 (Olck).

(*b*)   Isid. *Etym.* 20. 9. 9 (*De vasis repositoriis*). 'The "*skip*" is a container made of rods, suitable for clearing away manure and carrying earth': *cophinus est vas ex virgulis, aptum mundare stercora et terram portare.*

(*c*)   *Corp. Gloss.* s.v. 'cophinus'. cophinus (*vel* cof-) κόφινος III 357. 54. corbis V 653. 50 (= Iuvenal. III 14). (s)qualum IV 319. 47. cophinos corbes (corbe *cod.*) V 495. 43.
          Note: the equation κόφινος = corbis is also found in the Greek Glossary.

(*d*)   Colum. 11. 3. 51 (on forcing cucumbers). 'Anyone who wants an unusually early crop should, as soon as mid-winter is past, provide well-manured earth in *baskets*, and give it a moderate quantity of water; then when the seeds have come up, he should set the baskets in the open air on warm and sunny days': *sed qui praematurum fructum cucumeris habere volet, confecta bruma stercoratam terram inditam* cophinis *offerat, modicumque praebeat humorem. deinde cum enata semina fuerint, tepidis diebus et insolatis . . . sub divo ponat.*

(*e*)   Juv. *Sat.* 3. 14f. (on Jews), cf. *ibid.* 6. 542f. 'Jews, whose furniture consists of a *basket* and some straw': Iudaeis quorum cophinus *faenumque supellex.*

(*f*)   Vegetius, *Mil.* 2. 25 (on the soldier's kit). '*Baskets* for carrying earth': cophinos, quibus portetur terra.

DISCUSSION

Shape

The shape of an earth-carrying basket (passages *b*, *f*) is determined by the requirements. The baskets used by Trajan's soldiers for digging ditches and constructing earthworks (see below) are of the usual conical shape, with flat bases, like fruit-picking baskets.

Size

Forc. (on passage *e*) defines *cophinus* as a 'large wicker basket or hamper, used in agriculture and gardening, for carrying earth, manure, fodder, etc.; in it the Jews kept their food for the sabbath, wrapping it in the straw to keep it warm.' D–S (I. 2, 1497, s.v. 'cophinus' κόφινος) are equally dogmatic: 'a basket of circular shape, light, large and deep. For carrying earth, dung, sand, etc.' These authorities take no account of the limits imposed on size where manual operations are involved, and the term 'hamper' has a misleading connotation of size. For moving earth around the garden (passage *d*) a container of the size of our 'half-bushel' basket would be about right. We have monumental evidence on this. On Trajan's Column there are numerous scenes of ditch-digging, involving the lifting and passing upwards of earth from below to form the breastwork, and the size of basket depicted may be roughly gauged from the size of the soldiers on the job (see below, 'Extant representations'). The nub of the matter was admirably put by Richmond (*PBSR* XIII (1935), 18f.): 'The size of the baskets is not large, being nicely calculated for convenience of working, even in heavy soil or rock, while the baskets themselves could be easily made or inexpensively renewed.' Whatever range of meaning is to be attached to the Greek term κόφινος (see Part III, Introduction, p. 107), it is clear that the Latin derivative has a restricted use, and is not a generic term. Columella's basket for forcing cucumbers implies a quite different shape and larger dimensions. Rich (*Dict. Ant.* s.v.) ignores passages *b* and *f*, and illustrates a very inadequate discussion of the remainder with a cut from an engraved gem in the form of a large, shallow ornamental bath used for growing flowers. Baskets of somewhat similar shape appear on a bas-relief depicting two porters with heavy loads on their backs, with much forward distortion of the body (Pl. 5*c*). The contents, probably soft goods for sale, are secured by a lattice-work of cords. There is of course no evidence that these very distinctive hampers were referred to as *cophini*.

Extant representations

The two illustrations given by D–S are an object-lesson in the arbitrary use of pictorial evidence. Fig. 1924, from a Greek vase, shows peasants bringing produce to market. One of the group is carrying a pair of deep, pear-shaped basketry containers of the pannier type on a pole balanced across his shoulders (see above, s.v. sirpiculus, p. 67). Fig. 1925 presents a rigid basket with a loop for handle, the material in it being, as D–S admit, unidentifiable. In dealing with containers, the monumental evidence must be correlated wherever possible with that from literary sources. In the present case, the latter are decisive. Digging and earth-moving operations on Trajan's Column: Cichorius, *Traianssäule*, Taf. XIX–XX. Porters' hampers: Rome, Palazzo Massimi; tomb of L. Calpurnius (3rd cent. A.D.).

Survival

(*a*) *Of the name.* It. 'cofano' (m.), Eng. 'coffin'. Hilgers s.v. 'cophinus' notes that the Mod. Gr. 'κοφίνιον' and the It. 'cofano' are of similar shape, deeper than they are wide, with flat bases. The word appears frequently in the New Testament, e.g. after the feeding of the five thousand, the remains are gathered up in twelve κόφινοι (Mt. 14. 20, etc.).

(*b*) *Of the basket.* Scheuermeier, *Bauernwerk*, II, 452, pl. 459, showing a man with a hamper for the transport of grain from Corigliano, Apulia. Local name, 'cofina'.

10. Vannus (-i, m.) (etym. dub., perh. conn. with *ventus*, wind, or Gr. αἴνω), *winnowing-basket*

See J. E. Harrison in *JHS* 23 (1903), 292–304; 24 (1904), 241–54; *BSA* 90 (1903–4), 144–7.

Fig. 25. Vannus

11. Vallus (-i, m.), dimin. of *vannus*, (i) = *palus*, stake; (ii) '*heading*' *machine* for harvesting grain (*AIRW*, pp. 157ff.)

(*a*)   *R-E* XIII 538–41 [Kroll]; largely on Gr. λίκνον (*vannus*).

(*b*)   *R-E* VI A. 1. 291–2 [Schleiermacher] (*vallus*).

(*c*)   Varro, *LL* 5. 138. 'The *winnowing-scoop* takes its name from flying, since, when they agitate it, the light material flies away from it': *vallum* a volatu, quod cum id iactant, volant inde levia.

(*d*)   *Corp. Gloss.* s.v. 'vannus'. (i) *vannus* βραστήρ ἤτοι λίκνον II 259. 58. βραστήρ III 263. 5. λίκνον II 359. 11; 361. 3 (*v. vannulus*). tablis (τάβλιν? *neutrum graecum exspectatur*: λίκνον?) II 517. 7. genus vasis II 596. 22. argumentum (machinamentum?) de vimine factum in modum scuti, necessarium tempore messis; vas purgatorium est et mundandi farris instrumentum. legitur et vallus. (ii) *vallus* palus acutus IV 294. 32; 399. 37. palus IV 188. 33; 577. 9. *vallos* palos V 334. 38; 400. 19 (cf. Serv. in Georg. I. 264) . . . *v.* vannus.

(*e*)   Varro, *RR* I. 23. 5. 'In yet another place thickets should be planted so that you may have osiers for making woven articles such as wicker wagon-bodies, *winnowing baskets*, and hurdles': et alio loco virgulta serenda ut habeas vimina, unde viendo quid facias, ut sirpeas, *vallos*, crates.

(*f*)   *Ibid.* I. 52. 2. 'After threshing the grain should be tossed from the ground when the wind is blowing gently with *winnowing-scoops* or shovels': iis tritis oportet e terra subiectari *vallis* aut ventilabris, cum ventus spirat lenis.

(*g*)   Colum. 2. 20. 4. 'It is better that the heads should be beaten with flails and winnowed with *winnowing-baskets*': ipsae autem spicae melius fustibus cuduntur *vannis*que expurgantur (so again at 2. 20. 5).

(*h*)   Serv. ad *Georg.* I. 166. MYSTICA VANNVS IACCHI id est cribrum areale.

DISCUSSION

The etymology of *vannus* is uncertain. There is also much uncertainty about the gender of its diminutive *vallus*; both masc. and neut. are attested, while E–M give only fem. The Glossary entry (passage *d*) is for once on the target, while Servius most certainly is not! The *vannus* is a flat basket of distinctive design, deep at the back, which is closed, and becoming shallower, towards the front, which is open. It is fitted with two handles, each attached to one of the sides. The operator separates the grain from the lighter chaff by shaking the contents with a slight forward and upward motion. By this movement 'the chaff and dirt work their way to the upper end of the basket and are discarded and the heavy grains collect at the lower end' (Hopfen, *FIATR*, pp. 127–8, fig. 93). It should be noticed that the typical action of rubbing the grains together also cleans the sample at the same time; the method is efficient but very slow (45 kg per hour as compared with 1,200 kg per hour achieved with a hand-driven winnowing-mill) (see Hopfen, p. 128).

Extant representations

The *vannus* is frequently shown on bas-reliefs: e.g.:

(1) Espérandieu, *Gaule*, VII, no. 5833; Rostovtzeff, *SEHRE*², pl. XXIV. 2, from the funeral monument of a rich merchant of Mainz, W. Germany, now in the R–G Zentralmuseum there (see Pl. 5*a*). Here one man is sifting grain in the basket, while another removes the winnowed grain for storage.

(2) Espérandieu, *Gaule*, VI, no. 5075; provenance unknown. A basket of unusual shape, being almost square, held by a standing woman. Rich's illustration (*Dict. Ant.* s.v. 'vannus'), said to have been taken from a marble bas-relief, is inaccurate, having no difference in depth between the two ends, and his account of the process resembles more that of tossing a pancake than of shuffling the material *inside* the basket!

Survival

(*a*) *Of the implement.* The fan is still in use in the less advanced countries of eastern Europe and in most parts of the Middle East.

(*b*) *Of the name.* Fr. 'vannette', a winnowing basket (for oats).

Vallus

There is no doubt that the diminutive form *vallus* as used in passages *e* and *f* is a winnowing scoop or shovel, used in an entirely different method of separating the chaff, that of throwing the material into the air against a gentle breeze (hence the alternative name *ventilabrum* = 'ventilating device', a country colloquialism). They may well have differed only in the material of which they were made, the *ventilabrum* being made of wood, the *vallus* of basketry (see *AIRW*, pp. 32f.).

Note on movable and removable framing

Providing protection for growing plants against extremes of heat and cold is a permanent problem for the grower. Under Mediterranean conditions, late spring and summer heat presented more difficulties than frost or snow. Nursery beds, especially for raising plants and trees with small seeds, were protected by removable timber frames mounted on forked sticks (*furcae*) and covered with interlaced reeds or fronds. The height above the seed-bed could be varied to suit particular conditions, as Pliny explains (passage *h* below) when commenting on Cato's directions for making this sort of frame (passage *e*). The term used for the frames was *crates*, which, in the sense of a wickerwork hurdle, was in common use as a movable fencing for stock (*crates pastorales*), for drying fruit in the sun (below, s.v. 'crates', passages *e–g*), and so on.

12. Crates (-ium, f.) (us. pl. M-L 2304) (etym. dub., perh. for *kr̥tya, basketry), (i) gen. *wickerwork*; (ii) sp. *hurdle*; dimin. **craticula** (-ae, f.), (i) *gridiron*; (ii) *wicker strainer*

Fig. 26. Crates stercorariae

Not in Isid. (exc. 19. 10. 7 – non-agricultural).

(*a*) *R-E* IV 2. 1682–5 [Olck].

(*b*) Varro, *LL* 7. 55. '"Congerro" ("chum") from "gerra", "wickerwork"; this is a Greek word, the Latin equivalent of which is *"cratis"*': congerro a gerra: hoc Graecum est in Latina *cratis*.

(*c*) *Corp. Gloss.* s.v. 'crates'. crates γέρρον, εἶδος ἀσπίδος περσικῆς II 262. 60 πλέγματα ἐκ ῥάβδων II 117. 30 . . . gaerdes (cirographa gloss. Werth.) *AS* cf. Gallée 336; v. suppl. cf. cautio. Cf. Isid. XIX. 10. 7.

(*d*) Cato 10 and 11 (cf. Varro, *RR* 1. 22. 3, quoting Cato). '4 manure *hurdles*': *crates* stercerariae IV.

(*e*) *Ibid.* 48. 2 (on shading a cypress-nursery). 'Level the ground with a board or with the foot, and place forked props around it. Lay poles on them, and place on the poles vine-canes or *fig-drying frames*, to keep off cold and sun': eam terram tabula aut pedibus complanato, furcas circum offigito, eo porticam intendito, eo sarmenta aut *crates ficarias* imponito, quae frigus defendant et solem.

77

(*f*) Varro, *RR* 1. 23. 5 (distribution of planting areas). 'In yet another place thickets should be planted so that you may have osiers for making woven articles such as wicker wagon-bodies, winnowing baskets and *hurdles*': et alio loco virgulta serenda, ut habeas vimina, unde viendo quid facias, ut sirpeas, vallus, *crates*.

(*g*) Colum. 12. 15. 1 (on drying figs); cf. 15. 4, 16. 2. 'The figs are thrown on these (reed frames) and *shepherd's hurdles* woven of straw, rushes or bracken, are placed ... so that they may stand up, and, leaning against one another, may form an arched roof, like that of a hut, and protect the drying figs from the dew, and at times from the rain': tum ficus inicitur, et *crates pastorales* culmo vel carico vel filice textae ... disponuntur, ut ... erigantur, et inter se acclines testudineato tecto more tuguriorum viescentem ficum a rore, et interdum a pluvia defendant.

(*h*) Pliny, *HN* 17. 71 (on sowing cypress-seed). 'Cato also advises erecting *hurdles* supported on forked stakes the height of a man, to intercept the sun, and thatching them with straw to keep off the cold': Cato et furcis *crates* imponi iubet altitudine hominis ad solem recipiendum atque integi culmo ad frigora arcenda.

(*j*) Hor. *Epod.* 2. 45–6 (duties of the farmer's wife). 'And shutting in the fertile flock with woven *hurdles* let her drain their full-filled udders':

> claudensque textis *cratibus* laetum pecus
> distenta siccet ubera.

(*k*) Calp. Sic. *Ecl.* 1. 37–9 (results of the new Golden Age). 'Although at night the shepherd refuses to enclose the sheepfolds with ashen *hurdles*': licet ... nocturnaque pastor/claudere fraxinea nolit praesepia *crate*.

(*l*) Cato 13. 1 (equipment for the press-room for oil). 'Two *wicker strainers*': *craticulas* duas.

DISCUSSION

The etymology is uncertain, but the basic meaning common to the numerous items to which it is applied (hurdle, trellis, wickerwork, etc.) is that of an open-work frame ('objet tressé ou à claire-voie', E–M s.v.). In farm equipment *crates* is used to denote a flat framework, consisting of interlaced material, which may be of straw, rushes, bracken or branches, according to the purpose required.

At one end of the scale are the heavy hurdles used to fence in the sheep (passages *j* and *k*), and the stout 'stretchers' for carrying manure on to the fields (passage *d*); at the other the much lighter type of frame used in the fruit-drying process (passage *g*) or simply to keep the heat of the sun off a bed of delicate seeds such as cypress (passages *e*, *h*). Among the interesting varieties is Virgil's *arbuteae crates*, which appears once on the farm (*Georg.* 1. 166) and once as a stretcher to carry a corpse (*Aen.* 11. 64). A similar type of lattice-work was employed in the building of internal partitions, which were plastered over, thus resembling our lath-and-plaster technique. Vitruvius (2. 8. 10) calls them *parietes craticii*; cf. also Pallad. 1. 18. 2 (for dividing grain stores). Virgil uses *crates* to indicate the structure of the honeycomb (*Georg.* 4. 214). For *crates* as a harrow see *AIRW*, pp. 146 ff.

The diminutive *craticula* (passage *l*) is used frequently elsewhere with the meaning 'gridiron' for grilling meat (Martial 14. 221, etc.). Trimalchio's lavish kitchen equipment includes a 'silver grill'! But this has no place in the press-room (see Brehaut *ad loc.* who suggests that the adjoining word 'carnarium' (ordinarily a meat-rack) will have been used to keep the rawhide press-ropes out of reach of vermin).

Extant representations

The best-known illustration is the panel from the Seasons Mosaic from St-Romain-en-Gal, which depicts two labourers carrying manure to the field on a *crates stercorariae* (see Pl. 5*b*). The *crates pastorales* used for fencing (passages *g* and *h*) are illustrated by D–S, s.v. 'crates', vol. 1. 2, fig. 2048, in the form of an enclosure for wild animals (E. Gerhard, *Antike Bildwerke* (5 Hefte, München, Stuttgart, Tübingen, 1827–37), pl. LXXX).

Survival

(*a*) *Of the ancient types of fencing.* Still much in evidence (1) as temporary fencing, (2) in tropical and sub-tropical climates, to protect seed-beds and young seedlings from fierce sunshine (common in south and west Africa), and for drying fruit (common in southern Europe and North Africa).

(*b*) *Of the name.* Eng. 'crate', orig. a wickerwork container for fruit, etc., later a wooden container for fruit, with open lath-work; It. 'graticcio', a hurdle.

13. Plaustrum (-i, n.), also **plostrum** (Cato), *two-wheeled cart* (contrast *plaustrum maius* – the four-wheeler)

(*a*) *R-E* XX 2. 2551–6 (G. Herzog-Hauser).

(*b*) Varro, *LL* 5. 140 (on wheeled vehicles). '"Plaustrum", "cart", from the fact that unlike those I have mentioned above it is "open" ("palam") not to a certain extent, but completely, since the objects carried in it, such as stone, wooden beams and building material, "shine through" ("perlucent")': *plaustra ab eo quod non ut in his quae supra dixi ex quadam parte sed ex omni palam est, quae in eo vehuntur quod perlucent, ut lapides, asseres, tignum.*

Fig. 27. Plaustrum minus

(*c*) Isid. *Etym.* 20. 12. 3 (*De vehiculis*). 'A *cart* ("plaustrum") is a two-wheeled vehicle for carrying loads; and is called cart ("plaustrum") because it runs on wheels, as if one were to say "pilastrum"': *plaustrum vehiculum duarum rotarum, quo onera deferuntur. et dictum plaustrum, quia volvitur, quasi diceret pilastrum.*

(d) *Corp. Gloss.* s.v. 'plaustrum'. plaustrum ἅμαξα II 151. 55, etc. plostrum ἅμαξα II 152. 16; 504. 61. plaustrum κρόταλον II 355. 41; III 262. 30. . . . plaustrum vehiculum IV 145. 18; 419. 38. genus vehiculi V 384. 7 (*postrum*). rota (rheda?) aut carrum vel vehiculum IV 548. 24 etc. carpentum IV 548. 25; V 321. 33.

(e) Cato 2. 7 'He should sell . . . an old *cart*': *plostrum vetus . . . vendat.*

(f) *Ibid.* 62. 'You should have as many *carts* as you have teams, either of oxen, mules or donkeys': *quot iuga boverum, mulorum, asinorum habebis, totidem plostra esse oportet.*

(g) *Ibid.* 10. 2 (olive-yard inventory). '3 *four-wheeled carts*': *plaustra maiora* III. Cf. 11. 2 (the vineyard inventory, requiring '2 *carts*' (*plostra* II).

(h) Vitruv. *De Arch.* 10. 1. 5 (on essential machines). 'Transport of produce would not have been possible without the invention of *wagons* and carts on land, and ships on water': *portationesque eorum non essent, nisi plostrorum seu serracorum per terram, navicularum per aquam inventae essent machinationes.*

> *Note:* There does not appear to be any clear distinction in usage between the terms *plaustrum* and *serracum* (passage *h*). Herzog-Hauser (*R-E* s.v. 'plaustrum') follows Cicero (ap. Quintil. 8. 3. 21) in regarding *serracum* as a vulgar equivalent (*sordidum nomen*) of *plaustrum*.

(j) Virgil, *Georg.* 3. 585–6 (cf. Ov. *Trist.* 3. 10. 59). 'And over the lofty mountains they pull with straining necks the creaking *carts*':

> montisque per altos
> contenta cervice trahunt stridentia *plaustra.*

(k) *Ibid.* 2. 444–5 (on the uses of timber). 'From such trees the husbandmen turn spokes for wheels, from these they fashion solid drums for *wagons*':

> hinc radios trivere rotis, hinc tympana *plaustris*
> agricolae.

(l) Ovid, *Fasti* 6. 677–80 (the return of the drunken flute-players). 'Without delay the banqueters began to move their limbs, reeling with the heady wine; their shaky legs either stood or teetered. But the master bids them set off, then picked up the laggards and dropped them in a *wagon*; upon the *platform* was a wide basket':

> nec mora, convivae valido titubantia vino
>   membra movent dubii stantque labantque pedes.
> at dominus 'discedite' ait, *plaustro*que morantes
>   sustulit: in *plaustro* scirpea lata fuit.

DISCUSSION

The word is derived from a root which appears in Skt. *plavas*, a ship, and in Gk. πλέω, 'I sail', the swaying motion of a wheeled cart being naturally linked with that of a ship in motion. Both Varro and Isidore are, as often, wide of the mark. *Plaustrum* is properly a platform on wheels, which could be readily adapted for carrying different kinds of material. Varro's derivation from *palam*, 'open', is absurd, but his definition of the *plaustrum* as 'open on all sides' is very much to the point. In small-scale husbandry the basic items of equipment, which are relatively expensive to make (see *Ed. Diocl. Title* xv, 31–47 for relative costs), must be pressed into service for several tasks, not custom-built for occasional use. The load could be either fastened down on the platform, or contained in a large basket-body (*scirpea lata* – passage *l*). Other arrangements included a rail fixed to the sides to keep the load in position, and vertical boards added to make a more solid enclosure than that furnished by a basket. Homer's wagon 'fitted with an upper section' (ἀπήνην ... ὑπερτερίῃ ἀραρυῖαν) was presumably a removable container, possibly of basketry (*Od.* 6. 70). The commonest type of wagon, as displayed on bas-reliefs and wall-paintings, was of the tumbril type, having two wheels, which were not constructed with felloes and spokes, as in the racing or war chariot, but formed out of a solid drum (*tympanum*) of timber (passage *k*). These primitive wheels, usually built up from three pieces of timber, were fixed securely to the axle, so that both revolved together; hence the epithet *stridens*, 'creaking', commonly applied to a wagon on the move (passage *j*). Cato's *plaustrum maius* (passage *g*) was a larger, four-wheeled cart. Cato's four-wheeler will have been a very clumsy vehicle, with solid wheels fixed to the axles, and without benefit of a swivel-table for the front pair. This refinement, like many other advances in transport, was apparently a Gallic invention, and did not reach Rome before the beginning of our era (Haudricourt and Delamarre, *L'Homme et la charrue à travers le monde* (Paris, 1955), pp. 155 ff.). It is interesting to note that the critic Probus (1st century A.D.) commenting on Virgil, *Georg.* 1. 163 ('tardaque Eleusinae matris volventia plaustra') says that the *plaustrum* had neither spoked wheels nor a free-running axle. Even after the invention of the swivelling front axle, with the front and rear pairs of wheels remaining the same in diameter, the former had only a limited turning circle, since they could not pass beneath the chassis (see now Vigneron, *Le Cheval*, vol. 1, p. 115, against des Noëttes' rigid view).

Extant representations

Wheeled vehicles, whether for merchandise or passengers, are common subjects on funerary monuments. The detailed structure is not always easy to determine, e.g. whether or not a four-wheeler is equipped with a swivel-table or not. A very high level of technique is noticeable in the Gallo-Roman series (see Espérandieu, *Gaule*, 3175, 3232, 3685, 5499, 6193).

(1) *Primitive two-wheeler with solid wheels.* Part of a funerary monument from Sulmona, Abruzzi, Italy. Sulmona, Museo Civico. The cart has a shallow frame, on which is mounted a large *culleus*. Rostovtzeff, *SEHRE²*, pl. III. 5, p. 20. R. makes no comment on the load (see further Part III, s.v. 'culleus', pp. 139 ff.). See also Pl. 7.

(2) *Similar type, but with four solid wheels.* From a sculptured relief from Ephesus, now in the British Museum (Smith, *Catalogue of Sculptures*, II, no. 1285) (Rostovtzeff, *SEHRE²*, pl. XLVI. 3; Pl. 6b).

(3) *Heavy-duty four-wheeler*, loaded with a very large cask (*cupa*) and drawn by a pair of mules. Langres, Museum. Note the heavy frame, and the unusual design of the wheel-bosses. Espérandieu, *Gaule*, 5. 3685; Rostovtzeff, *SEHRE²*, pl. XXVIII. 3.

(4) *Four-wheeler* of light design, with spoked wheels; empty, but furnished with staves along the sides to take timber (see Rostovtzeff's note *ad loc.*). Found at Carnuntum. Now in the museum of Altenburg. Rostovtzeff, *SEHRE²*, pl. LXXIV. 2.

Extant specimens

Many identifiable metal parts of wagons have survived, and may be seen, often in great quantity, in the museum collections. Wooden portions are naturally of rare occurrence, but a number of cart wheels have survived, some in a remarkably good state of preservation. Among the best preserved are those found within or near the boundaries of the Roman fort at Saalburg, near Frankfurt-am-Main. See *Saalburg jahrbuch* III (1912), Taf. XVI: a wheel with ten spokes, a well-turned hub, and a heavy-duty one-piece felloe, from the nearby fort of Zugmantel.

14. Teges (-etis, f.), *cover, mat*

No entry in *R-E*.

Not in Varro, *LL*; not in Isidore.

(a) *Corp. Gloss.* s.v. 'teges'. ψίαθος, σκέπασμα II 195. 54. ψίαθος III 21. 6, etc. καλύβη III 261. 50 (unde?). coopertorium IV 290. 34, etc. a tegendo V 397. 40

(Non. 414. 25). tegetis vestis v 655. 2 (Iuvenal. 5. 8; 7. 221). tegete coopertoria IV 290. 40. coopertoria, mattae, v 485. 40.

(b)   Varro, *RR* 1. 22. 1 (list of tools, utensils, etc.). '(They include also) things
made of hemp, flax, rushes, palm and bulrushes, such as wagon ropes, bands
and *mats*': quae fiunt de cannabi, lino, iunco, palma, scirpo ut funes, restes,
tegetes.

(c)   Colum. 5. 5. 15 (on protecting vines against hot winds). 'Indeed, my uncle
... used to shelter his vines around the rising of the Dog-Star with *mats*
made of palm, because ... unless the vines are shaded by covers the fruit
is scorched as if by a fiery breath': patruus meus ... sub ortu Caniculae
palmeis *tegetibus* vineas adumbrabat, quoniam ... nisi teguminibus vites
opacentur, velut halitu flammeo fructus uratur.

(d)   *Ibid.* 12. 52. 9 f. (requirements for the olive harvest). 'There must be ...
reeds and *mats* for receiving the olives': cannae, *tegetes*, quibus oliva
excipitur.

(e)   *Ibid.* 12. 52. 10 (the olive harvest). 'The olives will have to be stripped off
by hand in fine weather, then sieved and cleansed on *mats* and reeds spread
under them': sereno caelo manibus destringi olivam oportebit, et sub-
stratis *tegetibus* aut cannis cribrari et purgari.

DISCUSSION

With raw material in the form of rushes (*iuncus*) readily available, and a
plentiful supply of labour, usually female household slaves, on hand, the
owner of a slave-run estate could have a good supply of matting for the
wide variety of purposes mentioned in the sources, corresponding closely
to their use in tropical countries today, where similar conditions obtain.

Material

Pliny (*HN* 21. 112) follows closely Theophrastus' account (*HP* 4. 12. 1 f.)
of the rush known as mariscus, which was widely used for matting. The
plant, usually identified as *Gladium mariscus* R.Br. (André, *Lexique*, s.v.),
is common in many parts of Europe, and in northern areas preferred to
straw for thatching.

Method of manufacture

Matting was either of the simple plain-weave type, the material being
plaited without a frame, or with a frame, resembling wickerwork. Our
references are concerned exclusively with the former type, but examples
of the latter type survive from Roman times (see below, 'Extant specimens'). Plain-weave matting is probably much older than basketry, mud-
impressions having been identified dating from the sixth millennium B.C.
(Forbes, *SAT*, IV, 178).

Uses

Apart from the passages cited above, the Glossary reference to *teges* = καλύβη, a hut or cabin, suggests that matting was used for making cheap outdoor buildings, such as shepherds' huts, like the straw 'capanne' which are still to be seen in parts of southern Italy. The materials used were freely available, and included reeds, palm-fronds and rushes (see Varro's list, passage *b*).

Extant representations

I know of no extant representations of matting.

Extant specimens

Fragments have survived from Egyptian sites and are to be found in all the major collections. The Flinders Petrie collection at University College London contains a fine oval mat of the Roman period from Kahun (Inv. U.C. 7493).

Survival

Movable covers like that mentioned by Columella (passage *c*) are regularly used by nurserymen even in northern latitudes, to protect seedlings in nursery-beds.

Under hot conditions, as Columella explains (5. 5. 14), the vines should not be heavily trimmed, so that the clusters can be protected by their own foliage; if the vine is deficient in foliage, the fruit should be protected by leaves (*frondes*), and sometimes with straw. He then goes on to mention the use of palm-frond matting, as used by his uncle, who is described as 'a most industrious farmer of the province of Andalusia' (*loc. cit.*). Similar conditions to those described by Columella are common in the wine-growing districts of South Africa as well as in parts of Spain and Provence, where hot, parching winds can do immense damage. The self-supporting vines which now predominate in all wine-producing countries except Italy are much more difficult to protect, and they are usually left to take their chance. In areas of large-scale production such as Provence or the Rioja region of Spain, such losses have to be measured against the high cost of providing adequate protection.

The list of hard basketry items concludes with an exceedingly common, and indeed essential, piece of farm equipment, the wickerwork beehive (*alvus, alvarium*), and a movable cucumber frame fitted with glazing (*speculare*), first mentioned by Columella.

15. Alvus (-i, f.) (Varro, Colum., Pliny), **alvarium** (-i, n.) (Virg., Colum.), *beehive*

Not in Varro, *LL*; not in Isid.

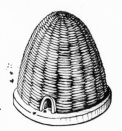

Fig. 28. Alvus

(*a*) *R-E* s.v. 'Biene' III 1. 438–50 [Olck]; *ibid.* s.v. 'Bienenzucht' III 1. 450–1 [Olck].

(*b*) Varro, *RR* 3. 16. 15. 'Some people build round *hives* of osiers, others of wood and bark, others by hollowing a tree, others make them of earthenware, and still others build them square out of fennel stalks': alii faciunt (*alvos*) ex viminibus rotundas, alii e ligno ac corticibus, alii ex arbore cava, alii fictiles, alii etiam ex ferulis quadratas.

(*c*) Colum. 9. 5. 6. 'If the place is rich in cork-trees, we shall doubtless make the most serviceable *hives* from their bark, because they are neither cold in winter nor hot in summer; if it abounds in fennels, containers can be just as conveniently woven from these … If neither of these materials is available, they can be made of plaited osiers': sive illa (scil. regio) ferax est suberis, haud dubitanter utilissimas *alvos* faciemus ex corticibus, quae nec hieme frigent, nec candent aestate; sive ferulis abundat, … aeque commode vasa texuntur. si neutrum aderit, opere textorio salicibus connectentur.

(*d*) Virg. *Georg.* 4. 33–5. 'The *hives* themselves, whether you have them made from hollowed bark sewn together, or of pliant withies woven, should have their entrances narrow':

> ipsa autem, seu corticibus tibi suta cavatis,
> seu lento fuerint *alvaria* vimine texta,
> angustos habeant aditus.

DISCUSSION

Materials

The chief requirements in a beehive are that it should be (*a*) proof against extreme variations of temperature, (*b*) easily movable, (*c*) made of durable material. Bark is given first place by both Varro (*RR* 3. 16. 17) and Columella (passage *c*). They also agree in condemning earthenware as the worst material of all, on the ground that it is too good a conductor of heat and cold. Bark, fennel and withies all have the advantage of providing adequate ventilation. Varro (*RR* 3. 16. 16) mentions that those made of withies are smeared inside and out with cow-dung in case the bees are put off by the rough surface. The chief defect of the basketry hive must surely have been the difficulty of preventing contamination. Varro advises a light smoking and sweeping three times a month (*ibid.* 17).

Design

The ovoid shape, culminating in a point, so standardized that the English form has long been used to designate other articles with the same profile (e.g. the beehive tombs of Mycenaean Greece), is too familiar to require description. The basketry was evidently so woven over the frame as to provide adequate aeration of the interior, essential to the health of the bees. For details of the construction see Columella 9. 6. In addition to several very small entrances, the hive needed a removable section at the back for inspection and withdrawal of the full combs. Varro (3. 16. 15) notes that some beekeepers make rectangular hives of fennel-stalks, thus anticipating the modern shape.

Extant representations

Rich (*Dict. Ant.* s.v. 'alveare') shows a specimen of the conical basketry hive, taken from a bas-relief, for which he gives no provenance, and which I have not been able to trace.

Extant specimens

Rich (*Dict. Ant.* s.v. 'fori') shows a bronze beehive shaped like an *urna*, containing four floors. In spite of the rare design, and the fact that it is said by Rich to have been discovered at Pompeii, I have not been able to trace it.

Survival

'Sir George Wheeler ... in the seventeenth century described the Athenian beehive as made of wicker, with combs which were built down from bars placed along the top, and this type was normal in Greece up to World War II. It may have resembled the ancient type' (W. Kendrick Pritchard, *Hesperia* 25 (1956), 260, s.v. σμῆνος – one of many valuable discussions of implements and equipment mentioned in the Attic Stelae). Bee-skeps of the same pattern were still to be seen in many parts of Britain up to the early part of this century. They have now been completely superseded by the box-type hive, introduced by Langstroth in 1851, which has the dual advantage of making inspection and removal easy, as well as enabling the bee-keeper to extend the accommodation by adding fresh tiers.

16. Specularis lapis, translucent stone, mica, used for glazing cold frames.

No entry in *R-E*.

Not in Varro, *LL*.

(*a*) Isid. *Etym.* 16. 4. 37. 'It is called *transparent stone*, because it admits light like glass; first discovered in Hither Spain near the city of Segovia. It is found beneath the soil, whence it is extracted, hewn and split into as many thin sheets as you like': *specularis lapis* vocatus est quod vitri more transluceat; repertus primum in Hispania citeriori circa Segobricam urbem. Invenitur enim sub terra et effossus exciditur atque finditur in quamlibet tenues crustas.

(*b*) Colum. II. 3. 52–3 (on raising early vegetables). 'It is also possible, provided it is worth the trouble, to have wheels put under larger containers, so that they can be brought out (into the open) and taken indoors again with less labour. In any event, they will have to be covered with *transparent panes*, so that even in cold weather when the sky is clear they can be safely brought out to get the sun': possunt etiam, si sit operae pretium, vasis maioribus rotulae subici, quo minore labore producantur, et rursus intra tecta recipiantur. sed nihilo minus *specularibus* integi debebunt, ut etiam frigoribus serenis diebus tuto producantur ad solem.

(*c*) Pliny, *HN* 19. 64 (on growing cucumbers). 'There was never a day when he (the emperor Tiberius) was not supplied with them, since his kitchen-gardeners had the cucumber beds mounted on wheels which they moved out into the sun, and on wintry days brought back under the cover of protecting *panes of translucent stone*': nullo quippe non die contigit ei, pensiles eorum hortos promoventibus in solem rotis olitoribus rursusque hibernis diebus intra *specularium* munimenta revocantibus.

(*d*) *Ibid.* 36. 160. '*Transparent stone* . . . can be split into any type of thin sheets': *specularis lapis* . . . finditur in quamlibeat tenues crustas.

DISCUSSION

The first references to panes of semi-transparent mica (*lapis specularis*) occur in authors of the first century A.D. (e.g. Seneca, *Ep.* 90; *QN* 4. 13). Windows glazed with manufactured glass probably antedate the reign of the emperor Tiberius (A.D. 14–37) (see passage *b*), but the material was at that time probably too costly for widespread use. Cf. Pliny, *HN* 36. 194.

8

SOFT BASKETRY

Fig. 29. Fiscus

1. Fiscus (-i, m.), flexible container, *bag*, *sack*; esp. (i) for oil-pressing ('ad exprimendum oleum' *TLL*); (ii) *purse*, *money-bag*; dimin. **fiscina** (-ae, f.), **fiscella** (-ae, f.), **fiscellus** (-i, m.), with sim. gen. and special meanings

(*a*)   *R-E* VI 2. 2385 [Rostowzew]. No mention of the primary meaning!

(*b*)   Varro, *LL* 5. 139. 'Vessels in which are carried crops or other necessaries are called *sacks* from this, taking their name from carrying ("a ferendo")': quibus comporta[n]tur fructus ac necessariae res, de his *fiscina* a ferendo dicta.

(*c*)   Isid. *Etym.* 20. 9. 7. 'The "fiscus" is the public purse; from which the words "fiscellae" and "fiscinae" take their names ... "Fiscus" however stands in the primary position, "fiscina" being a derivative, and "fiscella" a diminutive': *Fiscus* sacculus est publicus, unde et *fiscellae* et *fiscinae* dicuntur ... fiscus autem primae positionis est, derivatum fiscina, diminutivum fiscella.

(*d*)   *Corp. Gloss.* s.v. 'fiscus' only in the sense of 'treasury'.

(*e*)   *Ibid.* s.v. 'fiscina'. fiscina σπορίς II 436. 16. genus cofini V 295. 2. saccus, sarcina. Virgilius (*Georg.* I 266): nunc facilis rubea texatur fiscina virga. V 201. 3. a fisco per dirivationem: est autem fiscus publicus sacculus V 21. 4.

(*f*)   *Corp. Gloss.* s.v. 'fiscella'. κάρταλλος II 72. 20, etc. τάλαρος II 451. 20; κάλαθος II 337. 12; σπυρίς II 436. 16 etc. a fiscina diminutive V 201. 2. forma ubi casei exprimuntur IV 519. 12 etc. *fiscellam* vas viminis gracilis factum V 200. 29 (*om. cod. Palat. an* gracile? cf. Verg. *Ecl.* X 71). *fiscella⟨m⟩ scirpeam* iunceam contextam in modum navis V 569. 19 (*Vulg. Exod.* II 3) *fiscillum* cofinum diminutive a fisco V 628. 69. *fiscellus* mollis casei appetitor V 599. 41 = *Osb.* p. 239 (cf. Festus Pauli, p. 90. 2); *ubi* fiscello O. Muellerus.

(*g*)   Colum. 12. 52. 10 (cf. 49. 9) (on pressing olives). 'The olives, when they have been carefully cleaned, must be taken down to the press, and enclosed, while still whole, in new *rush bags* and put under the presses, to be squeezed for the shortest possible time': tum (olivam) diligenter emundatam protinus in torcular deferri, et integram in *fiscis* novis includi prelisque subigi, ut quantum possit paulisper exprimatur. Cf. Colum. 12. 18. 2-3; Pallad. 11. 19. 1 (for grapes).

(*h*)   Colum. 12. 54. 2 (on making oil for ointment (*unguenta*)). 'Next break up the olives in a hanging mill, and set them either on the discs of the press, or in a new *bag*': deinde suspensa mola olivam frangito eamque vel in regulas vel in novo *fisco* adicito. Cf. *ibid.* 12. 51. 2; 12. 52. 8; Ulp. *Dig.* 19. 2. 19. 2.

(*j*) Cato 13 (equipment for the press-room). '— new and — old *bags*': *fiscinas novas* —, *veteres* —. Cf. *ibid.* 26; 67. 2; 68; 153 (*fiscinas olearias Campanicas*); 135. 2 (*fiscinae Campanicae . . . fiscinas Romanicas*).

(*k*) Colum. 12. 39 (on making raisin wine). 'Afterwards tread the grapes with your feet, and squeeze them in a new *rush bag*': postea pedibus proculcato, et in *fiscina* nova uvas premito.

(*l*) Virg. *Georg.* 1. 266. 'Now let the pliant *bag* be woven of briar twigs': nunc facilis rubea texatur *fiscina* virga.

(*m*) Colum. 12. 18. 2 (on preparing for the vintage). 'If the farm is a large one, and the vineyards and plantations are extensive, you must keep up a continuous supply of woven *baskets* and treat them with pitch': si ager amplius, aut vineta aut arbusta grandia sunt, perenne . . . *fiscellae* texendae et picandae.

(*n*) *Ibid.* 12. 38. 6 (on making myrtle-wine). 'Next enclose the berries in a *bag* made of linen, and press them': mox *fiscello* lineo inclusas exprimito. (Cf. 7. 8. 3 and 6.)

(*o*) Pallad. 4. 10. 10 (on making pomegranate wine). 'You will carefully clean the ripe pips, put them in a *bag* made of palm leaves, squeeze them in a screw-press, and cook them gently': grana matura purgata diligenter in palmea *fiscella* mittes, in coclea exprimes et leniter coques.

(*p*) Tibullus 2. 3. 15f. (on making cheeses). 'There was the *cheese-bag* woven from the bulrushes' light stems, and here and there through their texture a passage was made for the whey':

tunc *fiscella* levi detexa est vimine iunci
raraque per nexus est via facta sero.

(*q*) Cato 54. 5 (on the regime for the working oxen). 'When they once taste green food, they are always looking for it, and they must wear *muzzles* to stop them going for the grass when ploughing': nam viride cum edunt, semper id exspectant, et *fiscellas* habere oportet, ne herbam sectentur, cum arabunt. Cf. Pliny, *HN* 18. 177: boves . . . *fiscellis* capistrari oportet.

r) Varro, *RR* 2. 2. 14 (on breeding of sheep). 'They also prevent the rams from mounting the ewes by tying over their genitals *bags* made of rushes or other material': deterrent ab saliendo et *fiscellas* e iunco aliave qua re quod alligant ad naturam.

DISCUSSION

Terminology

Fiscus and its compounds were generally distinguished in meaning from *corbis* (see the introductory discussion to this section (above, pp. 53f.)). Here, as elsewhere, the lexica and dictionaries of antiquities are far from satisfactory, and translators, by using the general term 'basket' for items belonging to either group, merely add to the confusion. For similar difficulties in the classification of implements see *AIRW*, 'Hoes', pp. 36ff. In passages where the material is specified (as *iunceus*, *lineus*, etc.) the precise meaning is not usually in doubt. We begin then with a list of the *materials* from which the containers are made.

The material

Most frequently mentioned are *iuncus* (rushes), and *linum* (linen); at 11. 2. 90, when giving a list of jobs for winter evenings, Columella writes: 'If the district is well-stocked with palm-trees or esparto grass, *frails* and baskets can be made': 'sive palmae spartive fecunda est (regio), *fiscinae sportaeque* (fieri debent)'. The term 'frail', used here by the Loeb translator, is appropriate, since it denotes a flexible basket, made of rushes, used for packing dried fruit (see *OED*, s.v. 'frail'). The *OED* entry s.v. the less common term 'bass' points in the same direction: 'bass 2. mat, hammock, flat plaited bag or flexible basket'. In all the passages cited above, whether directly or by implication, it is the flexibility of containers of this type that is the common factor; they are pliant (Virgil's 'facilis fiscina'), they can be squeezed very tight in the olive-press or in cheese-making, and so on. LSJ on the synonym τάλαρος (passage *f* – *fiscella* = τάλαρος) are misleading: 'basket of wicker-work in which new-made cheeses were placed so as to let the whey run off', which conveys the impression of rigid, rather than flexible, basketry (see further below, 'Extant representations'). Of course, neither τάλαρος nor *fiscus* and its derivatives are used exclusively of soft, flexible containers by non-technical writers (e.g. when used for fruit or flowers (LSJ s.v.). Taking the terms individually, it would appear that *fiscus* is essentially a bag; it is very common in the sense of purse or money-bag (cf. Augustine, *Comm. in Ps.* 146. 17: 'fiscus saccus est'). In range of meaning the form *fiscina*, which is adjectival in origin, stands midway between *fiscus* and its diminutives *fiscellus* and *fiscella*. In Cato it is the standard term for the bag in which the grapes and olives are pressed, and thus a synonym for *fiscus*. The other uses bring it very close to *fiscella* (e.g. 'panniers' at Pliny, *HN* 34. 66). Numerous non-technical references suggest the meaning 'basket' rather than 'bag', e.g. Cic., *Pro Flacco* 41, and Virgil, *Georg.* 1. 266, an ordinary fruit-basket; Colum. 10. 307, a flower-basket (cf. the references above to τάλαρος). Pliny (*HN* 18. 314) employs the term loosely of a *corbis pabulatorius*: so too Ovid (*Fast.* 4. 754).

Fiscella, though commonly used, like *fiscus*, of the container in which the grapes are enclosed for pressing (Colum. 12. 18. 2 – also for making raisin wine or pomegranate wine, Pallad. 11. 19. 1; 4. 10. 10), is also used of a muzzle made of woven material (Cato 54. 5; Pliny, *HN* 18. 177). Again it is used in another specialized sense of a finely-woven bag which can be suspended in a liquid, allowing its contents to percolate into the liquid (e.g. Cato 23. 3 – for making resinated wine; *ibid.* 24 – for making salted Greek wine; *ibid.* 88 – for making pure table salt).

Extant representations

The flexible containers used in the pressing of grapes and olives are frequently represented on the monuments: (1) Rich (*Dict. Ant.* s.v. 'torcular') shows a primitive method of pressing the grapes. A gang of men are shown in the act of lifting a heavy stone, using a piece of tree-trunk as a crowbar. The *fiscella* full of grapes has been placed beneath the stone. (2) *RF*, pl. 56, shows one of the panels from the Seasons Mosaic from St Romain-en-Gal. Here the very large container beneath the primitive lever-press operated by two men is out of scale with the press-beam. Rich (*Dict. Ant.* s.v. 'fiscella') is very misleading. His illustration is taken from a wall painting from Herculaneum (Museo Borbonico, vol. VI, tav. XX), showing a cylindrical basket lying on its side, and another upright. Nearby are two capons. This is surely a 'stuffing scene', as described by Varro (*RR* 3. 9. 19–21); the contents of the baskets will be one of the cereal compounds mentioned by him, not cheese.

Extant specimens

Well-preserved specimens have been found in tombs of the Roman period in Egypt. From Hawara comes a flat frail with four shells on the edge, fitted with rope handles (Dept. of Egyptology, University College London: Cat. U.C. 28048 – see Petrie, *Objects of Daily Use* (B.S.Arch., Egypt), London, 1927, pl. XLI, 167. This specimen is 15 cm wide and 7 cm high; another from the same collection (Cat. U.C. 28049) is 27 cm wide and 15 cm high (Pl. 4a).

2. Saccus (-i, m.) (fr. Gr. σάκκος; cf. Sem. *saq*, 'woven material'), dimin. **sacculus** (-i, m.), (i) *sack, bag*; (ii) *filter* (cf. *saccare*, to filter, strain); (iii) *small bag, purse*

Not in Varro, *LL*; not in Isidore.

(*a*) *R-E* I A. 2. 1622–4 [Hug].

(*b*) *Corp. Gloss.* s.v. 'saccus'. *saccus* σάκκος II 429. 35. ὑλιστήρ II 462. 48. σάγος, σακάλιον, σάκκος, βαλάντιον II 269. 43 (unde?). μάρσιπος III 327. 63; 530. 50. *saccum* μαρσίπιον III 327. 62; 530. 69. *saccus vinarius* ὑλιστήρ II 177. I.

(c) Cic. *In Verr.* II 1. 38. 95 (list of requisitions by Verres). 'When the villain was requisitioning from the communities corn, hides, overcoats and *sacks*': cum iste civitatibus frumentum, coria, cilicia, *saccos* imperaret.

(d) Colum. 9. 15. 12 (method of straining honey). 'A wickerwork basket, or a *bag* rather loosely woven of fine withies shaped like an inverted cone, of the type used for straining wine, is hung up in a dark place, and then honeycombs are piled into it one by one': saligneus qualus, vel tenui vimine rarius contextus *saccus*, inversae metae similis, qualis est quo vinum liquatur, obscuro loco suspenditur; in eum deinde carptim conferuntur favi.

(e) *Ibid.* 12. 17. 2 (on making vinegar from figs). 'After this they should let it (the vinegar) percolate through small rush baskets or *sacking made from broom*': postea in iunceis fiscellis vel *sparteis saccis* percolent.

(f) Pliny, *HN* 14. 137 (new ways of stimulating a thirst for wine). 'More than that, in order to absorb more wine, we break its strength with *filters*, and think up other ways of stimulating thirst': quin immo, ut plus (vini) capiamus, *sacco* frangimus vires, et alia inritamenta excogitantur.

(g) Horace, *Sat.* 2. 3. 148–9 (the doctor revives a miserly patient). 'He bids them bring in a table and tip out his *bags* of cash':

mensem poni iubet atque
effundi *saccos* nummorum.

(h) Martial, 10. 74. 6. 'He carries off fifteen *sackfuls* of gleaming gold': quindecim . . . ferventis auri . . . aufert saccos.

(j) Edict. Diocl. 11. 1. 2. 1. 'For goat's or camel's hair': de saetis caprinis sibe camelinis. 2. 'Hair, woven into bags or *sacks*': pili neti ad zabernas vel *saccos*. 'Bags, for clothing, or *sacks*, a pair, weighing thirty pounds, den. 400': zabernarum sibe *saccorum* par habens pondo triginta den. 400.

DISCUSSION

Saccus is evidently a generic word for a flexible bag, made of woven material, ranging in size from a money-bag (passage *b*: Gr. βαλάντιον) to a grain-sack (passage *c*). In its largest form it was, and still is, the ordinary container for transporting grain and flour. Rich (*Dict. Ant.* s.v. 'saccus') defines it as 'a large bag or sack, made of coarse linen cloth'. This is much too restricted: goat's hair and camel hair were also used (passage *j*).

Saccus vinarius. The wine-strainer, made apparently of linen (Hor. *Sat.* 2. 4. 54), or of finely-textured basketry (passages *d, e*), was the usual means employed to remove impurities from the wine. Hug (passage *a*) says the filtering was done when transferring the wine from *dolium* to *amphora*, adding three references to support his statement that Roman methods of wine-making were inferior to those of the Greeks, and therefore their wines needed much straining. None of the passages he cites, viz. Plut. *Symp.* 6. 7, Pollux 6. 18 and 10. 75, Schol. Aristoph. *Plut.* 1087, supports his claim. From passage *f* it seems that the Romans thought filtering also removed harshness from wine (if this is the meaning of 'vires'). In his commentary on the passage André (Budé edition) points out that filtering caused some loss of bouquet, and that the filters were impregnated with myrtle-oil, which both trapped the lees and perfumed the wine (Budé ed., p. 150).

Saccus nivarius. The snow-strainer, used for filtering the wine through snow-water in order to cool it: 'the cloth, with a lump of snow upon it, being placed over the wine-cup, and the liquor then poured upon the snow, and made to filter through the cloth into the cup (Mart. *Epigr.* 14. 104)', Rich, *Dict. Ant.* s.v.). See below, s.v. 'colum', p. 101.

Sacculus. The diminutive form appears to have been the ordinary word for a purse containing the small change needed for daily transactions (Pliny, *HN* 2. 137, Catull. 13. 8, etc.). It was also used with the meaning 'strainer'. See Cic. *Fin.* 2. 23, and J. S. Reid's long note to the passage, citing the opinion of the learned Catius (Hor. *Sat.* 2. 4. 53 f.) that the best clearing agent, which avoids loss of bouquet (*sapor*) is an egg. This method is still in use (see Billiard, *La Vigne*, pp. 510f.).

Extant representations

Saccus (i). Frequent on monuments: (1) A panel on Trajan's Column (Cichorius, *Traianssäule*, Taf. 124, nos. 338–9) has a vigorous scene of soldiers filling and carrying sacks of grain. (2) A tomb fresco from Ostia now in the Vatican, depicting a grain lighter (*navis codicaria*), the 'Isis Giminiana', loading corn for Rome. The sacks are being carried aboard the lighter and there checked (for quality and possible adulteration, as well as for weight) by a tally-clerk in the presence of the skipper. B. Nogara, *Le Nozze Aldobrandini*, Milano, 1907, pl. 46; Meiggs, *Ostia*, fig. 25e, p. 295; D–S IV, 930, fig. 5984. (3) A relief in the cathedral at Salerno, S. Italy, depicting the unloading of a ship. Among the basketry depicted on the Sens relief (Pl. 4c) are three identical items, usually taken to be heaps of grape-refuse (G. Julliot, *Musée Gallo-Romain de Sens*, p. 97). It seems more likely that they are large strainers. (See also Pl. 4c.)

Saccus (iii) = money-bag. Rich (*Dict. Ant.* s.v.) has an example copied from a bas-relief, which had been used as a street-sign to show the way to the *aerarium*, and carries the inscription VIATOR AD AERARIVM. *sacculus*. Rich (*Dict. Ant.* s.v.) shows an example of the draw-string purse from a Pompeian wall-painting (provenance not stated).

Survival

(a) *Of the object.* (1) *saccus.* Sacks of goat's hair are still used in Spain. (2) *sacculus.* The draw-string leather money-bag is still in use in the southern Mediterranean, and is still on sale in most parts of north Africa.

(b) *Of the name.* In many languages, e.g. Ital. 'sacco', 'sacca', Fr. 'sache', Eng. 'sack', 'satchel', with a similar range of meanings.

Fig. 30. Capistrum

3. Capistrum (-i, n.), dimin. **capistellum** (fr. *capere*, 'contain, hold'), (i) *halter, headstall*; (ii) *muzzle* (cf. *fiscella*); (iii) *holding-rope* for the press (Cato); (iv) *band, tie* for vines (Colum.)

Not in Varro, *LL.*

(a) *R-E* III 2. 1511–13 [Olck].

(b) Isid. *Etym.* 20. 16. 4. '*Halters* derive their name from the head ("caput") of beasts of burden': *capistri a capite iumentorum dicti.*

(c) *Corp. Gloss.* s.v. 'capistrum'. φορβεά II 472. 50, etc. φορβειά II 97. 38 (φορβια). kapistrum quod agnis aut furonibus in caput imponitur V 214. 18. V. armentarius cilo⟨ter⟩. V. uteri capistrum. cilo⟨ter⟩ camus, capistrum II 573. 11 (*corr. Loewe.* Cf. Nettleship, 'contr.' p. 410). armentarius ... capistrorum factor II 568. 8 (*male versum adscito* φορβεά *capistrum*). Cf. ἁμαξοποιός armentarius (contam. cf. carpentarius) III 201. 41.

(d) Varro 2. 6. 4 (on breeding and rearing asses). 'During the next (i.e. the second) year the young are allowed to be with their dams at night, and are loosely tied with a *halter*, or something of the kind': *proximo anno noctibus patiuntur esse cum his (scil. matribus) et leniter capistris aliave qua re habent vinctos.*

(e) Calp. *Ecl.* 1. 40–1 (effects of the new golden age). 'Yet the robber will not lay an ambush against the sheep-folds, nor drive off the stock when their *halters* are loose':

> non tamen insidias praedator ovilibus ullas
> afferat, aut laxis abiget iumenta *capistris*.

(f) Virgil, *Georg.* 3. 188f. (the training of the colt). 'In turn let him yield his mouth to a pliant *halter* while he is still weak and timid':

> inque vicem det mollibus ora *capistris*
> invalidus etiamque tremens.

(g) Virgil, *Georg.* 3. 398–9 (on rearing kids). 'Many even keep their new-born kids away from their dams, and from the beginning fasten their mouths with iron-spiked *muzzles*':

> multi etiam excretos prohibent a matribus haedos
> primaque ferratis praefigunt ora *capistris*.

(h) Edict. Diocl. 10 (for leather goods – *De loramentis*). 'Halter for mules 80 den. Combined bit-and-bridle for mules 120 den. Pack-saddle for a hinny

350 den.': capistrum mulare den. octaginta. frenum mulare cum capistello den. centum biginti. sagma burdonis den. trecentis quinquaginta.

(*j*) Cato 12 (equipment for the olive-press). 'Five *holding ropes*': *capistra* V.

(*k*) Colum. 4. 20. 3 (on tying the vines). 'Therefore when the vine has been drawn straight up to the top of the stake, it is tied to it with a *band*, so that when laden with its fruit it may not slide down and grow bent': quare cum ad summum palum recta vitis extenta est, *capistro* constringitur, ne fetu gravata subsidat curveturque.

DISCUSSION

The derivation (from *capere*, 'contain') is clear; the primary meaning is that of 'halter' or 'headstall', that is, a simple, or more complex, piece of harness to 'contain' the head, so that the animal can be controlled either by a simple rope, for breaking-in a colt (passages *d, f*), or by a complete bridle, defined as the 'headgear of the harness ... consisting of headstall (*capistrum*), bit (*frenum*) and rein (*lorum*)' (*OED* s.v. 'bridle'. The secondary meaning is that of 'muzzle', that is, a band or cage around the mouth to prevent biting, eating or rooting. On the strength of the etymology of the corresponding Greek term φορβειά (passage *c*), Smith (*Dict. Ant.* s.v. 'capistrum') suggests that the meaning 'nosebag' may have been the primary one. But this has nothing to do with *capistrum*!

The halter and headstall

The material for these will have varied with the requirements; thus Virgil's 'pliant halter' (*mollia capistra*) (*f*), usually wrongly translated 'muzzle', was presumably of soft leather (so Hooper–Ash *ad loc.*). Diocletian's Edict (passage *h*) includes *capistra* for horses and mules under the heading of leather harness (*loramenta*). We have no description of a Roman headstall, but representations in art show a basic pattern of muzzle-strap and forehead-strap connected by a pair of cheek-straps, the halter proper, whether of rope or leather, being attached through a ring to the near-side cheek-strap.

The extension of the meaning to include an enclosed muzzle, fastened round the muzzle-strap, is a natural one (see further Xen. *Equ.* 5. 1–3, a clear description of the putting-on of the bridle).

The muzzle

By an easy extension of meaning *capistrum* was also used of a band or cage to prevent the animal from biting, eating or rooting. Muzzles were commonly worn by oxen while ploughing, to prevent them from nibbling the grass, the verb *capistrare* being used frequently in this sense (e.g.

Colum. 6. 19. 2; Pliny, *HN* 18. 177). See further s.v. 'fiscella' (above, pp. 88–91). Iron-spiked muzzles (passage *g*) will have been of hard material, perhaps of basketry, forming a rigid cage. For a full discussion of head-stalls and muzzles see Vigneron, *Le Cheval* (1968), I, 34 ff.

Derivative uses

(1) *capistra* = 'holding-ropes' for the olive-press (passage *j*). Cato's detailed account of the 'holding-ropes' (*capistra*) for use in the olive-press (135), which are made of plaited thongs of rawhide, indicates that the meaning is closely related to that of 'halter'. See further 'Notes on ropes and cordage', Part I, p. 31.

(2) *capistrum* = looped strap for vine-stocks (passage *k*). Columella's use of the term is characteristically precise; when the vines have been pruned, staked and yoked, the first job of the binder (*alligator*) is to 'keep the vinestock straight, and not allow it to follow the curve of the prop'. The vine is therefore pulled straight up to the top of its stake, and there tied with a 'halter' (*capistrum*), to keep the head of the vine up, and prevent it sagging with the weight of the fruit. He does not describe the fastening, but the use of the term suggests a looped tie, resembling a simple halter.

Extant representations

I know of no representations of muzzles. Headstalls are rare on monu-ments, since equines, whether used as pack animals or in wheeled transport, are usually displayed in full harness. But there is a scene of preparation for a sacrifice on Trajan's Column, in which four horses are shown wearing headstalls, the second from the left of the panel being particularly well represented, with the head almost completely in profile (Pl. 6*a* and Cichorius, *Traianssäule*, Taf. 91, nos. 238–40; cf. Taf. 99, no. 259).

4. Clitellae (-arum, f.), later **sagma** (-atis, n.) pair of *panniers*, *pack-saddle*: a wooden frame for hanging sacks etc.

Not in Varro, *LL*; not in Isid., but *sagma* is defined at 20. 16. 5 as taking its name from the 'spreading of saddle-cloths', and the terms 'sumpter horse' (*caballus sagmarius*) and 'sumpter hinny' (*mula sagmaria*) are given in support. A *sagma burdonis* (for a hinny) is priced in the Edict (11. 4) at 350 den.

(*a*)   *R-E.* No entry s.v. 'clitellae'; *R-E* s.v. 'sagma' 1 A. 1752 [Fiebiger].

(*b*)   Fest. s.v. 'clitellae' p. 52 L; p. 59 M. '*Panniers* is the name given not only to the containers in which loads are carried strapped on the backs of mules, but also to a place in Rome and some places on the Flaminian Way which resemble them in their continual steep ascents and descents': *clitellae* dicuntur non tantum eae quibus sarcinae conligatae mulis portantur, sed etiam locus Romae propter similitudinem et in via Flaminia loca quaedam devexa subinde et adcliva.

(c) Plautus, *Most.* 778–82 (a new idea in trade). 'He's carrying his *panniers*, and here's another old man carrying them. I've started up a brand-new business, and a pretty good one. Muleteers, you know, have pannier-carrying mules, but I've got pannier-carrying men':

> vehit hic *clitellas*, vehit hic autem alter senex.
> novicium mihi quaestum institui non malum;
> nam muliones mulos clitellarios
> habent, at ego habes homines clitellarios.

(d) Hor. *Sat.* 1. 5. 47 (en route from Rome to Brindisi). 'Next at Capua, where the hinnies lay down their *panniers* at an early hour':

> hinc mulae Capuae clitellas tempore ponunt.

(e) Phaedrus 1. 15. 7ff. (change of government only a change of masters). 'Then, hesitating, the ass said : "Tell me, d'you think the winners will put two pairs of *panniers* on me?" "No", said the old man; "What's the difference, then, whom I serve, so long as I carry only one pair of panniers?"':
at ille lentus 'quaeso, num binas mihi / *clitellas* impositurum victorem putas?' / senex negavit: 'ergo quid refert mea / cui serviem, clitellas dum portem unicas?'

DISCUSSION

The pannier-carrying mule and donkey are so familiar a sight in southern Europe and the Middle East that a description is unnecessary. The material used in antiquity varied then, as now, according to the contents. Their importance in commercial transport is emphasized by Varro (*RR* 2. 6. 5) and elsewhere. More familiar is Virgil's homely picture of the donkey-driver loading his donkey with cheap apples for market and coming back from town with a return load in the form of a quernstone or a lump of pitch (*Georg.* 1. 274–5).

Design

Two types of pack-saddle are presently in use in many countries, (a) a wooden frame covered with leather or heavy cloth, with rings attached to hold the suspended loads; (b) a covering of soft yet strong material, moulded to the animal's back, and opening out into a capacious bag at either side; less often seen in Europe than (a), but still common in North Africa and the Middle East. For full discussion of the evidence see Vigneron, *Le Cheval*, I, pp. 130ff. Both types can be readily identified from monuments of the classical period (see below, 'Extant representations'). Mules thus equipped are commonly loaded with up to 150 kg of goods, and approximately similar loads were carried in antiquity. These compare favourably with the maximum permitted load of 492 kg for heavy wagons (*angariae*) on the Cursus Publicus, as laid down in the Theodosian Code (*Tit.* 8. 5. 17).

Extant representations

(1) *Panniers:* Bronze statuette from the Pulsky Collection, now in the British Museum (Walters, *Catalogue of Bronzes*, no. 1790; Pl. 8 *a*).

(2) *Hard frame:* Vigneron, *Le Cheval*, 1, pl. 56b (Lehmann-Hartleben, *Die Traianssäule* (Berlin/Leipzig, 1926), pl. 11).

5. Capisterium (-i, n.), *cleansing vessel* for grain

Not in Varro, *LL*; not in Isidore.

The term occurs only once:

(*a*) *R-E* III 2. 1510–11 [Olck].

(*b*) Colum. 2. 9. 11 (on treatment of the grain after threshing). 'When there is a particularly good yield, everything that is threshed out should be cleaned in a *cleansing vessel*, and the grain that settles to the bottom because of its weight and size should always be kept for seed': cum rursus amplior messis provenerit, quicquid exteretur *capisterio* purgandum erit, et semper, quod propter magnitudinem ac pondus in imo subsederit, ad semen reservandum.

DISCUSSION

The lexicographers relate this word to the Greek σκαφιστήριον, a hollow vessel. Ancient commentators, followed by some modern editors, have wrongly assumed that Columella is referring to a vessel with perforations in the bottom, like an ordinary sieve. But this makes no sense of Columella's account; if the vessel had holes in the bottom, how would the larger and heavier grains have settled? Rich (*Dict. Ant.* s.v.) thinks that water was possibly employed: but water must have been essential to the operation. Whatever its design, the *capisterium* was evidently a dual-purpose contrivance, since it both cleaned the grain and sorted the seed-corn from the rest.

Monuments

I know of no representation of a vessel answering to the requirements.

6. Colum (-i, n.), (i) *strainer*, for removing the scum from the must, etc.;
(ii) *sieve* (metal)

Fig. 31. Colum

Not in Varro, *LL.*

(a) *R-E* IV I. 590–2 (Mau).

(b) Isid. *Etym.* 14. 13. 'Baskets, frails and *strainers* for the wine-press, through
which the must flows. These get their name from the process of percolation':
qualos corbes *cola*que prelorum, per *quos*[1] mustum fluit, a colando dictos.

(c) Cato 11. 2 (inventory of vineyard equipment). 'Three wicker strainers,
three strainers to take off the flower': cola vitilia III, cola qui florem demat
III.

(d) Colum. 11.2.70 (collecting equipment for the vintage, etc.). '(The manager
must see that) the lids and *strainers* and all the other things which are
essential to the proper making of must (are properly washed and dried)':
tum et opercula *cola*que et cetera, sine quibus probe confici mustum non
potest. . .

(e) *Ibid.* 12. 19. 4 (preparations for making must); cf. *ibid.* 12. 38. 7. 'The man
in charge of boiling this (the must) should have ready in advance *strainers*
of rushes or broom': itaque qui praeerit huic decoquendo, *cola* iuncea vel
spartea . . . praeparata habeat.

(f) *Ibid.* 12. 38. 7 (on making myrtle-wine). 'They then squeeze the bruised
berries through a bag of linen, and after straining the juice through a rush
strainer they put it in small flagons': tum per lineum fiscum, quod pertri-
verant, exprimunt, et per *colum* iunceum liquatum sucum lagunculis . . .
condunt.

(g) Virg. *Georg.* 2. 241–2 (on testing soils). 'Take down from the grimy walls
close-woven baskets and *strainers* for the wine-press':

tu spisso vimine qualos
*cola*que prelorum fumosis deripe tectis.

(h) Martial 14. 103 (accompanying the gift of a wine-strainer). 'Take my advice
and weaken with my snow the strong cups of Setian wine; with a poorer
vintage you can dye (i.e. discolour) a linen sieve':

Setinos, moneo, nostra nive frange trientes
pauperiore mero tingere lina potes.

(j) Pomp. *Dig.* 34. 2. 21 (on the validity of legacies). 'In the case of silver
drinking vessels, there is some doubt whether it (the legacy) includes only
vessels which can be drunk from, or whether it also includes items acquired
for making the preparations for drinking, such as *snow-strainers* and
decanters; but it is more reasonable to include these as well': in argento
potorio, utrum id dumtaxat sit, in quo bibi possit, an etiam id, quod ad
praeparationem bibendi comparatum est, veluti *colum nivarium* et urceoli,
dubitari potest; sed propius est, ut haec quoque insint.

[1] quae? *Mynors, fortasse recte.*

DISCUSSION

There is much confusion about the various instruments to which this term is applied. Although the basic meaning of the word, which denotes a fine dripping or 'percolating' process, is clear enough, it is used of a variety of items not described by the writers who mention them. In order to avoid confusion I have included the *colum nivarium*, a special kind of wine-strainer, which was made of metal, and is, strictly speaking, out of place here.

Design and operation

The use of this term was, as the related verbs *colare* and *percolare* indicate, restricted to the filtering or skimming of liquids (for the related types of sieving and sifting instruments see the entries s.v. 'crates' and 'cribrum'). The word appears in Cato's vineyard inventory in two forms (passage *c*): (1) a general strainer, made of wickerwork, (2) a finer one specially used for taking off the 'flower' (Fr. 'fleur de vin'), a fungus which sometimes affected the wine in cask, and must be skimmed off to prevent contamination. Each of these operations would postulate a wide-mouthed vessel of concave shape. But the inverted cone design assumed by Rich (*Dict. Ant.* s.v.) for all the operations mentioned, is not necessary, except where extraneous matter is to be trapped by pouring into a narrow container, as in straining gravy into a gravy-boat. Our kitchen sieve or colander, on the other hand, which is used for the reverse process of running off liquids, need only be hemispherical.

Basketry strainers (cola prelorum, etc.). The passages cited above have been selected as representative of a range of utensils having much the same function, that of filtering out unwanted material. Prominent among them are the 'vat-strainers' (*cola prelorum* – passages *b* and *g*), mentioned in Cato's inventory as 'wicker strainers' (*cola vitilia*). These strainers, which were used immediately after the first pressing in the treading-vat (*forus, linter*), were designed to trap the skins and pulp, leaving the must to drain away. This material was then discharged into earthenware containers to be taken to the lever-press (*torcular, prelum*), or screw-press (*cochlea, Graecanica*) for pressing. A finer type of strainer made, not of wickerwork, but of rushes or broom (passage *e*), was used for the quite different process of skimming off the scum which rises to the top of the liquor during the boiling of the must to produce the preserve known as *defrutum*. These strainers were made with a much closer mesh, as may be seen from Columella's account of the making of myrtle-wine (passage *f*). Cato's 'skimmer' (passage *c*) may well have been a large flattish spoon or ladle

53/82

made of perforated metal. That it was made of a different material from
the wicker strainer used to strain the mixture after treading may be
inferred from the text. The *cola vitilia* of passage *c* were presumably made
to fit the mouth of the *dolium*.

The colum nivarium. It is well known that the Romans, like the Greeks,
ancient and modern, preferred to drink their wine in almost every state
except its natural one. They mulled it, they resinated it, they spiced it.
When they wanted it chilled, as well as watered, the device they used was
a convex metal strainer, very like our tea-strainer, as surviving examples
make clear. Snow was placed in the strainer, and the wine was poured
through the snow. Only full-bodied wines could stand this treatment: as
Martial explains (passage *h*), wine of poorer quality would simply be
strained through a linen sieve (*saccus linteus*) to remove impurities, staining
the linen bag in the process. See further p. 93 s.v. *saccus nivarius*.

Extant representatives

(1) *colum vinarium.* Rich (*Dict. Ant.* s.v. 'colum') shows the same illustration as for *saccus vinarius*, but the object depicted is a basket, and does not
conform to the requirements described above. D–S, I. 2, 1332, fig. 1728,
show a basketry vessel of deep and narrow dimensions, widening to a
bulb at the base. This is only part of a scene depicted in full on a bas-
relief from the Villa Albani, Rome, showing, to l. a man carrying a
basket of grapes to the press, next to him, another pouring the grapes in;
c. three men treading; to their r. a man pouring the proceeds of the
treading through a filter; at extreme r. another man discharging the skins
and husks into an earthenware container. For other details of the processes,
see Part Three, Introduction, pp. 112ff.

(2) *colum nivarium.* Rich (*Dict. Ant.* s.v. 'colum') is quite misleading, and
offers no illustration that meets the requirements. D–S, s.v. 'colum', II,
1332, figs. 1730–4, provide a number of excellent illustrations of various
types found in excavations, some of them very elaborate. Note particularly
a bronze specimen from Pompeii now in the National Museum at Naples
(fig. 1730), showing the holes distributed in an artistic pattern (Museo
Borb. II, pl. LX; cf. *ibid.* III, pl. XXXI, no. 5c – another elegant specimen of
similar design). Most elaborate of all those depicted is a strainer now in the
Museum at Nîmes, Provence, with a delicately curved handle terminating
in a duck's head, the attachment to the actual strainer being in the form
of the forepart of a lion, holding the strainer in its paws (fig. 1732).

PART TWO

Survival

(*a*) *Of the name.* It. 'colare', to 'filter', 'colatoio', a 'strainer', Eng. 'colander'.

(*b*) *Of the utensil.* The close resemblance of the *colum nivarium* to our tea-strainer is presumably the result of similarity of function. It may be noted that wine-jugs fitted with silver pourers were often equipped with a strainer. I have one in my possession which is very useful for pouring wine-cups.

7. Cribrum (-i, n.) (fr. *cernere*, 'separate'), (i) gen. *sieve*; (ii) sp. *flour-sifter, bolter*

No entry in *R-E*.

Not in Varro, *LL*. Not in Isidore, except with the meaning 'flour-sifter'.

(*a*) Cato 25 (on selecting grapes). 'Sift the grape-refuse every day, while it is still fresh, through a bed stretched on cords, or make a *sieve* for the purpose': vinaceos cotidie recentis succernito, lecto restibus subtento, vel *cribrum* illi rei parato.

(*b*) *Ibid.* 48. 2 (on making a cypress nursery). 'Make ridges five feet wide, spread crumbled manure on them, hoe it in, and pulverize the clods. Flatten the ridges, and hollow it out slightly; then sow the seed as thickly as flax, *sifting* earth over it a finger's breadth deep': porcas pedes quinos latas facito, eo stercus minutum addito; consarito glebasque comminuito. porcam planam facito, paulum concavam. tum semen serito crebrum tamquam linum, eo terram *cribro* incernito altam digitum transversum. (Cf. *ibid.* 151; Pliny, *HN* 17. 73, etc.)

(*c*) Colum. 8. 5. 16 (on the treatment of newly hatched chicks). 'The chicks should be placed in a *sieve* made of vetch or darnel, which has already been used, and should then be fumigated': cribro viciario vel etiam loliario, qui iam fuerit in usu, pulli superponantur, deinde . . . fumigentur.

(*d*) Ulp. *Dig.* 33. 7. 12. 10 (on the *instrumentum fundi*). 'Also the *sieves*, and the wagons for hauling out the dung (are included)': et cribra et plaustra, quibus stercus evehatur (continentur).

(*e*) Edict. Diocl. (Aphrodisias), Col. ii 11. 22 ff. (= ch. 15. 11. 56 ff.). '*Sieve* for the threshing-floor, leather: den. 250': cribrum areale coriacium; '*sieve* for the finest meal, leather: den 400': cribrum pelli[c]eum simulare; '*sieve*, largest size, woven: den. 200': cribrum textile maximum; and four other types, variously tariffed.

(*f*) Varro, *Men.* 69. 'So that a new *sieve* may hang on a new peg': ut novum cribrum novo paxillo pendeat.

(*g*) Cato 76. 3 (recipe for making *placenta*). 'When you have dried out the cheese completely, knead it in a clean mixing-bowl, and make it as fine as possible. Then take a clean *flour-sifter*, and force the cheese through it into the bowl': ubi omne caseum bene siccaveris, in mortarium purum manibus condepsito comminuitoque quam maxime. deinde *cribrum farinarium* purum sumito caseumque per cribrum facito transeat in mortarium.

DISCUSSION

The sieve (*cribrum*) is distinct from the strainer (*colum*), the former being used for the separation of dry material, the latter for material in suspension. Sieving and sifting is done by shaking the material in a container with holes or slats so as to release the finer material, leaving the residue in the container.

Shapes and sizes

Sieves of different sizes and varying mesh were as important on the farm as in the kitchen or bakery. Diocletian's Price Edict (passage *e*) lists six 'standard' types, with their maximum prices. Not all the types mentioned are known from surviving specimens, but we may classify them as follows: (1) the large, circular riddle with a deep rim, as still used by gardeners for sifting earth (passage *b*); (2) the 'sieve for threshing' (passage *e*), which was used for sifting the ears of corn left on the floor among the straw after threshing, will have been of this type; (3) the small flour-sifter (passage *g*); the type can be identified from surviving specimens (see below).

Materials

As with other forms of basketry, sieves to suit various purposes were made in a variety of materials. Columella (passage *c*) mentions vetch and darnel, used for plaiting over the frame, which would be of rigid material. The Roman sieve reproduced by Forbes (*SAT*, IV, fig. 24, p. 182), for which he gives neither an account of the materials used, nor an approximate date, nor the size nor provenance (!), appears to have been made by plaiting over bundles of reeds with raffia-like material. Three of the seven types listed in the Edict (passage *e*) are of leather, the most expensive being a flour-sifter (*c. simulare*), made of high-grade leather with fine perforations. The ordinary flour-sifter for domestic use (*c. farinarium*) was made of earthenware (see Pl. 2*a*).

Hilgers (fig. 29, p. 55) shows an extant specimen which formed part of a 'baking outfit' (Fig. 33). The sifter could be hung on the wall when not in use (passage *f*) (see below, 'Extant specimens').

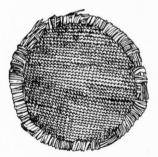

Fig. 32. Cribrum (*a*)

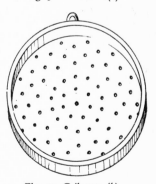

Fig. 33. Cribrum (*b*)

Uses

It is interesting to observe that in two of the passages cited, pieces of equipment are being used for purposes other than those for which they were designed; it is typical of Cato (passage *a*) that he should recommend using a mattress of cords for sieving the grape-refuse, with the alternative of making a proper sieve! The same thrifty attitude is also reflected in the improvised 'house' for newly-hatched chickens (passage *c*).

Extant representations

Of the flour-sifter: Sarcophagus of P. Nonius Zethus in the Museo Chiaramonti, Rome (Amelung, *SVM*, 1, pl. 84: *ibid.* (Text) 1. 4, no. 685) (see Pl. 2*a*). On the r. hand panel flanking the dedication, upper, r., a large sieve (original of rushes? – see below, s.v. 'Extant specimens'), with a prominent flange.

Extant specimens

Type (i): Forbes, *SAT*, IV, 182, fig. 24; made of woven rushes (Fig. 32). No details of size or provenance given. Type (ii): Hilgers, fig. 29; Paoli, *Vita romana*, p. 147, pl. 81.

Survival

(*a*) *Of the name.* It. 'crivello', a sieve.
(*b*) *Of the instrument.* Circular riddles made of withies were in use for sifting grain as late as the 18th century in England, and the type may still be seen in parts of southern Europe; see Scheuermeier, *Bauernwerk*, 1, 138, fig. 313, where it is described as universal in the Marche, Lazio, Campania, Lucania and N. Calabria.

PART THREE

UTENSILS MADE OF EARTHENWARE, STONE, METAL, WOOD AND LEATHER

(I) CLASSIFICATION PROBLEMS

The articles appearing in the first two sections of this survey of farm equipment have been broadly classified in terms of the material used in their manufacture, and more precisely in terms of the kind of operations for which they were required. Where the categories overlap, or spill over into one another, or where the same term was employed to denote a wide variety of items, suitable cross-references have been provided. The items of equipment discussed in this section, however, display such great variety in their shapes, their sizes, and the materials from which they were made, as well as in the uses to which they were put, that a strictly alphabetical order of presentation has been chosen as causing the least amount of confusion. Many utensils of a particular design were made in metal as well as in earthenware, and these variations are duly noted in the text. In this section, as elsewhere, it has been no easy task to establish the size and shape of some of the items, and even more difficult to distinguish specific from more generalized references in the sources. The Roman writers themselves, even when writing on technical questions, were often, and quite naturally, casual in their language, and it is therefore unwise to attempt too great a degree of precision in differentiating one from another, or to assume that a particular utensil or container was always used for its original purpose (that is, assuming that the original purpose can be determined: the linguistic evidence on which some modern writers have leaned heavily is notoriously unreliable). This problem has been neatly summed up for us by D. A. Amyx in the following observation: 'The real problem is perhaps to determine *what was not called a kophinos*. On this latter question, our position is, as usual, far from secure' (*Hesperia* 27 (1958), 190).

A further difficulty arises from the fact that earthenware containers have been hitherto studied almost exclusively from the aesthetic and decorative points of view, and very little work has so far been done on the identification and classification of the pots and pans used in everyday Roman life. In this department Greek studies are more advanced than Roman; the excavation of the Athenian Agora has led to much careful and systematic research for which there is as yet no parallel in Roman studies.

(2) ON THE ASSOCIATION OF THE NAMES OF VESSELS
WITH THEIR FORM AND FUNCTION

It is natural for lexicographers and compilers of reference works for students to produce neatly classified lists of objects, each with an appropriate text-figure, thus creating an impression of certainty of identification where none exists. I have drawn attention earlier in this book to some of the difficulties involved in sorting out the various basketry containers mentioned in our sources. With earthenware these problems seem to increase both in quantity and diversity. The best starting-point for discussion is in the introduction to Barbara Philippaki's monograph, *The Attic Stamnos* (Oxford, 1967). The author begins with a forthright statement: 'Most of the names given to Greek vases are merely conventional' (p. xvii). 'It is only natural', the writer continues, 'that contemporary authors and inscriptions do not take the trouble to define the vases they refer to, common things of everyday life. The later authors who try to do so were in no better condition than we are' (*ibid.* p. xviii). I believe, on the contrary, that we are in a rather better position than Dr Philippaki suggests, since we have access to vast quantities of specimens in the museums, while many of the vessels referred to in late commentators or lexicographers had long ceased to be manufactured when they wrote. Dr Philippaki next provides the reader with a list of names of vases which have been securely linked to a specific shape by the evidence of inscriptions on the bases themselves. Her list includes the following names which are relevant to the present enquiry: *hydria, amphora, kantharos, kalathos,* and *krater. Stamnos,* however, belongs to a different class: 'for the shape of vase discussed here, there is no reason to call it a *stamnos*' (*ibid.* p. xix). If this is the position in relation to Greek vessels, where both name and vessel appear together, it has been, until recently, even more difficult for the student of Roman material; as H. B. Walters pointed out long ago (*HAP* II, 472), 'there is ... no clear line of distinction to be drawn between the various forms of drinking-cups or of jugs or dishes, as is the case with Greek vases'. Hölder's classification and grouping of forms into urns, jars, jugs, etc. (1897) nevertheless provided a useful basis for further study, and Hilgers has recently produced a comprehensive catalogue of the Roman names, with complete coverage of the literary references, with good, though not complete, archaeological links. His interpretations, however, often strain the evidence, as we shall notice later. Further progress can now be made in the identification of form and name with the publication of John Hayes' systematic account of late Roman pottery (*Late Roman Pottery*, Oxford, 1971), and M. H. Callender's monograph on the Roman *amphora* (*Roman Amphorae*, Oxford, 1965) shows what can be done by detailed study of one of the most important forms. It may of course be argued that what has been attempted in the present study is largely wasted effort. What the historian needs is accurate analysis of the content of hoards of commercial vessels, showing the distribution of containers of different capacities, and so on. Does it matter whether a jug was called a *hydria*, an *urceus* or an *urna*? But the purpose of this study is not primarily to help towards the solution of problems in economic history; the main aim has been to gather together the basic literary and lexical references to various items of equipment, to identify them where possible and match them with the archaeological material. In many cases nothing more has been achieved beyond the exposure of traditional identifications or explanations as erroneous or unproven, while here and there the points established may help to provide a more secure basis for those engaged in economic or social history.

(3) PREPONDERANCE OF WINE AND OIL MANUFACTURE IN THIS SECTION

More than half of the forty or more items discussed are connected with the processing of wine and oil. There is much confusion among translators and lexicographers about the meaning of some of the terms, and the nature of many of these operations. Since the correct identification of a particular instrument or vessel depends on a proper understanding of the whole process of making wine or oil I have thought it best to give a detailed account of each process, introducing the technical terms at the appropriate point in the sequence of operations. Some of these operations (e.g. pressing) are common to both wine- and oil-making. In order to avoid unnecessary repetition and cross-referencing, I have prefaced this section with an account of the process of making wine (below, pp. 112ff.). The oil-making process, with its complex variety of milling and pressing devices, does not lend itself to this treatment, and the whole subject is dealt with in Appendix A. The reader will find a short account in the discussion s.v. 'lacus', pp. 158ff.

(4) ON THE SIZES OF THE VARIOUS CONTAINERS

It is of course well known that some of the containers described in this section were also used as standard measures of volume. But this does not mean that all vessels bearing the same name were standardized as to volume. The best-known illustration of this lack of standardization occurs in the various uses of the word *amphora*. In its original Greek form the word denotes a two-handled vessel of earthenware, used mainly for the transport and storage of wine. In its most characteristic form the amphora was of quite small diameter in relation to its height, and terminated in a point, making it possible to store numerous varieties of wine for sale to the public in a relatively small space, as in the well-known examples of surviving wine-shops at Pompeii. See the section on the *amphora* (below, pp. 122 ff.). But the *amphorae* recovered in recent years from numerous excavations on the sea-bed of the Mediterranean show great variety both in shape and size (see e.g. the complete plan of the wreck of a Byzantine merchantman discovered by the Pennsylvania expedition, the contents being accurately plotted and sampled, as shown by G. F. Bass in *Archaeology under Water*, London, 1966, fig. 34, with detailed discussion, pp. 108–48; most of the *amphorae* in the hold are of the round-bellied type).

There was also a standard amphora, used as a measure of volume for liquids by both Greeks and Romans, the former standard, at 9·18 gallons, being 1½ times the capacity of its Roman counterpart, which was equivalent to the *quadrantal* at 6·12 gallons.

(5) LEGAL EVIDENCE ON SIZES AND TYPES

Much valuable information on the sizes and types of containers is furnished by the legal Codes, especially in numerous passages which set out to define what items may or may not be included in a legacy of wine, since there was evidently much divergence of legal opinion on whether certain items were to be regarded as part of the *instrumentum fundi*, which included both physically immovable items, and items which were thought to be essential to the normal running of the estate. Many of these texts are included in the select evidence for particular containers (see e.g. s.v. 'aenum'). Two longer passages from the Digest are included here, since they provide useful information on a number of matters of general concern.

(1) Pomp. *Dig.* 33. 6. 2 (on testamentary dispositions). 'In the case of *storage jars* I do not think it correct that a bequest of wine should also include the storage jars, especially if they have been sunk in the storage area, or are of a size which makes them difficult to move. In the case of *vats* or *troughs*, I think one must concede that they should be included (in the legacy), unless they are similarly immovable in the field, as if they formed part of the fixed equipment of the farm. *Wineskins* do not have to be included in a bequest of wine; nor, in my opinion, should *large wineskins* be included either': in *doliis* non puto verum, ut vino legato et dolia

debeantur, maxime si depressa in cella vinaria fuerint, aut ea sunt quae per magnitudinem difficile moventur. in *cuppis* autem sive *cuppulis* puto admittendum et ea deberi, nisi pari modo immobiles in agro velut instrumentum agri erant. vino legato *utres* non debebuntur: nec *culleos* quidem deberi dico.

(2) Proc. *Dig.* 33. 6. 15 (on testamentary dispositions). 'The testator bequeathed the wine with the jars (containers). Trebatius says that the wine in the *jars* should not be included (in the bequest), holding that there is a difference between the words of the testator and his intention. But "dolia" (*storage jars*) are not included in the category of "vasa vinaria" (wine vessels); nevertheless I would not agree with Trebatius' contention that the wine which was in the "dolia" (in cask), that is, wine which was not in "vasa vinaria", was excluded from the legacy. I believe the correct opinion is that in the case of a person to whom wine has been bequeathed "cum vasis" (with the vessels), the legacy includes the "*amphorae*" and "*cadi*" in which we keep the wine after it has been run off ("diffusa"). When we decant wine into "*amphorae*" and "*cadi*" we do so with the intention of keeping it there until we have occasion to use it, and it goes without saying that we sell it with these containers; but when we put it into *storage jars* ("dolia") our intention is different; surely it is with the intention of decanting it later into "*amphorae*" and "*cadi*", or of putting it up for sale, excluding the storage jars': vinum cum vasis legavit. negat Trebatius quod in *doliis* sit deberi et sensum legatoris alium putat esse, verborum alium: ceterum *dolia* in vasis vinariis non sunt, tamen non concederem Trebatio vinum quod in *doliis* esset, id est quod in vasis non esset, non esse legatum. illud verum esse puto, cui vinum cum vasis legatum erit, ei *amphoras cados* in quibus vina diffusa servamus, legatos esse: vinum enim in *amphoras* et *cados* hac mente diffundimus, ut in his sit, donec usus causa probetur, et scilicet id vendimus cum his *cadis* et *amphoris*: in *dolia* autem alia mente coicimus, scilicet ut ex his postea vel in *amphoras* et *cados* diffundamus vel sine ipsis doliis veneat.

(6) ON THE RANGE OF USE OF PARTICULAR CONTAINERS OF THIS CLASS

It is particularly important to observe that many of the containers mentioned in this section, as in earlier sections of the book, were used for more than one purpose. Brief reference has already been made to this aspect (above, p. 107), but the matter is of more than passing interest, particularly where any attempt is to be made to examine the wider economic aspects, such as that of trade in a particular commodity. In fact, some of the commonest types of vessel used in Roman commerce were put to an astonishing variety of uses. Taking the commonest of all earthenware containers used in commerce, the *amphora*, we find that it is still too frequently assumed or implied, even in official Reports on archaeological finds, that these vessels were seldom used to hold commodities other than wine, and occasionally oil. In a recent study of amphora-stamps, M. H. Callender drew attention to this misconception, and included in his survey a list of proven contents totalling thirty separate items, ranging from honey to cleansing cream (*lomentum*). The references in the text to variety of contents known for each of the vessels discussed is not exhaustive, but the commonest attested uses are noted, and reference is made to less common, but important uses.

(7) FROM VINTAGE TO STOREROOM

(1) *From the vineyard to the treading-vat*

The vintager (*vindemiator*), armed with a small crescent-shaped hook (*falcula vineatica, unguis ferreus*), removed the ripe clusters, placing them in a basket (*corbula* – Varr. 1. 15 etc., *qualus vindemiatorius* – Dig. 33. 7. 8). These would be small enough to be easily carried round the vineyard. As these were filled their contents were emptied into larger baskets (*quali exceptorii*, the term used in the *Digest* to distinguish them from the *q. vindemiatorii*). The larger baskets were then carried by pack-donkey or by wagon (as on the Cherchel vintage mosaic) to the treading-vat (*forus, linter*) for the first stage of the conversion of grapes into wine. We also have references to wooden troughs (*alvei, lintres, naviae*) which were used for conveying the contents of the picking-baskets to the treading-vats.

(2) *The treading*

The purpose of this preliminary treading of the grapes, which was quite distinct from the pressing, was to liberate some of the juice by this relatively gentle squeezing process, producing a 'mush' (*pes*) (which still contained a great volume of juice), making it easier to complete the next stage, that of mechanical pressing by lever- or screw-press without loss of juice. The juice expressed by treading was used for the boiling down of the must into *defrutum*, which was then used as a preservative or for giving body to poor wine (see Colum. 12. 19 for a complete account of this process).

The treading-vats were usually located in the same area as the pressing-rooms (Vitruv. 6. 6. 2), so as to avoid any waste of time between the two processes. The vat consisted of a rectangular tank made of stone with shallow sides, elevated to a height of three or four steps, as Palladius tells us (1. 18) from the receiving-tanks placed at either side. Sometimes these receivers were replaced by large pottery containers (*labra*), set immediately beneath the outlet-pipes (Virgil, *Georg.* 2. 6: 'plenis spumat vindemia labris'), which are clearly shown in several well-known representations (e.g. *RF*, pl. 59).

The treaders (*calcatores*), whose numbers varied between two and seven or more to a vat, worked bare-footed, supporting themselves either by means of ropes above their heads, or by crutched sticks (see e.g. *RF*, pl. 60), the rhythm of the task being promoted by a musical accompaniment. The process is admirably described in the *Geoponika* (6. 11: *RF*, p. 46). See Pl. 7.

(3) *The pressing*

After the vat had discharged its flow of new wine, the residue at the bottom was removed, and after straining through a *colum vinarium* was placed in flexible baskets (*fisci, fiscinae, fiscellae*), and set under the press (*prelum, cochlea*). The oldest type, the lever-press (*prelum*), is fully described by Cato (chs. 18–19), together with a complete inventory of materials required to build it, as well as constructional details both for the press itself and for the building in which it is to be housed. Equipped with a capstan (*sucula*) for lowering the press-beam (*torcular*), Cato's version of the press shows a more rational use of human strength than the more picturesque types represented on the monuments. But they took up an inordinate amount of space (the lever could be 40 feet long). The screw-press (*cochlea*) introduced, according to Pliny, some twenty years before the time of writing (*HN* 18. 317), was both technically more efficient and dispensed with the space-consuming lever. On these technical improvements see Appendix A, pp. 225 ff.

(4) *From the pressroom to the storage-jars*

From the pressroom the wine was channelled or piped to the *cella vinaria* for the first stage of vinification. This area was normally an open court-yard with a northerly aspect, a necessary orientation for keeping conditions as cool as possible during the first stage of the fermentation process, which lasted nine days (Pliny, *HN* 14. 124). On reaching the *cella vinaria* the newly pressed and as yet unfermented wine (*mustum*) was run off into earthenware containers, ranging in capacity from *dolia* or *orcae* of up to 200 *modii* (= 65 amphorae or more than 400 gallons) to the smaller *seriae*.

The process of getting the must from the pressroom to the individual storage jars in the *cella vinaria*, as practised on estate no. 3 Boscoreale, can be followed from stage to stage as a result of the high standard of excavation, and the accurate plans (as reproduced, e.g. by Mau–Kelsey, cf. *RF*, p. 423, fig. 5), enabling an accurate model to be constructed at the Museo della Civiltà Romana in Rome. The description that follows is taken from Cagnat–Chapot, *Manuel d'arch. rom.* 1 (1916), 365, with some modifications. 'One entered the cella (R) by mounting a flight of three steps (R 1), which began in the corridor (Q) half way down the east wall of the cella. The wall was relatively low, except alongside room S, where it was crowned by a balcony; on the street side (R2), it was no more than 2 metres high. The *cella* was open to the sky, to maintain a flow of fresh air; for the same reason the wall giving on to the street (R2), which faced SSE, was pierced by numerous apertures. The storage jars were buried in the earth in four double files, with enough space left for easy movement around them. There were single rows on the W and S sides. Along the wall dividing the cella from the courtyard (A) ran a long, stone-built vat (R3), pierced with holes which corresponded exactly with the rows of jars. At pressing-time, the workmen poured the must from the receivers (P2) into a tall basin (P3) in the west wall of the pressroom. The bottom of this basin was pierced by a hole, to which was fitted a pipe through which the liquid flowed out and across the corridor (Q), and, passing through the wall, discharged into the vat, and filled it. At each aperture in the vat, another longer pipe was fitted, which conveyed the contents of the vat to the different jars in succession.' Cagnat (*op. cit.*) notes that the same general lay-out has been observed on several provincial wine-farms; cf. the reconstructed farm in C. J. M. de Vogüé, *Syrie centrale*, Paris, 1865–97, 1, 38; and, for Algeria, L. Jacquot, 'Les hacendas romaines', in *Rec. de la Soc. arch. de Constantine*, 43 (1909), 9ff.

(5) *Storage arrangements*

It is often stated quite erroneously that only choice wines were kept for several years 'in cask', that is, in the large *dolia* in the cella vinaria. In his inventory of vineyard equipment (ch. 11) Cato calls for enough *dolia* to contain the product of five vintages of 800 *cullei*. Earlier in the book he advises the owner of a vineyard to provide 'many storage jars, so that it will be gratifying to wait for higher prices' (ch. 3). In this way the grower could offer wines from one to five years old to the wholesale purchaser straight from the 'cask'. The normal container for transporting bulk wine in Italy was the skin of an ox holding one *culleus* (140 gallons), mounted on a wagon frame. This was filled from a vat of one *culleus* capacity (*labrum culleare*), set on a high platform from which its contents could be discharged into the skin via the neck, as shown on a well-known wall-painting from Pompeii (see Rich, *Dict. Ant.* s.v. 'culleus'; Brehaut, p. 133).

In the northern provinces, however, bulk wine was transported in coopered casks (*cupae*), as Pliny (*HN* 14. 132) explains: 'In the Alpine regions, they put the wine in wooden casks (*vasa lignea*) bound with hoops, and in the depth of winter they even light fires to prevent the wine from freezing.' The vin ordinaire for mass consumption was ladled off into *amphorae* (capacity 6–7 gallons), whose projecting handles made it easy for the local innkeeper or retailer to convey his supplies by hand, as in the well-known terra-cotta relief from Pompeii showing two men carrying a full *amphora* of wine on a pole across their shoulders, the container being secured by means of a rope passing through the handles (see Rich, *Dict. Ant.* s.v. 'amphora'). The elongated shape and pointed feet of these vessels made it easy to stack them in the storeroom, either leaning against the walls, or with their spikes dug into the soft earth or sand, as they may be seen in surviving *tabernae* at Pompeii and Ostia (see Pl. 12*c*). Another method of storage was to stack them in tiers (*in cuneum*) on specially made racks (see *TLL*, s.v. 'amphora', and below, s.v. 'cadus', p. 129). Wines retained 'in cask' for a varying number of years were subsequently removed to the storerooms on the top floor of the farmhouse (*apotheca, cella superior*) to mature in a warm temperature. It was commonly thought that maturation could be speeded up by transferring the stored amphorae to a storeroom located above the smoke-room (*fumarium*), where timber was seasoned. Storerooms above the bath-house are also mentioned in this connection. Columella, the only surviving technical writer to mention the smoking process, notes that too much exposure to smoke is harmful: 'for this reason', he adds, 'there should be another loft (*tabulatum*), to which the wine may be removed, to prevent its becoming contaminated by too much smoking' (1. 6. 20).

(8) THE RETAILING OF WINE TO THE CONSUMER

Surviving representations provide valuable information on this important phase, and often present a lively and vigorous picture of different methods of handling, where the literary record has left us almost nothing. From these monumental sources we can identify at least two methods by which the grower disposed of his product to the retailer or the large private consumer, and a variety of methods employed in direct sales of small quantities of wine to individual purchasers. Transfer of wine from grower to retailer is vividly brought before us in a marble bas-relief now in Ince Blundell Hall, near Liverpool (Pl. 10*b*). Since this monument has sometimes been incorrectly interpreted, it should be pointed out that while many farmers disposed of their crop to a contractor 'on the tree' (Cato 147), many will no doubt have attempted to increase their income by providing sufficient storage 'in cask' (*in dolio*) to enable them to hold out for higher prices, as Cato had recommended (*ibid.* 3. 2). In the present case the owner of the vineyard is also a dealer in wine. The scene is laid in the open wine-maturation area (*cella vinaria*), and the wine is being sold, not from stocks held in *amphorae* by a wholesale dealer, but directly from the *dolia*, here shown embedded in the ground. The transaction is obviously not taking place in a wine-dealer's shop, as Callender supposed (*Roman Amphorae*, p. 144). The prospective buyer is shown (lower r. in the picture), enjoying a tasting before giving his order. At the top r. the grower is seated at a table, on which money is lying in some profusion. In his l. hand he is holding a manuscript (the price list?), and at his side is a tally-clerk with a book (the account-book?) in his hand. In the centre of the panel two slaves are actively occupied in filling an *amphora* from a *dolium* by means of a ladle (*trulla*).

Another method of bulk disposal, in which the wine was conveyed from the estate in the skin of an ox (*culleus*) set on a wagon, and later piped off into *amphorae* at the dealer's shop, can be understood, though without the liveliness of the Ince Blundell panel, by combining Cato's description (ch. 154) with the end process as depicted on a Pompeian mural (Fig. 38). Cato's description of the filling of the container is given at pp. 140f. s.v. 'culleus'. The painting shows a stationary four-wheeled cart, which is completely filled by the great wineskin. Two employees of the vendor are filling an *amphora*, piping it off from the skin through one of the hind feet; another *amphora*, waiting to be filled, is propped up against a wheel.

The sale of wine in small quantities is illustrated on a number of surviving reliefs, as well as in a single wall-painting from Pompeii. Since wooden casks were the normal containers for bulk supply in the northern provinces (see the discussion s.v. 'cupa', below, p. 143), it is somewhat surprising to find no representation of the 'bodega' method of filling small containers directly from the cask. This may be due to mere chance: the representations are few. Alternatively, it may be due to another factor; by the time that local wine-production began to develop in Gaul, the storage *amphora* in which wine had been regularly imported from Italy was already so much a part of the tradition of the trade that it continued to be the ordinary container both in the wine-selling establishment and in the taberna, where wine was sold for consumption on the premises. The 'off-licence' shop was no doubt very popular; but I know of only one representation of it, namely the Gallo-Roman bas-relief from Til-

Châtel, now in the Museum at Dijon. Here the wine-shop has a projecting counter, fitted with apertures, into which funnels are placed, The customer, a young man, places his container, a one-handled jug, beneath the orifice, and the server, a woman, fills the jug via the funnel. The same method is illustrated on a gravestone from Jünkerath in the Moselle area, now in the Landesmuseum, Trier (*TZ* 1932, 39). Leather bottles, used as containers from very early times, are still in widespread use, especially in Spain, for carrying smallish quantities of wine. They appear in the same retail sale context in another wall-painting from Pompeii; here the wine is being taken round from door to door in leather bottles loaded on to a cart (Helbig, *Wandmalereien*, Leipzig, 1873, no. 1487 cited by Déchelette–Grenier, *Manuel d'archéologie gallo-romaine*, VI, 2, 601, n. 3; the following pages give a brief but very instructive account of wine-transport containers, with notes on inscribed *amphorae*, and *amphora*-stamps).

1. **Ahenum** (-i, n.), also **aeneum** (-i, n.) and **aenum** (-i, n.), *cauldron*

See also below, s.v. 'cortina'.

No entry in *R-E*.

Not in Varro, *LL* (exc. *vas aeneum*).

Not in Isidore.

(a) *Corp. Gloss.* s.v. 'aeneum'. aeneum v 560. 19. caldarium dicimus, qui de aere est Papias. aenus λέβης III 498. 75. aena λέβης II 12. 2. aeni Vergilius: e foliis undam trepidi despumat aeni (Georg. I. 296) v 163. 50. aeni ollas quas [c]aulas dicimus v 163. 49. aena vasa aerea v 163. 44. ollas aeneas v 163. 5. aenis aeneis IV 11. 38.

(b) Cato 11. 2 (vineyard inventory); cf. 13. 1 (cap. 5 *amphorae*.), etc. '1 *copper cauldron* holding 20 *amphorae*': *ahenum* quod capiat culleum I.

(c) *Ibid.* 105. 1 (recipe for Greek wine). 'Pour 20 quadrantals of must into a *copper* or lead *cauldron* and heat': musti Q. XX in *aheneum* aut plumbeum infundito, ignem subdito.

(d) Colum. 12. 16. 1 (recipe for making raisins). 'They should then be heated in a *bronze cauldron* or a large new clay vessel': deinde *aeno* vel in nova fictili ampla . . . calefieri convenit.

(e) Paul. *Dig.* 33. 7. 8. 3. 'There is little difference between cooking pots and the *cauldron*, which hangs above the hearth: the latter boils the water for drinking, while the porridge is cooked in the former': nec multum differt inter caccabos et *aenum*, quod supra focum pendet: hic aqua ad potandum calefit, in illis pulmentarium coquitur.

(f) Ovid, *Fast.* 3. 821–2 (on the feast of Minerva). 'Worship this goddess, you who remove the stains from damaged garments; worship her, whoever you are that prepare *cauldrons* for (dyeing) fleeces':

hanc cole, qui maculas laesis de vestibus aufers;
hanc cole, velleribus quisquis *aena* paras.

(*g*) Statius, *Silv.* 1. 2. 151 (description of a mansion). 'Marble ... was there, and blocks that matched the deep sea in colour, and the stone that awakes the envy of Oebalian purple and the mixer of the Tyrian *cauldron*':

hic flexus onyx et concolor alto
vena mari rupesque nitent, quis purpura saepe
Oebalis et Tyrii moderator livet *aheni.*

(*h*) Seneca, *Herc. Oet.* 663–4 (on a middle-class wife). 'For her no soft wool twice dipped in Sidonian *cauldrons* drinks the scarlet dyes':

ne Sidonio mollis *aeno*
repetita bibit lana rubores.

DISCUSSION

The word *aes* gives the adjectival forms *aheneus, aenus* and *aeneus.* Both *aenum* (passage *d*) and *ahenum* (passage *b*) were commonly used alone as substantives (cf. our use of 'copper' meaning a copper coin or a copper boiler – the latter an exact parallel), with the meaning kettle or cauldron (see also s.v. 'vas', pp. 203–4). The principal use of these large vessels was for boiling down the must to produce a great variety of salted, spiced and sweetened wines, for which there was a heavy demand; these included Cato's Greek and Coan wines (*De Agri Cultura* 105, 112), preserved with brine, and mead (*mulsum*), a mixture of boiled-down must and honey (Colum. 12. 41). The boiling-down process involved removal of the scum, as Virgil explains in a delightful passage on country life at night, when the farmer is working late into the evening making torches, while his wife works away at her weaving, or 'boils down the sweet must on the fire, and with leaves skims off the surface of the bubbling *cauldron*':

et quidam seros hiberni ad luminis ignes
pervigilat, ferroque faces inspicat acuto;
interea longum cantu solata laborem
arguto coniunx percurrit pectine telas,
aut dulcis musti Volcano decoquit umorem
et foliis undam trepidi despumat *aheni.*   *Georg.* 1. 291–6

As the last three citations make clear, bronze kettles or cauldrons were also used in the process of dyeing. Large-scale dyeing of garments or fabrics was carried on in buildings equipped with large, oblong vats, the dyestuffs being prepared by extraction, usually at fairly high temperatures, in a cauldron, passing thence by channels into the vats. This sort of lay-out may be seen at Pompeii (Mau–Kelsey, pp. 397ff. and fig. 229: plan of a dye-works unearthed near the Stabian Gate – see further the useful discussion in D–S, s.v. 'tinctor', 'tinctura', vol. v. 1, 138 ff.; and below, s.v. 'lacus'). But the cauldrons mentioned by Statius and Seneca (passages *g* and *h*) were evidently used for a more exclusive process, the dyeing of whole fleeces in expensive purple dyes, which gave more uniform as well as more durable results, and required a double dipping (passage *h*). Cauldrons were also used for boiling the drinking water, which was apparently the normal household practice, to judge from several casual references in the Jurists (e.g. *Dig.* 33. 7. 12. 15: 'vas aeneum, in quo . . . aqua ad bibendum paratur (in instrumento esse videtur)', i.e. 'the essential equipment includes the cauldron for heating up (boiling?) the drinking-water for the establishment'). They were also used for maintaining water at a high temperature for making mulled drinks, as commonly in the *popinae*, like that unearthed and partially restored at Pompeii. In this case the kettle was built into the counter (see below, 'Extant specimens').

Extant representations

See below, s.v. 'cortina', p. 136.

Extant specimens

A well-preserved cauldron of bronze, now in the Louvre, Paris, is featured by D–S, 1. 1, p. 170, fig. 195. The handle has an eye in the centre to take the hook by which the cauldron could be suspended over the fire. The built-in taverna cauldron: E. C. C. Corti, *The destruction and resurrection of Pompeii and Herculaneum*, tr. by H. McGregor, London, 1951 (orig. ed. 1940), pl. 36, p. 197.

2. Alveus (-i, m.), (i) *deep, hollow vessel*; (ii) *trough, tray*; dimin. **alveolus** (-i, m.), *small trough*

Not in Varro, *LL.*

(*a*)   *R–E* 1 2. 1704–5 [Mau]. For the etymology, see s.v. 'alvus', Part II,   ff.

(*b*)   Isid. *Etym.* 20. 8. 8 (*De vasis vinariis et aquariis*). 'The same applies to the derivation of *basin*, "albeus", because ablution usually takes place in it': idem et *albeum*, quod in eo ablutionem fieri solitum est.

(*c*)   *Corp. Gloss.* s.v. 'alveus'. genus vasis trog (*AS*) II 566. 2. . . . fluminis medius canalis vel lignum excavatum in quo lavantur infantes v 439. 3.

(*d*)   *Corp. Gloss.* s.v. 'alveolus'. albiolus pelvis rotundus v 340. 56. alveolis discis v 652. 15 (*Iuvenal.* v. 88).

(*e*)   Cato 11. 5 (vineyard inventory). '40 sowing baskets or *trays*': quala sataria *alveos* XL.

(*f*)   *Ibid.* 12 (contents of the pressroom). '10 *trays*': alveos X.

(*g*)   Colum. 9. 15. 13 (on making honey). 'After that when the liquefied honey has been run off into a *trough* placed beneath the comb, it is transferred to clay vessels': deinde ubi liquatum mel in subiectum *alveum* defluxit, transfertur in vasa fictilia.

(*h*)   *Ibid.* 12. 50. 5 (on preserving olives). 'After forty days they should be spread out in a *trough* (*tray*)': post XL dies in *alveum* diffundi.

(*j*)   Pliny, *HN* 16. 54 (on making pitch). 'The other kind (of pitch) is made from the resin of the pitch-pine, which is made to boil in strong oak *troughs* with red-hot stones, or, if no troughs are available, with piled-up billets of wood, as in making charcoal': illa fit e piceae resina ferventibus coacta lapidibus in *alveis* validi roboris, aut, si alvei non sint, struis congerie, velut in carbonis usu.

(*k*)   Colum. 8. 5. 13 (on incubating chicks). 'The man who puts the eggs under must watch that he doesn't arrange the eggs one by one in the nest by handling; he must collect the total number on a *tray*, and then gently slide the entire clutch into the nest which has already been made': servet autem, qui subicit, ne singula ova in cubili manu componat, sed totum ovorum numerum in *alveolum* ligneum conferat, deinde universum leniter in praeparatum nidum transfundat.

(*l*)   *Ibid.* 4. 4. 2 (on vine-planting). 'Particular care must be taken not to make the planting-hole *trough-shaped* . . . a vine that is set down on its back, as if it were lying in a *trough* . . . is liable to be damaged': id enim praecipue observandum est, ne similis sit *alveo* scrobes . . . nam vitis supina et velut recumbens in *alveo* deposita . . . vulneribus obnoxia est.

(*m*)   Edict. Diocl. (Aphrodisias), Col. II 11. 12 (= ch. 15. 11. 49). '*Box* holding five *modii*: 150 den.': *albeum* quinquemodiale: ✕ centum quinquaginta.

DISCUSSION

The numerous meanings attached to this word (trough, basin, dug-out canoe, etc.: for a full list see D–S, s.v.), have two features in common, viz. the belly-like shape (cf. the Glossator's definition of the diminutive *alveolus* as 'pelvis rotundus'), and, where the material is wood, the method of construction by hollowing out, as in the dug-out bath (passage *c*). The word is used by Livy (1. 4. 6) of the primitive dug-out canoe in which the twins Romulus and Remus were exposed, and by Pliny (*HN* 37. 13) and other writers of various forms of board used for dice- or counter-games. These ranged from the primitive hollowed out and compartmented piece of wood still commonly used in many parts of the world, to more sophisticated trays with raised sides. The main uses of troughs on the farm were for picking-boxes (passage *e*), for collecting liquids such as honey or pitch (passage *g* and *j*), and for drying fruit in the sun (passage *h*). It is curious that while forty *alvei* appear in Cato's vineyard inventory to be used as picking-boxes as an alternative to baskets (passage *e*) there is no mention of any containers for carrying away the olives. The Edict entry (passage *m*) may well refer to a standard box employed for just this purpose (cf. Pliny's reference, at 15. 23 fin., to a reasonable twenty-four hour stint of olive-pressing by a team of four men of three 'batches' (*factus*), each of 100 *modii*. The troughs for the pressroom (passage *f*) come third from the end of the list, and are followed by ten wooden spades and five iron shovels: 'these last-mentioned implements', says Brehaut (p. 29, n. 3), 'would be used to handle the olives, the olive-pulp and the mass after it had been pressed'. The Glossary reference (v 439. 3 in passage *c*) suggests the late survival of a primitive rustic type of baby's bath. Passage *d* indicates, on the other hand, that the diminutive form *alveolus* was used to denote a toilet basin or infant's bath. In the public baths, the *alveus* denoted the hot slipper bath, which, from extant remains, included both horizontal and 'sit-up' types (see below, 'Extant specimens'). Maü (*R-E* s.v. 'alveus') mentions only three uses of the term, and gives no reference to any of the well-known agricultural uses.

The basic shape of the vessel, with its characteristic sloping sides, is well brought out by Columella (passage *l*) when he draws a contrast between a straight-sided planting hole and a trough-like one which discourages the newly planted cutting from growing upwards. The Loeb translator, H. B. Ash, has unaccountably taken 'velut' to refer exclusively to 'recumbens', so that the vine is wrongly stated to be lying in a real trough!

Extant representations

(1) *alveus* = bathtub. D–S s.v. 'alveus', vol. I, pt. I, p. 219, fig. 241, show a painted scene from the Baths of Titus, Rome, with a newly-born baby about to be bathed in a small oval shallow bath (see above, passage *b*); the adult-size bathtub, of which many examples survive (see below), does not appear to be represented on any surviving monument.

(2) *alveus* = sowing tray. The sower depicted on one of the famous wall-mosaic panels from a villa at Cherchel, Algeria (Bérard, *MEFR* 135 (1935), 118 ff.), has a shallow sowing tray slung from his neck.

(3) *alveus* = mortar for pounding corn. D–S (*loc. cit.* fig. 243) show a mortar from the well-known funeral monument of the baker, Eurysaces, still extant in Rome, and a prominent landmark in the city. The pounding mortar is also well illustrated on a red-figured Attic amphora now in Leningrad (see above, s.v. 'pila', etc., pp. 16 f.).

This type of vessel, hollowed out of a piece of timber, and bound with iron, is still in regular use in the rural districts of southern Africa, where it is used for crushing maize (see above, s.v. 'pilum' p. 9).

Extant specimens

Surviving bathtubs are very common. They are comprehensively discussed and illustrated in F. Squassi, *L'arte idrio-sanitaria degli antichi*, Tolentino, 1954, pp. 85–93 and figs. 89–107; S. includes a domestic bath of the 'sit-up' type. Rich (*Dict. Ant.* s.v. 'alveus' 6) shows a cross-section of a bath of this latter type *in situ* in the Forum baths at Pompeii.

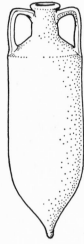

Fig. 34. Amphora (*a*)

3. Amphora (-ae, f.) (fr. Gr. ἀμφορεύς, 'two-handled jar'), (i) *storage jar* (for wine, oil, grain), (ii) unit of volume (= *quadrantal*)

Not in Varro, *LL.*

(*a*) *R-E* I 2. 1969–76 (as container) [Wernicke].

(*b*) *Ibid.* I 2. 1976 (as unit of volume) [Hultsch].

(*c*) Isid. *Etym.* 16. 26. 13. 'The *amphora* is so called because it is lifted on both sides. In Greek it is said to have taken its name from its shape, because its pair of handles seem to resemble ears': *amphora* vocata quod hinc et inde levetur. haec Graece a figura sua dicta dicitur, quod eius ansae geminatae videantur aures imitari.

(*d*) *Corp. Gloss.* s.v. 'amphora'. amphora κεράμιον II 16. 28; 347. 60, etc. ἀμφορεύς II 492. 33 *GR.L* (II 156. 6). ἄμφορον II 251. 32. modii tres III 488. 34; 509. 72. IV modios tenet V 340. 55.

(*e*) *CIL* IV 2551 (inscription on an *amphora*). C. Pomponio C. Anicio cos. ex fund. Badiano diff. id. Aug. bimum.

(*f*) Cato 10. 2 (oliveyard inventory). '2 oil *storage jars*': amphoras olearias II.

(*g*) *Ibid.* 11. 2. '4 *storage jars* covered with fibre': amphoras sparteas IIII.

(*h*) Colum. 12. 44. 5 (methods of preserving grapes). 'My uncle, Marcus Columella, used to order wide containers like dishes to be made from the clay of which *wine-jars* are made': Marcus Columella patruus meus ex ea creta qua fiunt *amphorae*, lata vasa in modum patinarum fieri iubebat.

(*j*) Horace, *AP* 21 (on consistency). 'A *wine jar* begins to take shape; as the wheel runs, why does a ewer turn up?':

amphora coepit
institui; currente rota cur urceus exit?

(*k*) Isid. *Etym.* 16. 26. 13. 'It holds a cubic foot of wine or water, but three Italian modii of grain': (*amphora*) recipit autem vini vel aquae pedem quadratum, frumenti vero modios Italicos tres.

DISCUSSION

The *amphora*, along with the oil lamp, is perhaps the most familiar of all earthenware objects surviving from Roman times. Since *amphorae* were exclusively employed for the bulk transport of oil and wine by sea, and this bulk traffic was a one-way affair, the disposal and distribution points contain enormous quantities of them. The result of two centuries of this traffic, arriving in Rome at the Tiber quays beside the Aventine hill, was a large, man-made mountain, the famous Monte Testaccio, consisting of vast quantities of dumped *amphorae*, the overwhelming majority of them originating in Spain (see below, p. 125). The biggest hoard so far discovered, which was found at Turin (*Augusta Taurinorum*), contained 1,350,000 amphorae filled with finely washed potter's clay (Callender, p. 41).

Shapes and sizes

While the long, slim shape made familiar from under-water recovery was very widely distributed, and may seem to be the most convenient shape for packing in the holds of merchantmen, as well as for stacking in the wine-shops, bulk transport in the later imperial period was dominated by the full-bellied globular type (see below, 'Transport', p. 125). Dressel (*CIL* xv. 2. 1 ff.) provides a Table identifying 45 different shapes, showing the immense variations of pattern resulting from the varying requirements of those who handled or consumed the contents of these widely used containers. A remarkable example of this variety of type is furnished by the finds at the *castra Praetoria*, home of the imperial bodyguard. Here were found no less than nineteen separate forms, ranging from the slim Augustan type to the globular type which became popular towards the end of the second century A.D. (Callender, p. xx).

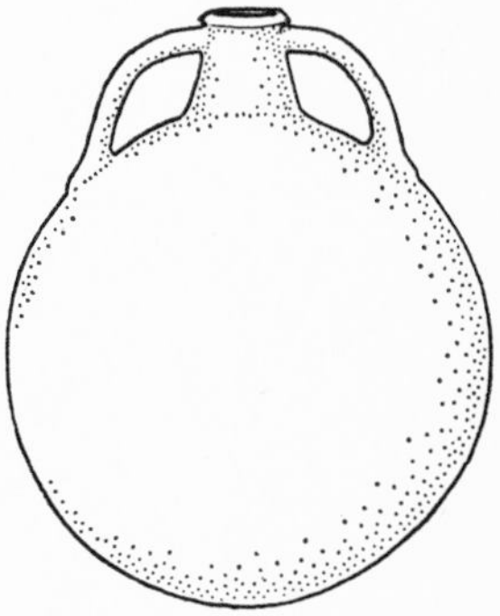

Fig. 35. Amphora (*b*)

Manufacture

Some *amphorae* were made entirely on the wheel, as may be proved by the typical 'rills' made in the process of building up. Others were hand-thrown, perhaps around a rope core. Many extant specimens show evidence of having been made in two sections, an upper and a lower, which were afterwards joined together. Callender (p. 42) cites evidence of visible finger-marks made by the potter kneading in the joints.

Treatment

The material was porous, and wine-amphorae seem always to have been coated with pitch (Pl. 15*c*), a procedure which, as M. Billiard sardonically remarks, 'while it left nothing to be desired on the score of impermeability, imparted to the wine a distinctive flavour intolerable to our palates, but which does not seem to have offended the taste of our forebears' (*L'Agriculture*, p. 243).

Use

With a capacity of just over six gallons, the *amphora* was the standard container both for storage prior to sale, and for transportation by sea to distant markets. While chiefly used for wine, *amphorae* were also used for the storage and transport of oil (passage *f*) and for corn (passage *k*). Callender (p. 37) provides a long list of inscriptions denoting contents, including olives (fresh, salted and preserved in boiled must), various kinds of fish-sauce (*garum, muria*), flour and honey.

Filling and pouring. After fermentation in the *cella vinaria* was complete (for the details of this process see below, s.v. 'dolium'), wine was decanted by ladling (Colum. 12. 28. 3, etc.) into *amphorae*, which were then conveyed to an upper storage chamber, there to remain uncorked so as to absorb the smoke from below, which was thought to accelerate the ageing process. For table use the wine was later decanted into *lagoenae* (q.v.). Both pouring through a funnel and tapping are attested. Bungs were made of raw clay, wood or cork (Pliny, *HN* 16. 34). A well-made wooden bung was found at Castlecary on the Antonine Wall in Scotland (Callender, p. 42, n. 2), and an amphora found at Silchester in Britain had been pierced and plugged with lead.

Protection in use. Cato's inventories mention fibre-covered *amphorae*, both for wine and oil (passage *g*), presumably for protection against the effects of hard, regular use in the working areas. Surviving examples show repair of cracks by the insertion of metal clamps, thus confirming Cato's reference to the topic (39. 1). The Landesmuseum in Trier (in the heart of a great vine-growing area) contains several representations of straw-protected *amphorae* of the later spherical type. Large wooden casks were normally used in the northern provinces for bulk wine transport, but the arrangement of these Trier *amphorae* in pyramids within a frame implies river-transport, perhaps from wholesaler to retailer (see Callender, pls. v *a* and *b*). From other monuments we learn that smaller containers of this type were enclosed in netting for transport in quantity, as they still are today in many parts of the world.

Storage arrangements

Bulk supplies of wine 'in cask' were evidently stored by wholesalers in the larger centres in single-storey 'caves' like the one discovered in Rome in 1789, where the *amphorae* were set out in rows in an upright position by partial burial in the ground (see below, 'Extant specimens'). More familiar to us is the arrangement adopted by the 'bottle-store' proprietor. As we know from establishments at Pompeii, the main stocks were kept in *amphorae* propped up against each other, and resting on their points, the back row against the wall, as shown in Pl. 12*c*. Quality wines normally had the date and provenance inscribed on the shoulder, as in passage *e*: 'In the consulship of C. Pomponius and C. Anicius. From the Badian estate. Bottled on August 13th. Two years old.' On racking and other methods of storage see Introduction, p. 115; also below, s.v. 'cadus', pp. 129f.

Transport of wine

Wine was conveyed in bulk from wholesaler to customer, or from port of entry from abroad to distribution points inland in river-barges or in wagons (see below, s.v. 'cupa' and 'culleus'). Over short distances, e.g. from sale depot to retailer, single 'commercial' *amphorae* were carried by two men, the vessel, weighing up to 55 kg, being suspended through the handles on a pole (see Pl. 12*b*). For bulk transport by sea, *amphorae* of the long, slender type were commonly racked in the hold herring-bone fashion, and bedded with straw, and it is in this arrangement that large quantities of them have lain undisturbed on the sea-bed of the Mediterranean until revealed by skin divers and brought to the surface. Recent underwater exploration of the wreck of a Byzantine merchantman off the coast of Turkey reveals the fact that most of the containers in this particular consignment were round-bellied and almost spherical, and distributed in quite a different manner in the hold (see G. F. Bass, *Archaeology under Water*, London, 1966, 152–3 and fig. 45). See also Pl. 9*b*.

The economics of handling

From the great variety of contents reported (see the full list in *CIL* xv. 4529–654, supplemented by Callender's list (pp. 37ff.)), it is clear that *amphorae* which had arrived full of wine were re-used on the estate; their value to the economical farmer is shown by references to instructions for repairing them (Cato 39 refers specifically to the repair of *dolia* by the use of lead strapping or oaken hoops), as well as by surviving specimens which show signs of having been repaired in antiquity (see e.g. Billiard, *La Vigne*, fig. 162). Oil-jars could not be refilled with other contents; and the dumping of thousands of globular *amphorae* from Spain to form the greater part of Monte Testaccio, bears eloquent testimony to the size of this sector of Rome's import trade at the height of the Empire. The hill has never been systematically excavated, and its value to the economic historian has yet to be fully assessed (see Callender, pp. 46ff.).

The amphora as unit of volume

The *amphora* was also used as a standard unit of volume for liquids, being equivalent to the *quadrantal* of two *urnae* (passage *j*). As a dry measure it was equivalent to three *modii Italici* (*ibid.*). A standard *amphora* was kept in the Public Record Office (*Tabularium*) on the Capitol: hence the term 'Amphora Capitolina' (Capitolinus, *Life of Maximinus* 4). The 'tonnage' of ships was also commonly registered in *amphorae* (e.g. Lentulus, *ap.* Cic. *Fam.* 12. 15. 2: 'ships, none of which registered less than two thousand *amphorae*'.

Extant representations

Very common on wall-paintings, reliefs and mosaics. The following are of particular interest: (1) A terra-cotta relief from Pompeii representing an inn-sign. The relief shows two men transporting an *amphora* of commercial type by means of a rope looped through the handles, and slung over a pole supported on their left shoulders, from the wine-merchant's to the inn (Pl. 12*b*). It will have made an appropriate and colourful advertisement for the establishment (Rich, *Dict. Ant.* s.v. 'amphora'). (2) Mosaic floor from the Piazzale delle Corporazioni, Ostia. The scene represents the transfer of cargo from an ocean-going vessel to a lighter (Pl. 9*a*); a stevedore is shown walking down a plank which connects the two vessels stern to bow, carrying an *amphora* balanced across his r. shoulder (Calza–Becatti, *Scavi*, IV, tav. CLXXXI, no. 106; *Hellas and Rome*, 196*a*; Meiggs, *Ostia*, pl. XXV (*a*)). (3) An 'off-licence' stall with two rows of *amphorae* on a relief in the Vatican (Pl. 12*c*). The Landesmuseum at Trier has a reconstructed group of *amphorae* covered with what looks like esparto-rope, stacked pyramid-fashion and enclosed in a criss-cross frame as in the hold of a ship (Callender, pl. V *a*) (Pl. 9*b*).

Extant specimens

Very large quantities have been found in private houses (especially at Pompeii), at the back of excavated wine-shops, and in the holds of sunken merchantmen. The house of M. Cassius (the so-called 'House of the Faun') at Pompeii contained a vast store of some 70 *amphorae* propped against the wall beneath the E. portico of the second garden; the *atrium* of the house of Emidius Rufus yielded more than thirty. Many are still to be seen in restored buildings at Ostia, Herculaneum and Pompeii, such as the so-called 'thermopolium' (Calza–Becatti, *Ostia*, p. 95; Meiggs, *Ostia*, pl. XXIX; *Hellas and Rome* (1959), 101 *b*). See also the shop attached to the Casa di Nettuno e Anfitrite at Herculaneum

(Maiuri, *Herculaneum*, Itinerario, 6th ed., trans. by V. Priestley, Rome, 1962, pl. XIX, 33).

For specimens recovered from wrecks see e.g. Bass (*op. cit.* above, p. 125), fig. 45. Underwater excavation has made these containers so easy to acquire that well-preserved, barnacle-encrusted specimens are often seen in use as ornaments.

4. Cadus (-i, m.) (fr. Gr. κάδος), (i) *wine-jar = amphora*; (ii) as measure = *amphora*; also **cadum** (-i, n.), *CGS* V 173, 33, 34 etc.

(*a*)   *RE* III 1. 1171–2 [Hultsch].

(*b*)   Varro, *LL* 9. 74 (only on the formation of the word).

(*c*)   Isid. *Etym.* 16. 26. 13 (*De mensuris*). 'The "*cadus*" is the Greek "amphora", containing three "urnae"': *cadus* est Graeca amphora, continens urnas tres.

(*d*)   *Ibid.* 20. 6. 4 (*De vasis vinariis et aquariis*). 'The bucket (?) ... the vessel which the Greeks call κάδος': situla ... quod vas Graeci κάδον vocant.

(*e*)   *Corp. Gloss.* s.v. 'cadus'. cadus ὑδρία II 462. 14. ὑδρία vel κάλπις (calipis *cod.*) III 496. 18; 505. 35. vas vinarius V 173. 35. genus vasis aenei V 173. 36. amphora semis IV 214. 45. situla aenea V 274. 45. vas V 493. 31. cadum graece quod latine situla vocatur V 173. 34. vas aereum sive cavum (caccabum H.) V 444. 13. vas ligneum V 173. 33. cado urna vel sicla (!) aenea V 444. 16. cada vas vinaria (vasa vin.?) IV 491. 5, etc. cados ambras (*AS*) V 349. 37. cadis vasis vinariis IV 432. 24 (= *Verg. Aen.* I 195). vasis V 444. 14.

(*f*)   Grom. p. 376. 10 (DE MENSURIS EXCERPTA). '3 "urnae" make a "*cadus*" or "*artaba*"': urnae tres *cadum* vel artabam faciunt.

(*g*)   Ov. *Met.* 12. 243 (the wedding of Peirithous). 'Wine gave them spirit. In the opening combat goblets and fragile *jars* and curved cauldrons were hurled in flight – objects once suited to feasting, but now to war and murder':

> vina dabant animos et prima pocula pugna
> missa volant fragilesque *cadi*, curvique lebetes,
> res epulis quondam, nunc bello et caedibus aptae.

(*h*)   Hor. *Odes* 3. 41. 18 (orders for dinner). 'Go, boy, and fetch ointment and garlands, and a *jar* that remembers the Marsian war':

> i, pete unguentum, puer, et coronas,
> et *cadum* Marsi memorem duelli.

(*j*)   Hor. *Odes* 3. 29. 1–5 (an invitation to dinner). '(Maecenas,) sprung from old Etruscan Kings, mellow wine in a *jar* as yet untilted ... has long been by me; lay aside delay':

> Tyrrhena regum progenies, tibi
> non ante verso lene merum *cado*
> ... iamdudum apud me est; eripe te morae.

(k) Stat. *Silv.* 4. 8. 39. 'Bring out a *jar* blackened with Alban smoke': Albano ... *cadum* sordentem promere fumo.

(l) Pliny, *HN* 5. 33. 'Large and *small oil storage jars* should be lined with olive lees': dolia olearia *cados*que amurca imbui.

(m) *Dig.* 33. 6. 15. 'We decant wine into "amphorae" and "cadi"': vinum in amphoras et *cados* diffundimus.

DISCUSSION

It seems clear from the evidence that the term *cadus*, like its parent κάδος, was used with an extremely wide range of meanings, both general and specific. In particular, the relationship between *amphora* and *cadus* has provoked endless discussion. Thus two of our passages (*c* and *f*) indicate that *cadus* was commonly used as a synonym for *amphora*, whether as container or as liquid measure. The equivalence may also be inferred from passage *g*, where goblets, *amphorae* and *lebetes* (the latter for mulling the wine), would be essential features of a banquet. It may also be pointed out that *cadus* is a natural substitute for *amphora* in poetic contexts, the cretic forms tending to restrict the use of the latter term, particularly in hexameter verse. It is worth noticing that κάδος does not figure in the list of 'standard' established names for pots (B. Philippaki, *The Attic Stamnos*, Oxford, 1967, pp. xviif.), nor does there seem to be any evidence of a distinction in Greek usage between κάδος and ἀμφορεύς (Sparkes, *Agora* XII. I, p. 201, n. I).

Shape

Used as a general term, the word, like *amphora*, may well have referred to a wide range of vessels, whose only common feature is the pair of characteristic handles. See the discussion of varieties of *amphora* design (above, p. 123).

Size

Here too there is evidence of much variation, complicated also by the fact that *cadus*, like *amphora*, was also a unit of volume. The *Digest* reference (passage *m*) might at first sight appear to be critical; here the terms are obviously not interchangeable, and the fact that lists of containers in the *Digest* commonly follow a descending order of size may lead to the conclusion that the *cadus* was a smaller sized *amphora*. If the *cadus* was a smaller version of the *amphora*, this might account for its frequent occurrence in the context of private wine-cellars, where its smaller size will have made it convenient. Even a full complement of nine such as sat down at

Nasidienus' dinner-party (Hor. *Sat.* 2. 8) could hardly have been expected to consume more than the equivalent of two bottles apiece, which would make a total for the evening of three gallons, or just under half an *amphora*. But we must be careful not to under-estimate the wine-consuming capacity of the ancient Romans! Hultsch (*a*) cites Columella (12. 28. 4) in support of the theory that a *cadus* was a Roman *amphora* holding two-thirds of a Greek *amphora*. But Columella, when he used the phrase 'cadus duarum urnarum' cannot have been thinking of a vessel holding only two *urnae*, because he goes on to talk of adding three *sextarii* (= half a gallon) of lees: the genitive is surely one of material, meaning that it had two *urnae* in it at the time. The only specific references to the size of the *cadus* are *Corp. Gloss.* V 214. 45 (passage *e*) where it is defined as half an *amphora*, and *Grom.* p. 376. 10 (passage *f*) which equates it both with the *amphora* and the *artaba* as a dry measure; these are mutually contradictory, which leaves the question of size still unsolved. There are many parallels to the case of containers of different sizes bearing the same name (see e.g. s.v. 'amphora' p. 123). Nor must the time factor be neglected. Later usage may have narrowed down the meaning, and standardized the size of the *cadus* as a regular unit of measurement representing half an *amphora*. But it is impossible on the available evidence to be more precise. See Callender, p. 3.

Materials

In common with numerous other vessels, the *cadus* was normally of earthenware, but could be made of bronze (twice in *Corp. Gloss* – passage *e*).

Uses

Primarily a container for stored wine, the *cadus* could, like the *amphora*, also be used for oil (Colum. 12. 53. 3), for grain (Pliny, *HN* 22. 121), and for legumes (*ibid*. 18. 307). Hilgers (p. 126) has collected fifteen different products contained in these vessels. There is some confusion among commentators about the use of *cadi* as wine-containers. Thus E. Saglio (D–S s.v.) wrongly refers to a mixing-bowl under this heading. Wine was not drawn out of the *cadus* by ladling, as from a mixing-bowl (see s.v. 'crater', 'creterra'), but poured by tilting it as it lay in its rack (cf. Horace's reference to the unopened *cadus* which will be tilted for the first time when Maecenas comes to dine with him (passage *j*). Racked *cadi* have been found *in situ* both in wine-shops and private houses. See e.g. J. J. Deiss, *Herculaneum* (1966), p. 106, on *amphorae* found in a wine-shop attached to the house of Neptune and Amphitrite: 'the amphorae of wine were laid lengthwise on a supporting wooden scaffold, cut to fit their shapes. They were reached by a ship's ladder of wood, which now dangles in space, carbonized ... one amphora is marked with an inscription quickly brushed in red: L. R. ANTIGONI.' For further discussion see Blümner, *Privataltertümer*, pp. 151 ff. Most of the standard dictionaries of antiquities are very uninformative on the matter of storage (see also s.v. 'amphora', pp. 124 f.).

Extant representations

On the assumption that *cadus* often appears as the term applied to a half-size *amphora* we may expect to find it in use as a distributing vessel in large establishments or on occasions where large numbers of people are drinking. It does not seem to be featured on Roman monuments, but there are several Greek vases where a small *amphora* appears as a serving-vessel. Two fine examples appear in Lullies' recent study *Der Dinos des Berliner Malers, Antike Kunst*, 14. Jahrgang, 1971, Heft 1, 44 f.; pl. 21. 2; pl. 23. 1. Each illustrates a similar scene, that of servants filling *deinoi* – the large carafes from which wine was ladled into the goblets. The *amphora* (*cadus*) on the earlier vase has a foot, that on the later one, a knob. The *cadus* is small enough for the servant to be able to carry it easily over his shoulder.

Extant specimens

See above, s.v. 'amphora', pp. 126 f.

5. Calcatorium (-i, n.) (from *calcare*, to tread; cf. *calcator*, Calp. Sic., *Ecl.* 4. 24), (i) *treading-vat* (late: cf. *forus, linter*); (ii) raised area in the *cella vinaria* (Pallad.)

Not in Varro, *LL*.

(a) *R-E* III. 1337 [Olck].

(b) Isid. *Etym.* 15. 6. 8 (*De operariis*). 'The vat, "forus", is the place where the grapes are trodden out, so called because the grapes are carried, "fera-tur", there, or because it is there that they are struck ("ferire") by the feet; hence it is also called the *trampling-place*': forus est locus, ubi uva calcatur, dictus quod ibi feratur uva, vel propter quod ibi pedibus feriatur; unde et *calcatorium* dicitur.

(c) *Corp. Gloss.* s.v. 'calcatorium'. calcatorium ληνός III 192. 46; 196. 62; 357. 56.

(d) Pallad. 1. 18. 1 (on planning and constructing the *cella vinaria*). 'The "cella vinaria" ... must be so arranged that it has the shape of the basilica itself, having a *platform* built on higher ground, with access by means of some three or four steps placed in between two tanks sunk on either side to receive the wine': cellam vinariam . . . habere debemus . . . sic dispositam, ut basilicae ipsius forma *calcatorium* loco habeat altiore constructum, ad quod inter duos lacus, qui ad excipienda vina hincinde depressi sint, gradibus tribus fere ascendatur aut quattuor.

(*e*) Serv. ad *Aen.* 4. 207 (on the meaning of 'Lenaeus'). '*Liber* is called "Lenaeus" because he presides over the wine-presses, which are called ληνοί in Greek. Schol. Dan.: From the treading-vat, ἀπο τῆς ληνοῦ, that is, from the tank': Liber Lenaeus dicitur, quia torculis praeest, qui et Graece ληνοί dicuntur . . . Schol. Dan.: ex *calcatorio* ἀπὸ τῆς ληνοῦ, hoc est, a lacu.

(*f*) Augustine, *comm. in Psalm.* 8. 2. 'Thus that cluster reaches the ears as if it were arriving at the wine-pressers' *treading-vat*': sic uva ista in aures venit quasi in *calcatorium* torculariorum.

DISCUSSION

Calcatorium is evidently the standard term in later Latin for the treading-vat, equivalent to the Greek ληνός and to the earlier Latin terms 'forus' and 'linter' (q.v.). The treading process, which was always carried out as an essential preliminary to the mechanical pressing (see Introduction, pp. 112 f.), is passed over with scarcely any mention by the classical writers, both technical and literary. But two surviving passages, both of them late, give valuable information which is not available from other sources. Thus in the very late compilation known as the *Geoponika* (ninth century A.D.), we have the only surviving description of the treading process, with much emphasis on the steps to be taken to avoid contamination of the must during the operation (see *RF*, p. 46), while in the first book of Palladius' *opus agriculturae* we get a detailed account of the organization of the *cella vinaria*. This includes the construction of what Palladius (passage *d*) calls a *calcatorium*, which is evidently a raised platform with kerbs, not the ordinary treading-vat of passages *b* and *c*. He also describes how the must is taken from there to the storage area by means of open conduits or pipes (I. I. 2). The arrangements suggest a big acreage under vines, and a large through-put of grapes. Commentators disagree on the meaning to be given to *calcatorium* here. Blümner (*Privataltertümer*, p. 578, n. 13) accepts without discussion the meaning 'winepress' ('die Kelter selbst'), ignoring Schneider's long note on our passage in his edition of 1795, where *calcatorium* is defined as 'locus editus in cella vinaria, ex quo vinum in dolia funditur'. The reader is left to imagine how the must is to reach this 'elevated position' after pressing. Rich (*Dict. Ant.* s.v.) rejects the well-attested meaning 'treading-vat', but he makes no mention of the other late passages cited above, and equates the 'platform' with Cato's 'suggestus' (ch. 134), which is in fact a loading platform for bulk supplies (see below, s.v. 'culleus', p. 140). In a recent discussion of the passage (*Vitruvius and Later Roman Building Manuals*, Cambridge, 1973, 8 ff.) Dr Hugh Plommer points out that Palladius makes no mention of a press, and thinks the *calcatorium* was a large treading-floor, 'with low kerbs and a tiled pavement', from which the must flows into two vats (*lacus*) and hence 'in masonry channels (*canales structi*), or earthenware pipes (*tubi fictiles*), into *dolia* placed at a still lower level'. His suggested reconstruction of this 'veritable basilica' is shown in his fig. 1.

Arrangement of the ordinary treading-vat

The main purpose in treading the grapes was to separate them from their stalks. This process, which is carried out far more efficiently nowadays by a machine (the Fr. 'égrapoir'), is quite distinct from that of pressing (see the Introduction, pp. 112 ff.). Two types of treading-vat are noticed in our sources: (1) a small portable vat, usually of wood (the *linter* – q.v.), (2) a large quadrangular basin made of stone (*forus*) (Pl. 7). Most of the surviving representations, which are numerous, especially in reliefs and mosaics, show the small portable type, which has earthenware jars as receivers (see below, s.v. 'linter', pp. 164–5). The various stages of wine-making came to play an important part in Christian teaching on the sacrifice of the Mass, and the passage from St Augustine, briefly cited above, is part of an elaborate allegorical treatment of the whole process, in which the various technical terms and operations are mentioned, and interpreted in contemporary theological terms. Here, as in other departments of ancient life, the ecclesiastical writers and commentators provide valuable information concerning matters on which the secular writers are often casual and uninformative.

6. Cisterna (-ae, f.) (deriv. of *cista* (cf. *caverna*); frequency of suffix -na in Etruscan suggests Etruscan origin (E–M, s.v. 'cisterna')), *reservoir, cistern*

Not in Varro, *LL*; nor in Isidore.

(a) *R–E* s.v. 'cisterna' III 2. 2606–7 [Puchstein].

(b) *Corp. Gloss.* s.v. 'cisterna'. cisterna λάκκος II 101. 16; 358. 15, etc. δεξαμενή II 268. 14 (cf. III 246. 25); III 200. 27; 357. 55; 365. 38.

(c) Pliny, *HN* 36. 173 (on constructing cisterns). '*Cisterns* should be constructed of five parts of clean sharp sand and two of the strongest lime, with pieces of flint each weighing not more than 1 lb. The floor and the walls should all alike be beaten down with ironclad baulks. It is better to build cisterns in pairs so that the impurities may settle in the first and the water pass through a sieve purified into the adjoining one': *cisternas* harenae purae asperae V partibus, calcis quam vehementissimae II construi, fragmentis silicis non excedentibus libras. ita ferratis vectibus calcari solum parietesque similiter. utilius geminas esse, ut in priore vitia considant atque per colum in proximam transeat pura aqua.

(d) Colum. I. 5. 2 (on the water supply for the farm). 'If there is a lack of running water, let a search be made for well-water close by, the well not to be too deep for raising the water, and the water not bitter or brackish in taste. If this too fails, and a rather meagre hope of a supply of running water makes it necessary, have capacious *reservoirs* built for human consumption, and tanks for the cattle. This rain-water is none the less very suitable for bodily health, and is regarded as outstandingly good if it is carried through earthenware pipes into a covered *cistern*': si deerit fluens unda, puteals quaeratur in vicino, quae non sit haustus profundi, non amari saporis aut salsi. haec quoque si deficiet et spes artior aquae manantis coegerit, vastae *cisternae* hominibus piscinaeque pecori struantur; quae tamen pluvialis aqua salubritati corporis est accommodatissima, sed ea sic habetur eximia, si fictilibus tubis in contectam *cisternam* deducitur.

DISCUSSION

The Roman agronomists devote a great deal of attention to the provision of a satisfactory water-supply, not only for human and animal consumption, but for the numerous other activities on the farm which require water. Although knowledge of the biological and other factors which cause the contamination of the supply was almost wholly lacking, the more obvious effects of taking water from a stagnant source were well known, including the fact that under normal climatic conditions in central and southern Italy, stagnant water provided a good breeding-ground for mosquitoes, including the malaria-carrying anopheles. Thus Varro (*RR* I. 12. 2) advises taking precautions if the farm is located in a swampy situation, 'because they are the breeding-places of certain minute creatures, which cannot be distinguished by the eye, which fly through the air and enter the body through the mouth and nose and cause serious diseases'. All the authorities agree that rain-water cisterns should only be used for human consumption in the last resort. The point is emphasized by a provision of the Roman legal code in relation to water-rights where the interdicts, which protect the user of water from rivers, wells, lakes or springs against improper interference with the flow, expressly exclude cistern water: 'for cisterns do not have a continuous supply of fresh water (*vivam aquam*)' (Ulp. *Dig.* 34. 22 (*de fonte*)). Pliny's recipe (passage *c*) is designed to provide a durable waterproof surface. For the repair of cisterns see Pallad. 2. 17. 3. Columella's recommendations can be precisely illustrated in many excavated farm sites (see below, 'Extant specimens'). More detailed specifications for securing a clean supply are mentioned by Vitruvius (8. 6. 14). For detailed discussion see now Plommer, *op. cit.*, 17 ff.

Extant specimens

Very numerous in excavations in all parts of the Roman empire.

On a small estate. At the Villa Pisanella near Pompeii was excavated a cistern more than twenty feet in depth, with a covered parapet. It was furnished with two outlet pipes, one leading to an open reservoir, the other to the interior of the farmstead, whence the water was piped to the various rooms (*RF*, p. 421, citing Crova, *Edilizia*, ch. 13).

A large system. A recent work by a hydraulic engineer working in Algeria mentions evidence on several Roman sites of elaborate water-catchment systems including collection basins (*lacus*), barrages and reservoirs, from which water was supplied both for urban consumption and land irrigation. See J. Birebent, *Aquae romanae: techniques d'hydraulique romaine dans l'est algérien*, Alger, 1964.

Fig. 36. Cortina

7. Cortina (-ae, f.), = Gr. λέβης, (i) *cauldron* (bronze) for boiling water, must, etc.; (ii) lead vessel for tapping *amurca*

W–H s.v. derive from *(s)ger-, to bend (cf. *cur-vus*).

Not in Isidore.

Corp. Gloss: no refs. exc. in the sense of Apollo's tripod (see *b* below).

(*a*)   *R–E* IV 2. 1660–1 (Mau).

(*b*)   Varro, *LL* 7. 48. 'In Ennius we find:

"What the hollow cauldron receives in its sky-bluish belly."

"Cava cortina", "hollow *cauldron*", is so called because that which lies between earth and sky resembles the shape of Apollo's tripod-cauldron; "cortina" derives from "cor", "heart", because it is from this cauldron that the first fortune-telling lots are thought to have been taken': apud Ennium:

quae cava corpore caeruleo (c)ortina receptat.

cava *cortina* dicta, quod est inter terram et caelum ad similitudinem cortinae Apollinis; ea a corde, quod inde sortes primae existimatae.

(*c*)   Cato 66. 1 (duties of the ladler in the olive pressroom). 'He shall place a lead *cauldron* in the vat for the oil to run into . . . . . . when you have removed the oil from the (lead) cauldron, drain out the dregs': *cortinam plumbeam in lacum ponito, quo oleum fluat . . . cum oleum sustuleris de cortina, amurcam deorito.*

(*d*)   Pliny, *HN* 15. 22 (on making oil). 'Consequently the oil must be ladled off several times a day, also skimmed off with a shell into lead *cauldrons*; bronze

is injurious ... from the cauldrons the oil must be poured off into pans':
quare saepius die capulandum, praeterea concha et in plumbeas *cortinas*;
aere vitiari ... ex cortinis in labra fundendum.

(e) *Ibid.* 35. 43 (on sources of pigments). 'Black is also produced from the black
deposit which sticks to the inside of bronze *cauldrons*': fit etiam ex flore
nigro, qui adhaerescit aereis *cortinis*.

(f) Plautus, *Poenulus* 1290 ff. (a threat to use physical violence). 'I'll cover him
with black bruises, and make him a sight blacker than the Ethiopians who
carry the water round the circus in *cauldrons* at the Games': ita replebo
atritate atrior multo ut siet quam Aegyptii qui *cortinam* ludis per circum
ferunt.

DISCUSSION

The literary references show that the *cortina* was primarily a vessel used
for boiling liquids over the fire, and therefore made of bronze or of lead,
the equivalent of our 'cauldron' (see s.v. 'ahenum', above, p. 118).

Shape

The passage from Varro (b) clearly defines the curved shape of the vessel,
suggested by the etymology, as resembling (1) the curved vault of the sky,
(2) the well-known vessel in which Apollo is said to have deposited the
bones of the Python. The *cortina* is thus a large, semicircular vessel, usually
with an open mouth, fitted with a looped handle. The common use of the
term 'kettle' is misleading.

Uses

Bronze cauldrons were regularly used for boiling water (see s.v.
'ahenum' (e)), for boiling down must (Colum. 12. 26. 1), and for melting
pitch for the lining of storage jars (Pliny, *HN* 16. 53). We learn from
Columella that *cortinale* was the standard term for the place where *defrutum* was made (1. 6. 19). On the process of making *defrutum* and its
various uses see Columella 12. 19 ff., where the specific terms *vasa defrutaria*
and *defrutarium* are used of these vessels. The legal writers seem to prefer
the term *aeneum* when referring to vessels used for boiling liquids (see the
references cited above, p. 117). Lead cauldrons (*cortinae plumbeae*) were
used in the oil-making process to remove the harmful dregs (*amurca*),
bronze vessels being rejected as contaminating the oil. The receiver was
sunk below the surface of the vat into which the oil flowed from the press,
and the oil ladled off (the Loeb editor (passage c) makes Cato's ladler
(*capulator*) 'skim off' the *amurca*, which is an impossibility!). For a lucid
account of the oil-making process, combining archaeological with literary

information, see Rich, *Dict. Ant.* s.v. 'torcularium'. The excellent plans and elevations are taken from Ruggiero's excavation report on the oil 'factory' at Gragnano, a work not readily available nowadays. Elsewhere we find *cortina* used of a cooking-pot (Pliny, *HN* 23. 60), also of a vessel used for carrying water in the circus, perhaps for watering-down the ponies after a race? (passage *f*). D–S have misunderstood the meaning of the other passage from Pliny (*e*), which does not refer to a cauldron used in the preparation of dyestuffs (this comes later, at 35. 150), but to deposits on the insides of bronze cauldrons, as sources of black pigments.

Extant representations

H. B. Walters, *Catalogue of Roman Pottery in the British Museum*, London, 1908, no. L. 92. A fragment of Arretine ware, found at Arezzo, Italy. This fragment, part of a mould for making pottery, shows a slave bending over a cauldron which is resting on a heap of stones, between which are sticks of wood forming a fire. With his left hand he shields his face against the heat (Pl. 12 *a*). The illustration provided by D–S is of a worker in a fullery stamping cloth in a bronze basin. But the container they illustrate is a *pelvis*, not a *cortina*. Perhaps the mistake arises from the earlier misunderstanding noted above. Rich's illustration is of a surviving specimen found at Pompeii (see below).

On Trajan's Column, Rome. Not a large specimen, but the shape, with a wide mouth and pronounced shoulder, is unmistakable. The panel (Cichorius, *Traianssäule*, Taf. 79, no. 285) shows soldiers bivouacking. In the bottom r. corner a soldier bends down beside a stream to fill a kettle.

Extant specimens

The Saalburg museum contains two good specimens of the large, flat-bottomed cauldron used for boiling must. One of these closely resembles the English heavy iron jam-making or preserving-pan (Pl. 32, Blümlein, *Bilder*, p. 93, Abb. 301). A fine specimen in bronze, recovered from the River Cherwell at Shipton-on-Cherwell, Oxfordshire, has a pair of rings instead of the more usual bucket-type handle. These enable the vessel to be carried by two men using a pole, as shown on a bas-relief from Certosa, near Pavia. See E. T. Leeds in *Archaeologia* 70 (1930), 3, pl. 1, and 25, fig. 9.

8. Crater (-ae, f.) (fr. Gr. κρατήρ), also **creterra** (-ae, f.), the usual prose form, (i) *mixing-bowl* (wine + water); (ii) *water basin* (? = *pelvis*); (iii) *oil vessel*

No relevant entry in *R-E*; the art. 'krater' (XI 2. 1612–16) refers only to the deriv. meaning *krater* = the constellation the 'Crown'. *R-E* s.v. 'urna' contains relevant discussion of a few problems.

Not in Varro, *LL*.

Fig. 37. Creterra

(a) Isid. *Etym.* 20. 5. 3. 'The *mixing-bowl*, "crater", is a cup with two handles; the word is Greek ... they were at first made from bundles of rods; hence they have been given the name "craterae" from the verb κρατεῖν because they hold themselves together': *cratera calix est duas habens ansas, et est Graecum nomen ... Fiebant autem primum a conexionibus virgarum; unde et dictae craterae ἀπὸ τοῦ κρατεῖν, id est quod se invicem teneant.*

(b) *Corp. Gloss.* s.v. 'crater'. *crater* κάνθαρος III 496. 49. *cratera* κρατήρ III 354. 47; 518. 15; III 270. 62. ποτηροπλύτης II 414. 47. patena V 422. 52 (*Clem. Rom. rec.* VIII 27; cratere: cf. *cod. Werthin. Gallée* p. 336; *V. suppl.*). *cratera vel obba est calix habens ansas* V 617. 38. *crater est* (crateres *codd.*) *vas, id est qui unum cadum* (*om. cod. Vatic.* 3321) *capit, cruas* III (qui vini capit urnas *Mai* VI 518) IV 30. 25. *crateres* πατάλαι (πατάναι?) III 323. 45. *calices vinarii* (vinarum *cod.*) V 495. 51. *vasa vinaria* IV 436. 7. *crateres fialas, scyphos, cantharos maiores* IV 491. 3. *vasa vinaria* IV 218. 11 (buttes vel vasa u. *d.*); 325. 53. *fialas, calices vinarii* (!) V 448. 22. *cratera* (?) *vas vinaria* (vasa u.?) *vel fiola, cantharos maiores* V 282. 9. *vas vinaria quod et galleta, anappum sc[l]alam* (*V. Isid.* XX 5. 5.) V 564. 48 (v. galenum, anaphus). *vas vinaria vel fialae* IV 491. 4.

(c) Non. p. 547. 'The "creterra", "*mixing-bowl*", is what they now call "situla", "bucket"': *creterra est quam nunc situlam vocant.*

(d) Non. p. 545. 27. '"Crateres", "*mixing-bowls*": vessels for oil': *crateres: vasa olearia.*

(e) Cic. *In Verr.* 5. 131 (depredations of Verres). 'He went off with some very fine bronze *mixing-bowls*': *crateras ex aere pulcherrimas ... abstulit.*

(f) Paul. *Dig.* 33. 10. 35 (on the essential furniture of a house). 'A silver *mixing-bowl* is not included in the furniture': *crateram argenteam non esse in supellectili.*

(g) Mart. 12. 32. 12 (a wretched array of household effects). 'Alongside a lantern and a *mixing-bowl* of cornel, a cracked chamber-pot was making water through its shattered side':

> et cum lucerna corneoque *cratere*
> matella curto rupta latere meiebat.

(h) Juv. *Sat.* 12. 4 (an outsize bowl). 'A *mixing-bowl* holding three gallons': *urnae cratera capacem.*

(j) Ovid. *Metam.* 5. 82 (a lethal weapon hurled by Perseus). 'With both hands he lifts a mighty *mixing-bowl*': *ingentem manibus tollit cratera duabus.*

(k)   Virgil, *Ecl.* 5. 68 (gifts for Daphnis). 'And I shall set up for you two *mixing-bowls* of rich oil': *craterasque* duo statuam tibi pinguis olivi.

DISCUSSION

Wine was very seldom drunk neat (*merum*), and a large container for mixing water in appropriate proportions with the wine was an essential part of the household equipment. The transliterated form *crater*, taken directly from the Greek, seems to have been the form preferred in poetry, while the form *creterra* was normal in, though not exclusive to, prose. It was made in many different materials, including bronze, silver and gold, as well as earthenware (passages *e*, *f*). See the full list of citations in Hilgers, pp. 156–9.

Shape

The basic shape is very familiar from the many surviving examples, being that of an inverted bell, with a wide mouth.

Size

The literary references, as often, seem to refer exclusively to unusually large sizes (passages *h*, *j*). The long list of Glossary entries (*b*) is a mine of either wrong or mutually contradictory information, mainly in the form of identifications with Greek vessels, ranging from *phialae* to *kantharoi*!

Operation

At formal dinners the strength of the mixture of water with the wine was determined by the Master of the Drinking (*arbiter bibendi*); before his guests arrive the host will have selected the wine, and ordered it down from the *apotheca*, or wine-store, which was normally not a cellar, but an upstairs room (see e.g. Horace, *Odes* 3. 21. 7–8, where the poet bids the jar 'come down' at the bidding of the *arbiter bibendi*, whose name is Corvinus). The water for mixing was kept in the pantry in *hydriae* or *urnae* (see the discussion under these headings). Both wine and water were ladled off into the mixing-bowls (*craterae*) by means of ladles (*trullae*), and from these into the decanters (*lagoenae*). Mulled wines, which were frequently served, were brought into the dining-room in the mixing-bowl, and distributed directly into the goblets, as with our punch. For wines served chilled, see s.v. 'saccus nivarius', Part II, pp. 92–3).

Material

While pottery was not uncommon, wealthy Romans, to judge from the notable finds at Pompeii, preferred bronze (see below, 'Extant specimens').

A cheap bowl of cornel-wood is included in the nondescript household gear of the miserly Vacerra (passage *g*).

Extant representations

A good specimen may be seen on a wall-painting from the tomb of Vestorius Priscus at Pompeii, depicting a collection of table silverware: H. Kähler, *Rom und Seine Welt*, München, 1958, Taf. 143 *a*; Hilgers, Taf. 5.

Extant specimens

Two fine specimens in bronze. Pernice, Bd. IV, p. 38; Abb. 47, 48; Taf. XI–XIII.

9. Culleus (-i, m.), = Gr. κολεός, -όν, (i) skin of ox used as *leather container* for liquids; (ii) as measure = 20 amphorae = 122 galls.

Fig. 38. Culleus

Not in Varro, *LL*.

(*a*) *R-E* IV 2. 1744–7 [Olck].

(*b*) D-S V, p. 614 s.v. 'uter', give numerous references to all types of wineskin including the *culleus*.

(*c*) Isid. *Etym*. 5. 27. 36. 'The large *wineskin* ("culeus") takes its name from "covering up" ("occulendo"), that is, from "closing" ("claudendo")': *culeus ab occulendo, id est claudendo dictus*.

(*d*) *Corp. Gloss*. s.v. 'culleus'. culleus ἀσκὸς βόειος, λάρναξ II 18. 41. culeus ἀσκὸς βόειος II 119. 39. μολγός III 24. 17. culleum ἀσκὸς ταύρειος II 248. 1. ὁ ταύριος ἀσκός II 103. 17 etc. The remainder of a long entry is concerned with the traditional punishment of parricides (being tied up in a *culleus*, etc.).

(*e*) *Grom*. p. 376. 13. duo chori *culleum* reddunt, quod sunt modia LX; cf. *Carm. de Pond*. 86:

> est et bis decies quem conficit amphora nostra
> culleus: hac maior nulla est mensura liquoris.

So frequently in agronomists (e.g. Cato 23. 2; 24, Varro, *RR* 1. 2. 7 (yield of ten *cullei per iugerum* of vines), etc.).

(*f*) Pliny, *HN* 7. 82 (on the feats of a proverbial 'muscleman'). 'But Vinnius Valens, who served as a centurion in the Praetorian Guard under the deified Augustus, made a habit of supporting the weight of carts loaded with "cullei" (*122 gallon containers*) of wine until they were emptied, and of picking up and lifting two-wheeled passenger coaches off the ground with one hand': at Vinnius Valens meruit in praetorio Divi Augusti centurio, vehicula vini *culleis* onusta, donec exinanirentur, sustinere solitus, carpenta adprehensa una manu retinere.

(*g*) Plaut. *Pseud*. 212–14 (a dire threat). 'If I don't get oil in *skins* delivered to me here right now, I'll have you put in a wineskin and delivered to the brothel tomorrow': si mihi non iam huc *culleis* oleum deportatum erit te ipsam culleo ego cras faciam ut deportere in pergulam.

(*h*) Ulp. *Dig.* 33. 7. 12. 1 (on the *instrumentum fundi*). 'Also included will be equipment provided for the export of produce (from the farm), such as pack-animals, road vehicles, ships, casks and *wineskins*': sed et ea, quae exportandorum fructuum causa parantur, instrumenti esse constat, veluti iumenta et vehicula et naves et cuppae et *culei*.

DISCUSSION

The word is connected with Gk. κολεόν, a scabbard. Like the Greek equivalent ἀσκὸς βόειος (passage *d*), *culleus* was used of the whole skin of an ox, used for transporting wine or oil, as depicted on a well-known painting from Pompeii, where it is shown filled, fastened at the throat and mounted on a wagon drawn by a pair of mules (see below, 'Extant representations').

As a liquid measure, the *culleus* was equal to 20 *amphorae* or 40 *urnae* (Colum. 3. 3. 10). In Cato's contract for the sale of wine in the jar it is stipulated that 41 *urnae* must be delivered for every *culleus* sold. Brehaut (p. 129, n. 1) thinks the additional half-amphora should be interpreted as a trade practice (cf. the now obsolete 'baker's dozen'). Olck (*R-E* s.v.) thinks that *dolia* will generally have held about one *culleus* (Cato 105. 1, cited in support of this view, mentions the making of Greek wine, and refers to a *dolium* with a capacity of 40 quadrantals (= 40 *amphorae*), and is nothing to the purpose). In fact *dolia* show a great range of size, from as small as 15 *amphorae* (= 92 galls.) to as large as 65 (= 400 galls.). Much more to the point is Columella's reference at 12. 18. 7 (a general account of preparations for the vintage), in which a specific quantity of pitch is stated to be 'enough for jars holding $1\frac{1}{2}$ cullei' – *sesquicullearibus doliis*, with the obvious implication that this was a common size of *dolium*. The term *cullearis* is used twice, once by Cato (154), and once by Vitruvius (6. 9). The first of these passages gives useful information about the measuring of wine in bulk: 'A trouble-free method for measuring out wine to the buyer: Make a vat for this purpose to hold one *culleus*. Provide it with four handles at the top so that it can be moved. Make a hole at the bottom; insert a pipe into it in such a way that it can be plugged tight. Make a hole at the top at the level where it holds exactly one *culleus*. Have it set on a platform among the storage jars so that the wine can run from it into the large wineskin [of the buyer]. Fill the wineskin, and then insert the plug': 'Labrum culleare illae rei facito, id habeat ad summum ansas IIII, uti transferri possitur. id imum pertundito; ea fistulam subdito, uti opturarier recte possit; et ad summum, qua fini culleum capiet, pertundito, id in suggestu inter dolia positum habeto, uti in culleum de eo[1] vinum salire possit. id inpleto, postea obturato.'

Extant representations

A wall painting from Pompeii shows, in the background, a *culleus* of wine set up in a four-wheeled cart (see above, s.v. 'plaustrum'), and secured in position by three wooden hoops attached to the wagon-frame at either side. The neck, from which the vessel was filled, has been bound tightly with several windings of cord. See Brehaut, 133 and Cato's instructions for filling the container at ch. 144. See also Fig. 38.

D–S v, p. 920, fig. 7514 show a two-wheeled cart fitted with vertical staves supporting a large *culleus* tied with cord at both ends. The original is a bas-relief from the former Lateran Museum, now in the Vatican, Rome. Cf. *ibid.* v, s.v. 'uter', p. 920, fig. 7239, large *culleus*, garlanded, and carried by four satyrs on a litter.

Survival

Rich (*Dict. Ant.* s.v.) states that 'a contrivance of precisely the same kind is still (*c.* 1895) employed in Italy for the transport and sale of oil' (see the passage from Vitruvius cited above).

10. Cupa (-ae, f.) (fr. Gr. κύπη (κύπελλον); cf. Skr. *kúpah*, 'hole'), (i) large wooden vessel, *cask*, *tun*; (ii) box-shaped component of an oil-mill (*mola olearia*)

Not in Varro, *LL.*

(*a*) *R–E* Suppl. III. 345 [Keune].

(*b*) Isid. *Etym.* 20. 6. 7 (*De vasis vinariis et aquariis*). '"Cupi" and "cupae", "tuns", take their name from taking, that is, receiving, water or wine; hence also the name "caupones", "innkeepers"': *cupos et cupas a capiendo, id est accipiendo, aquas vel vinum vocatas; unde et caupones.*

(*c*) *Corp. Gloss.* s.v. 'cupa'. cupa seu vagna βοῦττις μεγάλη, ἥν τινες γαυλὸν καλοῦσιν II 119. 15. vagna sive cuppa βοῦττις μεγάλη ... II 204. 11. cupa βοῦττις II 259. 336. βοῦττις graece, latine cupa II 119. 15. cupe (cupa?) vagna V 448. 49. bydin (*AS*) V 353. 45. cupas ubi ligeris V 638. 73 (= Non. 83. 19). cupas et cupos a capiendo . . . . . (vide Isid. (*b*)) copa vas vinarium, quod vulgo per u et per duo pp proferunt cuppam, sed melius per o et per unum p dicunt copam, copon (?) siquidem Graeci dicunt

Fig. 39. Cupa

---

[1] The MS reading, marked as corrupt by Keil, and emended to *de dolio* by Goetz, makes excellent sense (see Brehaut's note *ad loc.*). On the assumption that *dolium* in the phrase *de dolio* refers (as it usually does) to the storage jar, how can the wine run from this to a container placed *in suggestu*? *De eo* is surely correct.

profundum (?), a quo copam dicimus. vas vero balneatorium, non copa per o, sed cupa per u, eo quod nos intra se capiat v 584. 1. cupa κυψέλη III 366. 64.

(d) *CIL* v 985 (a freedman's property bequeathed to the guild of *Augustales*). 'My town and country estates together with 60 *tuns* of wine': ⟨praedi⟩a urbana et rus⟨tica cum vini c⟩upis LX.

(e) Pallad. 1. 18 (on constructing and equipping the *cella vinaria*). '(Channels or earthenware pipes are to run round the edges of the walls and discharge the flowing must into storage jars . . .) If there is a very large supply (of must), the intervening space will be broken up by *vats*, which . . . we can arrange to build on higher foundations above the level of the storage jars': si copia maior est, medium spatium *cupis* deputabitur quas . . . basellis altioribus impositas vel supra dolia possumus conlocare.

(f) Pliny, *HN* 16. 42 (on uses of various types of timber). 'Pitch pine is excellent for making split roof-shingles and *tuns*': piceae ad fissiles scandulas *cupas*que.

(g) Ulp. *Dig.* 33. 7. 8. 12 (on containers for bulk transport): see passage *h*, p. 140, s.v. 'culleus'.

DISCUSSION

The references to this term, which was apparently not current before Pliny's time, show that it was used of two different things, (1) a vat or tub, that is an open container used in the *cella vinaria* (passage *e*), (2) a butt or tun, that is a large closed container used for transporting wine in bulk, the equivalent of the Greek βοῦττις, which appears several times in the Glossaries (passage *c*). The only things these containers have in common is their size and the material of which they were made, viz. timber. The Thesaurus, which is not very precise in its distinction of the various passages cited, does emphasize the two meanings by the use of the terms *vas grande* and *dolium ligneum*.

(1) *cupa* = *vas grande* – a vat

Like the *dolia*, with which they are frequently associated in lists of cellar equipment (e.g. Scaev. *Dig.* 42. 93. 4; Ulp. *Dig.* 7. 1. 15. 6), *cupae* were regularly buried in the ground. Did the art of large-scale cooperage, associated with the wine industry of Gaul from the earliest surviving monuments, find acceptance in Italy, competing there with the traditional earthenware jars? Was there any change of taste over the centuries between Columella and Palladius, with 'wines from the wood', matured in cask, gaining favour over the peculiar bouquet imparted by the pitch-coated *dolia* and *amphorae*, which M. Billiard describes as 'insupportable à nos palats' (*L'Agriculture*, p. 243)?

(2) cupa = *dolium ligneum*, a cask, tun

It is interesting that our earliest surviving reference to the term comes in Hirtius' conclusion to Caesar's unfinished *Gallic War*, where, at the siege of Uxellodunum, the besieged townsfolk tried the experiment of filling these large barrels with a mixture of grease, pitch and shingles, which they then set on fire, preparatory to rolling them down towards the advancing enemy (*BG* 8. 42. 1). There are frequent references in the Glossaries, where *cupa* is equated with Greek βοῦττις (cf. 'butt') and with the late Latin word *vagna*. Passage *g* couples it with the wineskin (*culleus*) as a container for transporting wine, as so often depicted on reliefs and other monuments.

Extant representations

Wooden casks for the bulk transport of wine, which dominated the industry in the northern provinces, are often featured on Gallo-Roman monuments. The best-known examples are: (1) a relief from Neumagen, now in the Landesmuseum, Trier, showing an oared vessel loaded with four large casks; in the bows, the boatswain keeps time for the rowers by clapping his hands: in the stern, the pilot appears to be 'under the influence' (Rostovtzeff, *SEHRE*², pl. XXXIX 1). (2) a much smaller craft, containing only two casks and a steersman, the motive power for conveyance upstream being supplied by three men, each pulling on a separate rope attached to a post in the bows; from the Vaucluse district, now in the Musée Calvet, Avignon (*ibid.* pl. XXXIX, 5). (3) transport of wine by road is well illustrated by a vigorous bas-relief, now in the Musée St Didier, Langres, France, depicting a heavy four-wheeler, loaded with a single very large cask, and drawn by a pair of powerful mules (*ibid.* pl. XXVIII. 3).

Extant specimens

In view of the perishability of the material, the number of surviving *cupae* is remarkable. (1) A well-preserved specimen from Oberwesel, W. Germany, shows the usual construction of coopered staves bound originally with two double and three triple rows of withies nailed across. The bung-hole is clearly visible (Blümlein, *Bilder*, p. 93, fig. 303; Blümlein also shows (fig. 304) a well-made spigot, the handle of which is in the form of a cock). (2) The excavations at Silchester, an important communications centre in southern Britain, yielded three well-preserved *cupae* of silver fir, each six feet in height, which had been put to later use as well linings. They are now in the Duke of Wellington's loan collection at the City Museum, Reading; E. Hyams, *Dionysus*, New York, 1965, pl. 67, p. 176.

Fig. 40. Dolium

11. Dōlium (-i, n.), = Gr. πίθος, large *storage jar* for wine, oil, grain, etc. Not fr. *dŏlare*, 'to hew'. E–M (s.v.) cp. Irl. 'delb', 'form'; Bulg. 'delva', 'earthenware pot'.

Not defined by Isidore (20. 6. 7), who merely includes the word *dolium* in a list of *Vasa vinaria et aquaria*, with no etymology.

(a) R–E v 1. 1284–6 [Mau].

(b) Varro, *LL* 5. 5 = 37 (on the *falx sirpicula*). 'Rush-hooks ("falces sirpiculae") are so named from "sirpare", "to plait with rushes" ... thus broken *storage jars* are said to have been "sirpata", "rush-covered", when they are fastened together with rushes': falces sirpiculae vocatae a sirpando, ... sic sirpata *dolia* quassa, cum alligata his, dicta.

(c) *Corp. Gloss.* s.v. 'dolium'. dolium πίθος II 54. 46. doleum vas fictile ducentis decimatis (?) II siclos capere potest *gloss.* Werth. *Gallée* 338 (cf. *suppl.*). ludiolo (duliolum?) v 497. 30. dolei πίθος II 54. 42 dolia hydr⟨i⟩ae, vasa v 497. 29. doleta vascula sunt magna lapidea et vitrea alia capientes modia CC, alia C aliaque diversae magnitudinis sunt *gloss.*

(d) Cato 11 (vineyard inventory). '*Storage jars* for holding five vintages of 800 "cullei", 20 storage jars for storing grape-pulp, 20 for grain': *dolia* ubi quinque vindemiae esse possint culleum DCCC, dolia ubi vinaceos condat XX, frumentaria XX.

(e) Colum. 12. 18. 5 (preparations for the vintage). 'Large and small *storage jars* ... should be treated with pitch forty days before the vintage, a different treatment being given to those which are sunk below ground level and those which stand above it': *dolia* quoque et *seriae* ... ante quadragesimum vindemiae diem picanda sunt atque aliter ea quae demersa sunt humi, aliter quae stant supra terram.

(f) *Ibid.* 12. 4. 5 (on the making of preserving jars). 'These vessels ... should be made with wide mouths and of the same diameter right down to the bottom and not shaped like *wine jars*': haec vasa ... *fieri* oportet patenti ore et usque ad imum aequalia, nec in modum *doliorum* formata.

(g) *Ibid.* 12. 56. 3 (on pickling turnips). 'Then put (the turnips) into an *earthenware storage jar* coated with pitch, or a glass one': tum in *dolio* picato fictili, vel in vitreo componito.

(h) Pliny, *HN* 14. 134–5 (on wine-making). 'The shape of the *storage jars* is important: those which have wide bellies and mouths are less useful ... Thin wines must be kept in jars embedded in the ground, full-bodied wines in jars exposed above ground': quin et figuras (sc. *doliorum*) referre: ventriosa et patula minus utilia ... imbecilla vina demissis in terram *doliis* servanda, valida expositis.

(j) Cato 69 (recipes for farm and household). 'Steep the new *oil-storage jars* in this way. Keep them full of oil dregs for seven days, and see that you add oil dregs every day to keep them full. Then take out the dregs and dry the jars': *dolia olearia* nova sic imbuito. amurca inpleto dies VII, facito ut amurcam cotidie suppleas. postea amurcam eximito et arfacito. Cf. *ibid.* 10. 4 (*dolia amurcaria* as part of the equipment).

(*k*) Juv. *Sat.* 14. 308–10 (on Diogenes' 'tub'). 'The *jars* of the naked Cynic do not burn; should you break one, another house will be made tomorrow, or the same one will remain, soldered with lead':

dolia nudi

non ardent cynici; si fregeris, altera fiet

cras domus, aut eadem plumbo commissa manebit.

(*l*) Iav. *Dig.* 33. 7. 26 (*instrumentum fundi*). 'Trebatius Labeo thinks that *earthenware storage jars*, also those made of lead, which have earth heaped on them ... (should be included in the fixed equipment)': *dolia fictilia*, item plumbea, quibus terra adgesta est ... Labeo Trebatius putat.

(*m*) Pomp. *Dig.* 33. 6. 2 (on items to be included in a bequest of wine): see above, pp. 110–11.

DISCUSSION

dolium vinarium

The *dolium vinarium* was the largest type of wine-storage jar. After the mechanical pressing, the must was drawn directly from the *lacus torcularius* (the vat beneath the press) into these containers.

Shape and material. The characteristic shape, which is well known from many examples surviving *in situ* in the *cella vinaria* (see passages *e, h, l*), was dictated by the conditions. *Dolia* were pear-shaped, with their maximum width at the shoulder, to allow for the expansion of the contents during the earliest phase of fermentation (see Colum. 12. 44. 2). Baked clay is scarcely the ideal material for holding fermenting liquids: hence Varro's reference (*RR* 1. 13) to jars bursting 'fervore musti' (cited below, s.v. 'orca', p. 181). They also had a distinctive and pronounced 'lip' for easier fitting of the essential lids (see below). Wooden containers (*lignea vasa*) were used only in the Alpine regions according to Pliny (14. 132). See further the discussion s.v. 'cupa' p. 143.

Manufacture. 'The potters do not make all πίθοι on the wheel, only the small ones; the larger ones are built up from the ground from day to day in a warm room', *Geop.* 6. 3. 4. The difficulty of the task was proverbial: 'ἐν πίθῳ τὴν κεραμείαν μανθάνειν', Zenob. *Prov.* 3. 65 (cited by Mau, *R-E* s.v. 'dolium', v. 1. 1285).

Pitching. Another disadvantage, that of porosity, was overcome by coating the inside of the jars with pitch (*dolia picare*, passage *e*; see Pl. 15*c*), a practice which still survives in Portugal (see G. Pereira, *Les vignobles au Portugal*, Toulouse, 1932, p. 46). During the fermentation process the jars were left uncovered (Sen. *Ep.* 83. 16). They were not filled to the brim, the unfilled portion being smeared with *passum* (raisin wine) or *defrutum* (boiled must) to which had been added saffron and other herbs (see Cato

107). After the initial phase of fermentation, which usually lasted some nine days, the lids (*opercula*) were put on, and then sealed to exclude air, which caused rapid deterioration of the wine in cask (on this operation see Pliny, *HN* 14. 135; Macrob. *Sat.* 7. 12. 15 – cited below, s.v. 'operculum' p. 180).

Size of dolia. As the references show, *dolia* varied greatly in size, ranging in capacity from *c.* 10 to *c.* 65 *amphorae* (c. 60–400 gallons). Surviving specimens show a similar range, *dolia* holding 36 *amphorae* being quite common; the well-known specimens found buried *in situ* on farm no. 3 near Boscoreale are of medium size, with an average capacity of about 30 *amphorae*. Another well-known group at Ostia have their individual capacities marked. The marks of capacity survive in 23, and vary from a minimum of 28½ *a.* to a maximum of 47 *a.*, with an average of 40 *a.* Columella's account of the pitching process (12. 18. 5–7) refers to the amount of hard pitch needed to coat a jar holding 1½ *cullei* (= 30 *amphorae*), with the obvious implication that this was a common size.

Arrangement during fermentation. Macrobius (*Sat.* 7. 12. 15) mentions three ways of protecting the wine in the *dolia*: burying in the ground, roofing the jars over, coating the exterior of the jars with pitch and sealing up the lids. Climatic conditions were a determining factor: thus Pliny (*HN* 14. 133), 'in the more temperate countries, they place the wine in storage jars, which are either completely buried in the earth or in proportion to the climatic situation; this is how the wine is protected against the climate'. In warmer climates such as Campania the finest vintages were placed in smaller jars (*cadi*) in the open air, a practice which is still in vogue in the maturing of the *vinos soleados* of Madeira (see J. André's note to Pliny, *HN* 14. 133, in the Budé edition). For further discussion of these and other questions relating to the preservation of wines in antiquity see above, pp. 114–15 ff. The construction of such very large pottery containers (the largest, as we know from the story of Diogenes the Cynic (see passage *k*), were quite capable of holding a grown man in an upright posture), was costly in terms of man-hours. Cato (39) includes among bad-weather jobs on the farm those of 'mending the storage jars with lead straps, or binding them with bands of well-seasoned oak'.

dolium olearium, etc.

The same type of vessel was used for storing olive oil (passage *j*). The earthenware was porous, and needed to be proofed. In the case of oil-storage jars the newly made vessels were steeped in oil-lees (*amurca*) for a week (*loc. cit.*). They could also be used for the storage of grain, resembling the great *pithoi* in the long storage galleries of Knossos or Phaestos.

Diogenes' dolium. The 'tub' is presumably a northern version introduced to suit local conditions. Very large earthenware jars have continued to be made in Italy up to the present day; one may recall the delightful short story 'La Giara' by Luigi Pirandello of the man who was commissioned to make an enormous *dolium* for a customer, and was unable to get out of his self-made prison, and the legal complications that ensued when he demanded that the jar be broken to secure his release.

Extant representations

Dolia are very frequently represented on vases and bas-reliefs. Of outstanding interest is the front of a sarcophagus of the third century A.D. in the collection of marbles at Ince Blundell Hall, near Liverpool, England (Pl. 10*b*). See B. Ashmole, *Ancient Marbles at Ince*, Oxford, 1929, p. 298, pl. 46 (with full description of the scene); Rostovtzeff, *SEHRE*[2], pl. XXXIII. 2 (poor photograph, but good discussion). D–S s.v. 'vinarius', v, 896, fig. 7498: the scene depicted is a sale of wine on the estate of the grower, and is discussed in the Introduction (above, pp. 115–16).

Extant specimens

Dolia defossa (Pl. 10*a*) are preserved on many sites: (1) Boscoreale, no. 3, a model of which may be seen in the Museo della Civiltà Romana in Rome. (2) Ostia, Meiggs, *Ostia*, pl. XXV *d* (of Hadrianic date); details in *NS* 1903, 201 (G. Getti, who gives a complete ground-plan, and describes them as *dolia frumentaria*). Many show evidence of repair with lead strapping in the form of a cross. Four had factory marks, two bearing the names of the slaves in charge of the firing:

GENIALIS RASIN	RHODINVS
PONTICI·SER·FE	SER·FEC·

Survival

Roman methods of wine-making are still carried on in Bulgaria and other parts of Eastern Europe, and bured *dolia* may still be seen on many estates in these regions.

12. Forus (-i, m.) (cf. *foramen*, 'hole', *perforare*, etc.), also **forum** (-i, n.), lit. a hollowed-out space: (i) for wine-making, a *treading-vat*; (ii) esp. for oil-making, a *basin, sunken tank*

No entry in *R-E*.

Not in Varro, *LL*.

(*a*) (i) Isid. *Etym*. 15. 6. 8 (*De operariis* – on working-places). 'The *vat* ("forus") is the place where the grapes are trodden out, so-called because the clusters are "carried" ("feratur") there, or because it is there that they are "struck" ("ferire") by the feet; hence it is also called the "trampling-place" ("calcatorium")': *forus* est locus, ubi uva calcatur, dictus quod ibi feratur uva, vel propter quod ibi pedibus feriatur; unde et calcatorium dicitur.

(*b*)　*Corp. Gloss.* s.v. 'forus'. forus κατάστρωμα II 344. 15. fori ἀκροστόλιον II 224. 4. σηκὸς πλοίων (singulare non habet) II 430. 49. spatia in navibus IV 442. 49. Verg. *Aen.* IV 605; VI 412; V 543. 60. mediae partis navium, id est sedilia nautarum IV 73. 6.

(*c*)　(ii) Cato 18. 3 (construction of pressroom for olives). 'The whole *basin*[1] being five feet long, two and one-half feet wide, and a foot and one-half thick': totum *forum* longum P. V, latum P. II S, crassum P. I S.

(*d*)　(i) Varro, *RR* 1. 54. 2 (vintage and wine-making). '(A division must be made between grapes gathered for wine, and those selected for dessert) . . . therefore the gathered grapes are carried to the *wine-vat*, thence to go into the empty storage jar': itaque lecta defertur in *forum* vinarium, unde in dolium inane veniat.

(*e*)　(i) Colum. 11. 2. 71 (preparations for the vintage). 'He must prepare the wine-presses and *vats*, having had them carefully cleaned and washed': torcularia vero, et *fora* diligenter emundata lautaque . . . (praeparanda sunt).

(*f*)　(i) *Ibid.* 12. 18. 3 (preparations for the vintage). 'Next the receivers for wine and oil, and the *vats* and all the vessels must be . . . washed out': tum lacus vinarii et torcularii et *fora* omniaque vasa . . . eluenda sunt.

(*g*)　(ii) Pliny, *HN* 15. 23 (on oil-making). 'Four men at a time working in two *basins* can complete three pressings in a day and a night': factus tres gemino *foro* a quaternis hominibus nocte et die premi iustum est.

DISCUSSION

The difficulties involved in the interpretation of this term are not made any easier to unravel by the absence of any clear indications in the lexicographers. There is no entry in LS s.v. 'forus'. *OLD* s.v. 'forus' gives only the meanings 'narrow platform, deck or gangway', and (in pl.) rows of benches at the games, citing five of our references (*c–g*) under 'forum: 8 b: (in a wine- or oil-press) the space where the fruit was laid for pressing'. Forc. (s.v. 'forum III') has the remarkable entry: 'forum est etiam vasis vinarii genus, nempe torcularis, in quo ponuntur uvae, vel oleae prelo calcandae'! How part of the pressroom can be equated with a 'kind of vessel for wine' is not readily understood. No wonder the translators are at sea in attempting to attach a precise meaning to a term which a well-known dictionary, in an act of sweeping comprehensiveness, defines as 'bottle, cask, barrel, flagon, flask, vessel for holding wine'!

[1] The reference is to the hollow space provided to take the solid stone footings for the back posts of the press (see Brehaut, p. 39, n. 10).

If we examine the passages usually cited there does appear to be one common factor, that of a hollowed-out space, whether in the olive-press-room (passages *c* and *g*), where it must refer to the sunken area beneath the press, or in the wine-making section, where it must surely be the treading-vat, as Isidore so unequivocally informs us (passage *a*). That this was a common meaning of the word in later Latin is evident also from the Vulgate version of a well-known passage in Isaiah (63. 2): 'Why are your clothes all red, as though they have been in the full treading-*vat* of the pressroom?': 'quare rubra vestimenta tua, sicut de *foro* torcularis pleno conculcato (ὡς ἀπὸ πατητοῦ ληνοῦ, Vulg. sicut calcantium in torculari).' Columella's list of work to be done in advance of the vintage (passage *e*) refers to *fora* which have to be carefully cleaned and washed. The list is unfortunately not comprehensive, so that we cannot proceed to identify our word by a process of elimination. I know of no passage in Columella where the treading-vat is mentioned by name, and it seems not unreasonable to guess that *forus*, being grouped here with the instruments of the pressroom, is to be equated with *linter* = the treading-vat. Rich (*Dict. Ant.*) does not recognize the term *forus*. In his article on *forum* he describes *forum* 4 as 'a particular part of the press room, where wine or oil was made', and refers to his discussion s.v. 'torcularium' where each of the large basins into which the oil flows from the press is 'possibly termed *forum*'. This is clearly wrong: whatever the *forus* was, it was not identical with *lacus torcularius*. The Glossary references are irrelevant to our enquiry, since they are exclusively concerned with *forus* as a nautical term. In spite of much confusion among the commentators it seems evident to me that the term *forus* in the nautical sense derives from its position in what we call the 'waist' of a ship, so that there is a link between the two ranges of meaning to be attached to the term.

13. Gemellar (-aris, n.), a *container* with two compartments

No entry in *R-E*.

Not in Varro, *LL*; not in Isidore.

(a) *Corp. Gloss.* s.v. 'centum' (2). centum (sinum? *Goetz*). lacus vel gemellarium: vas ubi recipiebatur mustum v 617. 45.

(b) *Colum.* 12. 52. 10 (on ladling the newly pressed oil). '(After the first squeezing) the ladler must immediately empty out what has first flowed into the round tub, for this is better than a square leaden vessel or a built up *receiver with two compartments*': quod deinde primum defluxerit in rotundum labrum, nam id melius est, quam plumbeum quadratum, vel structile *gemellar*, protinus capulator depleat.

(*c*) Augustine, *Comm. in Psalm.* 80. 1. 'In these presses the oil is squeezed out unseen into *twin containers*, while the lees flow away openly into the public streets': in his (torcularibus) oleum eliquatur occulte in *gemellum*, amurca publice per plateas currit.

DISCUSSION

The *gemellar* was evidently a specialized container used in the manufacture of olive oil, during which much care was exercised to separate the oil from the lees, and to keep in separate containers the oil from the various pressings. From Columella's account of the process it appears that even a modest olive grove would require no less than ninety settling pans for the oil. Pottier (D–S s.v.) describes the *gemellar* as 'part of the press which receives the smooth (?) oil, while the lees run away outside'. But this is no more than a repetition of what Augustine wrote (passage *c*). See further Forbes, *SAT*, III, 104.

Extant representations

I know of none.

Extant specimens

At a recently excavated farm near Foggia in Apulia were found a pair of large containers sunk in the ground, linked by a pipe near ground-level, which may answer the requirements (from an unpublished report kindly communicated by Professor G. D. Barri Jones).

Fig. 41. Hama

14. [H]ama (-ae, f.) (fr. Gr. ἄμη = (1) 'shovel', (2) 'water-bucket', 'pail'), (i) gen. *water-bucket, pail*; (ii) *fire-bucket*; dim. **hamula** (-ae, f.), Colum., *small bucket*

No entry in *R-E*.

Not in Varro, *LL*.

(*a*) Isid. *Etym.* 20. 15. 3 (*De instrumentis hortorum*). 'The *bucket*': ama.

(*b*) *Corp. Gloss.* s.v. 'ama'. ama ἀμίς III 94. 2. amae vasa sunt in quibus sacra oblatio continetur *Papias*.

(*c*) Juv. *Sat.* 14. 305 (the cares of wealth). 'The millionaire Licinus bids his troop of slaves stand to all night long with *buckets* set out in order':

dispositis praedives *amis* vigilare cohortem
servorum noctu Licinus iubet.

(*d*) Pliny, *Ep.* 10. 33. 2 (report on lack of fire-fighting equipment in Nico-media). 'Apart from this (the apathy of the public) there is not a single fire engine anywhere in the city, nor a *fire-bucket*, nor any equipment for fighting a fire': et alioqui nullus usquam in publico sipho, nulla *hama*, nullum denique instrumentum ad incendia compescenda.

(e) Ulp. *Dig.* 33. 7. 12. 18 (items included in the *instrumentum fundi*). 'Mats, sponges, *fire-buckets* and brooms': formiones et spongias et *amas* et scopas.

(f) *Ibid.* 21. 'Pipes, grappling-hooks and *fire-buckets*': canales et harpagones et *amas*.

(g) Colum. 10. 387 (on selecting gourds). 'It will yield . . . a handy water *bucket* or a flask for wine': dabit illa . . . habilem lymphis *hamulam* bacchove lagoenam.

(h) Cato 135. 2 (where to buy equipment for the farm). '*Buckets*, oil-jars, water-pitchers . . . other bronze vessels should be bought at Capua and Nola': *hamae*, urnae oleariae, urcei aquarii . . . alia vasa ahenea Capuae, Nolae.

DISCUSSION

The distinction between *situla* and *hama* is probably one of size and weight, the former being the heavy-duty well-bucket, while the latter was the general purpose article included in the ordinary equipment of the kitchen and the garden toolshed. Cato's farm bucket was of bronze, but these would be too expensive for ordinary household purposes, perhaps even for a rich man's private fire-brigade (passage *c*), and may have been of wooden staves bound with hoop iron. This type is certainly common among surviving specimens (see below). Fire-fighting buckets may well have been made of leather, but I know of no evidence to support this suggestion.

Extant representations

The standard dictionaries offer no illustrations.

Extant specimens

Both bronze and wooden specimens are represented. Without suggesting that there was any hard and fast distinction between a *hama* and a *situla* I have set out the wooden specimens here, and those in bronze below, s.v. 'situla'. Roman Germany is again prominent as a source of surviving wooden containers. Thus Blümlein, *Bilder*, p. 83, Abb. 257, illustrates three surviving specimens, all made of wooden staves bound with broad iron hoops. Two are of conical shape, and nearly twice as deep as they are wide. The third is much more like a modern bucket. All three are equipped with 'eyes' to take a well-rope. Earlier (p. 39, Abb. 111) Blümlein illustrates an excellent chapter on wells and water-leading with an illustration of a well-bucket of cask-like shape, with four broad iron bands.

Fig. 42. Hydria

15. Hydria (-ae, f.) (fr. Gr. ὑδρία), *jug*, *ewer*, usually for water, but could be used for wine or grain

See also s.v. 'urceus', 'urna'.

No entry in *R-E*.

Not in Varro, *LL*.

(*a*) Isid. *Etym.* 20. 6. 4. '"Hydria", "ewer", a type of vessel for holding water, which takes its name from the derivation; the Greeks call water ὕδωρ': *hydria genus vasis aquatilis per derivationem vocata; ὕδωρ enim Graeci aquam dicunt.*

(*b*) *Corp. Gloss.* s.v. 'hydria'. hydria (vel ydr.) ὑδρία III 271. 1. urna IV 403. 40; V 545. 65. vas aquarium IV 197. 17 (cf. Isid. XX 6. 4). situla IV 298. 24. hydrias vasa terrena aquarum V 207. 41; 255. 22 (ydria).

(*c*) Cic. *In Verr.* 2. 2. 47. 'They declared that these costly silver *ewers*, as well as other items, had been given to Verres': *dicebant has argenteas pretiosas hydrias ... alia data esse Verri.*

DISCUSSION

As the Glossary references indicate, this loan-word from Greek is a late equivalent for the classical *urna*, and is often used in this sense by Christian writers. In the rare classical references the word is sometimes used, as in passage *c*, in its correct sense as a Greek vessel. The word was also used in a special and restricted sense to denote the urn filled with water from which the names of the tribes or centuries were shaken out to determine the voting-order in the Comitia. For the procedure see Taylor, *RVA*, 1966, p. 71; see also s.v. 'sitella', 'urna', below, pp. 189, 199.

The *hydria* as a type of container is defined by D–S (s.v. 'hydria') as follows: 'a large vessel for water, resembling the amphora in having two smaller handles on the sides, and the *oenochoe* in possessing a large vertical handle at the back, one end of which is fastened to the shoulder of the vessel, the other to the neck'. This of course is the rigid archaeologist's definition: we know of several variations. We are also well informed on the use of the *hydria*, since scenes of women drawing water from a fountain were favourite subjects with Greek vase-painters. When going to fetch water, women wore a soft pad (*cesticillus*) on their heads, using the two lateral handles for lifting the vessel. Girls are also frequently represented carrying them on the shoulder, as in the famous frieze on the Parthenon, representing the Panathenaic procession. See below, s.v. 'urna' p. 199.

Extant representations and specimens

See below, s.v. 'urna' pp. 199–200.

16. Infundibulum (-i, n.), also **infid-, infud-** (fr. *infundere*, 'to pour'),
(i) a *funnel* for pouring; (ii) a *hopper* (for the grain-mill)

No entry in *R-E*.

Not in Varro, *LL*; not in Isidore.

(*a*)   *Corp. Gloss.* s.v. 'infundibulum'. infundibulum χώνη II 83. 1; 479. 39; 504. 9 ... 6 variant spellings are noted, all w. equiv. χώνη) ... infundibulum tracter (*AS*) II 582. 42 (cf. Gallée 360).

(*b*)   Cato 10. 2 (oliveyard inventory). '2 *funnels*': *infidibula* II.

(*c*)   *Ibid.* 11. 2 (vineyard inventory). '2 *funnels*': *infidibula* II.

(*d*)   *Ibid.* 13. 3 (equipment needed in the oil cellar). '2 *funnels*': *infidibula* II.

(*e*)   Pallad. 7. 7 (how to smoke out the bees). 'Smoke is brought up to them, made from galbanum and dried cattle-dung, which may be conveniently raised by igniting coals in a cooking-pot. This vessel should be of such a shape that it can easily send out smoke as if from the narrow mouth of an upturned *funnel*': fumus admovetur ex galbano et arido fimo bubulo, quem in pultario factis carbonibus convenit excitare; quod vas ita figuratum sit, ut velut inversi *infundibuli* angusto ore fumum possit emittere.

(*f*)   Vitruv. *De Arch.* 10. 5. 2 (on the grain-mill). 'The *hopper* suspended above maintains the supply of grain to the mill': impendens *infundibulum* subministrat molis frumentum.

In addition, the term is twice used by Columella (3. 12. 3; 3. 18. 6) when comparing other operations with that of a funnel. The first of these examples is strangely classified by *TLL* as used in the special sense of a sieve (*cribrum*): the author is merely saying that excessively loose soil lets the rain pour through it as through a funnel.

DISCUSSION

(1)   *The funnel*

The shape of the vessel is traditional, and its use essential for the numerous occasions when liquids have to be poured from one vessel into another, particularly when the discharging vessel is larger than the receptacle. Rich (*Dict. Ant.* s.v. 'infundibulum') has a figure showing a funnel of pronouncedly bulbous shape, with a rather narrow orifice, taken from an original of glass found at Pompeii. The wide-mouthed type is represented in collections of ordinary household ware. Two are noted among finds in the late Roman levels in the Athenian Agora (see below, 'Extant specimens').

(2)   *The grain-hopper*

The most obvious arrangement for maintaining a steady flow of grain would be to mount a funnel on the top of the mill-housing. Rich (*Dict.*

Ant. s.v. 'infundibulum'), referring to the passage cited above from Vitruvius, thinks that the writer is referring to the upper millstone as representing a funnel. The upper millstone (*catillus*) is funnel-shaped, but Vitruvius, who is a practical man, and knows the parts of a grain-mill, is clearly not talking about the upper half of the mill itself; his hopper is 'suspended over' the machine. The well-known fragment of a marble relief from the Vigna delle tre Madonne, now in the Vatican, shows, above the *catillus*, a wedge-shaped object from which projects a short staff with a cord attached, identified by Amelung as a hopper, the staff being employed to control the flow of grain.

Extant representations

(1) *Of the funnel*: none known to me.

(2) *Of the hopper*: part of a sarcophagus from the Vigna delle tre Madonne, now in the Museo Chiaramonti; inv. no. 497, Taf. 68; Amelung, *SVM*, 1, 637; Moritz, *Grain-mills*, pl. 7, p. 77; *RF*, pl. 79.

Extant specimens

Of the funnel: H. S. Robinson, *Agora V*, Princeton, 1959, s.v. 'Coarse household ware', pl. 18, M 9 and M 119. The former of these two earthenware funnels which has its spout complete is distinctly convex in profile, while the latter is slightly concave. Both have wide mouths in relation to their depth.

Fig. 43. Labrum

17. Labrum (-i, n.) (condensed form of '*lava-brum*', fr. *lavare* 'wash'), (i) *vat, receiver*; (ii) *basin, bath-tub*; dim. **labellum** (-i, n.), *small vat, pan*

Not in Varro, *LL*.

(*a*) *R-E* XII I s.v. 'labrum' cols. 285–6 [Hug].

(*b*) Isid. *Etym.* 20. 6. 8. 'It is called "labrum", "basin" because infants are usually bathed ("labationem") in it; its diminutive form is "labellum", "*small bath*"': *labrum* vocatum quod in eo labationem fieri solitum est infantium, cuius diminutivum *labellum*.

(*c*) *Corp. Gloss.* s.v. 'labrum'. labrum λουτήρ II 362. 51; 500. 40; 544. 12, etc. λεκάνη, λουτήρ II 547. 58.

(*d*) *Ibid.* s.v. 'labellum'. labellum νειλάριον II 476. 10 labellum λουτηρίσκος II 362. 52; όλκίον III 325. 16.

(*e*) Cato 10. 4 (oliveyard inventory). '1 *vat* for steeping lupins': *labrum* lupinarium I. '1 wash-tub': *labrum* eluacrum I. (These are repeated in the vineyard list.)

(f) *Ibid.* 154 (a trouble-free method of measuring out wine to the buyer). 'Make a *vat* for this purpose to hold one *culleus*. Provide it with four handles at the top so that it can be moved. Make a hole at the bottom; insert a pipe into it in such a way that it can be plugged tight. Make a hole at the top at the level where it holds exactly one "culleus". Have it set on a platform among the storage jars so that the wine can run from it into the large wineskin [of the buyer.] Fill the wineskin, and then insert the plug': *labrum* culleare illae rei facito, id habeat ad summum ansas IIII, uti transferri possitur. id imum pertundito; eae fistulam subdito, uti opturarier recte possit; et ad summum, qua fini culleum capiet, pertundito, id in suggestu inter dolia positum habeto, uti in culleum de eo[1] vinum salire possit. id inpleto, postea obturato.

(g) Colum. 12. 52. 11 (on oil-making). 'In the oil-cellar there should be three rows of *pans*, one to contain the oil of the first quality, that is, of the first pressing; another for second quality, and a third for third quality . . . then, after the oil has stood for a very short time in the first *pans*, the ladler will have to strain it into the second and then into the next until he reaches the last (in the row)': sint autem in cella olearia tres *labrorum* ordines, ut unus primae notae, id est primae pressurae oleum recipiat, alter secundae, tertius tertiae . . . cum deinde paululum in *labris* primis constiterit oleum, eliquare id capulator in secunda labra debebit, et deinde in sequentia usque ad ultima.

(h) Virg. *Georg.* 2. 4–6 (invocation to Bacchus, Lord of the vine). 'Come hither father Lenaeus (here all things are full of thy bounty, for thee the field is in blossom laden with the vine-tendrils of autumn, for thee foams the vintage in the overflowing *vats*)':

> huc, pater o Lenaee (tuis hic omnia plena
> muneribus, tibi pampineo gravidus autumno
> floret ager, spumat plenis vindemia *labris*).

(j) Cato 88 (recipe for making salt from brine). 'Place this brine in *small pans* or flat dishes in the sun. Keep it in the sun until it solidifies. In this way the best salt is made': eam muriam in *labella* vel in patinas in sole ponito. usque adeo in sole habeto, donec concreverit. inde flos salis fiet.

(k) Colum. 12. 44 (how to preserve fresh table grapes). 'Then fill a new earthenware pan with the driest possible chaff, which has been sifted to rid it of all dust, and put the grapes on it. Then cover it with another pan': deinde *labellum* fictile novum impleto paleis quam siccissimis cribratis, ut sine pulvere sint, et ita uvas superponito: tum labello altero adoperito.

DISCUSSION

The basic shape common to a number of vessels to which this name is applied is clearly established by numerous surviving specimens of the round shallow toilet-basin set up at one end of the hot chamber of a set

---

[1] The MS reading, marked as corrupt by Keil, and emended to *de dolio* by Goetz, makes excellent sense (see Brehaut's note *ad loc.*) On the assumption that *dolium* in the phrase *de dolio* refers (as it usually does) to the storage jar, how can the wine run from this to a container placed *in suggestu*? *De eo* is surely correct.

of baths (Vitruv. 5. 10. 4; Cic. *Fam.* 14. 20, etc.), and to which the name *labrum* was applied. Isidore's derivation from *lavare* (passage *b*) is correct; the form is condensed, and quite unconnected with that of *lăbrum*, 'lip'. Round shallow pans of the same design were used in the making of oil (passage *g*) and of salt (passage *j*). In the oil-making process, the most difficult task was to get rid of the lees, and this was achieved by the tedious process of straining from one shallow pan to another, involving, as Columella explains (*loc. cit.*), the setting up of a row of thirty pans for each of the three qualities of oil. The capacity of oil lamps to burn clearly and steadily was sufficiently important to make these clarifying processes worth while. The term was also used to denote vats used for various purposes, such as steeping lupins to remove the bitter flavour and soften the tough fibres (passage *e*), and for receiving the grape-juice after treading, while *lacus* was usually applied to the larger receivers into which the must flowed after mechanical pressing (see below, pp. 158 f.). Passage *f* describes a very large vat designed to hold more than a *culleus* or *c.* 130 gallons. The diminutive *labellum* was applied to a number of smaller vessels of the same shape (passages *j* and *k*), including that used at tombs to receive libations for the dead (see Cic. *De Leg.* 2. 26. 66).

Extant representations

A good example of the shallow toilet-basin as used in the Baths is shown on a red-figure *krater* from Bari. The shallow basin is mounted on a fluted pedestal. To l., a girl washing herself over the basin; to r., a second girl fills the basin from a ewer (*Hellas and Rome*, 230 *a*): Rich (*Dict. Ant.* s.v. 'labrum') has a similar illustration. The above examples are Greek, but the surviving specimens from Roman sites show that the designs remain unchanged.

Extant specimens

(1) The *caldarium* of the Double Baths at Pompeii (Maiuri, *Pompeii*, Roma/Novara 1929, p. 49) contains a very large *labrum* set in an apse; immediately above the basin is a circular aperture, which could be opened by means of a metal disc (*clipeus*), according to the room temperature required (on this see Vitruvius 5. 10. 5). (2) Pompeii, House VII 12. 28; a square basin mounted on a fluted pedestal, resembling closely a modern toilet basin (Schefold, *Vergessenes Pompeji*, pl. 23, München, 1962). (3) A fine example in the Nymphaeum of the Erotes at Ostia (Calza–Becatti, *Ostia*, IV 2, 92, pl. 42, Roma, n.d. (1953)).

The fluted pedestal became virtually standardized at Pompeii; see Pernice, vol. 5, 1932, Taf. 24–34.

18. Lacus (-ūs, m.), lit. 'hollow', (i) *vat, receiver* for wine or oil; (ii) *cistern, tank* (= *cisterna*); (iii) *pond*, esp. for animals (= *piscina*); (iv) *storage bin, compartment*; dimin. **lacusculus** (-i, m.), *small bin, compartment*

Not in Varro, *LL* (except in sense of 'lake').

(a) *R-E* XII 1. 376 s.v. 'lacus' [Hug].

(b) Isid. *Etym.* 15. 6. 8 (*De Operariis*). 'It is called "lacus", "vat", because this is where the liquor from the fruit runs in': *lacus* dictus quia ibi decurrit frugum liquor.

(c) *Ibid.* 20. 14. 12. 'The *vat*, into which, after straining, flow the oil and wine that are forced out of the grapes or olives by squeezing': *lacus*, quo liquatum[1] profluat quod[2] ab uvis vel olivis torquendo oleum vinumque exigitur.

(d) *Corp. Gloss.* s.v. 'lacus'. lacus δεξαμενή II 268. 14. ληνός III 470. 29, etc. calcatorium, torcular, palus vel silanus IV 358. 57 ... lacus exceptoria [e] in qua aqua decurrit et scribitur una (uno G.) *c* Plac. V 31. 1 = V 80. 2 = V 112. 2 (*ubi* exceptoria *Deuerling*; *quamquam* exceptoria, ae *dicitur*). Cf. Serv. in *Aen.* VIII 74; *Georg.* IV 363.

(e) Cato 66. 1 (on oil-making). 'Place a lead cauldron in the *vat* into which the oil is to flow': cortinam plumbeam in *lacum* ponito, quo oleum fluat.

(f) Varro, *RR* 1. 54. 2 (operations of the vintage). 'When the grapes have been trodden, the stalks and skins should be placed under the press, so that any must remaining in them may be pressed out into the same *vat* (as the product of the treading)': quae calcatae uvae erunt, earum scopi cum folliculis subiciendi sub prelum, ut, siquid reliqui habeant musti, exprimatur in eundem *lacum*.

(g) Colum. 12. 18. 3 (preparations for the vintage and pressing). 'Next the *wine-vats* and the pressroom vats and treading-vats must be washed out ... with brine': tum *lacus vinarii* et torcularii et fora ... aqua marina ... eluenda sunt.

(h) *Ibid.* 1. 6. 13 (on granaries). 'But granaries are also divided off into *bins* to allow all the different kinds of legumes to be stored separately': sed et *lacubus* distinguuntur granaria, ut separatim quaeque legumina ponantur.

(j) Varro, *RR* 1. 13. 3 (on farm lay-out). 'In the outer yard there should be a pond for the soaking of lupins and other products which are put into better condition for use by immersion in water': in cohorte exteriore *lacum* esse oportet, ubi maceretur lupinum, item alia quae demissa in aquam ad usum aptiora fiunt.

(k) Colum. 12. 52. 3 (on making olive oil). 'However, since the large volume of berries defeats the efforts of the men working at the press, there should be a store-room with a raised floor, to which the fruit may be conveyed. This building ought to resemble a grain-store, and contain as many *bins* as the quantity of olives may require, so that each day's pressing may be kept apart and stored separately. The floors of these *bins* must be paved

---

 [1] liquatus *codd.*   [2] quo *codd.*

with stones or tiles and made sloping, so that all the moisture may flow quickly away through gutters or pipes': verumtamen quia interdum multitudo bacae torculariorum vincit laborem, esse oportet pensile horreum, quo importentur fructus; idque tabulatum simile esse debet granario, et habere *lacusculos* tam multos, quam postulabit modus olivae, ut separetur et seorsum reponatur uniuscuiusque diei coactura. horum *lacusculorum* solum lapide vel tegulis oportet consterni, et ita declive fieri, ut celeriter omnis humor per canales aut fistulas defluat.

DISCUSSION

The basic idea conveyed by this term is that of a hollow, whether natural or artificial. The main difficulties in interpreting its use are in passages concerned with the operations involved in the pressing of grapes and olives and the making of wine and oil. The various processes of pressing and liquefaction, since they inevitably leave various solid and semi-solid residues which have to be removed, require the use of a number of different types of vats and other receivers, whether singly or in combination. Here, as elsewhere, the writers are not always strict in their use of terms; *lacus* is but one among many words used with either a general or a specific meaning. Thus in passage *f* above, Varro is obviously referring to the receiver for the must as it comes out of the treading-vat, while at passage *g* Columella, who is normally more precise in his language than Varro, uses the specific adjectives *vinarius* and *torcularius* for the receivers for wine and oil respectively. For similar problems of identification see above, s.v. 'forus', pp. 148–9.

Three kinds of receiver may be distinguished: the vat (i), for wine, oil, etc.: the cistern (ii) for water storage: the bin (iv) for storing dry produce. Apart from these categories, two Roman writers also use the term *lacus* with the meaning 'pond', that is, 'a large body of water which rises and falls, opp. *stagnum*, a standing pool, etc.' (LS s.v.). *Lacus* (iii) is thus equivalent to *piscina*. In the account that follows I have attempted to sort out the types of vessel mentioned and to indicate the function of each in the operation concerned.

Lacus (i)

Used to denote various receivers for wine or oil (Columella's *lacus vinarius* and *lacus torcularius* (passage *g*), in which the product of the initial treading or pressing could settle before the next stage of processing into wine or oil. The Glossaries give the general synonyms of δεξαμενή and *exceptoria* (passage *d*), while Cato, in his usual manner, defines the receiver as 'lacus, quo oleum fluat' (passage *e*). For a general account of wine-making see the Introduction to this section (above, pp. 112 ff.). In the processing of olive oil, there are two difficult problems to be solved; these are: (*a*) the removal, without crushing, of the kernel (*nucleus*), which will otherwise impart a bitter flavour to the oil; (*b*) the separation of the oil from the lees (*amurca*), which, though a valuable by-product with all kinds of uses, also contaminates the oil. Removal of the kernel was effected in the mill (*trapetum, mola olearia*). The latter type of mill could be adjusted to suit the size of the berries (Colum. 12. 52. 6: part of a full and lucid account of the whole process). Separation of the lees was effected in a variety of ways: first, by ladling off the lighter oil from the *lacus* into a succession of shallow vessels or pans (*labra*), allowing it to settle at each straining, until the oil was completely clear of dregs; Columella (12. 52. 11–12) recommends no less than thirty pans for each of three pressings of the oil! An alternative to this tedious method was to provide a second vat at a lower level, and to trap the lees in a large vessel sunk in the floor of each vat. Though not described by any extant authority, this second method, which would speed up the process, was evidently used in large establishments, such as that excavated at Gragnano in the Sarno valley south of Pompeii (M. Ruggiero, *Scavi di Stabia*, Napoli, 1881, pp. 351 ff.; Rich, *Dict. Ant.* s.v. 'torcularium' – each with a detailed account of the buildings, including ground-plans and elevations). A third method, designed to cope with the problem arising where very large quantities of berries were coming forward, is described by Columella (above, passage *k*); see below, '*Lacusculus*'. For the whole series of processes, see below, Appendix A, pp. 225 ff.

Lacus (ii)

For *lacus* = cistern for water, see above, s.v. 'cisterna'.

Lacus (iii)

Used by Varro (passage *j*) of an outdoor pond with running water for cattle, geese and pigs to drink from and bathe themselves in, the oxen after work, the others on their return from pasture. Varro also prescribes a second pond in an outer yard 'for the soaking of lupins and other products which are made more serviceable by immersion in water' (*loc. cit.*).

Lacus (iv)

Used of bins (i.e. compartments) in the loft for dry storage of the various kinds of legumes kept for feed (passage *h*).

Lacusculus

The diminutive, with the specific meaning of a storage bin, is unique in this sense (passage *k*). The critical word here is *coactura*, which, as we shall see, has been misinterpreted by most commentators. The making of olive oil involved three processes, those of softening, milling and pressing. (For the whole series of procedures see Appendix A, pp. 225 ff.) Columella is here referring to the first two processes of softening and milling. He first recommends that the olives should be stripped, sifted and carefully cleaned to remove all impurities, then 'enclosed, while still whole, in new flexible frails, and put under the presses *for the shortest possible time*'. Salt must now be added to the resulting pulp, which is then put into the mill, the 'set' of the upper and lower stones being so adjusted as to prevent any crushing of the kernels (see Appendix A, p. 229). Great care had also to be exercised at each stage to get rid of the lees. The key word in the passage under discussion is *coactura*, which is usually translated as 'gathering', or 'picking' (Rich, *Dict. Ant.* s.v. 'lacusculus'). A moment's consideration will show that this cannot possibly be the correct meaning. If the olives have merely been gathered, the reference to the escape of the liquid (*umor*) will make no sense! In fact, *coactura* means not the day's *gathering*, but the day's *pressing*; the reason for the 'delaying action' of putting the day's pressing into the bins will surely have been the need to avoid a 'bottle-neck' over the whole process of oil-making, since the preliminary light pressing took much less time than the milling. This is what Columella means when he talks of 'the volume of the berries defeating the efforts of the workers'. In modern parlance, the operation with the bins is a 'delay and store' procedure, designed to even up the two operations.

Extant specimens

The most complete oil-processing plant known to the writer is that large establishment excavated at Gragnano in the Sarno valley south of Pompeii, and fully published by M. Ruggiero in 1881 (*Scavi di Stabia*, Napoli, 1881, 351 ff.). For a clear and succinct account of the pressroom operations, combining the evidence of Cato and Columella with the results of the Gragnano excavations, see Rich, *Dict. Ant.* s.v. 'torcularium'.

19. Lagoena (-ae, f.) (fr. Gr. λάγυνος), (i) *flagon, carafe*; (ii) later, *water-jug*; (iii) *boundary mark*; dim. **laguncula** (-ae, f.), Colum. 12. 38. 6

No entry in *R-E*.

Not in Varro, *LL*.

(a) Isid. *Etym.* 20. 6. 3 (*De vasis vinariis et aquariis*). '"Lagoena", "*flagon*", and "sicula", "pail", are Greek names, partially changed to turn them into Latin: the Greeks use the term λάγυνος, while we use "lagoena"; they use the term Σικελή, we use the term "sicula"': lagoena et sicula Graeca nomina sunt, inflexa ex parte ut fierent Latina. illi enim λάγυνος, nos lagoena; illi Σικελή, nos siculam dicimus.

(b) *Corp. Gloss.* s.v. 'lagoena'. lagoena λαγύνιον III 369. 13. vas vinarium V 629. 45. lagena vel orna sunt vasa V 620. 39. croog (*AS*) V 369. 4. laguna λάγυνος II 357. 65; III 24. 7; 326. 31. lagona paucali (*ubi* βαυκάλιον *Buechelerus*). II 563. 16. lacuna λάγυνος III 529. 33. lagonam vas lapideum ollo (olla?) id est crog (*AS*) V 416. 61 (de verb. interpret.). lagunam τὴν λάγυνον III 286. 10 = 656. 12. laguena et sigula graeca sunt nomina inflexa ex parte ut fierent latina: illi enim lagi, nos laguena, illi sicile, nos sicule vel secula dicimus V *praef.* XXXI. Cf. Isid. XX 6. 3.

(c) Colum. 12. 47. 2 (on preserving quinces). 'They should then be arranged in a new *flagon*, which should have a very wide mouth': in *lagoena* nova, quae sit patentissimi oris, . . . componantur.

(d) Mart. 7. 6. 5 (on Domitian's Law forbidding stalls projecting on to the street). 'No pillar is cluttered at its base with chained-up *flagons*':
nulla catenatis pila est praecincta *lagenis*.

(e) Pliny, *HN* 16. 128 (on the roots of trees). 'The fig-tree bristles with fine filaments . . . from these the mountain folk draw extremely fine threads and weave them into handsome *flagons* and other vessels': minutis haec capillamentis hirsuta ficus . . . e quibus montani praetenuia fila decerpentes, spectabiles *lagoenas* et alia vasa nectunt.

(f) Hor. *Ep.* 2. 2. 132–4. 'A man who was nice to his wife, one that could forgive his slaves their mistakes, and not get frantic if the seal of a flagon were broken':
comis in uxorem, posset qui ignoscere servis,
et signo laeso non insanire *lagoenae*.

(g) Mart. 4. 46. 8–9 (a collection of second-rate gifts). 'Lucanian sausages together with a Faliscan haggis and a Syrian *flagon* of black boiled-down must':
et Lucanica ventre cum Falisco,
et nigri Syra defruti *lagona*.

(h) Apuleius, *Metam.* 2. 15 (preparations for an evening's entertainment). 'And the flagon stood ready to hand, its neck opened with a wide, smooth cut, so that one could draw easily from it': et *lagoena* iuxta orificio caesim dehiscenti patescens facilis hauritu.

(j) Colum. 10. 383–7 (on growing gourds of different shapes). 'But if you are looking for a gourd of globelike shape which swells out vastly with ample

Fig. 44. Lagoena (a)

paunch, then choose a seed from the middle of the belly; this will produce capacious fruit fit to make a vessel for Narycian pitch or Attic honey from Hymettus, or a pail handy for water, or a *flagon* for wine': (nam si tibi cordi est)

> globosi
> corporis, atque utero nimium quae vasta tumescit,
> ventre leges medio; subolem dabit illa capacem
> Naryciae picis, aut Actaei mellis Hymetti
> aut habilem lymphis hamulam Bacchove *lagoenam*.

(*k*) *CIL* XIII 1008 k (inscription carved around the belly of a two-handled vessel). 'A full *flagon* for Martial': MARTIALI SOL[I]DAM LAGONAM.

(*l*) *Rev. Arch.* XVIII (1868), 225, pl. 23; Walters, *HAP*, II, 466 (circular pipe-shaped vessel with two handles with incriptions around either side). (1) 'Landlord, fill the *flagon* with beer': OSPITA REPLE LAGONA (sic!) CERVESA. (2) 'Innkeeper ...? be off; it's full'; COPOCNODI TVA BESES TREPLETA.

DISCUSSION

Design

Columella's interesting reference to gourds of different shapes (passage *j*), suggests that at least some vessels bearing the name were long-necked and swollen-bellied, resembling the 'crook-neck' gourd of which he writes. H. Couve (D–S III 2, s.v. 'lagoena') cites *Anth. Pal.* 9. 229 for the adj. μακροφάρυγξ, 'long in the throat', and *ibid.* 6. 248 for στειναύχην, 'narrow-necked', as applied to a λάγυνος, and describes the Greek vessel as a 'wide-bellied vase with a long narrow neck and a narrow mouth'. Passage *c*, with its reference to a very wide mouth (*patentissimum os*), suggests that this was an unusual feature. It has also been suggested by some etymologists that the word *lagoena* may be derived from the same root as Gr. λαγαρός, 'narrow-necked' (Plut. *Public.* 15; Xen. *Cyn.* 6. 5, etc.). See further Gabriel Leroux, *Lagynos*, Paris, 1913, pp. 75 ff. Many of the references cited by Leroux emphasize the length, as well as the narrowness, of the neck. The classical Greek vessel usually called οἰνοχόη (the word λάγυνος does not apparently occur before the fourth century B.C.) is a pouring vessel, with a long narrow neck, and a round, flattened belly, which resembles our port decanter, except for the addition of a handle. Identification of a particular vessel by the evidence of a specific name inscribed upon it is rare. The vessel with the dedication to one Martialis (passage *k*) as drawn by Walters (*HAP* II, fig. 217) has the characteristic shape of belly, but the neck is fairly short. The other inscribed vessel (passage *l*) is noted as extremely rare; it consists of a circular tube, with a mouth and two handles, and a small aperture at the base. The extraordinary shape and the amusing inscriptions suggest the possibility that it was used

Fig. 45. Lagoena (*b*)

in competitive beer-drinking, like our equally peculiar 'yard of ale' vessel. It also gives a salutary warning of the danger of over-confident attribution even when the name is inscribed on the vessel. Walters (*loc. cit.*) is clearly in error in classifying this curious container as an *ampulla*.

Taking all the varied evidence into account we can endorse the opinion that the *lagoena* was 'the most widely used handled jug, with a spout and either one or two handles' (Hilgers, pp. 64f.). There is also tangible evidence for much local variation in design.

Uses

The *lagoena* was used at the table for pouring wine directly into the goblet. Passage *f* shows that they were normally sealed, like our wine bottles, but for a different reason, to prevent any sampling of the contents by the butler before the wine was brought to table. Pilfering of wine by the domestic staff on a larger scale than this is attested in a letter from Cicero's brother Quintus to the confidential freedman-secretary Tiro. Admonishing the latter for failing to write to him, Quintus reminds Tiro that their mother was in the habit of sealing even the empty bottles, to prevent any being declared empty which had been illicitly drained of their contents! (Cic. *Fam.* 16. 26). The 'chained bottles' (*catenatae lagoenae*) of passage *d* were presumably part of the stock-in-trade of a wine-shop exposed on the street to save space inside, and with a chain passing through the handles to prevent theft by passers-by, as is still all too common in city markets. Passage *h* seems to imply that the flagon in question had somehow been treated to make the wine flow more easily, but the meaning of 'caesim' is not clear.

Extant representations

Not apparently common. Best-known is a fine floor mosaic (Pl. 11 *a*) found at Dougga (Thugga) in Tunisia, now in the Bardo Museum, Tunis. Poinssot, *Guide du Musée Alauoui*, 1 (1950), pl. xx. 3: *HGT*, pl. vii (in colour); Rostovtzeff, *SEHRE²*, pl. lxii. 1. The scene is taken to represent a drinks party preliminary to a banquet 'in a private house or a wine-shop' (Rostovtzeff *ad loc.*). Two hefty slaves, one clad only in an elaborate loincloth, are moving around among the guests, filling their shallow cups from large *lagoenae* with long, narrow necks, which they support on their shoulders, tilting the vessels adroitly by means of one of the handles – a dexterous performance even from a vessel furnished with a narrow mouth. Pouring from the shoulder is common throughout the Middle East.

Extant specimens

   Lagoenae showing minor variations on the general design established above are to be found in all the major Roman collections. The British Museum contains an excellent series (BM registration nos. 1856, 8–26, 263–6).

20. Linter (*-tris*, m.), also **lintris, lunter** (Cato), the earlier form, (i) gen. *trough, tub*; (ii) *wash-tub*; (iii) *treading-vat* (= *forus*); (iv) *boat*

Etym. dub., perh. conn. w. Norweg. 'ludr', a 'hollowed-out tree-trunk' (W–H *ad loc.*).

Not in Varro, *LL*; not in Isid. exc. as = 'boat'.

Corp. Gloss: only as = 'boat'.

(a) *R-E* XIII 1. s.v. 'linter', 718 [Hug]. *Note:* Hug accepts without discussion Servius' explanation of the term (passage *e*).

(b) Cato 11. 5 (vineyard inventory). '2 treading-vats (?)': luntris II.

(c) Tib. *Eleg.* 1. 5. 23–4 (Delia will learn the joys of farming). 'Or she shall watch the grapes in the brimming *vats*, and the quick feet treading the gleaming must':

> aut mihi servabit plenis in *lintribus* uvas,
> pressaque veloci candida musta pede.

(d) Virg. *Georg.* 1. 262 (on winter tasks). 'He carves *troughs* out of tree-trunks': cavat arbore *lintres*.

(e) Serv. *ad loc.* alii, lintres, quibus uva portabant, accipiunt.

DISCUSSION

There is considerable disagreement both about the derivation of the word, and about its meaning. Thus Rich (*Dict. Ant.* s.v. 'linter') defines it as a shallow-draught boat, used in marshes, with the secondary meaning of 'a trough employed at the vintage for carrying the grapes from the vineyard to the vat in which the juice was trodden out'. LS however derive it from the root of πλύνω (cf. πλυντήρ) 'to wash', making the meaning 'boat' secondary. Large vats were commonly made by carving them out of suitable timber (see s.v. 'labrum'). Commentators on passages *b* and *d* have assumed without argument that the objects referred to are troughs for carrying the grapes to the vats; thus Cato's pair of 'luntres' appear in Brehaut's translation as two 'dugout carriers', Billiard, *La Vigne*, p. 433 being cited in support of this interpretation. Hörle (*Hausbücher*, p. 247) suggests the meaning 'wine trough', whatever that may signify, while

Hooper–Ash refer to them as '2 trays'. The *Georgic* reference (passage *d*) would suit several different types of receptacle, but the Tibullus passage (*c*) undoubtedly refers to the treading-vat, with *linter* a synonym for *forus*. Postgate's 'trough into which the grapes were placed after pruning' is very wide of the mark. The weight of the evidence, though inconclusive, inclines me to the view that *linter* means a small, portable treading-vat, such as a smallholder would use, of the kind depicted on several Greek vases (see below, 'Extant representations').

Small-scale wine-production

The powerful emphasis laid by our authorities on commercial vine-growing may lead us to conclude, quite wrongly, that all the wine consumed was produced on large commercially run estates. But wine was very much a part of life for all classes of society, and not least for the small independent farmer, who will have found room on his few *iugera* for enough vines to provide a daily supply of wine for himself and his family. This, it seems, is the scale of operation reflected in the passages from Tibullus (*c*) and Virgil (*d*) where *linter* is used, assuming that the *linter* that Virgil's husbandman is carving out of a tree-trunk is also a treading-vat. For the farmer's own supply not even the simple lever-press, of the size depicted on the Seasons Mosaic from St Romain, would be needed. Wine is still made in some parts of Europe (Rumania and Bulgaria) by treading without subsequent pressing.

Extant representations

I do not know of any for the Roman period, and must therefore refer the reader to Greek evidence for this type of portable vat. *Münzen und Medaillen*, Auktion 40, 1969 ('Kunstwerke der Antike'), no. 87, a painted drinking cup (*kylix*) with the following scenes: (A) Sileni at the vintage. One Silenus, in front of the vinestock, appears to be saluting a cluster of grapes; to the r. two companions carry loads of grapes to the press in wide semicircular containers. (B) A Silenus treads the grapes in a vat which is standing on a table. Another carries a filled wineskin to set it on a donkey for transport to market.

Extant specimens

None known to me; since they were of wood, none is likely to have survived.

21. Metreta (-ae, f.) (= Gr. μετρητής, fr. μέτρον, 'measure'), (i) as measure of liquid capacity: norm. = 1½ *amphorae* (approx. 9 galls. or 45 litres); (ii) *tun, cask* (for wine)

(*a*) *R-E* Suppl. VII 448 [Becher].

(*b*) Isid. *Etym.* 16. 26. 9 (*De mensuris*). '"Metrum" is a liquid measure, taking its name from "mensura", "measuring", for μέτρον is the Greek word for measure. From this also it gets the name "*metreta*", just as "urna", "amphora" and similar words are the names of measures': metrum est mensura liquidorum: haec a mensura accepit nomen; μέτρον enim mensuram dicunt Graeci. et inde appellata *metreta*, licet[1] et urna et amphora et reliqua huiusmodi nomina mensurarum sunt.

(*c*) Cato 100 (on preparing jars for olive oil storage). 'If you are going to store olive oil in a new *nine-gallon jar*, wash it down with raw oil-lees, and shake the lees around for some time, to enable it to soak up the lees. If you do this the jar will not absorb the oil, and will be stronger': oleum si in *metretam* novam induturus eris, amurca colluito, agitatoque diu, ut bene combibat. id si feceris, *metreta* oleum non bibet, et firmior erit.

(*d*) Colum. 12. 22. 1 (how to preserve must with pitch). 'Put a "*metreta*" of liquid Nemeturican pitch in a tub or trough, then pour into the same vessel two *congii* of lye-ash and mix thoroughly with a wooden spatula': picis liquidae Nemeturicae *metretam* adde in labrum aut in alveum, et in eodem infundito cineris lixiviae congios duos, deinde permisceto spatha lignea.

(*e*) *Ibid.* 12. 47 fin. (on preserving white olives). 'For this method of preserving, new earthenware containers are prepared without pitch: to prevent them absorbing the oil, they are smeared with grease (?) as is done with *olive oil casks*, and are then dried out': huic autem conditurae vasa nova fictilia sine pice praeparantur: quae ne possint oleum sorbere, tamquam *olivariae metretae* imbuuntur liquamine: tum demum et assiccantur.

(*f*) Pallad. 11. 14. 7 (on preserving wine). 'To one "*metreta*" of best must add eight ounces of wormwood': in optimi musti *metreta una* . . . absinthii octo uncias . . . demittes.

(*g*) Juv. *Sat.* 3. 246–7 (on the dangers of walking about in Rome). 'One man buffets me with his elbow, another with a hard pole, one hits me on the head with a beam, another with a *barrel*':

> ferit hic cubito, ferit assere duro
> alter, at hic tignum capiti incutit, ille *metretam*.

DISCUSSION

The Greek term μετρητής was a liquid measure equivalent to an ἀμφορεύς (LSJ s.v. with numerous refs.). At 12. 53. 1 Columella calls for the use of a 'very large oil container' ('largest size of container'?), and subsequently

---

[1] *Lindsay, sine sensu*: sicut *fortasse rectius conieci.*

refers to the same vessel as a *metreta*. This seems to imply a vessel holding more than an *amphora*. A passage from Dioscorides (5. 82) has been cited as indicating that the *metreta* held 12 *congii* or 1½ *amphorae*. But the text is uncertain, and readings of 8 and 10 *congii* have been proposed. Brehaut, commenting on passage *c* above, thinks that Cato is not referring to a specific size, i.e. that *metreta*, when used of a container, meant a very large one, and presumably larger than an *amphora*. It is commonly assumed that the Roman *metreta*, as a liquid measure, represented a quantity of 1½ *amphorae*, but the evidence is insufficient to prove this. The scholiast on Juvenal 3. 246 (passage *g*) defined metreta as 'vas, quod amphoram capit'.

22. Modiolus (-i, m.) (dimin. of *modius*, q.v.), (i) a drinking-vessel shaped like a *modius*, a *tankard*; (ii) a *bucket* on a water-wheel; (iii) the box to carry the spindle of an oil-mill (*trapetum*); (iv) the cylinder of a water-pump

Not in Varro, *LL*; not in Isidore.

(*a*) *R-E* vi A. 2187–94 s.v. 'trapetum' [J. Hörle].

(*b*) *Corp. Gloss.* s.v. 'modiolus'. modiolus πλήμνη χοινικίς II 489. 5. χοινικίς ἡ τοῦ τροχοῦ II 477. 39. πλήμνη II 409. 47. Cf. χοινικίς foramen ligni, in quo volvitur rota vel modiolus rotarum III 262. 42 (unde?). modioli πλῆμναι III 173. 64; 262. 43 (πλουμαι *cod.*). nebae (*vel* nabae *AS*) v 371. 31.

(*c*) *Dig.* 34. 2. 36 (Scaevola on legacies). '"I charge the heirs on their honour to give my beloved wife Seia a gold goblet of her choice." My question is, where the inherited property contains only ladles, ordinary cups, *tankards* and drinking-bowls, can Seia make her selection from these categories of vessel?': 'Seiae dulcissimae poculum aureum quod elegerit fidei heredum committo ut darent'. quaero, cum in hereditate non sint nisi truellae, scyphi, *modioli*, phialae, an Seia de his speciebus eligere possit.

(*d*) Cato 20. 2 (how to mount the oil-mill). 'Make olive-wood *boxes* from the wood of the olive called "orchites" for the millstones, pour molten lead around them, and take care to fit them tight': modiolos in orbis oleagineos ex orcite olea facito, eos circumplumbato, caveto ne laxi sient.

(*e*) Vitruv. *De Arch.* 10. 4. 3 (on the water-raising wheel worked by the treadmill). 'Thus a wheel will be constructed around the axle, of such a size as will enable it to reach the height desired. Around the circumference will be attached square *buckets* strengthened with pitch and wax. Thus when the wheel is turned by operating the treadmill, the full buckets which have been carried aloft will, as they return to the bottom, without outside aid pour into the reservoir the water they have raised': sic rota fiet circum axem eadem magnitudine ut ad altitudinem, quae opus fuerit, convenire possit, circa extremum latus rotae figentur *modioli* quadrati pice et cera solidati. ita cum rota a calcantibus versabitur, modioli pleni ad summum elati rursus ad imum revertentes infundent in castellum ipsi per se quod extulerint.

(f) *Ibid.* 10. 4. 4 (on the undershot water-driven wheel). 'Wheels are also constructed in rivers ... around their outer edges are fixed fins. These, as they are struck by the force of the current, move on and compel the wheel to turn; thus, as they drink up the water with their *scoops* and carry it to the top (of the wheel)': fiunt etiam in fluminibus rotae ... circa earum frontes adfiguntur pinnae.[1] quae cum percutiuntur impetu fluminis, cogunt progredientes versari rotam, et ita *modiolis* aquam haurientes et in summum referentes.

(g) Vitruv. *De Arch.* 10. 7. 1 (on Ctesibios' water-pump). 'Two identical *cylinders* a short distance apart, with outlet pipes': *modioli* ... gemelli paulum distantes, habentes fistulas.

(h) *Ibid.* 10. 8. 1 (on Hero's water-organ). 'Bronze *cylinders*': aerei *modioli*.

DISCUSSION

The various objects designated by the term *modiolus* have a common basic shape, that of the *modius* (q.v.), though not all of them retain the characteristic form of that vessel, which is that of a cone, not a cylinder. Thus the tankard (passage *c*) retains the traditional shape, while the square *modioli* of the water-wheel (passages *e* and *f*) are in fact boxes fixed to the wheel, and having their sides corresponding to the *radii* of the wheel they also follow the profile of the corn-measure. On the other hand, Cato's axle-boxes for the oil-mill (*trapetum*) (passage *d*), and the cylinders used in the water-pump and water-organ (passages *g* and *h*) must be true cylinders.

Fig. 46. Modius

23. Modius (-i, m.) (from *modus* 'measure'), (i) as unit of capacity (dry measure) = approx. *l.* 8.7; (ii) the regulation-type *container* of this capacity in which corn was officially measured out

Not in Varro, *LL.*

(a) *R-E* s.v. 'modius' xv 2. 2328 (Becher); very inadequate.

(b) Isid. *Etym.* 16. 26. 10 (*De mensuris*). 'The "*peck*" ("*modius*") takes its name from the fact that it is in its own way ("*modo*") perfect. As a measure it is made up of forty-four pounds, that is twenty-two pints ("*sextarii*")': *modius* dictus ab eo quod sit suo modo perfectus. est autem mensura librarum quadraginta quattuor, id est sextariorum viginti duorum.

(c) *Corp. Gloss.* s.v. 'modius'. modius μέτρου ὄνομα II 130. 14. μόδιος II 372. 76, etc. μέτρον II 370. 4. χοῖνιξ III 366. 35; 379. 64. μέδιμνος III 263. 10. sextarii XVI v 371. 13 (cf. *GR.L.* VII 101. 13), etc.

(d) Cato 58 (ration scales for the farm workers). 'A "*modius*" of salt per year per person is sufficient': salis uni cuique in anno *modium* satis est.

---

[1] LS wrongly translate *pinna* as 'float', 'bucket'. The *pinnae* are of course the projecting 'fins' or 'paddles'.

(e) Cic. *In Verr.* 2. 3. 110 (profiteering on the Sicilian tithe). 'Two years later the tithe on the "ager Leontinus" was sold for 36,000 "medimni", that is, 216,000 *pecks* of wheat': agri Leontini decumae tertio anno venierunt medimnum XXXVI, hoc est tritici *modium* CC et XVI molibus.

(f) Corn. Nep. *Vita Attici* 2. 6 (munificence of Atticus). 'He made a present of corn to the whole population amounting to a gift of six *pecks* of wheat per head, a measure which at Athens is called a "medimnus"': nam universos frumento donavit, ita ut singulis VI *modii* tritici darentur, qui modus mensurae medimnus Athenis appellatur.

(g) Juv. *Sat.* 14. 126. 'He takes it out on his slaves' stomachs by giving short *measure*': servorum ventres *modio* castigat iniquo.

DISCUSSION

The design of the *modius* measure is familiar from numerous representations on coins and sculptured monuments. In addition, the surviving specimens provide details of its construction, as well as some food for speculation (see below, 'Extant specimens'). The *modius* was a standard, official measure of capacity in the form of a truncated cone, about the size of a two-gallon bucket, but narrower at the top than at the base, having a capacity of *c.* 8·75 litres. The specimen discussed below is made of heavy bronze, ¼ in. (6·35 mm) thick (see Fig. 46). The inscription declares it to be 'exact to 17½ sextarii'. Brazed to the metal rim at the top, and flush with it, is a three-pointed bronze plate, which acts as a defining bar for the purpose of levelling off the grain, and also prevents any illegal pressing down of the contents. Passages *e* and *f* show the relationship of the *modius* to the standard Greek unit of measurement for bulk grain, the *medimnus*. The *modius* had a capacity of exactly one-sixth of the *medimnus*. By natural extension the word was also used both generally and proverbially: thus Petronius (*Satyricon* 37), '*modio* nummos metiri', of a very rich woman; Cicero (*Att.* 6. 1. 16), 'pleno modio', meaning 'abundantly'.

Extant representations

The *modius* is frequently represented on Roman imperial coins, where the imperial message to the emperor's subjects touches on the vital question of Rome's corn supply. The best-known example is a bronze *quadrans* issued by the emperor Claudius (in H. Mattingly and E. A. Sydenham, *The Roman Imperial Coinage* (London, 1923–), I, no. 174; pl. 35, no. 12). There are numerous examples in mosaic on the floors of the Piazzale delle Corporazioni at Ostia (Pl. 16, see Calza–Becatti, *Scavi*, IV, tav. CLXXXV–CLXXXVII).

Extant specimens

A well-preserved *modius*, found at Carvoran, Northumberland, U.K., and now in the Clayton Memorial Museum at Chesters, Northumberland. Its capacity of 2·494 gallons (= 11·337 litres) is unexpected, since it exceeds the standard measure by one *choinix*, which is equivalent to an excess capacity over that of the standard *modius* of 10 per cent. The specimen is fully discussed and illustrated in F. G. Skinner, *Ancient Weights and Measures*, London, HMSO, 1967, pp. 69–72; Pl. XI *b*.

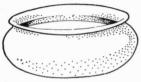

Fig. 47. Mulctrum

24. Mulctrum (-i, n.) (fr. *mulgere*, 'milk'), also **mulctra** (-ae, f.), **mulctraria** (-ium, n.pl.), **mulgarium vas** (n.), *milking-pail* (?), *milking bowl* (?)

No entry in *R-E*.

Not in Varro, *LL*.

(*a*) Isid. *Etym.* 20. 6. 7 (*De vasis vinariis et aquariis*). '*Milking pail* ("mulgarium vas"), in which the sheep are milked; also known as a "*milker*" ("mulctrum") from the fact that the milk is drawn off in it': *mulgarium vas* in quo mulguntur pecora: idem et *mulctrum*, ab eo quod in eo mulgitur lac.

(*b*) *Corp. Gloss.* s.v. 'mulctra'. mulctra mulgaria lactis IV 416. 27 (cf. Serv. in *Ecl.* III 30). mulcitra vas ubi lac mulgitur IV 121. 43 (cf. Isid. XX 6. 7); 259. 24 (mulcra). mulcra mulgarium (multarium), id est vas ubi lac mulgitur V 466. 31; 507. 37. multha celdre (*AS, de Clemente*) V 425. 28. mulcro vas in quo mulgitur V 224. 5. mulctra vas quo pecudes mulgentur V 224. 4. mulgarium v. mulctra. mulgaria vasa in quibus lac mulgitur V 224. 7.

(*c*) Colum. 7. 8. 1 (on cheese-making). 'The task of cheese-making must not be neglected, especially in remote parts of the country, where it is not convenient to take milk to the market in *pails*': casei quoque faciendi non erit omittenda cura, utique longinquis regionibus, ubi *mulctram* devehere non expedit.

(*d*) *Ibid.* 7. 8. 6 (on making goat's milk cheese). 'Some people, before they put the shackles on the nanny-goats, drop green pine-nuts in the *pails*, and then milk the goats over them, removing the nuts only after they have transferred the curdled milk into the moulds': nonnulli antequam pecus numellis induant, virides pineas nuces in *mulctram* demittunt, et mox super eas emulgent, nec separant, nisi cum transmiserint in formas coactam materiam.

(*e*) *Ibid.* 8. 17. 13 (special diet for fish). 'Equally suitable are any foods which closely resemble things that can easily be swallowed, such as curds fresh from the *milking-pail*, if the local situation or the low price of milk permit it': nec minus . . . quique sunt cibi sorbilibus proximi, ut e *mulctra* recens caseus, si loci conditio vel lactis annona permittit.

(*f*) Horace, *Epod.* 16. 49 (the Islands of the Blest). 'There the she-goats come unbidden to the *pails*': illic iniussae veniunt ad *mulctra* capellae.

(g) Virgil, *Georg.* 3. 176–8. 'Your cows, when they have given birth, will not, as in your fathers' day, fill up the snow-white *milking-pails*, but use up all their milk on their sweet offspring':

nec tibi fetae
more patrum nivea implebunt *mulctraria* vaccae
sed tota in dulcis consument ubera natos.

DISCUSSION

The term milk-pail conjures up in the mind a picture of the conventional country milkmaid with her wooden pail and three-legged milking stool. But the surviving representations of milking scenes, such as the milking of a cow in the Vatican Virgil, or the milking of a goat on the Istanbul mosaic, indicate a different method and different equipment. The milker in the Vatican MS is operating from behind, and milking the cow into a wide-mouthed, rather shallow earthenware vessel. The *mulctrum*, then, would be more accurately described as a milking bowl rather than a milking pail. D–S's 'sorte de terrine ou de jatte' is very close to the mark, but no ancient illustrations of the milking process are provided in the text; in fact the writer ends his very brief comments with the remarkable statement that 'on n'en connaît pas exactement la forme' (s.v. 'mulctra, mulctrare'). In the Polyphemus episode (*Od.* 9) Homer gives a detailed description of the interior of the Cyclops' cave: 'all his vessels were flowing with whey, bowls (γαυλοί) and tubs (σκαφίδες), manufactured, into which he would milk them' (9. 222–3). For γαυλός LSJ give the meaning 'milk-pail', 'water-bucket', noting that γαῦλος 'merchant-ship' takes its name from its round shape. The other term, σκαφίς, implies a wooden vessel made by scooping, a trough or tub. A vessel of the same rounded shape, the *sinum*, is referred to by Columella in his account of cheese-making (7. 8. 2). On balance, then, the literary evidence, such as it is, taken together with that of surviving representations of milking scenes, supports the view that the vessel used for milking was a bowl rather than a pail or bucket. But not all milk was made into cheese. In the introduction to his account of cheese-making Columella uses the word *mulctra* in reference to the conveying of liquid milk to market. This would seem to require a bucket-type container fitted with a lid. Lacking precise evidence, we must conclude that, while most references indicate that milking vessels were round-bellied, the term could also be used of a bucket-shaped vessel similar to our milking-pail. For pails and buckets see the passages cited below, s.v. 'situla', p. 188.

Extant representations

Milk pails, though unknown on Greek vases, are very common on vases from Apulia and other parts of S. Italy. These were used for carrying the milk. Bowls into which the animals were milked do not apparently occur; milking scenes were not a popular subject with the vase-painters. Two milking scenes are featured on extant mosaics: (1) A small panel from Zliten, Tripolitania: S. Aurigemma, *I mosaici di Zliten*, Africa Italiana 2, 1926, fig. 57; Rostovtzeff, *SEHRE²*, pl. LIX 2. The panel is extensively damaged but the shallow milking bowl can be made out (Pl. 11 *b*). (2) A milking scene from a mosaic in Constantinople: D. Talbot Rice, *The Great Palace of the Byzantine Emperors*, Edinburgh, 1949, p. 71, pl. 30 and fig. 11. The scene shows a man and a boy milking goats; on the r., a reed hut bound with cords; to l., a boy leaning forward to grasp the mouth of a tall, two-handled pitcher, brimming with milk. (3) A relief from a sarcophagus in the Museo delle Terme, Rome. The milker, a bearded man, wearing a loose tunic and cross-gartered, is seated on an upturned basket, and is shaded from the sun by a reed awning (cf. the lean-to shed in the Zliten mosaic). The goat is being milked into a round pot. (4) From The 'Good Shepherd' mosaic in Aquileia (Cabrol–Leclerq, 1953, 1, 884, fig. 199). In the centre a lamb; behind, a shepherd's crook, fitted with a hook, from which hangs a *mulctrum* of the same shallow, open type.

Extant specimens

In a group of pottery vessels from Rhitsona in Thessaly is a wide-mouthed, shallow bowl, 40 cm in diameter, described as 'a still-room bowl for settling the milk'. It has an upturned flange, presumably to prevent the contents from spilling (see Hilgers, p. 227, n. 34).

25. Nassiterna (-ae, f.) also, **nasiterna** (see *Corp. Gloss.*) (= *nasus* (?) or *nassa* (?) + *terna*: for the suffix cf. *cis-terna* etc.), *watering-pot*

No entry in *R-E*.

Not in Varro, *LL*; not in Isidore.

(a) Fest. 169 a 11, s.v. 'nassiterna', p. 168 L; p. 169 M. 'The *watering-pot* is a type of water-container with a handle and broad in shape, of the kind commonly used for watering-down horses. Plautus in the *Bacchides* (11, see below) and in the *Nervolaria* (*Stich.* 352, see below). Cato, too, in the speech he composed against Q. Sulpicius. "How often have I seen broken basins and *watering-pots*, ewers and chamber-pots without handles"': *nassiterna* est genus vasi aquari ansati et patentis, quale est quo equi perfundi solent. Plautus in *Bacchidibus* (11) ... et in *Nervolaria* (*Stich.* 352) ... et

Cato in ea oratione quam composuit in Q. Sulpicium. quotiens vidi trulleos *nassiternas* pertusos, aqualis matellas sine ansis.

(b) *Corp. Gloss.* s.v. 'nassiterna'. nassiterna γαλπις (κάλπις *vel* κάλπη *Labb.*) III 57. 23; 486. 10. nasiturna vas fictile ⟨d⟩uas aures habens II 587. 58. nasiterna vas aquarium *Plac.* V 34. 3 = v. 86. 9 (aquarium vas) = V 119. 33 (aquarium vas). Cf. *Festus* p. 169. 11; *Non.* 546. 5: nassiterna, vas aquale.

(c) Cato 10. 2 (oliveyard inventory); *ibid.* 11. 3 (vineyard inventory). '1 *watering-pot*': *nassiternam* I.

(d) Cato, *In Q. Sulpicium* (ap. Fest. s.v. 'nassiterna'). 'How often have I seen wash-basins and *watering-pots* with holes in them': quotiens vidi trulleos *nassiternas* pertusos.

(e) Varro, *RR* I. 22. 3 (Stolo quotes Cato on equipping an olive plantation). '(The owner should provide) five complete sets of oil-pressing equipment, and he (Cato) enumerates the items required, viz. of bronze: kettles, pitchers and a *watering-pot*, and so forth': ut faceret vasa olearia iuga quinque, quae membratim enumerat, ut ex aere ahenea, urceos, *nassiternam*, item alia.

(f) Plautus, *Bacchides* 11. 'Will someone please call out that filthy creature with *pail* and water?':

ecquis evocat
cum *nassiterna* et cum aqua istum impurissimum?

(g) Plautus, *Stichus* 352. 'A *watering-pot* and water here, someone, please. This guy's serving as sanitary commissioner without being elected to the job!':

ecquis huc effert *nassiternam* cum aqua? sine suffragio
populi aedilitatem hic quidem gerit.

(h) Plautus, *Miles* 581. 'By gosh I'll never take a nibble at the bait in that *trap*!': numquam hodie ex ista *nassa* hodie escam petam. (Schol.: *nassa* est piscatorii vasi genus, quo cum intravit piscis, exire non potest.)

DISCUSSION

The most popular derivation is from *nasus*, 'nose', and an augmentative termination, like *cisterna* from *cista*, 'thus meaning a vessel with a very long spout and not one with three spouts or three handles, as some have imagined' (Rich, *Dict. Ant.* s.v.). Among other implausible suggestions is that it is derived from *nassa*, a 'fish-trap' (W–H s.v.). A derivation from *nares*, 'nostrils', would be closer to the requirements (see below). A vessel with holes for distributing water over a surface will have been an essential piece of equipment on the farm or in the market garden, as well as for laying the dust on unpaved surfaces (passages *d* and *e*), and for watering-down horses after exercise (passage *a*). D–S s.v. 'hortus', III. 1, p. 287 refer to the well-known scene in Euripides' *Ion*, where Ion is presented cleaning the temple court with a sprinkling vessel (ἀπορραντήριον), but offer no evidence about its design.

Shape

The agricultural writers make frequent reference to the watering (*inroratio*) of seed-beds and plants, but Cato's inventories (*RR* 10 and 11) contain the only mention of the watering-pot itself (passage *c*). The Glossary entries are useless (passage *b*), and Festus' lengthy disquisition (passage *a*) gives no hint of the shape. D–S, s.v. 'topiarius', v, fig. 7012, p. 319, show a drawing of a two-handled earthenware pot with a short projection below one of the handles ending in a 'rose' for sprinkling. But they point out that the genuineness of the vessel illustrated is in question. Apart from this, the pot is very clumsy, the spout in particular being much too short for efficient use as a sprinkler. Until some solid evidence can be found, we must reluctantly conclude that we do not know anything definite about the shape of the *nassiterna*, beyond what may be inferred from its etymology. I am convinced that some device for distributing water in small droplets over seedbeds and young seedlings will have been as necessary to nurserymen in classical antiquity as it is today, but must add that at present we lack precise evidence. It is just possible that Roman gardeners used earthenware containers with perforations in the bottom and a single small hole at the top, with a body resembling that of a decanter. The earliest vessel of the type known to me is a mediaeval specimen, date. *c.* 1480, in the London Museum at Kensington Palace (Inv. A 1962). It was presumably filled by immersion, and the contents were released by removing the thumb from the small hole. The vessel in question has 'nostrils', and could therefore satisfy the etymological requirements. It does not however match Festus' description (passage *a*), and it lacks a handle.

Extant representations

None.

Extant specimens

None, apart from the dubious example cited by D–S (see above).

26. Oenophorum (-i, n.), also **oenophorus** (-i, m.) (fr. Gr. οἰνοφόρος), lit. *wine-carrier*, (i) (large) *wine-container*; (ii) *wine-case* for travelling; (iii) special type of decorated *flagon*

No entry in *R-E*.

Not in Varro, *LL*.

(*a*) Isid. *Etym.* 20. 6. 1 (De vasis vinariis et aquariis). 'The *wine-carrier* is a vessel for carrying wine; οἶνος is the word for wine. Hence the well known expression (Lucil. 139): "The bottom of the wine-carrier turns, so my opinion veers round"': *oenophorum vas ferens vinum*; οἶνος enim vinum est. de quo illud (Lucil. 139):

> vertitur oenophori fundus, sententia nobis.

(b) *Corp. Gloss.* s.v. 'oenophorum'. oenophorum οἰνοφόρον III 263. 15; 270. 44 (unde?).

(c) *Corp. Gloss.* s.v. 'vinarium'. vinarium οἰνοφορ⟨ε⟩ῖον II 381. 2. οἰνοφόρον III 197. 37, 263. 15, etc. ἀκρατοφόρον III 324. 47.

(d) Horace, *Sat.* 1. 6. 107–9 (on an ostentatious senator). 'Nobody is going to charge me with stinginess like yours, Tillius, when as praetor on the road from Tivoli you have a following of five slaves, carrying your chamberpot and your *wine-case*':

> obiciet nemo sordes mihi quas tibi, Tilli,
> cum Tiburte via praetorem quinque secuntur
> te pueri, lasanum portantes *oenophorumque*.

(e) Juv. *Sat.* 6. 425–8 (on a woman with a huge appetite for wine). 'At last she arrives with a flushed face, and with thirst enough to drink off a *wine-container* holding all of three gallons which is set down at her feet, and from which she tosses off a couple of pints before dinner to create a raging appetite':

> tandem illa venit rubicundula, totum
> *oenophorum* sitiens, plena quod tenditur urna
> admotum pedibus, de quo sextarius alter
> ducitur ante cibum rabidam facturus orexim.

(f) Persius, *Sat.* 5. 140–1 (preparations for a sea-voyage). 'Now you are all ready for off, loading up your slaves with packing-cloths and wine-case; "quick!", you cry, "all aboard!"':

> iam pueris pellem succinctus et *oenophorum* aptas
> ocius ad navem.

(g) Juv. *Sat.* 7. 11 (items in an auction sale). 'A *wine-case*, tripods, bookcases and cupboards': *oenophorum* tripedes armaria cistas.

DISCUSSION

'A basket or portable case for transporting small quantities of wine from place to place; especially for the supply of persons on a journey who preferred carrying their own wine with them to taking the chance of buying what they could upon the road': so Rich (*Dict. Ant.* s.v. 'oenophorum').

None of the references gives any specific information about the design of this type of container, which must have been a familiar sight on the road (passages *d*, *e*) or on the quayside (passage *f*); as common, in fact, as bookcases and cupboards at an auction sale (passage *g*). When wine was packed for carriage in relatively small quantities on a journey, one would expect the container to be a flagon encased in basketry, like the familiar Chianti-bottle of today, which has a long history. The proverbial expression cited by Isidore and attributed by him to the satirist Lucilius implies that the *oenophorum* was round, and that it was capable of turning. Does this mean a round receptacle slung, like other baggage items, behind the saddle of the mounted traveller, and turning round as he went on his way? Hilgers describes the vessel as 'clearly a flask or jug with handles', ignores the significant references to the use of the container by travellers (*d* and *f*), and compares it closely with the *lagoena*, noting that Martial (6. 89. 5) makes the two terms synonymous. But the passage will not bear this meaning. The most important inference to be drawn from the evidence is that, although *oenophorum* could be used to denote a large vessel for holding wine, as in passage *e*, where the 'record-breaking' lady needs a whole barrel to satisfy her thirst, the notion of a travelling container for wine to be consumed on a journey by road or by sea is implicit in two of the remaining passages, while something of the same sort is at least a likely item in the auction list in the last citation (*g*).

Size

The only reference I can find is the three-gallon container of passage *e*. This will have held the equivalent of eighteen of our wine bottles. Travelling containers will naturally have been of assorted sizes. Detailed study of representations of travellers on horseback or in vehicles might throw some light on the problems discussed here. The name is also applied to a well-known series of one- and two-handled flagons with relief decoration, the so-called 'oinophoroi'. See J. W. Hayes, *Late Roman Pottery*, London, 1972, pp. 411 ff. and pl. XXII *a*. The series is widely distributed, and apparently dates from the second and early third centuries A.D. (Hausmann, *Ath. Mitt.* 69–70 (1954–5), 138).

Fig. 48. Olla

27. Olla (-ae, f.), also older form **aula** (-ae, f.) (Cato, Plautus), = Gr. χύτρα, (i) *pot, jar* (gen.); (ii) esp. *cooking-pot* for vegetables, porridge, pulse, etc.; (iii) *olla ossuaria, urn* for ashes

(*a*) *R-E* VII 2. 2485–7 [F. Wotke]. E-M s.v. 'aulla': compare Skr. *ukhá* 'marmite'.

(*b*) Varro, *LL* 5. 108. 'Vegetables, "olera", take their name from a *pot*, "olla"': ab *olla* olera dicta.

(*c*) Isid. *Etym.* 20. 8. 1 ff. (*De vasis coquinariis*). 'The pot, "olla", takes its name from the fact that water bubbles up, "ebulliat", in it when fire is placed under it, as the steam rises higher. Hence the name "bubble", "bulla" is given to that which is held up in the water by the blast of the wind inside. The "dish", "patella", is a sort of wide vessel; it is in fact a *cooking-pot*, "olla", with a wider mouth. Cauldrons, "*lebetae*", are smaller *pots* made for culinary use': olla dicta pro eo quod ebulliat in ea aqua igni subiecto, ut altius vapor emittitur. unde et bulla dicitur, quae in aqua venti intus spiritu sustentatur. patella quasi patula; *olla* est enim oris patentioribus. lebetae sunt . . . *ollae* minores ad usum coquendi paratae.

(d) *Corp. Gloss.* s.v. 'olla'. olla χύτρα II 138. 26. . . . χαλκεῖον II 474. 56. λέβης III 204. 5. μηνίσκος III 500. 37; 530. 41 (nola vel olla). illa? alias vas ad coquendum v 228. 41. olla a bulliendo, unde et bullam v 574. 9 (*an* bulla *in his scribendum?*).

(e) Non. p. 543. *aula* quam nos *ollam* dicimus; et est capacissimum vas.

(f) Cato 81 (recipe for making pot-cake (*erneum*)). 'Pour (the mixture) into an earthenware pot, plunge it into a copper *cooking-pot* full of hot water, and boil over the fire': id indito in irneam fictilem, eam demittito in *aulam* aheneam aquae calidae plenam. ita coquito ad ignem.

(g) Plautus, *Mil.* 852–4 (a slippery cellar floor). 'But there was rather too much slippery space in the cellar. There was a *two-pound cooking-pot* there, and so, with those wine-jars handy, that pot often used to get filled up ten times over':

> sed in cella erat paulum nimi' loculi lubrici,
> ibi erat *bilibris aula*, sic propter cados
> ea saepe decies complebatur.

(h) Varro ap. Non. 15. 1. 'Watch the *pot of porridge*, in case it gets scorched': oculis observare *ollam pultis*, ne aduratur.

(j) Mart. 13. 8. 'Fill plebeian *pots* with emmer-pap from Clusium; when you are full and they are empty you can drink sweet must':

> imbue plebeias Clusinis pultibus *ollas*
> ut satur in vacuis dulcia musta bibas.

(k) Colum. 12. 8. 1 (on making sour milk cheese). 'Take a new *cooking-pot*, and make a hole in the bottom': *ollam* novam sumito eamque iuxta fundum terebrato.

(l) Mart. 12. 18. 19–21 (the pleasures of provincial life). 'When I get up, a fire, fed by a lordly pile of logs from a near-by oakwood, welcomes me, and my bailiff's wife crowns it with many a *cooking-pot*':

> surgentem focus excipit superba
> vicini strue cultus iliceti
> multa vilica quem coronat *olla*.

DISCUSSION

Olla (*aula*) was the name given to a cooking-pot made either of earthenware (cf. *ollae fictiles* at Colum. 8. 8. 7), or of metal, usually bronze (passages *d, e, f*). We have no specific reference to size or shape, but Cato's 'pot-cake' (passage *f*), with twelve pounds of ingredients mixed in a trough (*alveus*) then placed in a cooking-pot (*irnea*), which was then set in a bronze cauldron (*aula aenea*), for cooking as in a double boiler, would require a very large container, like the French 'bain-marie'. Other references imply small containers, and *olla* will have been a generic word like our 'pot', denoting a cooking pot of varying capacity. Columella's recipe for making sour milk cheese (passage *k*) demands a vessel with a flat bottom. Rich (*Dict. Ant.* s.v. 'olla') goes much further, and describes it as having 'a flat bottom, swelling sides, a wide mouth, and lid to cover it', adding that 'it was employed like the French pot-au-feu in many different culinary operations'. The term was also applied to the jars widely used for preserving different kinds of fruit (Colum. 12. 45. 2); hence the adjective *ollaris* applied to grapes preserved in pots (Mart. 7. 20. 9). Its most common uses were evidently for boiling vegetables (Sulp. Sev. *Dial.* 1. 13. 4: 'ollam cum holeribus sine igne fervere'; cf. Varro's absurd derivation of *olus* from *olla* (passage *b*), and porridge (passages (*h*), (*j*)). Unlike the *aenum*, or cauldron, which was slung from chains over the fire, the flat-bottomed *olla* was used on the stove. But for Martial (passage *l*), back in his native Spain, the pleasure of an open fire generously stoked with logs was enhanced by the fact that the *vilica*, in simple homely fashion, set her cooking pots among the logs. As with cooking utensils everywhere Roman pots were made in a variety of shapes and sizes to suit different culinary requirements. Hilgers (pp. 114f.) is wrong in claiming *aula* as a vulgar term for 'drinking-pot'. The point in the passages he cites is that an ordinary pot is being used for a different purpose (passages *g* and *j*). There are references to 'two-pound' (passage *g*) and 'four-pound' *ollae* (Plaut. *Aul.* 809), the weights presumably referring to the quantity of meal or pulse they were designed to contain, not, as LS, s.v. 'bilibris', to the weight of the pot itself. 'Find me a larger pot from close by', says a cook in a scene in the *Aulularia* (390), 'this one is (too) small: it doesn't hold enough' (cf. Columella's *angusta olla* at 9. 15. 5). Wotke (passage *a*) says the word is part of the popular vocabulary, not used by Virgil, Horace, or Ovid, who prefer the word *aenum*.

Extant representations

D–S s.v. 'olla' IV 1, 171–2, fig. 5395 shows an *ollarium* with funerary *ollae* in situ. *Ibid.* fig. 5396 shows an illustration of a funerary *olla* inscribed with the name of the deceased, now in the Louvre, Paris.

Extant specimens

A reconstructed kitchen in the house of the Vettii, Pompeii, showing a typical large cooking pot (*olla*) set on a tripod stand on the kitchen range, with other cooking vessels set aside in a corner adjoining: Mau–Kelsey, p. 267, fig. 125.

Note: the distinction between the various names may well turn out to be quite arbitrary, if we get fresh evidence; thus it is often stated that *olla* may be generally distinguished from *caccabus* in that the former is used for cooking the porridge (large-scale cookery) while the *caccabus* is essentially a pot for cooking vegetables in. But there is no proof of the distinction.

28. Operculum (-i, n.), also **operimentum** (-i, n.) (fr. *operire*, to cover), a *lid*, *cover*

Fig. 49. Operculum

No entry in *R-E*.

Not in Varro, *LL*, except 5. 167 in the sense of coverlets for beds. Not in Isid.

(a) *Corp. Gloss.* s.v. 'operculum'. operculum πῶμα II 138. 55; III 231. 4, etc. πωμάτιον II 426. 61. cooperimentum vasis II 588. 32. operculo σκεπάσματι II 138. 49.

(b) Cato 10. 2 (oliveyard inventory). 'One cauldron-*lid*': *operculum* aheni I. *Ibid.* 11. 2 (vineyard inventory). 'One cauldron-*lid*': *operculum* aheni I. *Ibid.* 11. 2 (vineyard inventory). 'Storage jars. . . . separate *lids* and covers for the jars': dolia . . . *opercula* doliorum et tectoria priva.

(c) Cato 104 (how to make wine for the *familia*). 'Put the *lid* on the storage jar and seal ten days later': *operculum* in dolium imponito et oblinito post dies X.

(d) Colum. 11. 2. 71 (preparations for wine-making). '(He must have ready in advance) the *lids* and strainers and all the other things essential to the proper making of the must': (cuncta praeparanda erunt) *opercula* colaque et cetera, sine quibus probe confici mustum non potest. Cf. *ibid.* 8. 8. 7.

(e) Pliny, *HN* 14. 135 (on methods of storing wine). 'The *lids* of the storage jars should be similarly treated with the addition of mastic or Bruttian pitch. The rule is that jars must not be unsealed in midwinter except on a fine day, and not when a south wind is blowing or when there is a full moon': sic *opercula* doliorum medicanda addita mastiche aut pice Bruttia. bruma aperiri vetant nisi sereno die, vetant austro flante lunave plena.

(f) Macrob. *Sat.* 7. 12. 15 (on protecting wine during fermentation). 'That is why the farmers, not content with setting their storage jars under a roof, bury them in the ground, and fortify them with *lids* coated on the outside, removing the wine as far as possible from contact with the air': unde agricolae dolia non contenti sub tecto reposuisse, defodiunt et *operimentis* extrinsecus illitis muniunt, removentes in quantum fieri potest a vino aeris contagionem.

DISCUSSION

Operculum (Gk. πῶμα) is the regular term for any kind of lid or cover for jars, cooking-pots, or similar vessels. As shown on monuments, they could be made to fit over the orifice, or where resistance to internal pressure was necessary, as in storage of fermenting wine (passage *c*), they could be flush-fitting, resting on an internal flange. Such covers were normally made air-tight by sealing with pitch or mastic (passages *c* and *e*). The point is strongly reinforced by Macrobius (passage *f*), who adds that it is difficult to keep wine from going off 'even in a full container' (*loc. cit.*). Cato's use of two separate terms (*operculum* and *tectorium*) in his reference to storage jars for grape-refuse and grain (passage *b*) may well imply the difference of type already mentioned; *operculum* will then refer to the internally fitting type, and *tectorium*, which is not otherwise used in this sense, to the 'cap' which fitted over the orifice. This would be the natural meaning of the latter term, since covers of this kind do make a sort of roof over the container.

Special types. Pliny's sliding cover (*operculum ambulatorium*, *HN* 21. 80) was 'a sliding or moveable lid, which might be depressed or raised, so as to cover exactly the contents in the vessel it belonged to, like that now used for snuff and tobacco jars. The Romans sometimes covered their beehives with lids of this kind, in order that the size of the honeycomb and hive might be exactly proportioned to each other' (Rich, s.v. 'operculum', p. 453). The term is twice employed by Apicius to denote a covered casserole dish: 4. 5. 200 (baked stuffed chicken) and 10. 1. 421 (stuffed baked fish).

Extant representations

Very common, and representing both the 'cap' and recessed types of lid.

Extant specimens

Both types are to be found in the major museum collections.

29. Orca (-ae, f.), (i) large earthenware *jar* for wine, oil, water, etc.; (ii) large *fish* (? walrus); dimin. **orcula** (-ae, f.), (i) small *jar* for preserving olives, salad, etc.; (ii) same type of vessel used as *boundary mark*

W–H s.v. 'orca': 'aus Gr. ὔρχη (äol. ὔρχη) f. irdenes Gefäss für eingesalzene Fische, wie auch urna (*urc-na), urceus; anders Svennung "orca" aus "urcea" (Kl. Beitr. 12)'.

No entry in *R-E*.

Not in Varro, *LL*.

(a) Isid. *Etym.* 20. 6. 5 (De vasis vinariis et aquariis). '"*Orca*" is a type of amphora; the smaller variety is called "urceus", and the diminutive is "urceolus"': *orca est amphorae species, cuius minore vocabulo urceus, diminutivo urceolus est.*

(b) *Corp. Gloss.* s.v. 'orca'. orca κεράμιον III 193. 66/7. κεράμειον III 270. 53 (unde?). est amphorae species cuius minoris vocabulum (-la *codd.*) orcius, diminutione orciolus est v 574. 37 (cf. Isid. xx 6. 5).

(c) Festus s.v. 'orca' p. 195 L; p. 182 M. 'The name "*orca*" is given to a very large marine animal. Vessels for holding figs are also called "*orcae*" from their resemblance; they are rotund and of identical shape': *orca genus marinae beluae maximum dicitur; ad cuius similitudinem vasa quoque ficaria orcae dicuntur: sunt enim teretia atque uniformi specie.*

(d) Varro, *RR* 1. 13. 6 (on the provision of storage). '(In the old days they ran the wine into a reservoir) because often, when new wine is laid down, the *butts*, as in Spain, and the large jars, as in Italy, are burst by the fermentation of the must': *quod saepe, ubi conditum novum vinum, orcae in Hispania fervore musti ruptae neque non dolea in Italia.*

(e) Colum. 12. 15 (on preserving figs). 'Set the figs in well-pitched *casks*': *in orcas bene picatas condere.*

(f) Hor. *Sat.* 2. 4. 64 ff. (Catius' recipe for sauce). 'The simple (sauce) consists of sweet olive oil, which should be mixed with full-bodied wine and brine, like that which gives such a powerful odour to your Byzantine *jar*':

> simplex a dulci constat olivo
> quod pingui miscere mero muriaque decebit
> non alia, quam qua Byzantia putuit *orca.*

(g) Pliny, *HN* 15. 82 (ways of preserving dried figs). 'Where there is a very plentiful supply, *large jars* are filled with them in Asia, and kegs in the city of Ruspina in Africa': *at ubi copia abundat, implentur orcae in Asia, cadi autem in Ruspina Africae urbe.*

(h) Cato 119 (recipe for *epityrum*). 'Make a confection of green, ripe and mottled olives as follows: remove the stones from green, ripe and mottled olives, and season as follows: chop up the flesh, add oil, vinegar, coriander, cummin, fennel, rue and mint. Place in an earthenware *jar*, cover with oil': *epityrum album nigrum variumque sic facito. ex oleis albis nigris variisque nuculeos eicito. sic condito. concidito ipsas, addito oleum, acetum, coriandrum, cuminum, feniculam, rutam, mentam. in orculam condito. oleum supra siet.*

(j) Grom. p. 337. 21 (on country estates alphabetically listed); cf. 344. 25 f. '(Estate listed as 'X') ... on a small mound beside the road you will find a small earthenware *jar* set up at a crossroads ... from there go straight along the valley': *in collicello circa viam orculam invenies in quatrifinio constituta* (sic). *ex eodem pergis recta valle.*

(k) Pers. *Sat.* 3. 48–50 (the poet's sole ambition as a schoolboy). 'The summit of my ambition was to know what that lucky top throw (of the dice) would bring me, how much that damnable deuce would sweep away – never to be balked by the narrow neck of the *jar*':

etenim id summum, quid dexter senio ferret,
scire erat in voto; damnosa canicula quantum
raderet; angustae collo non fallier *orcae*.

DISCUSSION

Orca

The shape and size of the *orca* can be determined, in general terms, by putting together the evidence furnished by Festus (passage *c*), and that of storage jars of corresponding type found *in situ*. Festus' adjective *teres* is synonymous with *rotundus*, meaning spherical or round-bellied, like the English 'tun' which is a cask of round-bellied shape (cf. the descriptive name Sir Tunbelly Clumsy given to the Falstaffian character in Sir John Vanbrugh's comedy *The Relapse* [1696]). A storage jar answering closely to the description was found at Pompeii and is now in the Naples Museum; it is almost completely spherical in shape, with a narrow flat base, measuring 5 feet in diameter compared with a height of 5 feet 7 inches. It is distinguished from the *dolium* (passage *d*), but whether in material or shape or in some other way is not clear. The editors and translators of Varro, while using different English terms such as 'butt' and 'jar', do not seem to notice the problem of identification: in fact the Loeb editors, using the same terms as Storr-Best, invert them, calling *orcae* 'butts', and *dolia* 'jars'. Hilgers (p. 235) sums up the evidence in the following words: 'Form: eine Art Amphora; länglich und rund, mit engem Hals, der orca (Art Walfisch) ähnlich.' But an elongated *amphora* would be the worst possible shape for holding fermenting must (passage *d*), and Persius' *orca* 'with a narrow neck' (passage *k*), surely means only that *some orcae* had narrow necks. This after all is the whole point of the game of throwing the knuckle-bones into the vessel!

The *orcula*

The diminutive is commonly used of a preserving jar of the same plump form as the larger vessel (passage *h*). It also appears unexpectedly along with two other earthenware vessels, in the pages of the land surveyors' manuals (passage *j*). The passage in which it occurs forms part of a list of country estates (*casae litterarum*), set out in terms of letters of the alphabet, the list in question being entitled *De casis litterarum montium*, though some of the estates described are on level plains. For further discussion see s.v. 'seria' (below, p. 187).

Extant representations and specimens

It will be evident from the discussion that while rejecting the common identification (based mainly on passages *a* and *k*) found in Rich (s.v.) and Blümner (*Privataltertümer*, p. 153), and accepted by Hilgers, I cannot distinguish this vessel from the general shape represented by the *dolium*. Rich's illustration (s.v.) is of an *amphora* with a particularly long neck; but the pointed base would not enable such a vessel to stand up unsupported. Its obvious instability will have quickly turned a receptacle for pitching into a target for shying!

The *orcula* as boundary marker (passage *j*) does not, unlike *lagoena* and *seria*, feature in the illustrations appended to certain of the MSS of the manuals of land surveying.

30. Pelvis (-is, f.) (cf. Skr. *pālavī*, 'vase'), shallow, round *basin*, esp. for washing, *toilet basin*

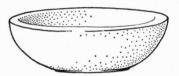

Fig. 50. Pelvis

No entry in *R-E*.

(*a*) Varro, *LL* 5. 119. '"Pelvis", "basin", takes its name from the washing of the feet, as if from "pedeluis", "foot-washer"': *pelvis* pede⟨l⟩uis[1] a pedum lavatione.

(*b*) Isid. *Etym.* 20. 6. 8. 'They are called "pelves", *basins*, because the feet are washed in them': *pelves* vocantur, quod pedes ibi lavantur.

(*c*) *Corp. Gloss.* s.v. 'pelvis'. pelvis λεκάνη II 144. 47; 359. 17, etc. νιπτήρ III 325. 20; 531. 22. λουτήρ III 196. 51; 270. 57; θερμοφύλαξ pelv⟨i⟩s III 203. 55 (*corr. a*; *v.* pigella). pelvis ab eo quod pedum pelluio sit (*vel* sunt), ut malluvium manuum *Plac.* V. 37. 20 + 21 (pelluis) = v 91, 23 = v 132. 35 (pellui). Cf. Varro *de l.l.* v 119; *Fest.* p. 246. 2; *Festus Pauli* p. 160. 4 *GRL* I 544. 15. Isid. xx 6. 8 pulvea (in serie pe—) vas rotundum in quo lavantur pedes II 589. 16 (pelluvia *H.*). pelves quod pedes ibi lavantur gloss. *Werth. Gallée* 341.

(*d*) Non. Marc. s.v. 'pelvis'. pelvis λεκάνη vas aquarium, variis rebus aptum.

(*e*) *Ibid.* 'The basin, "pelvis", is a water bowl in which different items are rinsed out': *pelvis* sinus aquarius in quo varia perluuntur.

(*f*) Pliny, *HN* 31. 27 (a test for badly-drained soils). '(They then resort to other tests.) They dig a hole five feet deep, and then bring there some pots made of unbaked clay, or a bronze *basin* smeared with oil, or a sheepskin, or a lantern burning and enclosed by leaves, and covered with earth; if the pots are found to be wet or cracked, if there is sweat on the basin, or if the lamp goes out without any failure of the oil-supply, or the sheepskin gets wet, these are sure signs of the presence of water': loco in altitudinem pedum quinque defosso ollisque figlino opere crudis aut peruncta *pelvi* aerea lanae

[1] *Scaliger*; pedelavis *Aldus*; *for* pedevis.

vellere[1] cooperto[2] lucernaque ardenti concamerata frondibus, dein terra, si figlinum umidum ruptumve aut in aere sudor vel lucerna sine defectu olei restincta aut etiam vellus lanae madidum reperiatur, non dubie promittunt aquas.

(g) Juvenal *Sat.* 3. 274–5 (on the risks of walking the streets of Rome at night). 'You can put up a piteous prayer in your heart that they'll be satisfied to fling down the contents of their wide *slop-basins*':

> ergo optes votumque feras miserabile tecum
> ut sint contenti patulas effundere *pelves.*

DISCUSSION

The identification of this vessel is not in dispute. As distinct from the large, pedestalled toilet basin (see s.v. 'labrum' above, pp. 155 ff.), it is the typical shallow basin used for a variety of purposes, including washing the feet (passages *a*, *b*) and rinsing clothes (passage *e*). *Pelves* were sometimes made of bronze (passage *f*). Rich (*Dict. Ant.* s.v.) notes that *pelvis* was the generic word while the specific terms *malluvium* and *pelluvium* were used to denote a hand-basin and a foot-basin respectively (see below, 'Extant representations'). Varro's derivation from *pes* and *luere* seems to be confirmed by the obvious derivation of *malluvium* and *pelluvium*. The basic shape, as reflected in that of the human pelvis, will have been shallow, wide and oval.

In this connection the Glossary entry s.v. 'alveolus' (see above, s.v. 'alveus', passage *c* = *Gloss.* v 340. 56, viz. 'alveolus pelvis rotundus') shows that round *pelves* were common; cf. the Glossary entry (above, passage *c*, 1. 5: 'vas rotundum in quo lavantur pedes'). There is a very interesting passage in Seneca (*QN* 1. 12. 1) where *pelves* filled with oil or pitch are used as reflectors for observing an eclipse of the sun, the dense liquid giving a less disturbed reflection than water.

Extant representations

D–S (s.v. 'pelvis' IV, 1, fig. 5548, p. 375) show a bas-relief depicting the familiar scene from Homer's *Odyssey* (19. 386 ff.), where the vessel is called a λέβης; LSJ, s.v. λέβης (2), note that it is also used of the bath in which Clytemnestra slew Agamemnon (Aesch. *Agam.* 1129). The vessel in which Eurycleia is washing Odysseus' feet (*ibid.* fig. 5549, p. 376) is small and round, and only large enough to accommodate the hero's feet.

---

[1] lanae vellere *add. Mayhoff.*

[2] *post* terra *transp.* cooperto *Detlefsen.* Jones (Loeb ed.) notes that the omission of *aut* before *lanae* is awkward, and suggests that Pliny may have forgotten to mention the sheepskin in his first list.

D–S s.v. 'fullonica', II. 2, 1350, fig. 3303, show a Pompeian painting, now in the National Museum, Naples, depicting a laundry establishment and its activities, including a woman (*fullonica*) getting rid of the dirt by treading the garments in a basin. D–S s.v. 'educatio' (II. 1, 479, fig. 2608) show a representation of a baby being bathed in a small round vessel with a heavy rim.

31. Seria (-ae, f.), dimin. **seriola** (-ae, f.), (i) *storage jar* of medium size (dist. fr. *dolium*); (ii) *preserving-jar* for salt meat, etc.; (iii) as *boundary marker*

Fig. 51. Seria

W–H s.v.: 'Fremdw. aus unbekannter Quelle.'

Not in Varro, *LL*.

(*a*) Not in *R-E*, s.v. but Mau, *R-E* V 1. 1285 s.v. dolium gives numerous references.

(*b*) Isid. *Etym.* 20. 6. 6 (De vasis vinariis et aquariis). 'The "*seriola*" is a straight-sided type of "*orca*" or an earthenware wine-jar first invented in Syria': *seriola est orcarum ordo directus vel vas fictile vini apud Syriam primo excogitatum.*

(*c*) *Corp. Gloss.* s.v. 'seria'. seria ἐπίπιθον III 24. 5. πιθάκνη II 407. 46.

(*d*) Cato 10. 4 (inventory of the oliveyard). '10 *smaller storage jars*': *serias* X (cf. *ibid.* 12. 3, *seriae* for the pressroom).

(*e*) *Ibid.* 13 (equipment for the pressroom for olives). 'One *smaller storage jar* for wine': *seriam* vinariam I.

(*f*) Varro, *RR* 1. 55. 5 (operations in the olive mill). 'Each heap (of olives) should pass in order of arrival through the *jars* and oil vessels to the mill': primus quisque acervus demittatur per *serias*[1] ac vasa olearia ad trapetas.

(*g*) *Ibid.* 3. 2. 8 (contents of a country villa). 'He had never seen there ... any wine-presses, vintage equipment, *oil-jars* or olive mills': nec tamen ibi se vidisse ... torcula, vasa vindemiatoria aut *serias* olearias aut trapetas.

(*h*) Colum. 12. 18. 5 (preparations for the vintage). 'The large and *medium-sized storage jars* and other vessels must be treated with pitch forty days before the vintage': dolia ... et *seriae* ceteraque vasa ante quadragesimum vindemiae diem picanda sunt.

(*j*) *Ibid.* 12. 28. 1 (how to make wine keep). 'Then into each *medium-sized storage jar*, which should contain seven amphorae, put an ounce and a third of the preparation': tum in *serias* singulas quae sint ampharum septenum addito medicaminis pondo unciam et scripula octo.

(*k*) Livy 24. 10. 8 (in a list of supernatural events). 'On the Vicus Iusteius an underground spring burst out, releasing such a volume of water that the *jars* and casks which were on the street were overturned and carried away as if by a violent torrent': et in vico Iusteio fontem sub terra tanta vi aquarum fluxisse ut *serias* doliaque, quae in eo loco erant, provoluta velut impetu torrentis tulerit.

[1] seria *Politian*, sena *Victorius*, sina *codd.* (*vid.* Colum. 7. 8. 2 – sinum lactis).

(*l*) Iul. *Dig.* 50. 16. 206. 'Vessels called "vinaria vasa" should properly be classed among the pressroom equipment. Large and *medium-sized jars* should be so classified, as long as they contain wine; when they contain no wine, they should cease to be included, since they are capable of being put to some other use, e.g. if grain is put in them': 'vinaria' vasa proprie vasa torcularia esse placet: dolia autem et *serias*, tamdiu in ea causa esse, quamdiu vinum haberent; cum sine vino essent,[1] desinere in eo numero esse, quoniam ad alium usum transferri possent, veluti si frumentum in his addatur.

(*m*) *Grom. Vet.* p. 341 (with fig. 300) (in a list of *Terminorum diagrammata*, that is, illustrations of different types of markers) '*Jar*': *seria*.

DISCUSSION

Terminology

In northern and central Europe large containers, both for liquids and solids, have traditionally been made of timber staves, so that there are no English equivalents for earthenware vessels of this type. The use of words like 'cask' and 'tun' is misleading. I have preferred the cumbersome but unambiguous term 'storage jar' with indications of relative size.

Shape

The etymology of the word is uncertain, so that no clue as to its shape is provided from this source. Varro and Isidore are strangely silent, and there is not even the usual set of 'multiple equations' in the Glossaries. The lexicographers are little better. LS describe the *seria* as a 'cylindrical earthenware vessel', but none of the references they cite gives any warrant for this statement, which seems to be no more than an obvious inference from Isidore (passage *b*). Forc. defines it as 'an earthenware vessel longer than it was broad, and full-bellied (*oblongum et ventriosum*)', but 'oblongum' has only a scholiast's authority (on *seria* at Pers. *Sat.* 2. 11), and there is nothing else in the passages cited to support either of these statements about the shape. Yet the word was in common everyday use, and described a common type of container: *seriae* appear not only in the usual inventories of agricultural equipment (passages *d* and *e*), but in casual references elsewhere both in the technical (passage *g*) and the non-technical writers (passage *k*). The last-named reference, from the historian Livy's account of a disastrous flood at Rome, is significant, since it refers to storage jars of two kinds, which were set out on the pavement in front of their premises by merchants for direct sale to the consumer 'ex cask', as in a Spanish 'bodega'. This makes the absence of any mention in the lexicographers all the more strange. A clue is furnished by the Glossary equation

[1] The vulg. *esse desinerent, in eo numero non esse* gives no sense.

with πιθάκνη = small pithos (passage c), suggesting that the seria may have been a smaller version of the dolium, perhaps distinguished from the larger vessel by some difference in shape. The vessel which appears in the manuscript illustrations to the Gromatici, where a jar with the name seria is classed among boundary marks (see also s.v. 'lagoena', 'olla'), is symmetrical in profile, resembling the preserving-jars described by Columella (12. 4. 5) as 'usque ad imum aequalia, nec in modum doliorum formata', so that the drawing seems not to conform to the requirements of a container for newly pressed wine, but closely to those of a preserving-jar (see also Isidore's first definition of seriola (passage (b)). Another possibility is that seriae were used to hold wine that was already fermented, in which case a vessel of asymmetrical profile would not be required (see above, s.v. 'dolium', p. 145, and further Blümner, Privataltertümer, p. 150, with full discussion of the evidence).

Size

The only specific reference to size is in passage (j). A capacity of 7 amphorae is not far short of the smallest dolium recorded (full list in Hilgers, p. 175). Columella's preserving-jar for salt pork (12. 55. 4f.) is called a seria, but we are not told how many pigs would fill it!

Uses

The evidence for its use covers a wide range, seriae being used both in the wine-cellar and in the olive pressroom (passages d, f, g). They were also used for storing grain (passage l), as well as for preserving ham (Cato 162. 1), and pork (Colum. 12. 55). Livy's story of the disastrous flooding caused by a burst spring shows that both seriae and dolia were used by shopkeepers.

The collection of surveyors' manuals and other material that has come down to us includes, amongst the items alleged to be latest in date, a treatise on boundaries (De terminibus). This work describes and illustrates with a set of drawings a large variety of boundary markers, amounting to some fifty separate items. Lagoena and seria appear in the list, but orcula, which appears as a boundary mark in an account of estate X (see above, s.v. 'orcula' p. 182) is omitted from this list. An earthenware container does not, on the face of it, look very suitable for the purpose. But boundaries had been regarded as sacred from very early times, and in the venerable Twelve Tables the penalty for removing one from a neighbour's property was 'excommunication' from the society of the Roman People. The vessel depicted as a seria has a wide mouth, the body is symmetrically curved, and it appears to have no handle, unless the draughtsman has not bothered to put one in.

Extant representations and specimens

    Grom. Vet. (ed. Blume), pl. 34, fig. 300. A row of storage jars in the Naples Museum (Pl. 13*a*) reflects the appropriate shape and size.

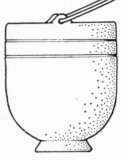

Fig. 52. Situla

32. Situla (-ae, f.), also **situlus** (-i, m.), (i) *bucket, pail* (for water); (ii) = *sitella, voting-urn*; dimin. **sitella** (-ae, f.), *voting-urn*

Not in Varro, *LL.*

(*a*) *R-E* III A. 1. 415–17, s.v. 'situlus, situla' [Leonard].

(*b*) Isid. *Etym.* 20. 6. 3 (*De vasis vinariis et aquariis*). 'The *bucket*, (so called) because to the thirsty ("sitientibus") it is suitable for drinking; this vessel the Greeks call a κάδος': *situla, quod sitientibus apta sit ad bibendum; quod vas Graeci* κάδον *vocant.*

(*c*) *Corp. Gloss.* s.v. 'situla'. situla κάδος II 185. 16, etc. ὑδροφόρος III 368. 7; 505. 34. κάλπις καὶ κάδος III 368. 208. ὑδρία vel κάλπις (calipis *vel* calapis *codd.*) vel κάδος III 496. 18; 505. 35. ὑδρία III 505. 30. sitla κάδος II 541. 52 (cf. cadus). situla sicla (cf. Arch. V. 468) aenea II 593. 14. linbaer (*AS*). V 390. 37. situla, situlus κάδος II 334. 25. situlus κάδος III 325. 9; 527. 23. νᾶνος III 325. 8; 531. 21. Cf. *Festus Pauli,* p. 176. 6.

(*d*) Cato 10. 2 (oliveyard inventory). 'One *water-bucket*': *situlum aquarium* I (repeated in the vineyard inventory – 11. 3).

(*e*) Veg. *Mulom.* 5. 30 (to treat a horse for rabies). 'You will set water by him in a *bucket* so that he does not hear the sound': *aquam . . . in situla appones ut non audiat sonitum.*

(*f*) Plautus, *Amph.* 671. 'If I get a *bucket*, I'll drain the whole life out of that well': *si situlam cepero, illi puteo animam omnem intertraxero.*

(*g*) Paul, *Dig.* 18. 1. 40. 6 (household inventory). 'The wheel for drawing the water is no less a part of the building than the *water bucket* (cf. Isid. *Etym.* 20. 15. 2: rope and *bucket*)': *rota quoque, per quam aqua traheretur, nihilo minus aedificii est quam situla* (cf. Isid. *Etym.* 20. 15. 2 *funis cum situla*).

(*h*) Fest. s.v. 'situlus', p. 185 L; p. 176 M; cf. Varro, *LL* 5. 119 s.v. 'vas aquarium'. 'The Greeks give the name "dwarf" to a low, shallow water-vessel; it is commonly known as the "bearded *bucket*". Dwarfs are called pygmies': *nanum Graeci vas aquarium dicunt humilem et concavum; quod vulgo vocant situlum barbatum unde nani pumiliones appellantur.*

(*j*) Plautus, *Casina* 359–60 (arrangements for a wedding). 'CHEL. Everything you ordered is on hand; wife, lots, *urn* and yours truly':

    CHEL.   adsunt quae imperavisti omnia
            uxor, sortes, *situla* atque egomet.

DISCUSSION

The dictionaries of antiquities are singularly unhelpful. In fact, neither D-S nor *R-E* (passage *a*) makes any reference to the surviving wooden buckets. At ch. 135 Cato's list of bronze articles to be purchased at Capua includes *amae* (pails) but no *situlae*. Since *situla aquaria* is the only bucket listed in the inventories (chs. 10 and 11) it might be assumed that the terms are interchangeable; but these lists are not completely exhaustive, and ordinary household pails, like the shovels, were simply taken for granted. Leonhard (passage *a*) cites a reference from the jurist Paul (*Sent.* 3. 6. 83) where the *situla* is described as a toilet article, used for sluicing the body while bathing. The issue is further confused by the fact that the term has been appropriated by archaeologists to denote a specific type of bronze vessel of cylindrical form, well known from the very ornate specimens recovered from excavations at Pompeii (see the illustrations to the D-S art. s.v.). The use of *situla* to denote an ordinary domestic bucket is well attested (e.g. passages *e*, *f* and *g*). The second meaning of *situla* (passage *j*) is rare, *sitella* and *urna* being the usual terms for the voting-urn: 'The receptacle was a *sitella* or an *urna*, terms which, like Plutarch's rendering ὑδρία (*Ti. Gracch.* 11. 1), describe water-carriers' (Taylor, *RVA*, p. 71).

Shape

The *situlae* attached to the water-wheel described by Vitruvius (10. 4. 4) will necessarily have been wider at the top than at the bottom; the same traditional shape will have been required for those used for bailing out the bilges of ships (Faust. Rei, *Serm.* 24, p. 319. 26), and for watering a horse (passage *e*). I do not know what special purpose could have been served by the concave, shallow, 'bearded' bucket of passage *h*.

Size

Vitruvius' hoist buckets held one *congius* or 0·75 gallons. Our domestic buckets commonly hold two gallons.

Extant representations

Situli are often featured on representations of wells with windlasses, e.g. a well and windlass from a marble sarcophagus from the Vatican cemetery, Rome. The pointed base enables the bucket to fill more readily.

Extant specimens

For wooden types, see above, s.v. 'hama', p. 151. Rich (*Dict. Ant.* s.v. 'situla') shows a bronze specimen, having the shape of an inverted bell, and terminating in a point. He gives no provenance. H. Wilsdorf (*Bergleute und Huttenmänner*, Berlin, 1952, p. 214, fig. 45) discusses an interesting bronze bucket from the mining district of Posada in Spain, which has thirteen irregularly disposed holes at the top. It is 22 cm in diameter, and 25 cm deep. These proportions closely resemble those of the wooden examples from Roman Germany.

33. Testa (-ae, f.), Gr. ὄστρακον, κεράμιον, (i) gen. piece of baked clay, *brick*, *tile* (cf. *opus testaceum*); (ii) gen. any type of *clay vessel*; (iii) broken fragment, *potsherd*

No entry in *R-E*.

Not in Varro, *LL*.

(*a*) Isid. *Etym.* 20. 4. 4 (*De vasis escariis*). 'Baked clay has assumed the name of "testa" (*sherd*), because while it was soft, it is made "toasted", and it has lost its connection with the old word, because it no longer is what it once was': argilla autem excocta *testae* vocabulum suscepit, quia, dum mollis esset, efficitur tosta, nec communicat cum vocabulo pristini generis, quia quod fuit non est.

(*b*) *Corp. Gloss.* s.v. 'testa'. testa ὄστρακον II 197. 54, etc. ostrago III 571. 32 . . . testa caput vel vas fictile v 526. 39; 581. 10. vasa argillacia quae igne[m] efficiuntur, tosta v 249. 1. Cf. Isid. xx 4. 4.

(*c*) Horace, *Odes* 3. 21. 1 ff. (address to a vintage wine in cask). 'Blessed *cask* that shared my birthday when Manlius was consul, come down when Corvinus bids me bring out a milder vintage':

> o nata mecum consule Manlio
> . . . pia *testa* . . .
> descende Corvino iubente
> promere languidiora vina.

(*d*) Ovid, *AA* 2. 696 (on the importance of maturity in a lover). 'Let people in a hurry drink the new wine, but for me let the *jar* laid down in consulships of ancient time pour out a vintage as old as my grandsire':

> qui properant, nova musta bibant; mihi fundat avitum
> consulibus priscis condita *testa* merum.

(*e*) Mart. 12. 93. 2 (on oil from Cordova). 'Cordova, more prolific than oily Venafro, nor less perfect than the *oil-jars* of Istria':

> uncto Corduba laetior Venafro
> Histra nec minus absoluta *testa*.

(*f*) Mart. 13. 7. 1–2 (on beans). 'If pale beans simmer for you in a red earthenware *pot* you can often say no to the banquets of wealthy hosts':

> si spumet rubra conchis tibi pallida *testa*
> lautorum cenis saepe negare potes.

(g) Pliny, *HN* 31. 114 (on nitron). '(Nitron) is burnt in an earthenware *pot*, fitted with a lid, to prevent it bursting out': (nitrum) uritur in *testa* opertum ne exultet.

DISCUSSION

Starting off from its basic meaning, a 'piece of baked clay' (*argilla tosta* – passages *a*, *b*), the word has developed a wide range of meanings, as the above examples show. Passages *c* and *d* suggest that it was a common synonym in poetry for *cadus*, the smaller type of storage jar for wine, as used in the private cellar of an individual householder (see above, s.v. 'cadus', pp. 127 ff.). It was also used (passage *f*) as a synonym for *olla*, the ordinary cooking vessel used on the kitchen stove, as well as for the outsize container inhabited by Diogenes the Cynic (see Juv. *Sat.* 14. 308 ff.). In the technical writers it is common as a synonym for *tegula*, a tile (e.g. Varro, *RR* 2. 3. 6, Vitruv. 2. 8. 19). The basic meaning is retained in the technical term *pavimentum testaceum*, a flooring made of broken pottery and poured concrete (Pallad. 1. 19. 1, etc.).

NOTE ON SCOOPS, SKIMMERS AND LADLES

The term 'ladle' is used of a number of instruments of broadly similar basic design, used in connection with the stirring of liquids under heat, or with the removal of material that rises to the surface during culinary or other processes. The basic shape is naturally that of a spoon, though the concave surface may be either solid for stirring, or pierced with holes like a colander for skimming and removing unwanted material. Ladles are usually distinguished from stirring-spoons by their greater depth, as well as by the vertical or near-vertical set of the handle in relation to the receptacle. As in other categories of instrument or container, rigid distinctions of form and function cannot be established among the range of terms employed.

Ladles

34. Trua (-ae, f.), Gr. τορύνη, *ladle, stirring-spoon*

(a) *R-E* vii A. 700–1 [Aug. Hug].

(b) Varro, *LL* 5. 118. '"Trulla", "*ladle*", from its similarity to "trua", a "*gutter*"; because the latter is large and the former small, they named it as if it were "truella", "*small trua*"': trulla a similitudine *truae*, quae quod magna et haec pusilla, ut true⟨l⟩la. Cf. Titin. and Pompon. ap. Non. 19. 17 f.

(c) Fest. s.v. 'antroare', p. 92 L; p. 9 M. 'They also give the name "*stirring-spoon*" to the implement used by cooks when stirring': *truam quoque vocant quo permovent coquentes exta.*

Fig. 53. Trulla

35. Trulla (-ae, f.), dim. of *trua*, Gr. τρυηλίς, (i) *ladle, dipper*; (ii) with or without the addition of *vinaria, cup-strainer*; (iii) builder's or bricklayer's *trowel*; (iv) *brazier*

(a) *R-E* VII A. 700–1 s.v. 'trua'.

(b) Isid. *Etym.* 19. 18. 3 (*De instrumento aedificiorum*). 'The *trowel* gets its name from the fact that it pushes and pushes away, that is it incorporates stones with lime or mud': *trullae nomen factum eo quod trudit et detrudit, id est includit calce vel luto lapides.*

(c) *Corp. Gloss.* s.v. 'trulla'. trulla ჳωμάλιστρος II 323. 1; III 20. 54, etc. κοτύλη (κοιντάλη *cod. em.* Boucherie) III 321. 58. τρύλλα[ς] II 460. 13. panna, cadia (cf. cazza *paulo post et* Diez I) id est ferrum unde parietes liniunt (!) II 595. 49. cazza ferrea V 517. 41. quod trudat, id est cludat cal[c]e vel luto lapides V 582. 15 (Isid. XIX 18. 3). crucae (*AS*) V 396. 3. scofl (*AS*) V. 396. 54.

(d) Cato 10. 2 (oliveyard inventory). 'One *ladle*': *trullam* I. *Ibid.* 11. 3 (vineyard inventory). 'One *ladle*': *trullam* I. *Ibid.* 13. 2–3 (inventory of requirements for the *cella olearia*). 'Three bronze *ladles*': *trullas* aheneas tres. 'Two wooden *ladles*': *trullas* ligneas II.

(e) Cic. *In Verr.* 4. 27. 62 (a lordly banquet). 'There was a wine utensil there, a ladle carved out of a single enormous precious stone, with a gold handle': *erat enim vas vinarium, ex una gemma praegrandi trulla excavata, manubrio aureo.* Cf. Varro, *LL* 5. 118: 'wine-*ladle*': *vinaria trulla.*

(f) Hor. *Sat.* 2. 3. 142–4 (Opimius the miser). 'Opimius, a poor man for all his stored up silver and gold, would, on holidays, drink wine of Veii from a *ladle* of Campanian earthenware, and on working days would drink sheer vinegar':

> pauper Opimius argenti positi intus et auri
> qui Veientanum festis potare diebus
> Campana solitus *trulla* vappamque profestis.

(g) Pliny, *HN* 37. 7 (a dipper worth a king's ransom). 'When the consular T. Petronius was facing death, he broke, to spite Nero, a myrrhine *dipper* which had cost him 300,000 sesterces, with the aim of disinheriting the emperor's table': *T. Petronius consularis moriturus invidia Neronis, ut mensam eius exheredaret, trullam myrrhinam HS CCC emptam fregit.*

(h) Livy 37. 11 (an effective fire-ship). 'The ships carried in front of them masses of blazing fire contained in iron *braziers* supported on a pair of poles projecting from their bows': *contis enim binis a prora prominentibus trullis ferreis multum conceptum ignem prae se portabant.*

DISCUSSION

The account in D–S v, 520, is unusually full; four meanings are distinguished from the literary references:

(1) *Trulla* as dim. of *trua*, 'a ladle or shell fitted with a long handle, somewhat resembling our soup-ladles' (passages *d*, *e*, *g*).

(2) Also used to denote a drinking-vessel (passage *f*).

(3) A brazier (containing live coals, supplied with air for combustion by holes pierced in its sides (passage *h*)).

(4) = *rutrum*, the builder's or plasterer's trowel. The shape of some extant specimens resembles closely the type in use today. In dealing with this meaning the Glossary editors seem to be curiously unaware of the fact that *trulla*, like the Eng. 'trowel', is used both of the bricklayer's and the plasterer's trowel, the latter meaning being correctly defined at *Gloss.* II 595. 49 'the trowel is the tool used for smearing' (i.e. plastering) 'interior walls' (passage *c*).

Rich (*Dict. Ant.* s.v.) devotes the greater part of his account to yet another meaning, which is rejected by D–S (s.v.) without discussion. Rich's entry is as follows (s.v. 'trulla 2'): 'A drinking-cup or table utensil employed for taking the wine out of a larger recipient, which contained a quantity mixed with snow. It was a species of *cyathus* of an improved character, being furnished with an inner case perforated as a strainer, and fitting into the hollow bowl of the cup, so that when adjusted together the two would form but one body, which might be conveniently dipped into the large vessel, and filled; then by removing the perforated case, any sediment or impurity deposited by the snow would be removed with it from the pure liquid left in the bowl.' The bowl was fitted with a hollow handle (Varro's *manubrium cavum* mistakenly attributed to the *trulleum* (see below, s.v. 'trulleum' passage *b*)). This double bowl may be regarded as an improvement on the wine-strainer known as the *colum nivarium* (on this see Part II, pp. 100 ff. s.v. 'colum nivarium'). These vessels were made in a variety of materials ranging from costly bronze (passage *d*) to common earthenware (passage *f*), and a prize specimen in precious stone (passage *e*).

36. Trulleum (-i, n.), Gr. χέρνιβον, *basin*, *slop-pail*

(*a*) *R–E* vii A. 707 [Aug. Hug]; also *trulleus*, *truleum*, *trullium*.

(*b*) Varro, *LL* 5. 118. 'From the same word (viz. "trua", "gutter") is named "truleum", "*basin*", because it resembles it in shape, except that it is wider, since it is to hold water, and that the handle is not hollowed save in the case of the *wine-basin*': ab eodem est appellatum *truleum*: simile enim figura, nisi quod latius est, quod concipiat aquam, et quod manubrium cavum non est nisi in *vinario truleo*.

(c) *Corp. Gloss.* s.v. 'trulleum'. trulleum est gutum (guttum *e*) et aquiminale χέρνιβον, ξεστόν (ξέστην *d* χερνιβόκεστρον *Mau*) ΙΙ 202. 31. trulleum χέρνιβον ΙΙ 476. 52; ΙΙΙ 324. 62 polybrum in quo manus perluuntur, quod in sinistra tenetur et aliud vas cum aqua in dextera v 655. 10 (Non. 547. 3).

(d) Cato 10. 2 (oliveyard inventory). 'One *slop-pail*': *trullium* I. *Ibid.* 11. 3 (vineyard inventory). 'One *slop-pail*': *trulleum* I.

(e) Pliny, *HN* 34. 7. 'The only genuine Corinthian vessels are therefore those which your connoisseurs sometimes convert into food dishes, and sometimes into lamps or even *slop-basins*': sunt ergo vasa tantum Corinthia, quae isti elegantiores modo ad esculenta transferunt, modo in lucernas aut *trulleos*.

DISCUSSION

As Rich points out (*Dict. Ant.* s.v.) this vessel is repeatedly mentioned by Cato, and always in conjunction with other vessels employed in washing, such as hand- and foot-basins, etc. Its close etymological connection with *trulla*, a perforated ladle or strainer (see above, p. 193), or a perforated brazier, makes it likely that it resembled our now obsolete slop-pail, which was recessed to take a perforated lid through which the dirty water could be poured from the toilet basin after use without splashing, and the contents concealed from view. The Glossaries (passage *c*) wrongly equate it with Gr. χέρνιβον, a hand-basin, while Varro (passage *b*) has confused this vessel with the special perforated ladle (*trulla*, Gr. τρύβλιον, or *trulla vinaria*), described and illustrated above.

Extant representations

Not very common. The slave filling an *amphora* from a *dolium* on the Ince Blundell relief is using a *trulla* (Pl. 10 *b*, see also Pl. 2 *d*).

Extant specimens

H. B. Walters, *Catalogue of Bronzes . . . in the British Museum*, London, 1899, no. 2461; found at Vaison-la-Romaine (Rom. *Vasio*) in 1836. Typical *trulla* with ornamental handle shaped into two Dolphins' heads. Diam. $4\frac{1}{2}$ inches (= 10·2 cm); length 8 in. = 20 cm.

37. Urceus (-i, m.) (see also *hydria, urna*), (i) vessel for drawing water, *ewer, pitcher*; (ii) *jug* for oil, wine, etc.; dimin. **urceolus** (-i, m.), *small jug for serving wine or water*

Apparently no entry in *R-E*; the word appears in its proper place in vol. IX A. I, but with no comment, and a direction to Suppl. IX, but there is no entry there.

(a) Isid. *Etym.* 20. 6. 5 (*De vasis vinariis et aquariis*). 'The "orca" is a kind of "amphora", of which the smaller size is called the "*urceus*" and the smallest the "*urceolus*"': orca est amphorae species, cuius minore vocabulo *urceus* diminutivo *urceolus* est.

(b) *Corp. Gloss.* s.v. 'urceus'. urceus στάμνος II 211. 53; 436. 40, etc. σταμνίσκος III 324. 46; 367. 78. ξέστης II 211. 40. udus (?) *c. post.* IV 196. 40. ortium σταμνίον III 289. 11 = 659. 20. orcium κεράμιον II 347. 60.

(c) *Ibid.* s.v. 'urceolus'. urceolus ξέστης, ξεστίον ὑποκοριστικῶς II 211. 45. urceolus πυθμήν III 271. 3. orciolus σταμνίσκος II 436. 39. ξέστης II 378. 5, etc., with variants urciolus, orciolum, urceolum.

(d) Varr. ap. Non. s.v. 'trulleum', p. 547. *urceolum* aquae manale vocamus, quod eo aqua in trulleum effundatur, unde manalis lapis appellatur in pontificalibus sacris.

(e) Cato 10. 2 (oliveyard inventory). 'Three water *pitchers*': *urceos* aquarios III (cf. 13. 1).

(f) *Ibid.* 11. 2 (vineyard inventory). 'Ten *pitchers* for grape-juice': *urceos* mustarios X.

(g) Paul, *Dig.* 33. 7. 18. 3 (list of farm equipment which passes to the legatee). 'The *pitchers* for pouring water into the cauldron are pressed into the same category, and thus continue in an endless chain of connection': urcei quoque, quibus aqua in aenum infunditur, in idem genus rediguntur, ac deinceps in infinitum . . . procedent.

(h) Ulp. *Dig.* 33. 7. 12. 1. '*Pitchers* and small pots in which preserved fruit is stored': *urceos* capsellas in quibus fructus componuntur.

(j) Horace, *AP* 21–2 (a metaphor from pottery-making). 'A wine-jar begins to be formed; as the wheel turns why does it emerge as a *pitcher*?':

amphora coepit
institui; currente rota cur *urceus* exit?

(k) Martial 14. 106 (a birthday present). 'Here is a present for you of a red *ewer* with a spreading handle; with this the Stoic Fronto used to fetch cold water.'

hic tibi donatur panda ruber *urceus* ansa;
Stoicus hoc gelidam Fronto petebat aquam.

(l) Colum. 12. 16. 4 (on preserving service-apples). 'At the same season service-apples should be carefully picked by hand and placed in *little pots* treated with pitch': eodem tempore sorba manu lecta curiose in *urceolos* picatos adicito.

DISCUSSION

Rich (*Dict. Ant.* s.v.) described the *urceus* as 'a vessel with handles, generally made of earthenware, and chiefly used as an ewer for filling other vessels with water. It is probably allied to ὕρχα and *orca* but there are no sufficient data by which to determine its precise form.' Most of these statements can be justified from the passages cited above; thus Horace's well-known allegory (passage *j*) is about a potter who started turning his wheel to make an *amphora*, and ended up by turning out an *urceus*, and passage *d* is good evidence for its normal use as a ewer or pitcher for filling other vessels with water. But the reference to handles in the plural raises difficulties. The Greek *hydria*, or water pitcher, which is very frequently represented on vases being carried to or from the fountain (see above, s.v. 'hydria', p. 152), had three handles, a pair of short handles on the shoulder for lifting the pitcher on to the carrier's head, and a much larger and wider handle, which commonly rose higher than the lip, for pouring. But Martial's red ewer (passage *k*) refers only to one 'spreading' (*panda*) handle; is this because the pouring handle was so prominent a feature in comparison with the pair of lifting-handles? Isidore (passage *a*) describes the *urceus* as a 'sort of *amphora*', and this is not at all inappropriate if the vessel is to be identified with the *hydria*, for the shapes of these two vessels are basically similar, the most obvious difference being the prominent looped handles of the *amphora*, which after all takes its name from this feature.

The great majority of the Glossary references (passage *b*) equate the *urceus* with the *stamnos*. The vessel conventionally called 'stamnos' nowadays has a high shoulder and a pair of handles, but for all we know the word *urceus* may have been commonly used in late Roman times for *hydria* (on the association of names with shapes see Introduction, pp. 108 f. and for the special difficulties connected with *stamnos* see B. Philippaki, *The Attic Stamnos*, Oxford, 1967, Introduction, pp. xvii–xix).

Shapes

As with many other vessels, there were numerous varieties, which cannot however be distinguished from surviving evidence. Thus Cato's Inventories (passages *e* and *f*) allow for pitchers for grape-juice (*urcei mustarii*) as well as the ordinary water-pitcher or *urceus aquarius*. The diminutive form *urceolus* was used either as a true diminutive (passage *l*), or with the special meaning of the ceremonial ewer (*aquaemanale*), used in the rain-making rite of the *lapis manalis*, when the magical stone was brought into the city during periods of severe drought (passage *d*). Hilgers' emphasis (p. 83) on *urceus* as covering two basically different shapes of vessel as denoted by his terms 'Krug', 'jug', and 'Topf', 'pot' or 'jar', is helpful (see his illustrations at pp. 84 and 85), but this does not solve the problem presented by the passage from Martial (*k*).

Sizes

Hilgers (p. 300) cites Plautus (*Miles* 831) for a capacity of 8 *heminae* (2½ litres). But the passage proves only that this quantity of wine was poured into the vessel! For a similar misinterpretation see above, s.v. 'cadus', p. 129.

The Digest reference

Passage *g* is part of a lengthy account of the principles on which various items are included in the list of essential equipment without which a farm cannot be properly run. The cauldron (*vas aeneum*) for heating the drinking water for the staff is essential: but to include also the pitcher with which it is filled is to start a backward progression that can only end in absurdity. The formula is reminiscent of 'The House that Jack Built', and the pitcher is the turning-point.

Extant representations

See above, s.v. 'hydria', and below, s.v. 'urna'.

Extant specimens

Vessels of both shapes have been found in large numbers. There is a good selection in the permanent display of Life in Roman London at the London Museum.

Survival

Of the name: It. 'orcio', 'pitcher'; 'orci(u)olo', 'small jar'.

38. Urna (-ae, f.), (A) as container, (i) *pitcher*, us. for water; (ii) *funerary urn* for ashes; (iii) *voting* or *lot-casting urn* (= *situla*, *sitella*); **urnalis** (-is) adj., holding one *urna* (Cato 13. 3, etc.); **urnalia** (-ium, n.pl.) *vessels* holding this amount (*Dig.* 33. 6. 16). (B) as unit of capacity = ½ *amphora* or 3 + galls.

R-E: no entry.

D-S: for illustr., see s.v. 'fons'.

(*a*) Varro, *LL* 5. 126 (on various kinds of tables). 'Besides there was a third kind of table for vessels ...; it was called an "urnarium", because it was here that they especially set and kept the "urnae", "*pitchers*", filled with water

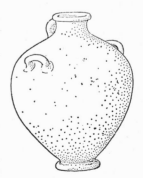

Fig. 54. Urna

in the kitchen . . . "Urnae", "*pitchers*", got their name from the fact that in drawing water they "dive" like an "urinator", "diver"': praeterea erat tertium genus mensae . . .; vocabatur urnarium, quod *urnas* cum aqua positas ibi potissimum habebant in culina . . . *urnae* dictae, quod urinant in aqua haurienda ut urinator.

(b) Isid. *Etym.* 16. 26. 14 (De mensuris). 'The "urna", "*pitcher*", is a unit of measurement which some people call a "quartarius", "four-congius measure". Properly however the "urna" is a vessel normally used for burying the ashes of the dead': urna mensura est quam quidam quartarium dicunt. proprie autem urna vas est, quae pro condendis defunctorum cineribus adhiberi solet.

(c) *Corp. Gloss.* s.v. 'urna'. urna κληρωτρίς, κάλπις, ὑδρία II 211. 49. κάλπη II 337. 50. . . . στάμνος II 436. 40 ἡμιαμφόριον II 324, 39, etc. ἡμικέραμον III 368. 34. (orna) . . . mensura, unde dicuntur sortes, quasi quartarium est IV 196. 5; 297. 53 (mensura *om.*) etc. . . . Cf. Isid. XVI 26. 14. urna ombar (vel ambaer *AS*) V 399. 30.

(d) Cato 11. 2 (vineyard inventory). 'Six *pitchers* covered with broom': urnas sparteas VI.

(e) Ovid, *Fast.* 3. 11–14 (Silvia comes to wash the sacred vessels). 'In the morning Silvia the Vestal made her way to the river for the washing of the holy vessels . . . she sets down the earthen *pitcher* from her head': Silvia Vestalis . . ./sacra lavaturas mane petebat aquas . . ./ponitur e summa fictilis *urna* coma.

(f) Prop. *Eleg.* 4. 11. 27–8. 'I shall speak for myself; if I lie, may the ill-starred *pitcher*, the sisters' punishment, weigh down my shoulders':

ipsa loquar pro me; si fallo, poena sororum
infelix umeros urgeat *urna* meos.

(g) Juv. *Sat.* 1. 163–4 (one may pillory the dead without fear). 'The subject of Achilles' death hurts nobody's feelings; nor does the long quest for Hylas, who tumbled in after his *pitcher*':

nulli gravis est percussus Achilles
aut multum quaesitus Hylas *urnam*que secutus.

(h) Cic. QF 2. 6. 'The senators' *voting-urn* acquitted him by an overwhelming majority, while those of the Knights were evenly balanced. The tribunes of the Treasury found him guilty': senatorum *urna* copiose absolvit, equitum adaequavit: tribuni aerarii condemnarunt.

(j) Hor. Od. 2. 3. 25–7 (of the inevitability of death and judgement). 'We are all driven to the self-same place; every man's lot is in the *urn*, and shaken there, to fly out sooner or later':

omnes eodem cogimur, omnium
versatur *urna* serius ocius
sors exitura . . .

(k) Ovid, *Trist.* 3. 3. 65 (on the disposal of the poet's ashes). 'But have my bones brought back in a tiny *urn*; thus shall my exile not outlast my death':

ossa tamen facito parva referantur in *urna*;
sic ego non etiam mortuus exsul ero.

DISCUSSION

The design and principal uses of this well-known vessel are not in dispute. There are three main types:

(1) *The ordinary water-pitcher* (Gr. ὑδρία). In its primary use, *urna* was the common pitcher, a narrow-necked, full-bodied vessel of earthenware (*fictilis urna*, passage *e*), or of metal, in which water was carried from the spring or river for domestic uses. Rich's description, and its accompanying illustration, cover all the essential points: 'it was carried on the top of the head [passage *e*], or on the shoulder [passage *f*], in the manner still practised by the women of Italy and Egypt; for which purpose it was furnished with three handles, as exhibited by the annexed engraving from an original of earthenware, – two at the sides, to assist in raising it, and one at the neck, by which it was held at the shoulder, or kept steady when tilted for pouring out' (*Dict. Ant.* s.v.). Apart from normal domestic uses drinking water was required for admixture with the wine at parties; Varro is cited twice (*LL* 5. 126; ap. Non. 544. 20) for the term *urnarium*, the table on which the *urnae* were placed. The water to be mixed in the proportions determined by the *arbiter bibendi* will have first been boiled, then mixed with the wine in the krater.

(2) *The cinerary urn*. Equally well-known is the vessel of similar shape (passage *k*), which served as a receptacle for the ashes collected from the funeral pyre. 'They were made of baked earth, alabaster, marble or glass' (Rich, *Dict. Ant.* s.v.).

(3) *The voting, or lot-casting urn*. For discussion of this vessel (passages *h*, *j*), see above, s.v. 'situla' (p. 189), and Rich, *Dict. Ant.* s.v. 'sitella'. Horace's phrase 'omnium versatur urna' (*j*) is neatly paralleled in the Tabula Hebana 23, where the tribal balls (*pilae*) are to be thrown into a 'revolving urn' (*urna versatilis*). See L. R. Taylor, *RVA*, p. 71.

Extant representations

The Greek water-pot known as the *hydria*, with which the *urna* is to be identified (see above, s.v. 'hydria', p. 152), is frequently depicted on monuments, especially in scenes of women drawing water from the public fountain. The best-known example of the type is a fine Attic black-figure *hydria*, showing a queue of women waiting their turn to draw water from the fountain Kallirhoe at Athens (D–S, II. 2, s.v. 'fons', fig. 3143). The full containers are carried vertically on the head, the empty ones horizontally. The cinerary urn is also well known from the monuments; see e.g. D–S IV. 1, fig. 5395 *b*. For representations of the voting-urn (*urna = sitella*) see Taylor, *RVA*, pl. V, nos. 2 and 3.

Extant specimens

Very common. See Erika Diehl, *Die Hydria*, Mainz, 1964; in particular pp. 146ff. on the hydria as receptacle for the ashes of the deceased; good examples of the latter, as found in the graves of ordinary Greeks, in Kurtz and Boardman, *Greek Burial Customs*, London, 1971, figs. 4–6, pp. 51–2. Professor Jocelyn Toynbee's *Death and Burial in the Roman World*, London, 1971, contains no specimens of this very common receptacle!

39. Uter (-tris, m.), = Gr. ἀσκός, *bag*, etc., made from the hide of various animals

Not in Varro, *LL*.

(a) No entry in *R-E* s.v. ἀσκός or 'uter', but Olck's article (*R-E* IV 2. 1742–7, s.v. 'culleus') is both informative and comprehensive, giving references for the smaller type of skins as well as for the *culleus*.

(b) Isid. *Etym*. 20. 6. 7. '*Bags*, "utres", take their name from the womb, "uterus"': *utres ab utero*.

(c) *Corp. Gloss.* s.v. 'uter'. uter ἀσκός (v. *margo*) II 212. 15; III 489. 53. uter utris, utreus, follis ἀσκός III 247. 55. utris ἀσκός II 212. 31, etc.

(d) *Dig*. 33. 6. 3 (on items included in a bequest of wine). 'When wine is left as a legacy, the *wineskins* will not be included, and I say that ox-hides ought not to be included either': *vino legato utres non debebuntur; nec culleos quidem debere dico*.

(e) Pliny, *HN* 28. 240 (how to stanch bleeding). 'The ash from a *goatskin*, provided that it has been used for wine, together with an equal weight of resin, which is a recipe for stanching the flow of blood': *hircini quoque utris, vinarii dumtaxat, cinis cum pari pondere resinae, quo genere sistitur sanguis.*

(f) Varro, *De Vita Populi Romani*, I (ap. Non. s.v. 'tina' p. 544). 'In very early days they used to provide at drinking parties first *skins* of wine, later large vessels called "tinae" (that is, vessels with elongated mouths and fitted with lids) or casks, and in the third phase, "amphorae"': *antiquissimi in conviviis utres vini primo, postea tinas ponebant (id est oris longi cum operculo) aut cupas, tertio amphoras.*

(g) Livy 21. 27. 5 (how Hannibal's Spanish troops crossed the river). 'The Spaniards with no effort packed their clothes in *wineskins*, placing their shields on top, and swam across the river lying on top': *Hispani sine ulla mole in utres vestimentis coniectis ipsi caetris superpositis incubantes flumen tranavere* (cf. Caes. *BC* 1. 48; Curt. 7. 5. 18).

(h) Pliny, *HN* 12. 31 (on *spina piperis* as a remedy). 'The best kind for medical use is the frothing type; this is imported from India in *leather bottles* made of camel skin or rhinoceros hide': *aptissimum medicinae quod est spumosum; Indi in utribus camelorum aut rhinocerotum id mittunt.*

DISCUSSION

The wear-resistant properties of the skins of animals, whether in the form of rawhide or tanned leather, their impermeability as compared with untreated earthenware, as well as their availability, have made containers of this material strong competitors as receptacles for liquids. The commonest article of this class mentioned in literature is the goatskin bag (Gr. ἀσκός), as carried by travellers on foot or on horseback, and containing a reasonable amount of wine or water for daily use (passages *d* and *e*). Olck (*R–E* s.v. 'culleus') notes that the practice of using pigskins to make small containers is still widespread in the Orient, and that water is kept cool in the familiar skin-bag of the water-carrier with the hair on the outside, while for wine the hairy side is turned inwards. We may observe (passage *d*) that these ordinary wineskins are excluded from legacies that automatically go to the heir who inherits a testator's stock of wine, on the grounds that they were used, not for storage, but for daily use. The same passage also makes clear the distinction between *utres* and *cullei*, the latter being the entire skin of an ox (see above, s.v. 'culleus' p. 140). Assuming that Varro's list (passage *f*) is in descending order of size, corresponding to a gradual reduction in consumption per head on these convivial occasions, these early wineskins may well have been made from the skins of pigs. The tenth Title of Diocletian's Edict (on leather goods) mentions 'first-grade *utres*' at 120 den. and olive-oil skins (*utres olearii*) at 100 den. The use of inflated skins as pontoons (passage *g*) is well known from ancient times. The Spanish troops in question were light-armed: even so, the 'odres' they swam over on will have been large enough to have sufficient buoyancy with their clothes packed inside. According to Caesar (*BC* 1. 48) Spanish soldiers were so accustomed to crossing rivers on skins that they never went on campaign without them. The larger type of 'odre' still used in Spain is made from sheepskin or goatskin. Leather-covered containers have a long history, as we may see from Pliny's account (passage *h*) of the use of camel or rhinoceros hide for the export of medicines.

Extant representations

D–S s.v. 'uter' gives no illustration of the small wineskin, but shows (v, 615, fig. 7239) a scene of Bacchic revelry from an Apulian *krater*, in which a number of satyrs are disporting themselves around a festal *culleus* of enormous dimensions, bound with straps and covered with ivy. The smaller wineskins are often to be seen on vases with Bacchic scenes; e.g. Furtwängler–Reichhold, *Griechische Vasenmalerei*, München, 1900–32, pl. 48 – a well-known *psykter* (wine-cooler) by Douris, now in the British

Museum. Here a delightful grouping of revelling Silenoi includes a Silenus squeezing a full wineskin held under his arm, and dexterously discharging its contents into the mouth of a kneeling companion. A fine Roman example was found in an *oecus* of a private house at Herculaneum (House of the Stags) – a marble statuette of a young satyr carrying an 'otre' on his shoulder. M. Brion, *Pompeii and Herculaneum*, tr. by J. Rosenberg, London, 1960, pl. 89.

Survival

(*a*) *Of the name.* It. 'otre', 'wineskin', 'goat-skin bottle'; Sp. 'odre', 'wineskin'.

(*b*) *Of the vessel.* Ubiquitous in Spain.

40. Vas (-is, n.), pl. **vasa** (-orum), (i) *container*: cf. our 'vessel'; (ii) *instrument or implement in general*; (iii) gen. *baggage*; dimin. **vasculum** (-i, n.), *small vessel* or *container*

R-E has only *vasa murrina*.

Note: vas is common in the technical writers with a variety of specific or general adjectives, such as *aquarius*, *vinarius*, etc. These are separately discussed below. The lexicographical references are given together for convenience.

Vas (gen.)

(*a*) Varro, *LL* 5. 119 (domestic animals). 'A *water-jug* they called a "futis", because with it in the dining-room they "poured on", "infundebant" [*scil.* the guests' hands] the water that had been brought': *vas aquarium* vocant futim, quod in triclinio allatam aquam infundebant.

(*b*) *Ibid.* 5. 120 (vessels on the dining-table). '*Vessels* on the eating-table': *vasa* in mensa escaria. These include *catinus*, *canistrum* and *tryblion*.

(*c*) *Ibid.* 5. 125 (the table for holding domestic vessels). 'A second variety of table for vessels was of stone, an oblong rectangle with a single column called a "cartibulum". When I was a boy this used to be placed in many houses near the roof-opening and on and around it were placed *bronze vessels*': altera vasaria mensa erat lapidea quadrata oblonga una columella; vocabatur cartibulum. haec in aedibus ad compluvium apud multos me puero ponebatur et in ea et cir⟨cum⟩ ea(m) aenea vasa.

(*d*) Isid. *Etym.* 20. 4. 1 (*De vasis escariis*). '*Vessels* ("vasa") take their name from eating ("vescendo"), because things to eat are served in them': *vasa* dicta a vescendo, quod in ea escae adponantur.

(*e*) *Corp. Gloss.* s.v. 'vas'. vas ἀγγεῖον, σκεῦος II 204. 45, etc.

(*f*) Ulp. *Dig.* 33. 7. 8 (list of farm equipment). 'The equipment of the farm includes ... *implements* used for cultivation, viz. ploughs, heavy and light hoes, billhooks, two-pronged drag-hoes and other similar items': in instrumento fundi ea esse ... *vasa*que utilia culturae, quae sunt aratra, ligones, sarculi falces putatoriae bidentes et si quae similia dici possunt.

(*g*) Colum. 12. 53. 2 (on the making of 'gleucine' oil). 'An *oil-vessel*, as large as possible, and either new or at any rate very solidly constructed, should be got ready': *vas oleare* quam maximum, et aut novum aut certe bene solidum praeparari oportet.

(*h*) Ibid. 11. 3. 52 (a glasshouse on wheels). 'It is also possible, if it is worth the trouble, to put wheels under fairly large *containers*, so that they can be brought out and taken indoors again with less labour': possunt etiam, si sit operae pretium, *vasis* maioribus rotulae subici, quo minore labore producantur, et rursus intra tecta recipiantur.

(*j*) Ibid. 12. 11. 1 (on making beeswax water). 'After the second yield of honey, the wax should be steeped in spring water or rain water; then the water should be squeezed out and strained and poured into a *lead vessel* and boiled, and all impurities removed with the scum': cum secundarium mel de favis fuerit exemptum, cerae ... aqua fontana vel caelesti macerentur. expressa deinde aqua coletur, et in *vas plumbeum* defusa decoquatur, omnisque spurcitia cum spumis eximatur.

(*k*) Dig. 34. 2. 20 (on testamentary dispositions). 'If *utensils* have been bequeathed, these include not only receptacles for containing prepared items of food or drink, but instruments providing support for anything; therefore salvers and hors d'œuvre trays are included': si *vasa* sint legata, non solum ea continentur, quae aliquid in se recipiunt edendi bibendique causa paratum, sed etiam quae aliquid sustineant: et ideo scutellas vel promulsidaria contineri.

(*l*) Hor. Ep. 1. 2. 54. 'If the *container* is not clean, whatever you pour into it turns sour': sincerum est nisi *vas*, quodcumque infundis acescit.

(*m*) Livy 27. 47. 8 (breaking camp in silence). 'The signal was given to strike camp (lit. pick up their *traps*) in silence': dato signo ut taciti *vasa* colligerent.

(*n*) Caes. BC 1. 66. 'On receipt of this information he ordered the signal to be given and the usual order for striking camp to be given out': quo cognito signum dari iubet et *vasa* militari more conclamari.

DISCUSSION

Basically the word *vas* is a generic term for a container of earthenware or metal, without differentiation of size or shape (for similar generic uses in basketry, see Part Two, s.v. 'corbis'). In addition, as the *Digest* passage shows, the usage has been extended so as to cover items which cannot be classified as containers (passage *f*). In more restricted applications the term is used by the technical writers to denote either the material of which the container is made (e.g. *vas plumbeum* in passage *j*), or the class of equipment to which it belongs (e.g. *vas oleare* in passage *g*). Also, by a useful and natural 'shorthand' process some of these adjectives came to be used quite regularly without the substantive (e.g. *aenum* = *vas aeneum* = cauldron). On this see s.v. 'aenum', p. 118. Varro's *vas aquarium* = *futis* (passage *a*) seems to be another case of a general term used with specific meaning: *vasa aquaria* are used elsewhere as a category comprising several vessels used for carrying or pouring water. The last two citations (passages *m* and *n*) show the most generalized usage of all, and one that is widely used in army contexts, where *vasa* = 'traps' or 'baggage'.

PART FOUR

MISCELLANEOUS

The items discussed, in order of presentation, are as follows: flails, *baculum*, *fustis*, *pertica* (i); the shepherd's crook, *pedum* (*baculum pastorale*); the ox-goad, *stimulus*.

The flail. Three methods of threshing the reaped grain are mentioned by our authorities, the choice of method being determined by the way in which the grain had been harvested. Where part of the straw was left attached to the heads of grain, the straw was removed by trampling with the hooves of animals, or by the use of various mechanical devices, the most common of which was the *tribulum* or threshing-sledge (see *AIRW*, pp. 152–6). Where the heads alone were cut off, leaving the straw for other purposes such as thatching, these were then taken indoors, and either beaten out with flails during the winter or trodden out by cattle (see Colum. 2. 20. 4). The process is mentioned only three times, twice by Columella and once by Pliny (see below, passages 1 (*c*), 2 (*c*), 3 (*f*)). No distinction is made between the three terms used, *baculum* (walking-stick), *fustis* (cudgel) and *pertica* (pole) being used indifferently.

1. Baculum (-i, n.), also **baculus** (-i, m.), (i) *walking-stick*; (ii) *flail* (cf. Fr. and Eng. 'baton')

(*a*) Isid. *Etym.* 20. 13. 1. 'The *walking-stick* is said to have been an invention of Bacchus, the discoverer of the vine, for men to lean on when under the influence of wine': *baculus a Bacco* (sic!) *repertore vitis fertur inventus, quo homines moti vino inniterentur.*

(*b*) *Corp. Gloss.* s.v. 'baculum'. *baculum* βακτήριον III 366. 39; 490. 30; III 198. 6. *fustem pastoralem* V 492. 26.

(*c*) Colum. 2. 20. 4 (on treatment of the grain after 'heading'). 'The ears themselves may be carried into the granary, and then, during the winter, be beaten out with *flails* or trodden out by cattle': *spicae ipsae possunt in horreum conferri, et deinde per hiemem vel baculis excuti vel exteri pecudibus.*

2. Fustis (-is, m.), (i) a *cudgel*; (ii) *flail*; (iii) *stake*

(*a*) Isid. *Etym.* 20. 13. 2 (*De reliquis quae in usu habentur*). 'Stakes, because they "stand" planted in the earth; the country folk call them "pali"': *fustes, quod praefixi in terram stent, quos palos rustici vocant.*

(*b*) *Corp. Gloss.* s.v. 'fustis'. *fustis* ῥάβδος, βάκλον II 74. 56, etc. ξύλον ἐν ᾧ τύπτομεν II 378. 33; ῥόπαλον III 263. 64, etc.

(*c*) Colum. *loc. cit.* (after referring to threshing with animals). 'It is better however that the ears themselves be beaten with *flails* and cleaned in winnowing baskets': *ipsae autem spicae melius fustibus cuduntur vannisque expurgantur.*

3. Pertica (*-ae*, f.), *rod, pole, staff* (cf. Eng. 'perch' as unit of land measurement), (i) *flail*; (ii) *vine-prop*; (iii) *surveyor's measuring-staff* (= *decempeda*); (iv) *perch for birds*

Note: Examples of the various meanings are given here for convenience. They include two references to *pertica* (ii), a vine-prop (see further above, pp. 19 ff.). For *pertica* (iii) = *decempeda* see above, p. 42.

Not in Varro, *LL*; Isidore mentions only *pertica* as measure of length (15. 15. 2).

(a) *R-E* xix. 1059–60 [A. Schulten]; cf. *ibid.* iii A s.v. 'Stab' [de Waele].

(b) *Corp. Gloss.* s.v. 'pertica'. pertica κανών, κάμαξ ii 148. 39. κανών, κοντός ii 493. 52, etc.

(c) Cato 33. 2 (on training the young vines). 'When the vine begins to climb the *support*, tie the young shoots': quae (vinea) iam in *perticam* ibit, eius pampinos teneros alligato.

(d) Varro, *RR* i. 8. 2 (varieties of vineyard). 'There are usually four kinds of "yokes" for vines, viz. *poles*, reeds, cords and vines': iugorum genera fere quattuor, *pertica*, harundo, restes, vites.

(e) Varro, *RR* i. 55. 2 (on harvesting olives). 'Those which cannot be reached by the hand should be beaten down, but struck with a reed rather than a *pole*': quae manu tangi non poterunt, ita quati debent, ut harundine potius quam *pertica* feriantur.

(f) Pliny, *HN* 15. 3. 11 (on harvesting olives). 'To knock the olives down with *poles*': oleas *perticis* decutere.

(g) Pliny, *HN* 18. 298 (after a description of harvesting methods for grain). 'After reaping the ears are beaten out in some places with threshing-sledges, in others by trampling with mares; elsewhere they are threshed out with *flails*': messa spica ipsa alibi tribulis in area, alibi equarum gressibus exteritur, alibi *perticis* flagellatur.

(h) Varro 3. 9. 7 (on the construction of hen-houses). 'Large numbers of *perches* should be run across the hen-houses, enough to accommodate all the hens': in caveis crebrae *perticae* traiectae sint, ut omnes sustinere possint gallinas. (Cf. Colum. 8. 3. 7; Pallad. 1. 26.)

DISCUSSION

Like the English words 'pole' and 'staff' *pertica* implies a straight piece of wood of circular section. In viticulture it is used either of a vertical prop (passages *c*, *d*), or of a cross-bar for 'yoked' vines (Colum. 4. 12. 1). On the use of flails (passage *g*) see above, s.v. 'baculum'. Varro disapproves of the use of *perticae* to bring down olives as damaging to the crop, and recommends the use of a light cane or reed (passage *e*; Pl. 14 *c*). Like the English derivative, the word is also found meaning a perch for birds (passage *h*), so that Columella (at 8. 3. 7) can quite naturally write of making perches of squared timber (*conquadratae perticae*) to give the roosting birds a better hold.

On flailing

The use of three general words to signify a flail indicates that the task was not carried out with a specially designed implement, but with a simple staff or stick. The action of beating the ears as they lie flat with an unjointed stick will have been very tiring. The first improvement, consisting of two sticks joined together by a leather hinge, belongs to post-classical times (first mentioned by St Jerome, *Comm. in Isa.* 19. 28, *Pat. lat.* vol. 24, col. 326). The jointed flail is a far more efficient instrument than the simple stick, since the lower portion can be made to strike the corn along its whole length, and the operator need not bend so far in order to bring the flail parallel to the ground (on this improvement see H. J. Massingham, *Country Relics*, Cambridge, 1939, 72–8).

4. Pedum (-i, n.), *shepherd's crook*; also **baculum pastorale** (Sil. Ital.)

Not in Varro, *LL*; not in Isidore.

(*a*) *R-E* XIX 54 [A. Hug].

(*b*) *Corp. Gloss.* s.v. 'pedum'. *pedum* καλαῦροψ II 527. 4. ... καλαῦροψ ποιμενικὴ ῥάβδος II 337. 22. generis neutri baculum pastoralem V 509. 44. ... fustis recurvus, quo pastores pedes ovium capiunt V 232. 6. baculum curvum est, quo pedes ovium detinentur, et pastorale gestamen V 232. 7. dicitur virga pastoralis, cui[us] uncus additur ferreus, qua pedes tondendarum ovium capiuntur, et in se habet pares nodos aere decoratos quaeque aliter clava appella[n]tur V 232. 8.

(*c*) Fest. s.v. 'pedum' 211 M; 231 L. 'The *crook* indeed is a stick with an inward curve, used by shepherds for catching sheep or goats by the foot: Virgil himself recalls it in the Bucolics when he says (5. 88): "But do you take up the crook"': *pedum* est quidem baculum incurvum, quo pastores utuntur ad comprehendendas oves, aut capras, a pedibus: cuius meminit etiam Vergilius in Bucolicis cum ait (5. 88): "at tu sume pedum".

(*d*) Servius. virga incurvata, unde retinentur pecudum pedes.

DISCUSSION

While the *pedum* appears frequently on monuments as the emblem of Pan, Faunus and other rustic divinities connected with sheep, I find only two literary references, namely in Virgil (*Ecl.* 5. 88), and Silius Italicus (*Punica* 13. 345), where Pan is described as carrying a *pastorale baculum* (cf. *Corp. Gloss.*, passage *b*). For a similar case see *AIRW*, s.v. 'forfex', pp. 119f.

Extant representations

D–S s.v. 'pedum', IV. 1, fig. 5538, p. 369; from a statue of a shepherd in the Vatican (not traceable). Rich (*Dict. Ant.*, s.v.) shows an example taken from a Pompeian wall-painting depicting Paris in the guise of a Phrygian shepherd; cf. Baumeister, *Denkmäler des klassischen Altertums*, 3 vols., München/Leipzig, 1885–93, fig. 1358. See also Pl. 14a.

Survivals

(a) *Of the word.* It. 'pastorale', a shepherd's crook (cf. *baculum pastorale* above).

(b) *Of the object. Baculum pastorale* is used to refer to the crozier in the Form of Presentation of a bishop-elect of the Roman Church. The oldest form of crozier was a wooden rod bent at the top with a point at the other end, known as the *pedum*, giving support to the suggested origin in the shepherd's crook, as against the other contender, the *lituus* of the Roman augur.

5. Stimulus (-i, m.), *goad*

Fig. 55. Stimulus

(a)   *R-E* III A. 2534–6 [Hug].

(b)   Isid. *Etym.* 20. 16. 6 (*De instrumentis equorum*). '*Goads* ("stimuli") take their name from fear (timor)': nam ex timore *stimuli* nuncupantur.

(c)   Colum. 2. 2. 26 (the ploughman's job). 'He should never provoke a bullock with the *goad*. This makes him irritable and liable to kick, but he may urge him on from time to time with the whip': numquam *stimulo* lacessat iuvencum, quae res taetratum calcitrosumque eum reddit, non numquam tamen admoneat flagello.

(d)   Tibull. 1. 1. 30–1. 'Yet I would not be ashamed from time to time to have grasped the double drag-hoe, or to have scolded the lazy oxen with the *goad*':

nec tamen interdum pudeat tenuisse bidentem
aut *stimulo* tardos increpuisse boves.

(e)   Pliny, *HN* 18. 179 (the ploughman's job). 'The ploughshare should be cleaned now and then with a *goad* tipped with a scraper': purget vomerem subinde *stimulus* cuspidatus rallo.

DISCUSSION

The ox-goad, as the surviving representations show, was usually a straight stick, with a spike embedded in one end. The double-ended instrument, used by the ploughman, which also had a flat scraper for cleaning the ploughshare (Pliny's 'stimulus cuspidatus rallo' (passage *e*)), is well known from monuments (below, s.v.). D–S (s.v. 'aratrum' I. 1, fig. 437) show a Greek ploughman using a right-angled goad. Columella's rejection of the goad in favour of the whip (passage *c*) is in keeping with the humane attitude he shows elsewhere to animals (cf. e.g. 7. 3. 16 – on the treatment of ewes at lambing-time). One may compare the ban against the use of the stick on flagging horses in the *Cursus Publicus* (*Cod. Theod. Tit.* 8. 5. 1–2).

Extant representations

D–S (IV. 2, s.v. 'rallum') notices three representations: (*a*) the well-known plough model from Arezzo, now in the Villa Giulia in Rome (fig. 5916); (*b*) another from the necropolis at Vulci, now in the Museo Nazionale at Naples (fig. 5917); a third (unillustrated) from Acerra (*Mon. Acad. dei Lincei* IX, pl. IV. 5). To these should be added the spirited scene on a mosaic panel from St Romain (Pl. 14 *b*).

CONCLUSION

I. THE ECONOMICS OF FARM MANAGEMENT

(1) *'Investment' farming*

It is obvious from the surviving evidence that the only types of farm unit that can be subjected to detailed analysis are the two 'model' production units worked by slave labour under a slave overseer, with occasional visits from the absentee owner, that is, the *oletum* and the *vinea* for which Cato has provided complete inventories of equipment, stock and personnel (*RR* 10 and 11). Since the aim in each case was to achieve the maximum possible degree of self-sufficiency, much attention is given at various points in the Handbook to sources of supply, as well as to the making and maintenance of plant and equipment produced on the estate. Detailed attention is also given to sources of supply of items which cannot be produced on the estate. Cato's list (135) includes clothing, shoes, iron implements, bronze utensils, ropes of fibre and leather, ploughshares, ploughs and yokes, wagon-frames, threshing-sledges, oil-mills and mill-stones for the grain-mill. Other miscellaneous items in the list include iron nails and bolts, and three specific items of earthenware, viz. roof-tiles (*tegulae*), large basins (*labra*) and large storage jars (*dolia*).

What does this list tell us about the economics of this type of enterprise? First, the manufacture of metal implements and utensils is not attempted, for the obvious reason that supplies are readily available at local centres of manufacture. There is a major centre for bronze at Capua, the largest manufacturing centre in Italy. Cales, close to Capua, is evidently a major source of supply for most iron implements, with a subsidiary centre a little further away at Minturnae. Venafrum, in the heart of Cato's country, specialized in spades. It was also the nearest source of supply for heavy earthenware items (*dolia*, *labra*, *tegulae*) which would require a large production unit, with a labour force and an output too large for the size of Cato's model units. Capua was also a centre for the manufacture of ropes and cordage. Rome, the most distant centre, was the recommended source of supply for clothing, footwear and threshing-sledges. Transport of heavy equipment by road was notoriously expensive. The heaviest single item required on the *oletum* was the olive-mill (*trapetum*). Cato names Pompeii and Nola as the best places to buy the mill (135); but earlier (22) he gives a complete breakdown of costs for the supply and carriage of a mill from Suessa and from Pompeii to a particular district; since the cost of cartage from Pompeii is four times that from Suessa, preference for a Pompeian mill might be dictated by superior quality or a more durable variety of stone. Varro (*RR* I. 55. 5) says that the millstones were made from 'hard, rough stone'. The cost of transporting a mill from Pompeii represented nearly 43 per cent of the total cost!

Manufacture on the farm. When we turn our attention to the long and varied list of items which were produced on the estate, and bear in mind also the requirements in grain and fodder for operating a farm where the main product was wine or oil (see *RF*, pp. 394 f.), we can see that it will not have been difficult to keep the labour force occupied through the different seasons of the year. The main items produced on the farm were (*a*) props, yokes, ties and other equipment connected with the vineyard, (*b*) containers, receivers of many different kinds made from timber, basketry or earthenware.

I have examined elsewhere (*RF*, pp. 394 ff.) the range of items, over and above the wine or oil, which formed the staple of Cato's two 'model' farms. The list is a lengthy one; and in view of the size of the labour force, even allowing for the jobs carried out by the women and children of the *familia*, the fact that so many pieces of equipment were purchased from outside is not surprising. Workshop production of pottery containers and iron implements by craftsmen settled on the estate was common on the large estates of later times (Varro had already noted that rich owners usually kept their own smiths and other essential craftsmen 'to prevent the farm-hands leaving their work and loafing about on working-days' (*RR* I. 16. 4)). Cato's units are, however, too small to justify the permanent addition to the farm budget of skilled men not fully employed, in an enterprise based on 'round the clock' working by all permanent employees.

Continuity of operation. The efficiency of the slave-run 'investment' farms on which the surviving agricultural writings are based depended in large measure on continuity of operation. The work-force, even on one of Cato's smaller units (11), represented a sizeable capital investment which, like a modern industrial plant, needed to be worked to full capacity. Hence the employment of contract labour for seasonal tasks for which additional hands were required for short periods. Interruption of normal working due to loss of, or damage to, tools and equipment had to be reduced to a minimum. Both these aspects are illustrated in the surviving texts. At 11. 1. 20, in the course of a lengthy account of the multifarious duties of the slave overseer, Columella mentions the following directions to be given to him by the proprietor: 'Furthermore during the holidays he should inspect the farm equipment (*instrumentum rusticum*) without which no work can be carried out, and he should make very frequent inspections of the iron implements (*ferramenta*). These he should always provide in duplicate, and having had them repaired from time to time, he should keep them locked up, so that, if any item suffers damage in the course of work, he may not need to borrow from a neighbour: it costs more than the price of these items if you have to call off the slaves from their work.' Again at 12. 52. 8 he gives a list of the equipment required for the olive harvest, stressing the need for all these items to be kept in greater quantity than required, 'because they wear out in use and become fewer and fewer, and if anything is missing when the time comes for it to be used, the flow of work is interrupted'.

Organization of work during slack periods. We have noticed above that advantage had to be taken of holiday periods for inspection, repair and maintenance of tools and other equipment. Elsewhere in the agronomists we find numerous scattered references to jobs to be undertaken during slack periods such as the depth of winter when outside work is impossible, and during the long hours of midwinter darkness, when daylight working is restricted. Thus in the Calendar of work for the second fortnight of November Columella recommends that some hours should be added at this time of the year to the short period of daylight, noting that many jobs can be properly done by artificial light (*in lucubratione*). A list of these items is appended.

List of jobs for slack periods.

Jobs for long winter nights (Colum. 11. 2. 90 ff.):

(1) Cutting and shaping of poles (*pali*) and squared props (*ridicae*).

(2) Making hives for bees (*alvaria*), if the district abounds in fennel (*ferula*) or bark (*cortex*).

(3) Frails (*fiscinae*) or baskets (*sportae*) to be made, if the district abounds in palm-trees (*palma*) or broom (*spartum*).

(4) Hard baskets (*corbes*) if there is plenty of brush (*virgulta*).

(5) Willows (*salix*) if cut the previous day can be cleaned (i.e. stripped of bark) by artificial light and prepared as ties for vines (*vitium ligamina*). At 4. 30 Columella estimates the amount of land required to provide sufficient material for props and ties as follows: 1 *iugerum* of osier-willows for binding 24 *iugera* of vines; 1 *iugerum* of reed-plantation (*harundinetum*) for providing yoke-frames for 20 *iugera* of vines; 1 *iugerum* of chestnut-trees (*castanetum*) for single-prop poles (*pali*). If the soil is unsuitable for

willow plantations broom (*genista*) may be grown for binding. 1 *iugerum* of land planted with chestnuts will yield 12,000 props (*statumina*). The wood is split to form stakes (*ridicae*) of squared timber, which are more durable in the ground than round poles.

Pliny also gives some information on winter jobs and jobs to be done at night (*HN* 18. 232–3).

(6) Felling timber is a winter job.

(7) Weaving wicker baskets (*quali*), hurdles (*crates*) and rush-baskets (*fiscinae*) (see (3) above).

(8) Cutting torches (*faces*).

(9) Preparing squared vine-props (*ridicae*) and poles (*pali*) (see (1) above). Pliny adds useful information on man-hours required for prop-making, viz. for *ridicae* 30 a day in the daytime, 5 in the night, 7 in the early morning. For poles the quantities are exactly doubled.

(2) *Subsistence farming*

I have noticed elsewhere (*RF*, pp. 346 ff.) that the smallholder living at subsistence level, and working his land the hard way with hand implements, continued to survive alongside the concentrated *latifundia* of later times. Yet the smallholder, though held up as a model for their supposedly degenerate contemporaries by idealists and reformers, remains in the background of the picture. Here and there we catch a fleeting glimpse of him: rising while it is still dark for the milking, and pressing the cheese at night so as to have it ready at daybreak for the journey to market (Virgil, *Georg.* 3. 400 ff.); or again in winter sharpening stakes by the firelight – a task for slaves on 'model' farms – while his wife plies her loom or boils down the must (*ibid.* 1. 291 ff.). Elsewhere (*Georg.* 1. 273 ff.) we get a vivid impression of another *rusticus* riding his ass to town with surplus oil or cheap apples to sell, and bringing back from town a millstone or a lump of pitch (*ibid.* 1. 273 ff.). To these may be added that remarkable work the 'Country Salad' (*Moretum*) by an unknown contemporary of Virgil, which conveys the whole atmosphere of country life at this humble level. Simulus, the owner of a tiny plot, is up at crack of dawn, 'fearing the wretched hunger of the approaching day' (4). In spite of his slender resources, he manages to keep a servant, an African woman of generous dimensions whose racial characteristics are faithfully portrayed (32–5). The worst of the day's preparatory activities are already over by the time she appears: the careful resuscitation of the fire from last night's embers, the withdrawal of the day's ration from the scanty pile of grain (*frumenti pauper acervus*, 16), the tedious grinding of the meal in a hand-mill, a single-handed task, in the course of which each hand relieves the other, while their owner solaces the tedium with a song (19–30). Then, after calling the maid to get the fire going properly and put on the pot, he sieves the grain and prepares the flour for baking in a primitive oven made by covering the dough with an arrangement of crocks within the hearth, and drawing the fire round and over them (39–50). The heart of the poem is the account (55–116) of the making of the salad (*moretum*) which gives it its name. The anonymous author presents here no Alexandrian conceit, but a genuine, unsentimental portrayal of country life.

(3) *Trade in materials and products*

In an interesting chapter Varro (*RR* 1. 16) discusses a number of questions relating to the neighbourhood in which the estate is situated. In choosing a farm three main points should be considered: (1) *Security:* he knows of some areas with excellent land which are ruled out because the neighbours are brigands, as in some parts of Sardinia and western Spain. (2) *Local markets:* the farmer needs a supply-centre for items not produced on his farm, and a market for his surplus products. A neighbouring town, or a wealthy estate in your neighbourhood, can supply you with some items more cheaply than if you were to produce them yourself. On the other side of the balance sheet, your neighbours can provide you with a market for your surpluses; the only items cited here (they are noted as examples) are props, poles or reeds. To these may be added seedlings and rooted cuttings from the tree-nursery or the vine-nursery; Columella includes the profit from the sale of the latter in his vineyard balance sheet (3. 3). (3) *Good communications:* are there accessible roads and navigable rivers? If there are, are they convenient for transporting your produce or not? Here Varro is echoing Cato's earlier statement: 'If possible, your farm should be on a south-facing slope, in a healthy situation, where there is an abundant supply of labour, near a flourishing town, the sea, or a river on which boats ply, or a good road' (*De Agri Cultura,* 1. 3).

River traffic. Our ancient sources tell us very little about the extent of river-borne commerce: 'river navigation poses an irritating problem. It existed, and played an important role but we cannot gauge its extent with precision' (J. Le Gall, *Le Tibre,* Paris, 1953, p. 58). There are several references to the use of the Tiber for transporting supplies of grain from Etruria and the neighbourhood during famines at Rome (Livy 2. 34. 5; 4. 52. 5–6, etc.). Farms with easy access to the Tiber or its tributaries are mentioned elsewhere (e.g. Cic. *Rosc. Am.* 7. 20, when the estate of the elder Roscius is stated to have included 13 farms, almost all with a frontage on the Tiber). Canals were also important; yet our sole authority for canal-haulage in Italy is the well-known passage in Horace, *Satires* 1. 5.

9–26, where the passengers were held up for several hours when the drunken bargee tied up the mule and went off to sleep! The subject of river and canal haulage by animals is fully discussed by P. Vigneron (*Le Cheval* (1968), pp. 143–7).

Commerce between estates. Cato preached the doctrine of economic self-sufficiency; yet, as we have seen, many necessities had to be purchased from outside suppliers in the towns. But there is no sign anywhere in the *De Agri Cultura* that its author was aware of the mutual advantages of commerce between one owner and another in the same district. In this matter, as we have noticed above, Varro's treatise represents a distinct advance in the direction of efficiency.

2. THE ECONOMICS OF TRANSPORT AND THE HANDLING OF MERCHANDISE

(1) *Factors affecting technical innovation and development*

The proverb 'Necessity is the mother of invention' makes a good starting-off point to this discussion. Taken in its narrowest and most literal sense, the theory that inventions only occur when necessity forces man to invent a new technique or process will not bear examination. But if we look at historical examples of the application and development of innovations, and take note of the remarkable, and often very long, time-lags between invention and application, we find ample evidence to support the hypothesis that 'man does not generally better his techniques until he experiences an urgent need to apply them' (P. Vigneron, *Le Cheval* (1968), p. 140). The best-known example of such a long time-lag reported from classical antiquity is concerned with the invention and diffusion of the undershot water-wheel. This device from the beginning of our era (the first mention of it in a classical author occurs in the middle of the first century B.C. (Lucretius, *De Rerum Natura* 5. 517)) made it possible to transmit the energy of flowing water by means of reduction-gearing into a horizontally placed millstone for grinding corn, and thus eliminated the drudgery of a task that had occupied men or animals over several millennia of time. Yet some two hundred years elapsed between the invention and its widespread application to milling. The history of technology abounds with these perplexing time-lag problems. The fact is that a method of operation, developed over a period of time, and making adequate use, without over-taxing them, of well-known techniques and existing resources of raw materials and power supplies, is likely to continue in operation until one or other of these resources becomes seriously in-adequate. The Egyptian pyramid-builders achieved their objectives using rather primitive techniques in quarrying, transporting and setting in position the great blocks of which these stupendous monuments are constructed. The results were impressive enough: the sides of the Great Pyramid are of uniform length to within 8″ in 756′; the maximum error at base level is no more than ½″, and the maximum deviation from the right angle 1/20th of a degree. They had plenty of manpower, good supervision, and plenty of time. Until the arrival of the barbarians at their gates the Romans had plenty of donkeys and worn-out horses to drive their mills. Today the Chinese build multi-storey hotels in Peking without the aid of machinery. They have an abundance of manpower.

(2) *Problems of load-carrying in classical times*

Forty years ago Lefebure des Noëttes announced that the invention of the horse-collar was a revolutionary step in the economic development of Europe, releasing mediaeval farmers and merchants from the severe limitations imposed on men's activities in the cultivation of the soil and in the movement of goods by the inefficient equine harness which had remained unchanged throughout classical times. That the ancient throat-and-girth harness limited the load-pulling capacity of horses and mules is an indisputable fact. What matters surely is not a limiting factor *per se*, but the role of these particular animals as load-pullers in the economy. Techniques of transport are closely interdependent: 'the pack-saddle competes with the harness, bovine with equine traction. River and coastwise transport and human porterage restrict the role of animals. In proportion as a particular technique is better adapted to geographical conditions, and is able to move goods at a lower price, it pushes other methods into the background' (P. Vigneron, *Le Cheval* (1968), p. 140). In simple, undeveloped communities the cheapest form of transport is a man (or a woman) with a load on his head, his shoulder or his back.

In many parts of Black Africa, where head-loading of merchandise still predominates, men carry head-loads of up to 25 kg a distance of 25 km in a day. Tibetan porters normally carry 36 kg on their backs, and the famous Sherpas of the Himalayas can carry loads of up to 18 kg to a height of 25,000 feet (personal communication from Christian Bonington; cf. R. Capot-Rey, *Géographie de la circulation sur les continents* (Géographie humaine, t. 20), Paris, 1946, p. 76). The extent to which human load-carriers were employed in Roman times in the transport of goods from place to place cannot be assessed. With the exception of the army, where heavy loads were carried for long distances by the legionaries, and the casual traveller with his *mantica* or *pera* on his shoulder, little information can be gained either from texts or monuments. But on the farm, porterage played a dominant role, as the foregoing pages have testified: in manuring the fields, in harvesting the grain, in the work of the vineyard, the orchard and the olive-grove, the man with the basket or the hurdle is in the foreground; again, in the processing and subsequent handling of the product, it is the man with the basket, sack or jar who dominates the daily activities. The same pattern of manual activity has persisted until recent times, in spite of more efficient animal harness, as M. Capot-Rey has reported of eighteenth-century France: 'One section of the rural population, the *manœuvres*, had only their arms for carrying the hay and the corn; even among landowners, many who lacked sufficient pasture to maintain a team of horses, did all their own transporting. It was on foot with his basket on his back that the vintager brought the grapes to the press . . . the milk was carried from the farm to the town and there distributed from door to door by sturdy peasants. Even the products of industry were sometimes carried on the back' (Capot-Rey, *op. cit.* p. 77).

(3) *The pack-saddle in the economy of transport*

Passing from human load-carrying to transport by animals, we find that load-carrying mules and donkeys, equipped with pack-saddles or panniers, played a much more important part in these operations than animal-drawn wagons. Here it was not, as Lefebure des Noëttes supposed, the inefficiency of equine harness that gave the load-bearing pack-mule the advantage over the wagon, but the geographical conditions of the Mediterranean region. In a short but valuable note, the geographer J. Sion gives a lucid appraisal of the problem: 'The Mediterranean lands, with their preponderance of broken terrain, are the realm of the pack-saddle rather than the cart . . . the pack-animal is better adapted to these lands of harsh and changing relief, and small-sized holdings where it makes fewer demands on limited resources than a good draught-animal' (J. Sion, 'Quelques problèmes de transport dans l'antiquité . . .', *Ann. hist. écon. et Soc.* 7 (1935), pp. 630–1).

3. THE PERSISTENCE OF BASIC ATTITUDES

Smallholders and peasant farmers have been bywords in all periods for frugality and parsimony. Lacking capital resources apart from his holding the subsistence farmer has at all times found it hard to keep his head above water. Conservative in outlook and averse to innovation, he has been at all times a model for moralists and the despair of reformers. When changing circumstances demand a change both of attitude and of method, ingrained habits and traditional attitudes persist; Cato the Censor was no peasant's son, nor were his business activities confined to the exploitation of his estates: if his biographer Plutarch is to be believed, he had money invested in a wide range of enterprises, which included hot springs, laundry establishments and pitch factories. Much of his handbook is based on the new investment farming which was imparting a new look to the agrarian economy of Italy as well as to the face of the countryside. Yet the text itself is curiously old-fashioned; apart from a liberal scattering of proverbial farming lore, there is a great deal of 'making do', much emphasis on the mending and re-use of worn or broken equipment, and here and there a meanness that goes beyond the traditional parsimony of the peasant. 'Making-do' items include a recommendation (25) to sieve the grape-husks through a cord-bed or to make a sieve for the purpose (the bed is quite suitable for the job, but the point is that it is offered as a first choice, not, as in the usual way, as a substitute for the proper equipment!). The best example is to be found at 38. 4; 'Sell your firewood and faggots. If you can't sell them and have no stone for making lime, make charcoal of them, and burn in the field the faggots and brush which are surplus to requirements. Plant poppies where you have burnt them.' The most striking example of the re-use of materials is to be found at 59, where the author, after giving a list of clothing-rations, recommends making patchwork out of the old, worn-out working garments (they have to last for two years before replacement). Columella's recommended issue is more generous: he includes an outer coat made of skin, with a thick hood for use in hard weather (11. 2. 95). Examples of sheer meanness are not infrequent in Cato; apart from the notorious advice to 'sell an old slave, a sickly slave and whatever else is superfluous' (2. 7) there is the sharp contrast between the special care devoted to the working oxen, and the indulgent treatment of the ploughmen who look after them, and the recommendation to give the hands 'windfall olives and rejects with little oil in them, issue them sparingly and make them last as long as you can' (58). I have indicated elsewhere (*RF*, pp. 450ff.) that the large landowners, 'who alone possessed the resources to initiate and promote the extension of new or improved techniques and methods', had no incentive either to increase productivity or to reduce costs by the introduction of less labour-intensive techniques at a time when there was both stagnation in the economy and an increasing shortage of labour to keep it going. The attitude of the middle-sized proprietor will also have contributed to this trend. The attitude towards shortage of labour, for which there are references as far back as Varro, seems to have remained unchanged: 'this is the best way to do the job; but if you are short-handed, then do it the following way' (see Colum. 4. 6. 2; Pliny, *HN* 18. 300; Pallad. 9. 3). The distance that separates our attitude from that of the Roman landowner is made abundantly clear in the paradoxical dictum of Pliny, who, after roundly condemning the absentee landlord and denouncing the use of chain-gang labour on the farm, adds the unexpected statement (it sounds proverbial) that 'moderation is the most valuable criterion in every walk of life. Good cultivation is essential, but optimum cultivation is ruinous, except where the farmer runs the farm with the aid of his own family, or employs people whom he will have to maintain in any case' (*HN* 18. 37–8). Yet the small-scale, intensive system of cultivation, with its combination of arable with animal husbandry, and its intercultivation of sown with planted crops, which takes up so much of the attention of the Roman writers on husbandry, and which has occupied so much of our attention in the foregoing pages, can still be identified in its essentials by anyone who travels in the Mediterranean region, for it represents a sound response to the conditions of soil and climate which are peculiar to the area.

PLATE 1

a. Pony drinking from a trough fed from a well by means of a swipe (*tolleno*). Mosaic from Oudna. Tunis: Bardo Museum.

b. Raising irrigation water from the Nile with the Archimedean screw (*cochlea*).

c. Oak cylinder-block of a double-action force-pump, showing the twin bronze cylinders. From the Roman theatre, Trier. Trier: Landesmuseum.

PLATE 2

a. Fine and coarse flour-sieves (*cribra*), mortars and other milling equipment. Part of the front of the sarcophagus of P. Nonius Zethus. Rome: Vatican.

b. Donkey-mill (*molae asinariae*). Relief panel from a mausoleum on the Isola Sacra, Ostia.

c. Stone *mortarium* for grinding grain from the military base of Trimontium (Newstead), Scotland. Edinburgh: National Museum of Antiquities of Scotland.

d. Bronze wine-strainer (*trulla*) from Vasio (Vaison-la-Romaine), Provence. London: British Museum.

PLATE 3

a. Vine-trellis (*pergula*) with grape-clusters and a bird eating the fruit. Part of a floor-mosaic from Cherchel, Algeria. Cherchel Museum.

b. Worker carrying grapes in a fruit-picking basket (*qualus*). Part of the pergula mosaic from Cherchel.

c. Life on an African farm. To l., seasonal offerings to the mistress of the estate. In foreground, r., a fence (*vacerra*) enclosing an orchard. Dominus Julius Mosaic, Carthage. Tunis: Bardo Museum.

PLATE 4

a. and *b.* Hard (*sporta*) and soft (*fiscus*) types of basket from Roman Egypt. Department of Egyptology, University College London.

c. Wine-making equipment from Agedincum (Sens) in central France, including full and empty grape-baskets, mortars (*mortaria*), a fork, and piles of *marc de raisin*. Part of the frieze of a funeral monument. Sens: Museum.

PLATE 5

a. Winnowing grain with the *vannus*; carrying away the sifted grain in a basket (*corbis*). From the funeral monument of a merchant of Moguntiacum (Mainz), W. Germany. Mainz: Zentral-Museum.

b. Two labourers carrying manure to the fields on a hurdle (*crates stercorariae*). From a Gallo-Roman seasons mosaic from Vienne. St-Germain-en-Laye: Nat. Museum of Antiquities of France.

c. Two slaves carrying merchandise in netted baskets (*cophini*). Relief from the tomb of L. Calpurnius Piso. Rome: Palazzo Massimi.

PLATE 6

a. Oxen for sacrifice wearing muzzles (*capistra*). Relief from Trajan's Column, Rome.

b. Road transport in Asia Minor. Four-wheeled goods wagon drawn by mules, followed by a two-wheeler drawn by oxen. From Ephesus. Both vehicles are loaded with heavy sacks. London: British Museum.

PLATE 7

Vintage scenes. To l., two-wheeled cart with solid wheels and wicker-work body, carrying grapes to the press; above, picking grapes; to r., treading vat (*forus, labrum*). Rome: Palazzo Mattei.

PLATE 8

a. Braying donkey equipped with basketry panniers (*clitellae*). Bronze statuette.
London: British Museum.

b. Wicker-work farm cart of traditional pattern. Seen on a farm near Porec,
Istrian Peninsula.

PLATE 9

a. Dock-worker carrying a wine-*amphora* from a merchantman (r.) to a lighter (l.).
Ostia Piazzale delle Corporazioni.

b. In foreground, *r.*, replica of riverbarge loaded with wine-casks (*cupae*); behind, stacked *amphorae*,
encased in basketry for sea transit. Trier: Landesmuseum.

PLATE 10

a. Oil-storage jars (*dolia olearia*) deeply buried in the ground, Ostia.

b. Sampling and sale of wine direct from the *cella vinaria*. In centre, ladling out wine into an *amphora*; top r., tally-clerk with notebook; bottom r., a buyer enjoys a tasting. Relief from Ince Blundell Hall, near Liverpool.

PLATE 11

a. Nubian slaves serving wine from flagons (*lagoenae*) to guests at a fashionable party. Mosaic from Dougga, Tunisia. Bardo Museum, Tunis.

b. Goatherd, seated r., milking a goat into a shallow bowl (*mulctrum*). Mosaic from Istanbul, Palace of the Emperors.

PLATE 12

a. Man superintending the boiling of a cauldron (*cortina*) on a fire. Fragment of a terracotta plaque. London: British Museum.

b. Two men carrying an *amphora* full of wine on a pole. Inn-sign from Pompeii.

c. Roofed market stall with stacked *amphorae*. Bas relief. Rome: Vatican Museum.

PLATE 13

a. Storage jars (*seriae*). Naples: National Museum.

b. Toilet basin (*labrum*) in the changing room (*apodyterium*)
of the Forum Baths, Herculaneum, Insula VI.

c. Cook-shop (*thermopolium*) in Herculaneum, Insula V,
nos. 15–16. The six storage jars (*dolia*) in the counter base
contain remains of cereals and vegetables.

PLATE 14

a. Pastoral scene on a Roman sarcophagus. In centre, shepherd with his crook (*pedum*); to l., shepherd feeding his dogs.

b. Ploughman directing his team with a long goad (*stimulus*).

c. An African farm-worker tapping down olives with long canes. Detail from the Oudna Mosaic (cf. Pl. 1 (*a*)).

PLATE 15

a. Basket-making. To l., a labourer brings a bundle of osiers (*salix*); to r., in front of a building, a second man weaves a basket over a frame of crate-rods. From the Seasons Mosaic, Vienne.

b. Pressing the grapes with the simple lever-press. The man to the l. is leaning out to obtain greater purchase.

c. Pitching wine-jars. To l. a worker smears the inside of a storage-jar with pitch; to r. a second man stirs the liquid pitch on the fire.

PLATE 16

To l. a labourer brings a full sack of grain to be measured: c., a *modius* measure; beside it an official with a document in his r. hand; with his l., he runs through the sample. Ostia: Piazzale delle Corporazioni.

APPENDIXES

APPENDIX A

ON THE MAKING OF OLIVE OIL

Most of the standard works of reference mention the lever press (*torcular*), the screw press (*cochlea*) and the oil mill (*trapetum*). But these were by no means the only devices used in the manufacture of this immensely important product, which, apart from its important culinary uses, provided the classical world with the equivalent of soap and electric light. We have at our disposal a considerable amount of evidence, both literary and archaeological, concerning its manufacture, but there are textual difficulties, as well as problems of identification of the parts of some of the machines, and the surviving representations have been misinterpreted. The best general treatment of the subject is that of E. Besnier (D–S s.v. 'olea, oleum'), the only full critical discussion of the sources that of A. G. Drachmann (*Ancient Oil-Mills and Presses*, Copenhagen, 1932), which is indispensable. J. Hörle's study (*Catos Hausbücher*, Paderborn, 1929) is confined to Cato's press and mill, and suffers in consequence, while R. J. Forbes's treatment (*SAT*, III, 101–4; 130–8; 147–8) is most unsatisfactory, since the two related processes are treated quite separately and somewhat perfunctorily, with little attention to the archaeological evidence. The account that follows is based on Besnier's article, supplemented, particularly on the subject of the evolution of the different types of mills and presses, by Drachmann's masterly study. The basic literary and archaeological evidence is listed at the end of the Appendix.

TECHNICAL PROBLEMS INVOLVED IN OIL-MAKING

The processes involved are rather more complicated than those required in wine-making. In both cases the liquid must be 'expressed', from the fruit. In wine-making varying degrees of pressure can be applied, from gentle treading to severe squeezing which leaves only the grape-skins and the crushed pips for use as cattle-feed (see above, pp. 112 f.). The making of oil, on the other hand, involves the removal, *without crushing*, of the kernel, and the separation from the oil of the commercially useful but highly contaminating *amurca* or lees. To avoid deterioration before milling 'each day's picking should be immediately placed under the millstones and the press-beam' (Colum. 12. 52. 3), but where there is a very large harvest, a 'delay and store' procedure will be necessary (for details see above, s.v. 'lacusculus'). Careful provision is to be made at this stage to allow the *amurca* to flow away.

1. *Gathering the olives*

The olive harvest falls conveniently into place in the farmer's calendar, well after the completion of the vintage (early in November, according to Columella (11. 2. 83) and Palladius (11. 10), and on into December, depending upon the district). In gathering the fruit, Roman practice seems to have shown some improvement on that of the Greeks who, as can be seen on a well-known black-figure vase (Forman Collection Sale Catalogue, London, 1899, p. 62, no. 323) merely tapped the branches with canes. This would certainly result in harmful bruising of the fruit, even if, as is still the practice in Italy, sheets were spread out under the trees. Varro (*RR* 1. 55. 1) insists on picking by hand when the berries can be reached from ground level or from ladders and with bare, rather than gloved, hands. Fruit that cannot be reached by hand should be lightly struck with a reed (*harundo*) rather than a pole (*pertica*) (see Pl. 14*c*). Harsher methods, according to Varro, will knock off branches and thus diminish next year's crop. Hence the well-known saying that the olive fails to bear a good crop every other year. One may well suspect that practice did not match precept, especially on large estates.

2. *Treatment of the berries before milling*

(*a*) *Cleaning the berries*. Much attention is given in Columella's account of the processing of olives (it is in fact the most detailed one) to the methods employed for removing all extraneous material before the berries were passed on to the mill. They must first be stripped of their stalks (*destringi*) by hand in fine weather, then sifted (*cribrari*) and cleansed (*purgari*) on mats and reeds which have been spread under them. As soon as they have dried out (three days at most are allowed for this), they are passed on to the next stage, that of softening.

(*b*) *Softening the berries*. The next stage in the process was to soften the berries before removing the kernel in the mill. Various methods are mentioned, including (1) steeping the berries in hot water (Pliny, *HN* 15. 23); (2) subjecting them to very light pressure in the lever-press (Colum. 12. 52. 10); see the discussion s.v. 'lacus', p. 160. I believe that the second method, for which Columella is our sole authority, was introduced to avoid the ill-effects of the hot-water treatment. Nevertheless, this method continued in use, for the *Digest*'s inventory (19. 2. 19. 2) of items to be furnished to the tenant by the landlord includes a kettle (*aenum*) for the hot water. At this stage natural salt was usually added to the pulp at the rate of two *sextarii* per *modius*, according to Columella (12. 52. 10), which is equivalent to one part in eight. The purpose was to prevent the oil from thickening (Pliny, *HN* 15. 18).

3. *Removing the kernel*

Columella (12. 52. 6–7) mentions four methods of making oil. These are (1) the oil-mill (*mola olearia*); (2) the revolving mill (*trapetum*); (3) the 'clog and vat' (*solea et canalis*); and (4) the 'little bruising device' (*tudicula*). The first three of these methods are set out in order of preference without technical descriptions, while the fourth, presumably the only method not familiar to Columella's readers, is given a cursory and highly inadequate description, which is followed by some comments on the difficulties involved in its use. The *trapetum* (2) is described in detail by Cato (20 ff.), with a full set of instructions for building it, and an estimate of cost (22). We have no surviving literary evidence for the other three, but we have two extant representations of the *mola olearia* (1). We shall begin by disposing briefly of nos. 3 and 4, and then proceed to examine the major questions arising in connection with the design and operation of nos. 1 and 2.

Canalis et solea (3). The lexica are wide of the mark; LS, s.v. 'solea', followed by the Loeb translator, render *solea* as 'a kind of wine-press'. Both ignore the copula 'et', which is surely vital: whatever it turns out to be, *canalis et solea* must refer to a unit made up of two parts. D–S (s.v. 'olea, oleum', IV I, 166) suggest that Columella is referring to a primitive treading operation, and cite Hesych. s.v. 'κρουπεζούμενος' and Phot. s.v. 'κρουπέζια', each of whom supports the identification by defining κρουπέζια as 'wooden sandals' (i.e. 'clogs') 'with which they trample the olives' (ὑποδήματα ξύλινα μεθ' ὧν τὰς ἐλαίας πατοῦσι). *Solea* will then be a 'clog', and *canalis* a 'vat'. The method is certainly primitive, wasteful, and much less appropriate than the parallel process of treading the grapes. Yet there is monumental evidence to support it: in the Rondanini relief, as described by Drachmann (*AOMP*, p. 68), there is a 'square container full of fruits, which are presumably olives...in the container stands an amorine; his left knee is lifted, *as if he was stamping the olives, which is absurd*' (italics mine). Later in the discussion Drachmann confirms from a similar relief (fig. 22, p. 152) the view that the berries 'are undeniably olives, not grapes', but prefers to leave what he calls the contradiction unresolved rather than believe the evidence of his eyes![1]

Tudicula (4). Columella merely tells us that this device resembled an upright threshing-sledge (*tribulum*), noting that it does the job 'reasonably well' (*non incommode*), except for the fact that it often goes out of order, and that 'the operation is obstructed if you put just a few too many berries in' (12. 52. 7). The underside of a threshing-sledge was studded with hard flints for bruising and breaking up the straw to release the heads of grain. A *tribulum* set upright with the flints facing inwards could have formed one of the long sides of a container (we note that it could be overfilled), in which the berries were somehow rubbed as in a grater over the roughened surface in such a way as to release the kernels. The etymology, from *tundere*, to 'bruise, bray, as in a mortar' (LS, s.v. 'tundo' B) is in keeping with this idea, but how the upright *tribulum* was fitted, and how the device operated cannot be determined from the very limited evidence.

Trapetum (2). The design of the 'revolving mill' (fr. Gr. τρέπω, 'I turn, revolve') is abundantly clear, both from Cato's detailed specification (20ff.) and from the specimens that have survived either intact or partly damaged. There is a detailed inventory of the latter in Drachmann, *AOMP*, pp. 7ff. Basically the *trapetum* consisted of a heavy stone mortar (*mortarium*), fitted with a central pillar (*milliarium*), surmounted by a long rectangular piece of hard wood (*cupa*) made of beech or elm, which pivoted at its centre on a projecting iron pin (*columella*), the exposed wooden surface of the *cupa* being protected against the wear of the iron pivot by means of a replaceable sheath of iron (*fistula ferrea*), see Cato 21. 'The middle of the *cupa* is left square, to rest on the *milliarium*, while the two arms are made into axles for the millstones (*orbes*), and the ends are made into handles' (Drachmann, *AOMP*, p. 28). The kernels were separated from the berries by the revolving action of a pair of stones of circular form (the *orbes*), which had a flat inner, and a convex outer, surface, the latter being shaped so as to correspond precisely with the concave curvature of the inner surface

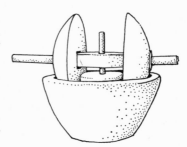

Fig. 56. Trapetum

[1] Paton, *JHS* 18 (1898), 209: 'the simplest oil-press, which is still in use in many of the Turkish villages in Anatolia, consists only of a stone or wooden trough in which the bags of crushed olives are placed, with a wooden plank above them, on which men stand to press out the oil. The trough is of oblong form, and is furnished with a spout by which the oil runs into a wooden tank. There is a similar one in the garden of Getsemane.'

of the mortar in which they were made to revolve. A tight fit of axles to *orbes* was secured by wooden 'navels' (*modioli*), set into the square holes with lead, and by metal bushes at either end of the navels (for details see Drachmann, *AOMP*, p. 27). Ring-washers (*armillae*) and a special type of wedge-guards (*cunici*) were also fitted at the inner and outer junctions of the *cupa* with the *orbes* to prevent wear, and there was an adjusting wedge (*librator*) for setting the

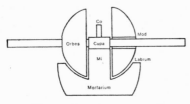

Fig. 57. Catonian trapetum

gap between the stones and the mortar. The purpose of these various washers and wedges will be evident from a glance at the accompanying figure representing a cross-section of a Catonian *trapetum* (Fig. 57). The critical gaps are those that separate the revolving stones from the bottom of the mortar and from the central pillar. Cato's instructions are very precise here: 'the *orbis* should be at least one inch from the bottom of the *mortarium*; between the *orbis* and the *milliarium* there should be a distance of one inch' (Cato 22). Very slight wear between *cupa* and *columella*, or any slackening of the tight joints between *orbis* and *cupa* could cause the stone to wobble and graze the surface of the mortar.

The above account of Cato's *trapetum* is based on the detailed analysis made by Drachmann of the various parts of the mill and the methods employed in its construction. Cato's text abounds with problems of identification of the terms he uses, and it is clearly corrupt in a number of places. Drachmann's reconstruction involves the rejection of that offered by J. Hörle (*Hausbücher*), which was also adopted by Paul Thielscher (*Des Marcus Catos Belehrung über die Landwirtschaft*, Berlin, 1963).

The account given by Forbes (*SAT*, III, 147 ff.) is both inadequate and confused (e.g. at p. 103 he states that the distance between stone and kernel could not be regulated in the *mola olearia*, while at p. 148 the reader is told that 'many Roman agronomists prefer the more adjustable *mola olearia* where no fixed distance between *orbes* and *mortarium* existed').

Mola olearia. The term is quite general in its meaning, and there are indications in the record of modifications and improvements in the basic design. None of the agronomists has given a description of this type of mill, but the archaeological evidence is quite convincing. The mill is known from three sarcophagus reliefs, it was the only type known in the eighteenth century, and modern mills built on the same principle are still extant in several places. From this evidence it is clear that the *mola olearia* 'consisted of two cylindrical mill-stones, rotating on a horizontal axle which was carried by a vertical beam, that turned round also, and was placed in the middle of the flat surface on which the grinding took place' (Drachmann, *AOMP*, p. 42). The Rondanini relief shows a broad, shallow mortar standing on a foot which broadens out at the base, and a very thick and long *columella* coming up from the transverse *cupa*. This end of the sarcophagus is unfortunately incomplete, and only one of the two cylindrical millstones survives. There is one obvious drawback in the device as depicted here: both stones and mortar have flat surfaces; this means that any tendency to wobble (caused e.g. by wear on the *cupa*) would have the inevitable result of causing the olive-kernels to be crushed. Evidence from later times shows that the secret whereby the berries were squeezed without crushing the kernels had been lost after the classical period: 'the olives were crushed, stones and all, and yielded a large amount of inferior oil' (Drachmann, *AOMP*, p. 44). But the latest of the three surviving representations, a sarcophagus from

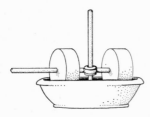

Fig. 58. Mola olearia

Arles in Provence (Espérandieu, *Gaule*, I, 143, fig. 176) shows a vertical feature, presumably a beam with a bearing at either end, which would enable the *cupa* to be set at any required height, and to hold the stones secure against any tendency to wobble on the spindle. We must now return to Columella's account (12. 52. 3 ff.). At 52. 6 he explains his preference for the *mola* over the *trapetum* as follows: 'mills make it very easy to organize the process; they can be lowered or even raised to suit the size of the berries, and so prevent crushing of the kernel, which spoils the flavour of the oil'. Drachmann (*AOMP*, p. 143, fig. 9) has a somewhat simplified drawing of the *mola*, showing how the millstones were mounted on a short cross-member which passed through the upright baulk of timber, making adjustment of the height an easy matter, either where the cross-member goes through the vertical stanchion, or where the lower pivot of the upright enters the short *milliarium*. It has commonly been assumed, without supporting evidence, that the *trapetum* could be so adjusted. Cato certainly gives careful instructions for adjusting the *orbes* and the *mortarium*. Drachmann (*AOMP*, p. 44) demonstrates the impossibility of upward or downward adjustment save by considerable structural alteration (e.g. lowering the height by taking a strip off the *cupa*). In any case a change in the height of the *orbes* would alter their curvature in relation to the curvature of the *mortarium*; it is essential that these should match if the critical distances are to be maintained.

Respective capabilities of trapetum *and* mola. One important difference between these two devices is now obvious: while the defects of the primitive *mola olearia* were capable of, and did indeed undergo, notable improvements, both in the stability of the millstones and in the capacity to deal with berries of varying sizes, the design of the *trapetum* rendered it incapable of developing this flexibility. In fact, the only technical improvement that can be traced from existing remains is in the design of the millstones. A glance at Fig. 57 will show that Cato's *orbes* were unnecessarily bulky for the task they had to perform. A significant reduction in bulk (and therefore in weight) could be achieved simply by narrowing the curvatures, as in the later Pompeian specimen shown at the r. of Fig. 59. This would in turn result in a corresponding reduction in the weight of the *mortarium*.

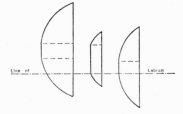

Fig. 59. Trapetum stones compared

Cato's discussion of the cost of a *trapetum* (22. 3–4) shows that the cost of transporting a complete outfit from Pompeii to the farm (distance not given) represented 43 per cent of the total cost! We have no similar estimates for the *mola olearia*, but its 'standard' millstones will have been less expensive to make.

4. Extraction of oil

The result of removing the kernel by any of the methods described above is to produce a 'mush' (*sampsa*). The next stage is that of removing the oil and separating it from the lees (*amurca*). The oil had to be 'expressed', that is, squeezed out of the mush under pressure, either by a lever and ropes, a lever and screw, a direct screw or a system of wedges. In the lever press the material to be squeezed was placed as close as possible to the fulcrum, the free end of the lever being brought down either by ropes wound over a capstan, or by a screw passing through the free end of the lever. Both the direct-screw press and the wedge press required a heavy frame to take the thrust. The information in our sources enables us to trace a number of stages in the technical development of these presses in the search for more efficient methods of extracting the oil. Four varieties of lever press can be distinguished in the literary sources, but the wedge press is known to us only from a wall-painting. In describing them I have adopted, with some modifications, the nomenclature of A. G. Drachmann, whose study of these devices largely supersedes all previous work, and whose conclusions still hold the field (*AOMP*, Part II, pp. 50–121).

The lever press. Our authority for the development of the lever press is an important passage in Pliny's *Natural History* (18. 317) where he summarizes the development, and refers to four types of press: (1) the simple lever; (2) the lever and screw; (3) the weighted screw; (4) the direct screw. These will now be discussed in turn.

(1) *The simple lever press.* The press-beam (*prelum*) is drawn down by means of ropes and leather thongs (*funibus vittisque loreis*) and handspakes (*vectibus*). This is the type of press for which Cato (18) gives full specifications; it would serve equally well for grapes or olives (see Pl. 15*b*). Its most primitive form is well displayed on an early Greek black-figure vase (Forbes, *SAT*, III, fig. 28, p. 111), which shows the beam bent down at the free end by the weight of two heavy boulders, while a man lies further along the beam to give some extra pressure; the grapes are built up in layers separated by flat slabs of wood. The Catonian press (Fig. 60) shows two improvements on this primitive 'tree-trunk' press: first the setting up of massive vertical standards at either end, anchoring them into the floor to take the thrust; secondly, the substitution of ropes, pulleys and a capstan for the clumsy stone weights. For the ropes used see above, Part I, s.v. 'funis' and 'lorum'. For the press-house and the technical details of the press see Rich, *Dict. Ant.* s.v. 'torcular'; Drachmann, *AOMP*, pp. 99–121 (where Cato's tortuous and baffling account is teased out and clarified).

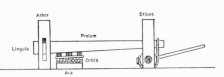

Fig. 60. Catonian lever press

(2) *The screw-and-lever press (type a).* The next development was to find a better method of raising and lowering the press-beam. This was done by using a screw instead of ropes and a capstan. The earlier form of this (Fig. 61), mentioned by Pliny as a Greek invention dating back a hundred years from his own day (*NH* 18. 317), had a spar (*malus*), equipped with a screw thread fixed to the floor of the pressroom and passing through the free end of the lever. On the screw above the beam was a nut, which was attached to the beam. The screw must have been fixed to the floor in such a way that it could turn without giving way upwards. The lever could then be moved up or down by turning it by means of handles fixed on it below the lever. Drachmann (*AOMP*, p. 54) explains Pliny's use of the word *stella* (see 18. 317) as meaning that there were four handles slotted into the screw so as to form a star. Pliny (*loc. cit.*) goes on to describe a variation of this type of screw-and-lever press.

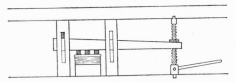

Fig. 61. Lever and screw press (*a*)

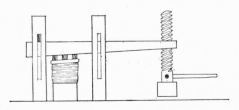

Fig. 62. Lever and screw press (*b*)

(3) *The screw-and-lever press (type b).* In this improved version (Fig. 62), the screw, instead of being attached to the floor, is made fast to a weight of stone (*arcae lapidum*), which is made to hang clear of the floor, making the task of lowering the press-beam very much easier. It also eliminated a defect in the

earlier version. Since the end of the press-beam does not come down in a straight line, but describes an arc, the screw will tend to be forced out of the vertical as the press-beam descends, causing both friction and jamming. In addition, the improved press simplifies the problem of raising the heavy beam after the pressing is complete. Cato's press was lifted by pulleys, whereas the earlier screw press involved heavy manual action on the screw itself. With the new version, the press-beam is lifted up by simply turning the screw in a contrary direction, while at the same time the suspended weight is lowered to the ground (see Fig. 62).[1]

(4) *The direct-screw press.* The next advance was to use the screw for *direct pressure* on the berries; if the screw could be adequately anchored to withstand the severe reverse pressure as the squeezing process reached its maximum, the long, clumsy space-filling lever could be eliminated. This problem had already been tackled by the Greeks, and two types of direct-screw press are mentioned, along with two of our earlier types, in the third book of the *Mechanika* of Hero of Alexandria. The Greek text of this portion of Hero's work has been lost, and the account survives only in an Arabic translation. The investigator is here involved with difficulties in the interpretation of the technical terms for the parts of the press; and there is some manuscript corruption as well. The main lines, as expounded by Drachmann (*AOMP*, pp. 63 ff.), are fairly clear. Hero's single-screw press, which was a portable affair, was contained within a rectangular frame, closely resembling a letter-press (see Fig. 63). His twin-screw press has a movable beam, which comes down as the screws are turned, and is not enclosed in a frame (see Fig. 64). Both presses have one indispensable feature in common – the provision of a female screw-thread in the beam itself. Hero devotes the last chapter of his *Mechanika* to the method of making an inside screw thread such as would be needed to make nuts or to thread the inside of a beam. In his lengthy study of the matter Drachmann (*AOMP*, pp. 77 ff.) argues for the hypothesis that the screw nut was not invented before about A.D. 50 (the endless screw goes back as far as Archimedes, some three centuries earlier).

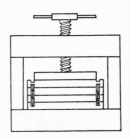

Fig. 63. Hero's single-screw press

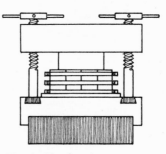

Fig. 64. Hero's twin-screw press

(5) *The 'congeries' press.* Pliny's fourth press, the 'congeries' press, is a screw press built inside a frame, with a single screw in the middle, and this certainly required a stationary horizontal beam with a female thread cut through it (see

---

[1] Paton (*JHS* 18 (1898), 211) notes that the screw-and-lever press which has the suspended weight has one advantage over the direct-screw press: since maximum pressure is applied at once, there is no possibility of strain, whereas in the direct-screw press unlimited pressure can be applied. He also records that in the weighted press the maximum can never be very great – in fact no more than that of the suspended stone. Drachmann (*AOMP*, pp. 120 f.) estimates the force exerted by the Catonian lever press at 10·296 kg. In the absence of detailed specifications it is not possible to make any comparative studies of this aspect in relation to the other types of press.

Fig. 65). Pliny's account (18. 317 fin.) shows that this press is identical with Hero's single-screw press (no. 4, p. 8), except for the 'superstructure'. The word 'congeries' (Drachmann's rendering, fr. *congerere*, 'to pile together, heap'), is used of any rough assemblage of material, especially stone. In Hero's small press the reverse pressure could easily be taken up by the members of the timber frame; but the upthrust of a large wine- or oil-press was a very different matter. Drachmann (*AOMP*, p. 58) regards it as an inexpensive solution of the problem used where an existing lever press of the old type was being converted into a direct-screw press. The type is well known from later times (examples cited by Drachmann, *loc. cit.*). Paton (*JHS* 18 (1898), 210 f.) provides an interesting account of an old-fashioned lever-and-screw press on the island of Kalymnos near Rhodes which was replaced by a direct-screw press around 1890, adding (*art. cit.* 211, n. 1) that it 'had recently been converted into a more modern type'.

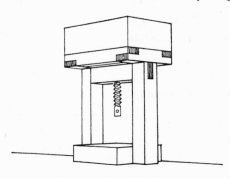

Fig. 65. Congeries press

(6) *The wedge-and-beam press.* This type of press, which is not mentioned by any of the literary sources, is represented on two well-known wall-paintings, from Herculaneum and Pompeii respectively (see Fig. 66). The press consists of a heavy square wooden frame, resembling that of Hero's single-screw press (above, p. 231). The container filled with mush is set at the bottom. The remainder of the frame is occupied by a series of wooden floors (*tabulata*), separated from each other by rows of heavy timbers, which are circular in section. The necessary pressure is applied by the use of wedges driven in by mallets. Both representations are fanciful, with *amorini*

Fig. 66. Wedge-and-beam press

as operators, and one can only guess at the structure of the press; the vertical members were presumably anchored into the ground, but the major pressure would have been on the top horizontal, and there is no way of determining how the thrust was countered. Structural weakness may have caused it to be abandoned, which would account for its exclusion from the texts (Columella's list at 12. 52. 6 seems to be comprehensive).

THE LITERARY EVIDENCE

Cato 18 (instructions for making a pressroom (*torcularium*) with four presses).

Ibid. 20–2 (how to set up an olive-mill (*trapetum*)).

Note: The design of the press is essentially the same whether olives or grapes are to be pressed; at ch. 19 Cato gives the different dimensions needed for the pressing of grapes.

Pliny *HN* 18. 317 (types of wine-press, including some recent improvements in their design).

Cato 64–7 (on harvesting the olives and making oil).

Columella, *RR* 12. 52. 6 (pros and cons of four different methods of making oil).

Pliny, *HN*, 15. 21–3 (brief and muddled account of oil-making, quoting Cato, but confusing his account).

THE ARCHAEOLOGICAL EVIDENCE

(1) *Surviving items of equipment*

Trapetum found at Stabiae: now in the National Museum at Naples (Drachmann, *AOMP*, fig. 3).

Trapetum found at Boscoreale in 1891. Now *in situ* at the Porta Marina, Pompeii (Drachmann, *AOMP*, figs. 4 and 6).

Trapetum found at Oliaro in 1799; sent to Pompeii. Now in Naples (?) (La Vega, *Descrizione del ritrovamento e ristaurazione di un antico molino di olio.* Napoli, 1783, 59–71; Tav. i–iii).

Trapetum found at Casa di Miri in 1780 (*Antichità di Ercolano*, Torino, 1792). See the full discussion of these items by Drachmann (*AOMP*, 7–22).

Mortarium and set of *orbes* found on the roads to Gragnano and St Leo.

(2) *Monuments representing pressing and milling*

The Rondanini Relief. This appears to be one of two surviving representations of Columella's *mola olearia* (above, p. 228) which was worked by a pair of cylindrical stones.

For a similar relief see the notes made by G. Zoega *Apparatus ad Bassirelievi*, Ny Kgl. Saml. Fol. 357 b vii, pag. 184 d, describing an apparatus which was at one time in the Museo delle Terme in Rome. Drachmann thinks that the Rondanini is a copy of the Zoega relief (*AOMP*, 69).

Brondsted's relief. On this see Drachmann, *AOMP* 42, and refs. cited there.

APPENDIX B

TREES, SHRUBS AND PLANTS AS SOURCES OF RAW MATERIALS

BY MALCOLM BONNINGTON

The materials used by the Romans for making basketware and related items of farm equipment were derived from a number of trees, shrubs and plants. It was the prudent farmer, according to Varro's precepts, who ensured, by cultivating the necessary copses, thickets and crops, that he had at his disposal whatever he required for the smooth running of his establishment. Failing this, his only recourse was to such second-best materials as the wildness of nature yielded, and which may well have lacked the required degree of firmness or flexibility.

APPENDIX B

RAW MATERIALS MENTIONED IN OUR SOURCES

Pliny and Columella together identify in their writings an extensive range of flora from which the withies (*vimina*) or the twigs (*virgae*) were obtained; other writers named additional varieties of the material used. Broadly the sources of information may be categorized as follows:

(*a*) *Trees*: principally the willow (*salix*), which was regularly cultivated in plantations (see e.g. Cato's list of profitability, ch. 1. 7); also holm-oak (*ilex*), hornbeam (*carpinus*), elder (*sambucus*), chestnut (*castaneus*), ash (*fraxinus*), strawberry-tree (*arbutus*), lime (*tilia*), hazel (*corylus*), birch (*betulla*), cork oak (*suber*), and palm (*palma*).

(*b*) *Shrubs*: bramble (*rubus*), butcher's broom (*ruscus*), Spanish broom (*genista/spartum*), and the chaste-tree (*agnus castus, vitex*).

(*c*) *Waterside plants*: reeds (*harundo/canna*), rush (*iuncus*), galingale (*cyperus*), bulrush (*scirpus*), sedge (*ulva/carex*) and marsh-mallow (*hibiscus*). Several of these plants were cultivated in beds (see the terms *harundinetum* and *iuncetum*).

(*d*) *Field plants*: bracken or fern (*filix*), darnel (*lolium*), vetch (*vicia*), flax (*linum*) and hemp (*cannabis*). The straw (*culmus*) of some field crops (e.g. fennel (*ferula*)), was also used, where not required for bedding or thatch.

(*a*) *Trees*

The willow was without doubt the most extensively used and the most versatile of the woods employed; its pliability and variation in thickness render it ideal for weaving and fashioning into a whole range of items. As Pliny indicates (16. 174), its branches furnished vine-props, its bark vine-ties, and its osiers or shoots anything from tapes or basketry of the finest texture to stronger wickerwork, and many pieces of farm equipment, The toughness of an osier, it was found, could be controlled, either by soaking it in a pond if greater suppleness was required, or by burying it for a fortnight in a manure heap to increase its rigidity. Willow is light in weight, takes a good polish, endures a buffeting without splitting or breaking, and will stand bending at right-angles; what could be more ideal for basketry?

Since the Romans were familiar with several species of 'salix' – and in Italy today over two dozen species, discounting their varieties and hybrids, may be identified – some acquired special applications. However, the difficulty of identifying those species is compounded further by the inconsistency among the Roman authorities, so that only the broadest of inferences are possible.

The bark was commonly peeled from the slim 'short-rods' of the Amerian willow for tying the vine-canes to their supports. The rods of this whitish willow, which may be identified with the Common Osier (*Salix viminalis* L.), are called 'short' by modern growers (or 'soft-tops' or 'fine-tops') as there is a greater quantity than usual of pith around the rods. Growing up to ten metres in height it can in one season produce shoots of up to four metres, whereas in two or three years the rods are sturdy enough for modern hampers and basket-furniture. The traditional pollarding of willows, normally at about three metres, to provide a succession of osier-rods, was also the practice of the Romans; but they lopped the tree at half this height. Cato (6. 4) and Varro (1. 24. 4), however, recommend for vine-ties the Greek Willow, which had an additional use as a binding for a graft on a fruit-tree. The mention of yellow shoots by Columella (4. 30. 4) leads quickly to the identification of the Greek Willow as the Yellow-Eyed or Yolk-of-Egg Willow (*Salix vitellina* L.), the branches and thin twigs of which are bright yellow. Used unpeeled they are the toughest osiers grown; today 'they are sold for tie-rods, to market-gardeners, nurserymen and celery growers' (S. C. Warren-Wren, *Willows* (Newton Abbot, 1972), p. 89). This variety of the large White Willow, together with the shrubby Purple Willow (*Salix purpurea* L.), the slender tough branches of which sprout purplish shoots at first, later growing into smooth olive-grey rods, became the source of a large percentage of Roman wickerwork. From these could be fashioned everything from the clumsiest of hurdles to the most delicate of meshes. Some artefacts must certainly have demanded nimble fingers; Pliny speaks, for example, of wickerwork sheaths being woven for the swelling gourds or cucumbers in order that different shapes may be induced (*HN* 19. 70).

As is still the practice in Palestine today, osiers were also woven into beehives, the insides of which were lined with a coating of cow-dung; straw skeps of this type have long been used by bee-keepers until recent times.

Other less pliable timbers found their uses on the farm. The holm-oak and the hornbeam were shaped into handles for tools, and from the elder and chestnut were cut props for the trailing vines; but the ash, often the source of Roman javelin-shafts, produced tool-handles, vine-props and wickerwork pens for enclosing sheep. Such enclosures were also constructed from the bitter-fruited strawberry-tree, of which Pliny suggested one taste was enough (*HN* 15. 99).

Vines were trained up elms and poplars (both black and white varieties), while for ties and ropes the subcortical layer of wood from the lime tree was sufficiently pliable. According to Pliny (*HN* 16. 176) vines themselves and hazels twisted to provide extra strength also gave a material suitable for binding. For the crate-rods of a basket, the ribs around which the osier-rods were woven, twigs were taken, as were the magistrates' rods of office, from the silver birch. The bark of the spongy and deeply furrowed Cork Oak (*Quercus suber* L.) was preferred to withies, bricks or jars for beehives, particularly as it resists extremes of temperature. The bark (*cortex*) when stripped from the tree, where it grows again, could be flattened into sheets of up to three metres square (Pliny, *HN* 16. 34); the beehive of the desired shape was then constructed from portions of the bark sewn together. Often the bee sought a natural habitat within the hollows of this small tree (*suber*), or of the Holm-Oak (*ilex*) (Virg. *Georg.* 2. 452–3) to which it is almost identical in leaf, acorn and cup. Apart from its marine uses as floats for fishing-lines or anchor-cables, this cork was also shaped into stoppers for oil-casks or wine-jars. Finally, the less rigid palm-tree yielded the fronds that were woven into boxes, baskets, mats and ropes. They were plucked after the harvest, dried indoors for four days, then by being exposed on the ground day and night, the fronds were blanched and thus prepared for manufacture. Pliny speaks of forty-nine species, one of which gave a soft, broader leaf that proved extremely useful for weaving (Pliny, *HN* 13. 39) and may be identified as the *Chamaerops humilis* L., the only palm truly indigenous to Europe. Common in Sicily, it was deliberately cultivated, although it bore no fruit.

(b) Shrubs

The bramble is hardly an ideal material for basketry, but there is evidence that the Romans were reduced to hacking off the thorns with thorn-cutters so that the brambles could be used for plaiting (Colum. *RR* 4. 31. 1). This tedious task must only have been undertaken where a more suitable material was not to be found. Vine-props were also derived, if the condition of the region permitted it, from 'vepres', which has been taken as a generic term for wild plants (see *AIRW*, 89).

Similar to the bramble is the Butcher's Broom (*Ruscus aculeatus* L.). This hardy evergreen perennial which produces inconspicuous green flowers and cherry-like berries continues to grow around Italian lakes in the shady spots it prefers. It has sharp spines and is not very suitable for withies, yet Virgil (*Georg.* 2. 413–14) implies that it is used in the vineyard along with willows and reeds. The *ruscus* which Pliny includes in a list of wild plants not further discussed and names for the medicinal properties of the root, he later (*HN* 23. 166) identifies with the wild myrtle (*oxymyrsine* or *chamaemyrsine*) which he observes was utilized by country people for brooms. He notes its red berries which render possible the identification of the *ruscus* as Pliny's unnamed shrub ('frutices sanguinei' at 16. 176), which was an additional source of withies; thus Virgil's implication is confirmed.

A larger shrub with yellow pea-like flowers is the Spanish Broom. The slender, virtually leafless, branches that resemble rushes were praised as the most sensitive of vine-ties; they were firm, yet very pliant, and did not cut into the vine-canes as willow- or elm-ties tended to do. The other advantage was that it abounded in the dry areas where willow would not grow. The Spanish Broom in fact belongs neither to the Genista family, as does the Needle Furze (or Petty Whin), nor to the spine-free Cytisus family of the English Broom. Called 'spartum' after the Greek 'spartos', Spanish Broom was woven into a variety of baskets, sacks and strainers, as well as into nets in order to give pomegranate trees some protection against birds (Colum. 12. 46. 2), and slippers for oxen with injured hoofs, to keep them dry (*ibid.* 6. 12. 2). The terms 'spartos', 'spartum' were also used of esparto grass. On the confusion between these plants, and the variety of products for which they were used, see Part I, section 4, pp. 29–30.

Like the willow is the smaller Chaste-tree, the shrub with the unnecessarily double cognomen of 'agnus castus' since both words allude in Greek and Latin respectively to the shrub's widely fabled, but improbable, power to protect feminine virtue. The pliable shoots of this late-flowering ornamental shrub, still used by the inhabitants of Greece and Crete for weaving into baskets, were woven by the Romans into baskets and wickerwork hurdles. Known also to the Romans as *Salix Marina*, and flourishing in waterside and coastal areas, the Chaste-tree may well have served both farmers cultivating land that bordered the sea and fishermen, for whom it provided tackle in the way that 'smaller beds exist in the Devon seaboard coombes for the provision of material required for the making of lobster pots' (Warren-Wren, *op. cit.* p. 86).

(c) Waterside plants

When Varro recommended the cultivation of a willow-copse (*salictum*) for the sake of its material uses, he in the same breath recommended a reed-thicket (*harundinetum*), for the cane (*calamus*) of the reed, traditionally the source of roofing thatch, was also frequently cut for use in the vineyard. Such canes, often longer than the height of a man, provided an overhead trellis when tied in bundles to give uniform thickness, or in pairs were used as props for the trailing vine, which sometimes was bound by reed-leaves, notably in Liguria, or by split reeds. The varieties known to the Romans were probably the Sweet Flag (*Acorus calamus*), the Common Reed (*Arundo phragmites*) and the Great Reed

(*Arundo donax*). If such reed-thickets are not given the necessary attention, the reeds become 'slender and like the "canna"', the common name for the bastard reeds that crowd the banks of the cool Mincio in Virgil country. These too were cut for vine-props, baskets and for knocking down olives from the trees on to the rush mats spread below.

Many more artefacts were made out of rush, which enjoyed an application second only to the willow; Roman writers mention the following: strainers (*colum*), bags (*fiscus*), fishing baskets (*sporta*), hand baskets (*calathus*), flower baskets (*fiscina*), fish baskets (*nassa marina*) and mats (*teges*); many of these could have been located on a Roman farm.

Four types of rush may be identified. The most useful for wickerwork as it is soft and fleshy, according to Pliny, is the Round Headed Club Rush (*Scirpus holoschoenus* L.), which grows up to 1½ m. Secondly but inferior in bushiness, thickness and height, there is the Black Bog Rush (*Schoenus nigricans* L.). In salt water grew the Sea Rush (*Juncus maritimus* L.) or the Sharp Sea Rush (*Juncus acutus* L.) from which fishing baskets were plaited. Any of these four rushes may well have been chopped down by the farmer's *falx sirpicula* for basket-weaving (see *AIRW*, s.v. 'falx sirpicula', p. 89). According to Pliny (21. 112), Mago the Carthaginian also identified the Mariscan Rush (*Gladium mariscus* R.Br.), better known in England as the Fen Sedge. It still grows in many parts of Europe and North Africa, and is noted as extremely suitable for making matting.

In addition 'iunci' were used for letting down spices into a large oil-jar, and, like many other materials, for vine-ties. For this latter purpose, according to Pliny (*HN* 17. 209) 'all Greece' used the *iuncus* or sedge or the triangular rush that they called 'cyperos', to which our nearest equivalent is the Sweet Galingale (*Cyperus longus* L.). Yet another reed, distinguished from the 'iuncus' by Varro and Columella, but not by Virgil, who not once in his main works uses the word, was the 'scirpus'. Used by boatmen on the River Po as a sail-beam, this tall Common Bulrush or Clubrush (*Scirpus lacustris* L.) was worked into hampers, mats, bags and thatched roofs.

Two words were employed to describe the marsh-sedges that were also used for vine-ties, and, in the absence of timber, for ropes and nets: 'carex' and 'ulva' (or 'sagitta', a nickname prompted by its arrowhead shape). *Carex* is now the term for the largest genus of sedges, but although at one point Columella speaks of it together with bracken as needing to be uprooted (Colum. 2. 2. 13), for the drying of figs he suggested forming a cloche from shepherds' hurdles that were woven of straw, sedge or ferns as a protection against rain and dew (Colum. 12. 15. 1). Palladius (12. 7. 22) also advised the preservation of chestnuts by shutting them up in rather dense baskets (*sportae*) shaped from marsh-sedge.

The other waterside plant known to have been used for baskets is one of the Malvaceae, the pink-blossomed Marsh Mallow (*Althaea officinalis* L.) to which Dioscorides gave the name 'hibiscus'. Its medicinal value was important (Plin. *HN* 19. 89; 20. 29), but his reference to the parsnip-like root raises questions about the reliability of his information or the identity of the 'hibiscus' he was discussing. It is clear from a reference in Virgil's *Eclogues* (10. 71) that the strong fibres in the Marsh Mallow's erect stems were woven into the type of basket that might allow the whey to be separated from the curdled milk.

APPENDIX B

(d) Field plants

Certain plants from the fields, either cultivated or wild, were also turned into farm equipment. The Romans, whose ploughs failed to extirpate it with their shallow shares, found bracken a curse. It proved difficult to check, and needed to be constantly uprooted by hand, a task a boy could do, suggested Columella. Yet the farmer turned his enemy to his advantage, and with his toothed bracken-cutter gathered the rife bracken (*Pteris aquilina* L.) or the hardy fern (*Polystichum filix* L.) to be used within pens to protect sheep from the hard ground and disease, or for cloches to cover drying figs. Darnel (*lolium*) too was not always as 'infelix' as Virgil would have it (*Georg.* 1. 154); Columella (*R.R.* 8. 5. 16) speaks of the use in the hen-house of a sieve made of darnel or vetch, in which to place the newly-hatched chicks so that they may be fumigated. Straw, which could be derived from any of the cereals or fodder-grasses, was also recommended for fig-cloches. Second only to cork, and preferred for beehives above the ubiquitous willow-osier, were the stout stalks of the fennel (*Ferula communis* L.) which in its wild state reaches a height of 2 m, or when cultivated grows even taller. Sometimes used for seasoning food, the fennel produced, when its pithy-centred stalks were dried, the lightest of woods, which gave splints for broken bones, walking-sticks for old men, but to mischievous schoolboys meant the dreaded cane (Martial 14. 80.). By the farmer they could readily be cut to form his square, shallow hives (Varro, *RR* 3. 16. 15).

The cultivation of flax seemed to Pliny so vital to Mediterranean development that he saw it in a category of its own, between agriculture and horticulture. The use of the extracted fibres for sails, nets and clothes is well attested. Nevertheless the agronomists speak of more lowly farm uses; its uniform thread made it ideal for nets for fishing, bird-catching and hunting, while it provided the tinier net-bag by which spices were let down into a large oil-jar or through which myrtle juice was squeezed. For dipping pomegranates into hot sea water in a process designed to preserve the fruit longer during storage, flax (or rush) provided the string, while it also tied together small rosemary bunches in fermenting must.

Hunting nets were also made of hemp, which was recommended by Varro for the well-supplied farm, together with flax and rushes. These would provide the whole range of rope-work needed, from the heavy ropes (*restes, funes*) to the more slender strings (*lineae*). See Part I, section 4, pp. 29–38.

With all these materials being used on different Roman farms in order to provide comparable equipment, the principal factor was clearly the availability of the raw material. Perhaps nowhere is the importance of such a factor pinpointed more plainly than in Pliny's observation that in Gaul the flour-sieve was made from horse-hair, from flax in Spain and from papyrus and rushes in Egypt. The availability of these trees, shrubs, waterside and field plants thus governed the choice of any particular material for any particular artefact; and the correlation of artefacts and materials was so local that it allows no meaningful classification of general use.

In an era when all equipment was handmade, patterns were arbitrary and shapes and sizes numerous. Only two conclusions therefore may be made, in the form of broad generalizations about the Roman practice of equipment-making with respect to the materials used: first that the harder woods and the thicker withies or osiers gave the sturdier basketware, while more pliant osiers, rushes and reeds provided the finer, softer items; secondly, there is abundant evidence of compliance with the doctrine of maximum use of available raw material, as is shown by the recommendation to store grapes in the sawdust of poplar, ash and pine, and to hollow out gourds as containers. It was the imprudent farmer who failed to abide by the doctrine.

SELECT BIBLIOGRAPHY

Bennett, R. and Elton, J. *A History of Corn-milling*. London and Liverpool, 1898.

Billiard, R. *L'Agriculture dans l'antiquité d'après les Géorgiques de Virgile*. Paris, 1928.

La Vigne dans l'antiquité. Lyons, 1913.

Birebent, J. *Aquae romanae*. Alger, 1966.

Bloch, M. *Land and Work in Mediaeval Europe*, selected papers by Marc Bloch, trans. by J. L. Anderson. London, 1967, 136–68.

Blümlein, C. *Bilder aus dem Römisch-Germanischen Kulturleben*, 2nd ed. Munich–Berlin, 1926.

Blümner, H. *Die römischen Privataltertümer*. Munich, 1911 (Handb. d. klass. Altertumswiss., Bd. 4, Abt. 1. 2, Tl. 2).

Technologie und Terminologie der Gewerbe und Künste bei Griechen und Römern, 4 Bde. Leipzig, 1875–87.

Bradford, John, *Ancient Landscapes*. London, 1954.

Cagnat, R. V. and Chapot, V. *Manuel d'archéologie romaine*, 2 vols. Paris, 1916–20.

Callender, M. H. *Roman Amphorae*. Oxford, 1965.

Crova, B. *Edilizia e tecnica rurale di Roma antica*. Milan, 1942.

Daumas, M. *Histoire générale des techniques*, vol. 1. Paris, 1964.

Déchelette–Grenier, *Manuel d'archéologie gallo-romaine*, vol. VI, 1 and 2. Paris, 1934.

Drachmann, A. G. *Ancient Oil Mills and Presses*. Copenhagen, 1932.

Feldhaus, F. M. *Die Technik der Antike und des Mittelalters*, 2nd ed. Munich, 1965.

Forbes, R. J. *Studies in Ancient Technology*. Leiden, 1955– .

Haudricourt, A. G. and Delamarre, M. J.-B. *L'Homme et la charrue à travers les âges*, 3rd ed. Paris, 1955 (Géographie Humaine, vol. 25).

Hayes, J. W. *Late Roman Pottery*. London, 1971.

Hilgers, W. *Lateinische Gefässnamen: Bezeichnungen, Funktion und Form römische Gefässe* . . . (*Bonner Jahrbücher*, Beiheft 31). Düsseldorf, 1969.

Hölder, Oscar, *Die Formen der römischen Thongefässe*. Stuttgart, 1897.

Hörle, J. *Catos Hausbücher*. Paderborn, 1929.

Jacobi, H. Römische Getreidemühlen, *Saalburgjahrbuch* III (1912), 75–95.

Krause, J. *Angeiologie*. Halle, 1854.

Mau, A. *Pompeii: its Life and Art*, trans. by F. W. Kelsey. London, 1907.

Moritz, L. A. *Grain-Mills and Flour in Classical Antiquity*. Oxford, 1958.

Neuburger, A. *The Technical Arts and Sciences of the Ancients*, trans. by H. L. Brose. London, 1930.

Paoli, U. *La vita romana*, 9th ed., trans. by W. Macnaughton. London, 1968.

Parias, L. H. *Histoire générale du travail*, vol. 1. Paris, 1959.

Pernice, E. (ed.), *Die Hellenistische Kunst in Pompeii*, 6 vols. Berlin (Deutsches Archäologisches Institut), 1925–38.

SELECT BIBLIOGRAPHY

Prêcheur-Canonge, Th. *La vie rurale en Afrique romaine d'après les mosaïques.* Paris/Tunis, 1962 (Publ. de l'Univ. de Tunis, Fac. Lett., sér. 1, vol. 6).

Rich, A. *A Dictionary of Roman and Greek Antiquities.* 4th ed. London, 1874.

Rostovtzeff, M. I. *Social and Economic History of the Roman Empire,* 2nd ed. trans. by P. M. Fraser, Oxford, 1958.

Scheuermeier, P. *Bauernwerk in Italien, der italienischen und rätoromanischen Südschweiz,* Eine sprach- und sachkundliche Darstellung landwirtschaftliche Arbeiten und Geräte. Erlenbach/Zürich, 1943.

Skinner, F. G. *Ancient Weights and Measures.* London, 1967.

Vigneron, P. *Le Cheval dans l'antiquité gréco-romaine,* 2 vols. Nancy, 1968.

White, K. D. *Agricultural Implements of the Roman World.* Cambridge, 1967.

A Bibliography of Roman Agriculture. Reading, 1970.

Roman Farming. London, 1970.

Wright, D. *Baskets and Basketry.* London, 1959.

GENERAL INDEX

* Signifies main reference

Agora, Athenian, 107, 153
attitudes, basic, persistence of, 220–1*
augur, 210

bag, 91–4*; goatskin, 201
'bain-marie', 178
bark of trees, 53, 65, 85
barley, 14
basil, 4, 5
basilica, 132
basin, 120, 183–5* (*pelvis*), 193–4 (*trulleum*); hand-, 184; foot-, 184
basketry, 52–3; sources of supply of, 233–9; ?as protection, 176
baskets: fruit-picking, 61, 73; work-, 72; cheese-making, 72; earth-carrying, 73; for whey, 237
baskets, making of, 52, 54–5*
bass, 90
bath, 120, 155–6
bathtub, 121, 122
bee-hives, 52, 85–6*, 180; material for, 235
beer-drinking, 162
bin, 158, 159
boat, 164
bookcase, 175
bottles: chained, 163; leather, 117
bouquet, of wine, 93
box: part of oil-mill, 167, 168; part of water-wheel, 168; axle-, 168
bracken, 238
bramble, 26; for basketry, 235
brazier, 193
bread, 10, 11
bronze, 53; for containers, 129, 134–5, 138, 151, 169, 184, 193; manufacture of, 213
broom, 26, 52, 53, 69, 100, 216
bucket: well-, 151; fire-fighting, 151; on water-wheel, 167, wooden, 189; bronze, 189; hoist-, 189
bucket-yoke, 51, 67–8
bungs, 124
bushel-measure, 168–70
butt (tun), 142, 182*

camels, in transport, 52
canals, 217–18

cane, for vine-props, 236
capacity: of *creterrae*, 138; of *dolia*, 113, 140; of *oenophora*, 176; of *amphorae*, 126; of *ollae*, 178; of *cadi*, 128–9; of *seriae*, 187; of *situlae*, 189
capstan, 38
cargo, transfer of, 126
cart: 4-wheeled, 116, 117, 141; donkey-, 51; mule-, 51
cask, 53; wine-, 51, 143
casserole, 180
catalogues, xii
cauldron, 118–19*, 178, 197, 204
centuriation, 41
cheese, 171, 178
chestnut: bark of, 65; trees, 215
Christ-thorn, 26
cistern, 132–4*, 158; supplies from, condemned, 133
climate: effect of, on storage, 146; importance of, 222
codes, legal, 110
coins, 169
communications: importance of, 217; by river, 217; by canal, 217
containers: woven, supply of, 52; earthenware, 53, suppliers of, 213; basketry, 53–4*; for manure, 67; for provisions, 69; capacity of, 176; classification of, 107 ff.; distribution of, 109; uses of, 112; stacking of, 115, 124; repair of, 125, 146; as boundary marks, 161, 182, 187
continuity of operation, 214–15
control mechanism: for grain-milling, 154; for oil-making, 160
cooking, arrangements for, 176 ff.
cooking-pot, 176–9
craftsmen, on estates, 214
crate-rods, 53, 54; materials for, 235
crook, shepherd's, 172
cucumbers, 74
cupboard, 175
cylinder, of water-pump, 167
cypress, 4, 5

darnel, 103
decanter, 138
decanting, of wine, 124

INDEX OF GREEK WORDS

GREEK TERMS APPEARING IN LATINIZED FORM

INDEX OF LATIN WORDS

urnarium, 199
uter, 111, 200–2*; u. olearius, 201

vacerra, 27
vallus, 75–6*
vannus, xi, 75–6*
vas, 111, 167; v. vinarium, 111, 145, 148; v.
  ligneum (= cupa), 115; vasa defrutaria,

135; v. grande, 142; v. aeneum, 197,
  204, v. plumbeum, 203; v. oleare, 203
ventilabrum, 77
vilica, 178
vindemiator, 112
virgultum, 215
vivarium, 26

BOTANICAL TERMS

acorus calamus, 236
agnus castus = vitex = salix marina, 234,
  235*
Althea officinalis L., 237
arbutus, 234
arundo donax, 26, 236–7
arundo phragmites, 236

betulla, 234

calamus, 236
canna, 234, 237
cannabis, 29, 234
carex = ulva, 234, 237
carpinus, 234
castaneus, 234
Chamaerops humilis L., 235
Cladium mariscus L., 237
cortex, 215; for beehives, 235; for woven
  materials, 235
corylus, 234
culmus, 234
cyperos, 234, 237
Cyperus longus L., 237
cytisus, 236

ferula, 6, 215, 234; F. communis L.,
  238
filix, 234; Polystichum filix L., 238
fraxinus, 234

genista = spartum (1), 216, 234, 235*

harundo, 208, 234
hibiscus, 234, 237

ilex, 234, 235
iuncus, 29, 83, 90, 234, 237; I. maritimus
  L., 237; I. acutus L., 237

linum, 29, 90, 234
lolium, 234, 238
lygeum spartum, 29

paliurus australis, 26
palma, 90, 215, 234
Polystichum felix L., 238
Pteris aquilina L., 238

Quercus suber L., 235

rosa sempervirens, 26
rubus, 26, 234
ruscus aculeatus, 26, 234, 236*

salix, 215, 234; S. viminalis, 234; S. vitellina L., 235; S. purpurea L., 235
sambucus, 234
Schoenus nigricans L., 237
scirpus, 67, 234, 237; S. holoschoenus
  L., 237; S. lacustris L., 237
spartum (1) = genista, 69, 90, 215, 234
spina, 26
stipa tenacissima, 29
suber, 234, 235

tilia, 234
triticum: vulgare, 14; durum, 14

ulva = carex, 234, 237

vepres, 236
vicia, 234
vitex = agnus castus, 234

LIST OF PASSAGES CITED

LIST OF PASSAGES CITED